THE WORLD
AS WILL AND IDEA

VOLUME II

THE WORLD
AS WILL AND IDEA

By

ARTHUR SCHOPENHAUER

VOLUME II

*CONTAINING THE CRITICISM OF THE
KANTIAN PHILOSOPHY AND THE
SUPPLEMENTS TO THE FIRST
BOOK AND PART OF
THE SECOND BOOK
OF VOLUME I*

Paucis natus est, qui populum ætatis suæ cogitat

Sen.

LONDON

ROUTLEDGE & KEGAN PAUL LIMITED

BROADWAY HOUSE, 68 - 74 CARTER LANE, E. C.

Translated from the German by
R. B. HALDANE, M.A.
and
J. KEMP, M.A.

First Published 1883
Tenth impression
1957

REPRINTED BY LITHOGRAPHY IN GREAT BRITAIN BY
JARROLD AND SONS LTD, NORWICH

CONTENTS

APPENDIX.

SUPPLEMENTS TO THE FIRST BOOK.

FIRST HALF.

THE DOCTRINE OF THE IDEA OF PERCEPTION.

SECOND HALF.

THE DOCTRINE OF THE ABSTRACT IDEA, OR OF THINKING.

CONTENTS.

SUPPLEMENTS TO THE SECOND BOOK.

Appendix.

CRITICISM OF THE KANTIAN PHILOSOPHY.

———

C'est le privilège du vrai génie, et surtout du génie qui ouvre une carrière, de faire impunément de grandes fautes.—Voltaire.

IT is much easier to point out the faults and errors in the work of a great mind than to give a distinct and full exposition of its value. For the faults are particular and finite, and can therefore be fully comprehended; while, on the contrary, the very stamp which genius impresses upon its works is that their excellence is unfathomable and inexhaustible. Therefore they do not grow old, but become the instructor of many succeeding centuries. The perfected masterpiece of a truly great mind will always produce a deep and powerful effect upon the whole human race, so much so that it is impossible to calculate to what distant centuries and lands its enlightening influence may extend. This is always the case; for however cultivated and rich the age may be in which such a masterpiece appears, genius always rises like a palm-tree above the soil in which it is rooted.

But a deep-reaching and widespread effect of this kind cannot take place suddenly, because of the great difference between the genius and ordinary men. The knowledge which that one man in *one* lifetime drew directly from life and the world, won and presented to others as won and arranged, cannot yet at once become the possession of mankind; for mankind has not so much power to receive as the genius has power to give. But even after a successful battle with unworthy opponents, who at its very birth contest the life of what is immortal and desire to nip in the bud the salvation of man (like the serpents in the cradle of Hercules), that knowledge must then traverse the circuitous paths of innumerable false constructions and distorted applications, must overcome the

attempts to unite it with old errors, and so live in conflict
till a new and unprejudiced generation grows up to meet
it.   Little by little, even in youth, this new generation
partially receives the contents of that spring through a
thousand indirect channels, gradually assimilates it, and
so participates in the benefit which was destined to flow
to mankind from that great mind.   So slowly does the
education of the human race, the weak yet refractory pupil
of genius, advance.   Thus with Kant's teaching also; its
full strength and importance will only be revealed through
time, when the spirit of the age, itself gradually transformed and altered in the most important and essential
respects by the influence of that teaching, will afford con-
vincing evidence of the power of that giant mind.   I have,
however, no intention of presumptuously anticipating the
spirit of the age and assuming here the thankless *rôle*
of Calchas and Cassandra.   Only I must be allowed, in
accordance with what has been said, to regard Kant's
works as still very new, while many at the present day
look upon them as already antiquated, and indeed have
laid them aside as done with, or, as they express it, have
left them behind ; and others, emboldened by this, ignore
them altogether, and with brazen face go on philosophising
about God and the soul on the assumption of the old
realistic dogmatism and its scholastic teaching, which is
as if one sought to introduce the doctrines of the alchemists
into modern chemistry.   For the rest, the works of Kant
do not stand in need of my feeble eulogy, but will themselves for ever praise their author, and though perhaps
not in the letter, yet in the spirit they will live for ever
upon earth.

Certainly, however, if we look back at the first result of
his teaching, at the efforts and events in the sphere of
philosophy during the period that has elapsed since he
wrote, a very depressing saying of Goethe obtains confirmation : " As the water that is displaced by a ship
immediately flows in again behind it, so when great minds

have driven error aside and made room for themselves, it very quickly closes in behind them again by the law of its nature" (*Wahrheit und Dichtung*, Theil 3, s. 521). Yet this period has been only an episode, which is to be reckoned as part of the lot referred to above that befalls all new and great knowledge; an episode which is now unmistakably near its end, for the bubble so long blown out yet bursts at last. Men generally are beginning to be conscious that true and serious philosophy still stands where Kant left it. At any rate, I cannot see that between Kant and myself anything has been done in philosophy; therefore I regard myself as his immediate successor.

What I have in view in this Appendix to my work is really only a defence of the doctrine I have set forth in it, inasmuch as in many points that doctrine does not agree with the Kantian philosophy, but indeed contradicts it. A discussion of this philosophy is, however, necessary, for it is clear that my train of thought, different as its content is from that of Kant, is yet throughout under its influence, necessarily presupposes it, starts from it; and I confess that, next to the impression of the world of perception, I owe what is best in my own system to the impression made upon me by the works of Kant, by the sacred writings of the Hindus, and by Plato. But I can only justify the contradictions of Kant which are nevertheless present in my work by accusing him of error in these points, and exposing mistakes which he committed. Therefore in this Appendix I must proceed against Kant in a thoroughly polemical manner, and indeed seriously and with every effort; for it is only thus that his doctrine can be freed from the error that clings to it, and its truth shine out the more clearly and stand the more firmly. It must not, therefore, be expected that the sincere reverence for Kant which I certainly feel shall extend to his weaknesses and errors also, and that I shall consequently refrain from exposing these except with the most careful indulgence, whereby my language would necessarily become weak and insipid through circumlocution. Towards a living writer such indulgence is needed, for human frailty cannot endure even the most just refutation of an error, unless tempered by soothing and flattery, and hardly even then; and a teacher of the age and benefactor of mankind deserves at least that the human weakness he also has should be indulged, so that he may not be caused pain. But he who is dead has thrown off this weakness; his merit stands firm; time will purify it more and more from all exaggeration and detraction. His mistakes must be separated from it, rendered harmless, and then given over to oblivion. Therefore in the polemic against Kant I am about to begin, I have only his mistakes and weak points in view. I oppose them with hostility, and wage a relentless war of extermination against them, always mindful not to conceal them indulgently, but rather to place them in the clearest light, in order to extirpate them the more surely. For the reasons given above, I am not conscious either of injustice or ingratitude towards Kant in doing this. However, in order that, in the eyes of others also, I may remove every appearance of malice, I wish first to bring out clearly my sincere reverence for Kant and gratitude to him, by expressing shortly what in my eyes appears to be his chief merit; and I shall do this from a standpoint so general that I shall not require to touch upon the points in which I must afterwards controvert him.

———

Kant's greatest merit is the distinction of the phenomenon from the thing in itself, based upon the proof that between things and us there still always stands the *intellect,* so that they cannot be known as they may be in themselves. He was led into this path through Locke (see *Prolegomena zu jeder Metaph.,* § 13, Anm. 2). The latter had shown that the secondary qualities of things, such as sound, smell, colour, hardness, softness, smoothness, and the like, as founded on the affections of the senses, do not belong to the objective body, to the thing in itself. To this he attributed only the primary qualities, *i.e.*, such as only presuppose space and impenetrability ; thus extension, figure, solidity, number, mobility. But this easily discovered Lockeian distinction was, as it were, only a youthful introduction to the distinction of Kant. The latter, starting from an incomparably higher standpoint, explains all that Locke had accepted as *primary qualities, i.e.*, qualities of the thing in itself, as also belonging only to its phenomenal appearance in our faculty of apprehension, and this just because the conditions of this faculty, space, time, and causality, are known by us *a priori*. Thus Locke had abstracted from the thing in itself the share which the organs of sense have in its phenomenal appearance ; Kant, however, further abstracted the share of the brain-functions (though not under that name). Thus the distinction between the phenomenon and the thing in itself now received an infinitely greater significance, and a very much deeper meaning. For this end he was obliged to take in hand the important separation of our *a priori* from our *a posteriori* knowledge, which before him had never been carried out with adequate strictness and completeness, nor with distinct consciousness. Accordingly this now became the principal subject of his profound investigations. Now here we would at once remark that Kant's philosophy has a threefold relation to that of his predecessors. First, as we have just seen, to the philosophy of Locke, confirming and extending it; secondly, to that of Hume, correcting and making use of it, a relation which is most distinctly expressed in the "*Prolegomena*" (that most beautiful and comprehensible of all Kant's important writings, which is far too little read, for it facilitates immensely the study of his philosophy); thirdly, a decidedly polemical and destructive relation to the Leibnitz-Wolfian philosophy. All three systems ought to be known before one proceeds to the study of the Kantian philosophy. If now, according to the above, the distinction of the phenomenon from the thing in itself, thus the doctrine of the complete diversity of the ideal and the real, is the fundamental characteristic of the Kantian philosophy, then the assertion of the absolute identity of these two which appeared soon afterwards is a sad proof of the saying of Goethe quoted above; all the more so as it rested upon nothing but the empty boast of intellectual intuition, and accordingly was only a return to the crudeness of the vulgar opinion, masked under bombast and nonsense, and the imposing impression of an air of importance. It became the fitting starting-point for the still grosser nonsense of the clumsy and stupid Hegel. Now as Kant's separation of the phenomenon from the thing in itself, arrived at in the manner explained above, far surpassed all that preceded it in the depth and thoughtfulness of its conception, it was also exceedingly important in its results. For in it he propounded, quite originally, in a perfectly new way, found from a new side and on a new path, the same truth which Plato never wearies of repeating, and in his language generally expresses thus: This world which appears to the senses has no true being, but only a ceaseless becoming; it is, and it is not, and its comprehension is not so much knowledge as illusion. This is also what he expresses mythically at the beginning of the seventh book of the Republic, the most important passage in all his writings, which has already been referred to in the third book of the present work. He says: Men, firmly chained in a dark cave, see neither the true original light nor real things, but only the meagre light of the fire in the cave and the shadows of real things which pass by the fire behind their backs; yet they think the shadows are the reality, and the determining of the succession of these shadows is true wisdom. The same truth, again quite differently presented, is also a leading doctrine of the Vedas and Puranas, the doctrine of Mâyâ, by which really nothing else is understood than what Kant calls the phenomenon in opposition to the thing in itself; for the work of Mâyâ is said to be just this visible world in which we are, a summoned enchantment, an inconstant appearance without true being, like an optical illusion or a dream, a veil which surrounds human consciousness, something of which it is equally false and true to say that it is and that it is not. But Kant not only expressed the same doctrine in a completely new and original way, but raised it to the position of proved and indisputable truth by means of the calmest and most temperate exposition; while both Plato and the Indian philosophers had founded their assertions merely upon a general perception of the world, had advanced them as the direct utterance of their consciousness, and presented them rather mythically and poetically than philosophically and distinctly. In this respect they stand to Kant in the same relation as the Pythagoreans Hicetas, Philolaus, and Aristarchus, who already asserted the movement of the earth round the fixed sun, stand to Copernicus. Such distinct knowledge and calm, thoughtful exposition of this dream-like nature of the whole world is really the basis of the whole Kantian philosophy; it is its soul and its greatest merit. He accomplished this by taking to pieces the whole machinery of our intellect by means of which the phantasmagoria of the objective world is brought about, and presenting it in detail with marvellous insight and ability. All earlier Western philosophy, appearing in comparison with the Kantian unspeakably clumsy, had failed to recognise that truth, and had therefore always spoken just as if in a dream. Kant first awakened it suddenly out of this dream; therefore the last sleepers (Mendelssohn) called him the "all-destroyer." He showed that the laws which reign with inviolable necessity in existence, *i.e.*, in experience generally, are not to be applied to deduce and explain *existence itself;* that thus the validity of these laws is only relative, *i.e.*, only arises after existence; the world of experience in general is already established and present; that consequently these laws cannot be our guide when we come to the explanation of the existence of the world and of ourselves.   All earlier Western philosophers had imagined that these laws, according to which the phenomena are combined, and all of which—time and space, as well as causality and inference—I comprehend under the expression "the principle of sufficient reason," were absolute laws conditioned by nothing, *æternæ veritates;* that the world itself existed only in consequence of and in conformity with them; and therefore that under their guidance the whole riddle of the world must be capable of solution. The assumptions made for this purpose, which Kant criticises under the name of the Ideas of the reason, only served to raise the mere phenomenon, the work of Mâyâ, the shadow world of Plato, to the one highest reality, to put it in the place of the inmost and true being of things, and thereby to make the real knowledge of this impossible; that is, in a word, to send the dreamers still more soundly to sleep.   Kant exhibited these laws, and therefore the whole world, as conditioned by the form of knowledge belonging to the subject; from which it followed, that however far one carried investigation and reasoning under the guidance of these laws, yet in the principal matter, *i.e.*, in knowledge of the nature of the world in itself and outside the idea, no step in advance was made, but one only moved like a squirrel in its wheel.   Thus, all the dogmatists may be compared to persons who supposed that if they only went straight on long enough they would come to the end of the world; but Kant then circumnavigated the world and showed that, because it is round, one cannot get out of it by horizontal movement, but that yet by perpendicular movement this is perhaps not impossible.   We may also say that Kant's doctrine affords the insight that we must seek the end and beginning of the world, not without, but within us.

All this, however, rests on the fundamental distinction between dogmatic and *critical* or *transcendental philosophy*. Whoever wishes to make this quite clear to himself, and realise it by means of an example, may do so very briefly by reading, as a specimen of dogmatic philosophy, an essay of Leibnitz entitled "*De Rerum Originatione Radicali*," and printed for the first time in the edition of the philosophical works of Leibnitz by Erdmann (vol. i. p. 147). Here the origin and excellence of the world is demonstrated *a priori*, so thoroughly in the manner of realistic-dogmatism, on the ground of the *veritates æternæ* and with the assistance of the ontological and cosmological proofs. It is indeed once admitted, by the way, that experience shows the exact opposite of the excellence of the world here demonstrated; but experience is therefore given to understand that it knows nothing of the matter, and ought to hold its tongue when philosophy has spoken *a priori*. Now, with Kant, the *critical philosophy* appeared as the opponent of this whole method. It takes for its problem just these *veritates æternæ*, which serve as the foundation of every such dogmatic structure, investigates their origin, and finds it in the human mind, where they spring from the peculiar forms which belong to it, and which it carries in itself for the purpose of comprehending an objective world. Thus, here, in the brain, is the quarry which supplies the material for that proud dogmatic edifice. But because the critical philosophy, in order to attain to this result, was obliged to go beyond the *veritates æternæ* upon which all the preceding dogmatism was founded, and make these truths themselves the objects of investigation, it became *transcendental* philosophy. From this, then, it also follows that the objective world, as we know it, does not belong to the true being of the thing in itself, but is merely its phenomenal appearance conditioned by those very forms which lie *a priori* in the intellect (*i.e.*, the brain), therefore it cannot contain anything but phenomena.

Kant, indeed, did not attain to the knowledge that the phenomenon is the world as idea, and the thing in itself is the will.   But he showed that the phenomenal world is conditioned just as much through the subject as through the object, and because he isolated the most universal forms of its phenomenal appearance, *i.e.*, of the idea, he proved that we may know these forms and consider them in their whole constitution, not only by starting from the object, but also just as well by starting from the subject, because they are really the limits between object and subject which are common to them both; and he concluded that by following these limits we never penetrate to the inner nature either of the object or of the subject, consequently never know the true nature of the world, the thing in itself.

He did not deduce the thing in itself in the right way, as I shall show presently, but by means of an inconsistency, and he had to pay the penalty of this in frequent and irresistible attacks upon this important part of his teaching.   He did not recognise the thing in itself directly in the will; but he made a great initial step towards this knowledge in that he explained the undeniable moral significance of human action as quite different from and not dependent upon the laws of the phenomenon, nor even explicable in accordance with them, but as something which touches the thing in itself directly : this is the second important point of view for estimating his services.

We may regard as the third the complete overthrow of the Scholastic philosophy, a name by which I wish here to denote generally the whole period beginning with Augustine, the Church Father, and ending just before Kant.   For the chief characteristic of Scholasticism is, indeed, that which is very correctly stated by Tennemann, the guardianship of the prevailing national religion over philosophy, which had really nothing left for it to do but to prove and embellish the cardinal dogmas prescribed to it by religion. The Schoolmen proper, down to Suarez, confess this openly; the succeeding philosophers do it more unconsciously, or at least unavowedly. It is held that Scholastic philosophy only extends to about a hundred years before Descartes, and that then with him there begins an entirely new epoch of free investigation independent of all positive theological doctrine. Such investigation, however, is in fact not to be attributed to Descartes and his successors,[1] but only an appearance of it, and in any case an effort after it. Descartes was a man of supreme ability, and if we take account of the age he lived in, he accomplished a great deal. But if we set aside this consideration and measure him with reference to the freeing of thought from all fetters and the commencement of a new period of untrammelled original investigation with which he is credited, we are obliged to find that with his doubt still wanting in true seriousness, and therefore surrendering so quickly and so entirely, he has, indeed, the appearance of wishing to throw off at once all the early implanted opinions belonging to his age and nation, but does so only apparently and for a moment, to assume them again immediately and hold them all the more firmly ; and so is it with all his successors down to Kant.

[1] Bruno and Spinoza are here entirely to be excepted. They stand each for himself and alone, and belong neither to their age nor their quarter of the globe, which rewarded the one with death and the other with persecution and insult. Their miserable existence and death in this Western world is like that of a tropical plant in Europe. The banks of the sacred Ganges were their true spiritual home ; there they would have led a peaceful and honoured life among men of like mind. In the following lines, with which Bruno begins his book *Della Causa Principio et Uno*, for which he was brought to the stake, he expresses clearly and beautifully how lonely he felt himself in his age, and he also shows a presentiment of his fate which led him to delay the publication of his views, till that inclination to communicate what one knows to be true, which is so strong in noble minds, prevailed :

> "*Ad partum properare tuum, mens*
> *ægra, quid obstat ;*
> *Seclo hæc indigno sint tribuenda*
> *licet ?*
> *Umbrarum fluctu terras mergente,*
> *cacumen*
> *Adtolle in clarum, noster Olympe,*
> *Jovem.*"

Whoever has read this his principal work, and also his other Italian writings, which were formerly so rare, but are now accessible to all

Goethe's lines are, therefore, very applicable to a free independent thinker of this kind:

> "Saving Thy gracious presence, he to me
> A long-legged grasshopper appears to be,
> That springing flies, and flying springs,
> And in the grass the same old ditty sings." [1]

Kant had reasons for assuming the air of also intending nothing more. But the pretended spring, which was permitted because it was known that it leads back to the grass, this time became a flight, and now those who remain below can only look after him, and can never catch him again.

Kant, then, ventured to show by his teaching that all those dogmas which had been so often professedly proved were incapable of proof. Speculative theology, and the rational psychology connected with it, received from him their deathblow. Since then they have vanished from German philosophy, and one must not allow oneself to be misled by the fact that here and there the word is retained after the thing has been given up, or some wretched professor of philosophy has the fear of his master in view, and lets truth take care of itself. Only he who has observed the pernicious influence of these conceptions upon natural science, and upon philosophy in all, even the best writers of the seventeenth and eighteenth centuries, can estimate the extent of this service of Kant's. The change of tone and of metaphysical background which has appeared in German writing upon natural science since Kant

through a German edition, will find, as I have done, that he alone of all philosophers in some degree approaches to Plato, in respect of the strong blending of poetical power and tendency along with the philosophical, and this he also shows especially in a dramatic form. Imagine the tender, spiritual, thoughtful being, as he shows himself to us in this work of his, in the hands of coarse, furious priests as his judges and executioners, and thank Time which brought a brighter and a gentler age, so that the after-world whose curse was to fall on those fiendish fanatics is the world we now live in.

[1] Bayard Taylor's translation of "Faust," vol. i. p. 14.—TRS.

is remarkable; before him it was in the same position as
it still occupies in England. This merit of Kant's is connected with the fact that the unreflecting pursuit of the
laws of the phenomenon, the elevation of these to the
position of eternal truths, and thus the raising of the
fleeting appearance to the position of the real being of the
world, in short, *realism* undisturbed in its illusion by any
reflection, had reigned throughout all preceding philosophy, ancient, mediæval, and modern. Berkeley, who,
like Malebranche before him, recognised its one-sidedness,
and indeed falseness, was unable to overthrow it, for his
attack was confined to *one* point. Thus it was reserved
for Kant to enable the idealistic point of view to obtain
the ascendancy in Europe, at least in philosophy; the
point of view which throughout all non-Mohammedan
Asia, and indeed essentially, is that of religion. Before
Kant, then, we were in time; now time is in us, and so on.

Ethics also were treated by that realistic philosophy
according to the laws of the phenomenon, which it regarded as absolute and valid also for the thing in itself.
They were therefore based now upon a doctrine of happiness, now upon the will of the Creator, and finally upon
the conception of perfection; a conception which, taken
by itself, is entirely empty and void of content, for it
denotes a mere relation that only receives significance
from the things to which it is applied. "To be perfect"
means nothing more than "to correspond to some conception which is presupposed and given," a conception which
must therefore be previously framed, and without which
the perfection is an unknown quantity, and consequently
has no meaning when expressed alone. If, however, it is
intended tacitly to presuppose the conception "humanity,"
and accordingly to make it the principle of morality to
strive after human perfection, this is only saying: "Men
ought to be as they ought to be,"—and we are just as
wise as before. In fact "perfect" is very nearly a mere
synonym of "complete," for it signifies that in one given

case or individual, all the predicates which lie in the conception of its species appear, thus are actually present. Therefore the conception "perfection," if used absolutely and in the abstract, is a word void of significance, and this is also the case with the talk about the "most perfect being," and other similar expressions. All this is a mere jingle of words. Nevertheless last century this conception of perfection and imperfection had become current coin; indeed it was the hinge upon which almost all speculation upon ethics, and even theology, turned. It was in every one's mouth, so that at last it became a simple nuisance. We see even the best writers of the time, for example Lessing, entangled in the most deplorable manner in perfections and imperfections, and struggling with them. At the same time, every thinking man must at least dimly have felt that this conception is void of all positive content, because, like an algebraical symbol, it denotes a mere relation *in abstracto.* Kant, as we have already said, entirely separated the undeniably great ethical significance of actions from the phenomenon and its laws, and showed that the former directly concerned the thing in itself, the inner nature of the world, while the latter, *i.e.,* time, space, and all that fills them, and disposes itself in them according to the law of causality, is to be regarded as a changing and unsubstantial dream.

The little I have said, which by no means exhausts the subject, may suffice as evidence of my recognition of the great merits of Kant,—a recognition expressed here both for my own satisfaction, and because justice demands that those merits should be recalled to the memory of every one who desires to follow me in the unsparing exposure of his errors to which I now proceed.

It may be inferred, upon purely historical grounds, that Kant's great achievements must have been accompanied by great errors. For although he effected the greatest revolution in philosophy and made an end of Scholasticism, which, understood in the wider sense we have indicated, had lasted for fourteen centuries, in order to begin what was really the third entirely new epoch in philosophy which the world has seen, yet the direct result of his appearance was only negative, not positive. For since he did not set up a completely new system, to which his disciples could only have adhered for a period, all indeed observed that something very great had happened, but yet no one rightly knew what. They certainly saw that all previous philosophy had been fruitless dreaming, from which the new age had now awakened, but what they ought to hold to now they did not know. A great void was felt; a great need had arisen; the universal attention even of the general public was aroused. Induced by this, but not urged by inward inclination and sense of power (which find utterance even at unfavourable times, as in the case of Spinoza), men without any exceptional talent made various weak, absurd, and indeed sometimes insane, attempts, to which, however, the now interested public gave its attention, and with great patience, such as is only found in Germany, long lent its ear.

The same thing must once have happened in Nature, when a great revolution had altered the whole surface of the earth, land and sea had changed places, and the scene was cleared for a new creation. It was then a long time before Nature could produce a new series of lasting forms all in harmony with themselves and with each other. Strange and monstrous organisations appeared which did not harmonise either with themselves or with each other, and therefore could not endure long, but whose still existing remains have brought down to us the tokens of that wavering and tentative procedure of Nature forming itself anew.

Since, now, in philosophy, a crisis precisely similar to this, and an age of fearful abortions, was, as we all know, introduced by Kant, it may be concluded that the services he rendered were not complete, but must have been negative and one-sided, and burdened with great defects. These defects we now desire to search out.

First of all we shall present to ourselves clearly and examine the fundamental thought in which the aim of the whole "Critique of Pure Reason" lies. Kant placed himself at the standpoint of his predecessors, the dogmatic philosophers, and accordingly he started with them from the following assumptions :—(1.) Metaphysics is the science of that which lies beyond the possibility of all experience. (2.) Such a science can never be attained by applying principles which must first themselves be drawn from experience (*Prolegomena*, § 1); but only what we know *before*, and thus *independently of* all experience, can reach further than possible experience. (3.) In our reason certain principles of this kind are actually to be found: they are comprehended under the name of Knowledge of pure reason. So far Kant goes with his predecessors, but here he separates from them. They say: "These principles, or this knowledge of pure reason, are expressions of the absolute possibility of things, *æternæ veritates*, sources of ontology; they stand above the system of the world, as fate stood above the gods of the ancients." Kant says, they are mere forms of our intellect, laws, not of the existence of things, but of our idea of them; they are therefore valid merely for our apprehension of things, and hence they cannot extend beyond the possibility of experience, which, according to assumption 1, is what was aimed at; for the *a priori* nature of these forms of knowledge, since it can only rest on their subjective origin, is just what cuts us off for ever from the knowledge of the nature of things in themselves, and confines us to a world of mere phenomena, so that we cannot know things as they may be in themselves, even *a posteriori*, not to speak of *a priori*. Accordingly metaphysics

is impossible, and criticism of pure reason takes its place.
As opposed to the old dogmatism, Kant is here completely
victorious; therefore all dogmatic attempts which have
since appeared have been obliged to pursue an entirely
different path from the earlier systems; and I shall now
go on to the justification of my own system, according to
the expressed intention of this criticism. A more careful examination, then, of the reasoning given above will
oblige one to confess that its first fundamental assumption
is a *petitio principii.* It lies in the proposition (stated
with particular clearness in the *Prolegomena,* § 1): "The
source of metaphysics must throughout be non-empirical;
its fundamental principles and conceptions must never
be taken from either inner or outer experience." Yet
absolutely nothing is advanced in proof of this cardinal
assertion except the etymological argument from the word
metaphysic. In truth, however, the matter stands thus:
The world and our own existence presents itself to us
necessarily as a riddle. It is now assumed, without more
ado, that the solution of this riddle cannot be arrived at
from a thorough understanding of the world itself, but
must be sought in something entirely different from the
world (for that is the meaning of "beyond the possibility
of all experience"); and that everything must be excluded
from that solution of which we can in any way have
immediate knowledge (for that is the meaning of possible
experience, both inner and outer); the solution must
rather be sought only in that at which we can arrive
merely indirectly, that is, by means of inferences from
universal principles *a priori.* After the principal source
of all knowledge has in this way been excluded, and the
direct way to truth has been closed, we must not wonder
that the dogmatic systems failed, and that Kant was able
to show the necessity of this failure; for metaphysics and
knowledge *a priori* had been assumed beforehand to be
identical. But for this it was first necessary to prove that
the material for the solution of the riddle absolutely can-

not be contained in the world itself, but must be sought for only outside the world in something we can only attain to under the guidance of those forms of which we are conscious *a priori*. But so long as this is not proved, we have no grounds for shutting ourselves off, in the case of the most important and most difficult of all questions, from the richest of all sources of knowledge, inner and outer experience, in order to work only with empty forms. I therefore say that the solution of the riddle of the world must proceed from the understanding of the world itself; that thus the task of metaphysics is not to pass beyond the experience in which the world exists, but to understand it thoroughly, because outer and inner experience is at any rate the principal source of all knowledge; that therefore the solution of the riddle of the world is only possible through the proper connection of outer with inner experience, effected at the right point, and the combination thereby produced of these two very different sources of knowledge. Yet this solution is only possible within certain limits which are inseparable from our finite nature, so that we attain to a right understanding of the world itself without reaching a final explanation of its existence abolishing all further problems. Therefore *est quadam prodire tenus*, and my path lies midway between the omniscience of the earlier dogmatists and the despair of the Kantian Critique. The important truths, however, which Kant discovered, and through which the earlier metaphysical systems were overthrown, have supplied my system with data and materials. Compare what I have said concerning my method in chap. xvii. of the Supplements. So much for the fundamental thought of Kant; we shall now consider his working out of it and its details.

Kant's style bears throughout the stamp of a pre-eminent mind, genuine strong individuality, and quite

exceptional power of thought. Its characteristic quality
may perhaps be aptly described as a *brilliant dryness*, by
virtue of which he was able to grasp firmly and select the
conceptions with great certainty, and then to turn them
about with the greatest freedom, to the astonishment of the
reader. I find the same brilliant dryness in the style of
Aristotle, though it is much simpler. Nevertheless Kant's
language is often indistinct, indefinite, inadequate, and
sometimes obscure. Its obscurity, certainly, is partly
excusable on account of the difficulty of the subject and
the depth of the thought; but he who is himself clear to
the bottom, and knows with perfect distinctness what he
thinks and wishes, will never write indistinctly, will never
set up wavering and indefinite conceptions, compose most
difficult and complicated expressions from foreign languages to denote them, and use these expressions constantly
afterwards, as Kant took words and formulas from earlier
philosophy, especially Scholasticism, which he combined
with each other to suit his purposes; as, for example,
" transcendental synthetic unity of apperception," and
in general " unity of synthesis " (*Einheit der Synthesis*),
always used where "union" (*Vereinigung*) would be quite
sufficient by itself. Moreover, a man who is himself
quite clear will not be always explaining anew what has
once been explained, as Kant does, for example, in the
case of the understanding, the categories, experience, and
other leading conceptions. In general, such a man will
not incessantly repeat himself, and yet in every new exposition of the thought already expressed a hundred times
leave it in just the same obscure condition, but he will
express his meaning once distinctly, thoroughly, and exhaustively, and then let it alone. " *Quo enim melius rem
aliquam concipimus eo magis determinati sumus ad eam
unico modo exprimendam*," says Descartes in his fifth
letter. But the most injurious result of Kant's occasionally obscure language is, that it acted as *exemplar vitiis
imitabile;* indeed, it was misconstrued as a pernicious

authorisation.   The public was compelled to see that what is obscure is not always without significance; consequently, what was without significance took refuge behind obscure language.   Fichte was the first to seize this new privilege and use it vigorously; Schelling at least equalled him; and a host of hungry scribblers, without talent and without honesty, soon outbade them both.   But the height of audacity, in serving up pure nonsense, in stringing together senseless and extravagant mazes of words, such as had previously only been heard in madhouses, was finally reached in Hegel, and became the instrument of the most barefaced general mystification that has ever taken place, with a result which will appear fabulous to posterity, and will remain as a monument of German stupidity.   In vain, meanwhile, Jean Paul wrote his beautiful paragraph, " Higher criticism of philosophical madness in the professorial chair, and poetical madness in the theatre" (*Æsthetische Nachschule*); for in vain Goethe had already said—

> "They prate and teach, and no one interferes;
> All from the fellowship of fools are shrinking;
> Man usually believes, if only words he hears,
> That also with them goes material for thinking."[1]

But let us return to Kant.   We are compelled to admit that he entirely lacks grand, classical simplicity, *naïveté, ingénuité, candeur.*   His philosophy has no analogy with Grecian architecture, which presents large simple proportions revealing themselves at once to the glance; on the contrary, it reminds us strongly of the Gothic style of building.   For a purely individual characteristic of Kant's mind is a remarkable love of *symmetry,* which delights in a varied multiplicity, so that it may reduce it to order, and repeat this order in subordinate orders, and so on indefinitely, just as happens in Gothic churches.   Indeed, he sometimes carries this to the extent of trifling, and from love of this tendency he goes so far as to do open

[1] "Faust," scene vi., Bayard Taylor's translation, vol. i. p. 134.—TRS.

violence to truth, and to deal with it as Nature was dealt with by the old-fashioned gardeners, whose work we see in symmetrical alleys, squares, and triangles, trees shaped like pyramids and spheres, and hedges winding in regular curves. I will support this with facts.

After he has treated space and time isolated from everything else, and has then dismissed this whole world of perception which fills space and time, and in which we live and are, with the meaningless words "the empirical content of perception is given us," he immediately arrives with one spring at *the logical basis of his whole philosophy, the table of judgments.* From this table he deduces an exact dozen of categories, symmetrically arranged under four heads, which afterwards become the fearful procrustean bed into which he violently forces all things in the world and all that goes on in man, shrinking from no violence and disdaining no sophistry if only he is able to repeat everywhere the symmetry of that table. The first that is symmetrically deduced from it is the pure physiological table of the general principles of natural science— the axioms of intuition, anticipations of perception, analogies of experience, and postulates of empirical thought in general. Of these fundamental principles, the first two are simple; but each of the last two sends out symmetrically three shoots. The mere categories were what he calls *conceptions;* but these principles of natural science are *judgments.* In accordance with his highest guide to all wisdom, symmetry, the series must now prove itself fruitful in the syllogisms, and this, indeed, is done symmetrically and regularly. For, as by the application of the categories to sensibility, experience with all its *a priori* principles arose for the understanding, so by the application of *syllogisms* to the categories, a task performed by the *reason* in accordance with its pretended principle of seeking the unconditioned, the *Ideas* of the reason arise. Now this takes place in the following manner: The three categories of relation supply to syllogistic reasoning the three only possible kinds of major premisses, and syllogistic reasoning accordingly falls into three kinds, each of which is to be regarded as an egg out of which the reason hatches an Idea; out of the categorical syllogism the Idea of the *soul*, out of the hypothetical the Idea of the *world*, and out of the disjunctive the Idea of *God*. In the second of these, the Idea of the world, the symmetry of the table of the categories now repeats itself again, for its four heads produce four theses, each of which has its antithesis as a symmetrical pendant.

We pay the tribute of our admiration to the really exceedingly acute combination which produced this elegant structure, but we shall none the less proceed to a thorough examination of its foundation and its parts. But the following remarks must come first.

It is astonishing how Kant, without further reflection, pursues his way, following his symmetry, ordering everything in accordance with it, without ever taking one of the subjects so handled into consideration on its own account. I will explain myself more fully. After he has considered intuitive knowledge in a mathematical reference only, he neglects altogether the rest of knowledge of perception in which the world lies before us, and confines himself entirely to abstract thinking, although this receives the whole of its significance and value from the world of perception alone, which is infinitely more significant, generally present, and rich in content than the abstract part of our knowledge. Indeed, and this is an important point, he has nowhere clearly distinguished perception from abstract knowledge, and just on this account, as we shall afterwards see, he becomes involved in irresolvable contradictions with himself. After he has disposed of the whole sensible world with the meaningless "it is given," he makes, as we have said, the logical table of judgments the foundation-stone of his building. But here again he does not reflect for a moment upon that which really lies before him. These forms of judgment are indeed *words* and *combinations of words;* yet it ought first to have been asked what these directly denote : it would have been found that they denote *conceptions.* The next question would then have been as to the nature of *conceptions.* It would have appeared from the answer what relation these have to the ideas of perception in which the world exists ; for perception and reflection would have been distinguished. It would now have become necessary to examine, not merely how pure and merely formal intuition or perception *a priori*, but also how its content, the empirical perception, comes into consciousness. But then it would have become apparent what part the *understanding* has in this, and thus also in general what the *understanding* is, and, on the other hand, what the *reason* properly is, the critique of which is being written. It is most remarkable that he does not once properly and adequately define the latter, but merely gives incidentally, and as the context in each case demands, incomplete and inaccurate explanations of it, in direct contradiction to the rule of Descartes given above.[1] For example, at p. 11 ; V. 24, of the " Critique of Pure Reason," it is the faculty of principles *a priori;* but at p. 299 ; V. 356, it is said that reason is the faculty of *principles,* and it is opposed to the understanding, which is the faculty of *rules !* One would now think that there must be a very wide difference between principles and rules, since it entitles us to assume a special faculty of knowledge for each of them. But this great distinction is made to lie merely in this, that what is known *a priori* through pure perception or through the forms of the understanding is a rule, and only what results from mere

---

[1] Observe here that I always quote the " Kritik der reinen Vernunft " according to the paging of the first edition, for in Rosenkranz's edition of Kant's collected works this paging is always given in addition. Besides this, I add the paging of the fifth edition, preceded by a V. ; all the other editions, from the second onwards, are the same as the fifth, and so also is their paging.

conceptions is a principle. We shall return to this arbitrary and inadmissible distinction later, when we come to the Dialectic. On p. 330; V. 386, reason is the faculty of inference; mere judging (p. 69; V. 94) he often explains as the work of the understanding. Now, this really amounts to saying: Judging is the work of the understanding so long as the ground of the judgment is empirical, transcendental, or metalogical (Essay on the Principle of Sufficient Reason, § 31, 32, 33); but if it is logical, as is the case with the syllogism, then we are here concerned with a quite special and much more important faculty of knowledge—the reason. Nay, what is more, on p. 303; V. 360, it is explained that what follows directly from a proposition is still a matter of the understanding, and that only those conclusions which are arrived at by the use of a mediating conception are the work of the reason, and the example given is this: From the proposition, "All men are mortal," the inference, "Some mortals are men," may be drawn by the mere understanding. On the other hand, to draw the conclusion, "All the learned are mortal," demands an entirely different and far more important faculty—the reason. How was it possible for a great thinker to write the like of this! On p. 553; V. 581, reason is all at once the constant condition of all voluntary action. On p. 614; V. 642, it consists in the fact that we can give an account of our assertions; on pp. 643, 644; V. 671, 672, in the circumstance that it brings unity into the conceptions of the understanding by means of Ideas, as the understanding brings unity into the multiplicity of objects by means of conceptions. On p. 646; V. 674, it is nothing else than the faculty which deduces the particular from the general.

The understanding also is constantly being explained anew. In seven passages of the "Critique of Pure Reason" it is explained in the following terms. On p. 51; V. 75, it is the faculty which of itself produces ideas of perception. On p. 69; V. 94, it is the faculty of judging, *i.e.,* of thinking, *i.e.,* of knowing through conceptions. On p. 137 of the fifth edition, it is the faculty of knowledge generally. On p. 132; V. 171, it is the faculty of rules. On p. 158; V. 197, however, it is said : "It is not only the faculty of rules, but the source of principles (*Grundsätze*) according to which everything comes under rules ; " and yet above it was opposed to the reason because the latter alone was the faculty of principles (*Principien*). On p. 160; V. 199, the understanding is the faculty of conceptions; but on p. 302; V. 359, it is the faculty of the unity of phenomena by means of rules.

Against such really confused and groundless language on the subject (even though it comes from Kant) I shall have no need to defend the explanation which I have given of these two faculties of knowledge—an explanation which is fixed, clearly defined, definite, simple, and in full agreement with the language of all nations and all ages. I have only quoted this language as a proof of my charge that Kant follows his symmetrical, logical system without sufficiently reflecting upon the subject he is thus handling.

Now, as I have said above, if Kant had seriously examined how far two such different faculties of knowledge, one of which is the specific difference of man, may be known, and what, in accordance with the language of all nations and all philosophers, reason and understanding are, he would never, without further authority than the *intellectus theoreticus* and *practicus* of the Schoolmen, which is used in an entirely different sense, have divided the reason into theoretical and practical, and made the latter the source of virtuous conduct. In the same way, before Kant separated so carefully conceptions of the understanding (by which he sometimes means his categories, sometimes all general conceptions) and conceptions of the reason (his so-called Ideas), and made them both the material of his philosophy, which for the most part deals only with the validity, application, and origin of all these conceptions ;—first, I say, he ought to have really

examined what in general a *conception* is. But this very
necessary investigation has unfortunately been also neglected, and has contributed much to the irremediable
confusion of intuitive and abstract knowledge which I
shall soon refer to. The same want of adequate reflection
with which he passed over the questions: what is perception? what is reflection? what is conception? what
is reason? what is understanding? allowed him to pass
over the following investigations, which were just as inevitably necessary: what is it that I call the *object*, which
I distinguish from the *idea?* what is existence? what is
object? what is subject? what is truth, illusion, error?
But he follows his logical schema and his symmetry without reflecting or looking about him. The table of judgments ought to, and must, be the key to all wisdom.

I have given it above as the chief merit of Kant that he
distinguished the phenomenon from the thing in itself,
explained the whole visible world as phenomenon, and
therefore denied all validity to its laws beyond the phenomenon. It is certainly remarkable that he did not
deduce this merely relative existence of the phenomenon
from the simple undeniable truth which lay so near him,
" *No object without a subject,*" in order thus at the very
root to show that the object, because it always exists
merely in relation to a subject, is dependent upon it,
conditioned by it, and therefore conditioned as mere
phenomenon, which does not exist in itself nor unconditioned. Berkeley, to whose merits Kant did not do
justice, had already made this important principle the
foundation-stone of his philosophy, and thereby established
an immortal reputation. Yet he himself did not draw the
proper conclusions from this principle, and so he was
both misunderstood and insufficiently attended to. In
my first edition I explained Kant's avoidance of this
Berkeleian principle as arising from an evident shrink-

ing from decided idealism; while, on the other hand, I found idealism distinctly expressed in many passages of the "Critique of Pure Reason," and accordingly I charged Kant with contradicting himself. And this charge was well founded, if, as was then my case, one only knew the "Critique of Pure Reason" in the second or any of the five subsequent editions printed from it. But when later I read Kant's great work in the first edition, which is already so rare, I saw, to my great pleasure, all these contradictions disappear, and found that although Kant does not use the formula, "No object without a subject," he yet explains, with just as much decision as Berkeley and I do, the outer world lying before us in space and time as the mere idea of the subject that knows it. Therefore, for example, he says there without reserve (p. 383): "If I take away the thinking subject, the whole material world must disappear, for it is nothing but a phenomenon in the sensibility of our subject, and a class of its ideas." But the whole passage from p. 348–392, in which Kant expounded his pronounced idealism with peculiar beauty and clearness, was suppressed by him in the second edition, and instead of it a number of remarks controverting it were introduced. In this way then the text of the "Critique of Pure Reason," as it has circulated from the year 1787 to the year 1838, was disfigured and spoilt, and it became a self-contradictory book, the sense of which could not therefore be thoroughly clear and comprehensible to any one. The particulars about this, and also my conjectures as to the reasons and the weaknesses which may have influenced Kant so to disfigure his immortal work, I have given in a letter to Professor Rosenkranz, and he has quoted the principal passage of it in his preface to the second volume of the edition of Kant's collected works edited by him, to which I therefore refer. In consequence of my representations, Professor Rosenkranz was induced in the year 1838 to restore the "Critique of Pure Reason" to its original form, for in the second volume referred to he had it printed according to the *first* edition of 1781, by which he has rendered an inestimable service to philosophy; indeed, he has perhaps saved from destruction the most important work of German literature; and this should always be remembered to his credit. But let no one imagine that he knows the "Critique of Pure Reason" and has a distinct conception of Kant's teaching if he has only read the second or one of the later editions. That is altogether impossible, for he has only read a mutilated, spoilt, and to a certain extent ungenuine text. It is my duty to say this here decidedly and for every one's warning.

Yet the way in which Kant introduces the *thing in itself* stands in undeniable contradiction with the distinctly idealistic point of view so clearly expressed in the first edition of the "Critique of Pure Reason," and without doubt this is the chief reason why, in the second edition, he suppressed the principal idealistic passage we have referred to, and directly declared himself opposed to the Berkeleian idealism, though by doing so he only introduced inconsistencies into his work, without being able to remedy its principal defect. This defect, as is known, is the introduction of the *thing in itself* in the way chosen by him, the inadmissibleness of which was exposed at length by G. E. Schulze in "*Ænesidemus*," and was soon recognised as the untenable point of his system. The matter may be made clear in a very few words. Kant based the assumption of the thing in itself, though concealed under various modes of expression, upon an inference from the law of causality—an inference that the empirical perception, or more accurately the *sensation*, in our organs of sense, from which it proceeds, must have an external cause. But according to his own account, which is correct, the law of causality is known to us *a priori*, consequently is a function of our intellect, and is thus of *subjective* origin; further, sensation itself, to which we here apply the law of causality, is undeniably *subjective*; and finally, even space, in which, by means of this application, we place the cause of this sensation as object, is a form of our intellect given *a priori*, and is consequently *subjective*. Therefore the whole empirical perception remains always upon a *subjective* foundation, as a mere process in us, and nothing entirely different from it and independent of it can be brought in as a *thing in itself,* or shown to be a necessary assumption. The empirical perception actually is and remains merely our idea: it is the world as idea. An inner nature of this we can only arrive at on the entirely different path followed by me, by means of calling in the aid of self-consciousness, which proclaims the will as the inner nature of our own phenomenon; but then the thing in itself will be one which is *toto genere* different from the idea and its elements, as I have explained.

The great defect of the Kantian system in this point, which, as has been said, was soon pointed out, is an illustration of the truth of the beautiful Indian proverb: "No lotus without a stem." The erroneous deduction of the thing in itself is here the stem; yet only the method of the deduction, not the recognition of a thing in itself belonging to the given phenomenon. But this last was Fichte's misunderstanding of it, which could only happen because he was not concerned with truth, but with making a sensation for the furtherance of his individual ends. Accordingly he was bold and thoughtless enough to deny the thing in itself altogether, and to set up a system in which, not, as with Kant, the mere form of the idea, but also the matter, its whole content, was professedly deduced *a priori* from the subject. In doing this, he counted with perfect correctness upon the want of judgment and the stupidity of the public, which accepted miserable sophisms, mere hocus-pocus and senseless babble, for proofs; so that he succeeded in turning its attention from Kant to himself, and gave the direction to German philosophy in which it was afterwards carried further by Schelling, and ultimately reached its goal in the mad sophistry of Hegel.

I now return to the great mistake of Kant, already

touched on above, that he has not properly separated perceptible and abstract knowledge, whereby an inextricable confusion has arisen which we have now to consider more closely. If he had sharply separated ideas of perception from conceptions merely thought *in abstracto*, he would have held these two apart, and in every case would have known with which of the two he had to do. This, however, was unfortunately not the case, although this accusation has not yet been openly made, and may thus perhaps be unexpected. His "object of experience," of which he is constantly speaking, the proper object of the categories, is not the idea of perception ; neither is it the abstract conception, but it is different from both, and yet both at once, and is a perfect chimera. For, incredible as it may seem, he lacked either the wisdom or the honesty to come to an understanding with himself about this, and to explain distinctly to himself and others whether his "object of experience, *i.e.*, the knowledge produced by the application of the categories," is the idea of perception in space and time (my first class of ideas), or merely the abstract conception. Strange as it is, there always runs in his mind something between the two, and hence arises the unfortunate confusion which I must now bring to light. For this end I must go through the whole theory of elements in a general way.

The "Transcendental Æsthetic" is a work of such extraordinary merit that it alone would have been sufficient to immortalise the name of Kant. Its proofs carry such perfect conviction, that I number its propositions among incontestable truths, and without doubt they are also among those that are richest in results, and are, therefore, to be regarded as the rarest thing in the world, a real and great discovery in metaphysics. The fact, strictly proved by him, that a part of our knowledge is known to us *a priori*, admits of no other explanation than that this constitutes the forms of our intellect; indeed, this is less an explanation than merely the distinct expression of the fact itself. For *a priori* means nothing else than "not gained on the path of experience, thus not come into us from without." But what is present in the intellect, and has not come from without, is just what belongs originally to the intellect itself, its own nature. Now if what is thus present in the intellect itself consists of the general mode or manner in which it must present all its objects to itself, this is just saying that what is thus present is the intellect's forms of knowing, *i.e.*, the mode, fixed once for all, in which it fulfils this its function. Accordingly, "knowledge *a priori*" and "the intellect's own forms" are at bottom only two expressions for the same things thus to a certain extent synonyms.

Therefore from the doctrine of the Transcendental Æsthetic I knew of nothing to take away, only of something to add. Kant did not carry out his thought to the end, especially in this respect, that he did not reject Euclid's whole method of demonstration, even after having said on p. 87; V. 120, that all geometrical knowledge has direct evidence from perception. It is most remarkable that one of Kant's opponents, and indeed the acutest of them, G. E. Schulze (*Kritik der theoretischen Philosophie*, ii. 241), draws the conclusion that from his doctrine an entirely different treatment of geometry from that which is actually in use would arise; and thus he thought to bring an apagogical argument against Kant, but, in fact, without knowing it, he only began the war against the method of Euclid. Let me refer to § 15 of the first book of this work.

After the full exposition of the universal *forms* of perception given in the Transcendental Æsthetic, one necessarily expects to receive some explanation as to its *content*, as to the way in which the *empirical* perception comes into our consciousness, how the knowledge of this whole world, which is for us so real and so important, arises in us. But the whole teaching of Kant contains really nothing more about this than the oft-repeated meaningless expression : " The empirical element in perception is *given* from without." Consequently here also from the *pure forms of perception* Kant arrives with one spring at *thinking* at the *Transcendental Logic.* Just at the beginning of the Transcendental Logic (Critique of Pure Reason, p. 50; V. 74), where Kant cannot avoid touching upon the content of the empirical perception, he takes the first false step; he is guilty of the πρῶτον ψεῦδος. " Our knowledge," he says, " has two sources, receptivity of impressions and spontaneity of conceptions : the first is the capacity for receiving ideas, the second that of knowing an object through these ideas : through the first an *object* is given us, through the second it is thought." This is false; for according to it the *impression,* for which alone we have mere receptivity, which thus comes from without and alone is properly " given," would be already an *idea,* and indeed an *object.* But it is nothing more than a mere *sensation* in the organ of sense, and only by the application of the *understanding* (*i.e.*, of the law of causality) and the forms of perception, space and time, does our *intellect* change this mere *sensation* into an *idea,* which now exists as an object in space and time, and cannot be distinguished from the latter (the object) except in so far as we ask after the thing in itself, but apart from this is identical with it. I have explained this point fully in the essay on the principle of sufficient reason, § 21. With this, however, the work of the understanding and of the faculty of perception is completed, and no conceptions and no thinking are required in addition ; therefore the brute also has these *ideas.* If conceptions are added, if thinking is added, to which spontaneity may certainly be attributed, then knowledge of *perception* is entirely abandoned, and a completely different class of ideas comes into consciousness, non-perceptible abstract conceptions. This is the activity of the *reason,* which yet obtains the whole content of its thinking only from the previous perception, and the comparison of it with other perceptions and conceptions. But thus Kant brings thinking into the perception, and lays the foundation for the inextricable confusion of intuitive and abstract knowledge which I am now engaged in condemning. He allows the perception, taken by itself, to be without understanding, purely sensuous, and thus quite passive, and only through thinking (category of the understanding) does he allow an *object* to be apprehended: thus he brings *thought into the perception.* But then, again, the object of thinking is an individual real object; and in this way thinking loses its essential character of universality and abstraction, and instead of general conceptions receives individual things as its object: thus again he *brings perception into thinking.* From this springs the inextricable confusion referred to, and the consequences of this first false step extend over his whole theory of knowledge. Through the whole of his theory the utter confusion of the idea of perception with the abstract idea tends towards a something between the two which he expounds as the object of knowledge through the understanding and its categories, and calls this knowledge *experience.* It is hard to believe that Kant really figured to himself something fully determined and really distinct in this object of the understanding; I shall now prove this through the tremendous contradiction which runs through the whole Transcendental Logic, and is the real source of the obscurity in which it is involved.

In the "Critique of Pure Reason," p. 67–69; V. 92–94, p. 89, 90; V. 122, 123; further, V. 135, 139, 153, he repeats and insists: the understanding is no faculty of perception, its knowledge is not intuitive but discursive; the understanding is the faculty of judging (p. 69; V. 94), and a judgment is indirect knowledge, an idea of an idea (p. 68; V. 93); the understanding is the faculty of thinking, and thinking is knowledge through conceptions (p. 69; V. 94); the categories of the understanding are by no means the conditions under which objects are given in perception (p. 89; V. 122), and perception in no way requires the functions of thinking (p. 91; V. 123); our understanding can only think, not perceive (V. pp. 135, 139). Further, in the "Prolegomena," § 20, he says that perception, sensation, *perceptio,* belongs merely to the senses; judgment to the understanding alone; and in § 22, that the work of the senses is to perceive, that of the understanding to think, *i.e.,* to judge. Finally, in the "Critique of Practical Reason," fourth edition, p. 247; Rosenkranz's edition, p. 281, he says that the understanding is discursive; its ideas are thoughts, not perceptions. All this is in Kant's own words.

From this it follows that this perceptible world would exist for us even if we had no understanding at all; that it comes into our head in a quite inexplicable manner, which he constantly indicates by his strange expression the perception is *given,* without ever explaining this indefinite and metaphorical expression further.

Now all that has been quoted is contradicted in the most glaring manner by the whole of the rest of his doctrine of the understanding, of its categories, and of the possibility of experience as he explains it in the Transcendental Logic. Thus (Critique of Pure Reason, p. 79; V. 105), the understanding through its categories brings unity into the manifold of *perception,* and the pure conceptions of the understanding refer *a priori* to objects of *perception.* P. 94; V. 126, the "categories are the condition of experience whether of perception, which is found in it, or of thought." V. p. 127, the understanding is the originator of experience. V. p. 128, the categories determine the *perception* of objects. V. p. 130, all that we present to ourselves as connected in the object (which is yet certainly something perceptible and not an abstraction), has been so connected by an act of the understanding. V. p. 135, the understanding is explained anew as the faculty of combining *a priori,* and of bringing the multiplicity of given ideas under the unity of apperception; but according to all ordinary use of words, apperception is not the thinking of a conception, but is *perception.* V. p. 136, we find a first principle of the possibility of all perception in connection with the understanding. V. p. 143, it stands as the heading, that all sense perception is conditioned by the categories. At the same place the *logical function of the judgment* also brings the manifold of given perceptions under an apperception in general, and the manifold of a given perception stands necessarily under the categories. V. p. 144, unity comes into perception, by means of the categories, through the understanding. V. p. 145, the thinking of the understanding is very strangely explained as synthetically combining, connecting, and arranging the manifold of perception. V. p. 161, experience is only possible through the categories, and consists in the connection of *sensations,* which, however, are just perceptions. V. p. 159, the categories are *a priori* knowledge of the objects of perception in general. Further, here and at V. p. 163 and 165, a chief doctrine of Kant's is given, this: *that the understanding first makes Nature possible,* because it prescribes laws for it *a priori,* and Nature adapts itself to the system of the understanding, and so on. Nature, however, is certainly perceptible and not an abstraction; therefore, the understanding must be a faculty of perception. V. p. 168, it is said, the conceptions of the understanding are the principles of the possibility of experience, and the latter is the condition of phenomena in space and time in general; phenomena which, however, certainly exist in perception. Finally, p. 189–211; V. 232–265, the long proof is given (the incorrectness of which is shown in detail in my essay on the principle of sufficient reason, § 23) that the objective succession and also the coexistence of objects of experience are not sensuously apprehended, but are only brought into Nature by the understanding, and that Nature itself first becomes possible in this way. Yet it is certain that Nature, the course of events, and the coexistence of states, is purely perceptible, and no mere abstract thought.

I challenge every one who shares my respect towards Kant to reconcile these contradictions and to show that in his doctrine of the object of experience and the way it is determined by the activity of the understanding and its twelve functions, Kant thought something quite distinct and definite. I am convinced that the contradiction I have pointed out, which extends through the whole Transcendental Logic, is the real reason of the great obscurity of its language. Kant himself, in fact, was dimly conscious of the contradiction, inwardly combated it, but yet either would not or could not bring it to distinct consciousness, and therefore veiled it from himself and others, and avoided it by all kinds of subterfuges. This is perhaps also the reason why he made out of the faculties of knowledge such a strange complicated machine, with so many wheels, as the twelve categories, the transcendental synthesis of imagination, of the inner sense, of the transcendental unity of apperception, also the schematism of the pure conceptions of the understanding, &c., &c. And notwithstanding this great apparatus, not even an attempt is made to explain the perception of the external world, which is after all the principal fact in our knowledge; but this pressing claim is very meanly rejected, always through the same meaningless metaphorical expression: "The empirical perception is given us." On p. 145 of the fifth edition, we learn further that the perception is given through the object; therefore the object must be something different from the perception.

If, now, we endeavour to investigate Kant's inmost meaning, not clearly expressed by himself, we find that in reality such an object, different from the perception, but which is by no means a conception, is for him the proper object for the understanding; indeed that it must be by means of the strange assumption of such an object, which cannot be presented in perception, that the perception first becomes experience. I believe that an old deeply-rooted prejudice in Kant, dead to all investigation, is the ultimate reason of the assumption of such an *absolute object*, which is an object in itself, *i.e.*, without a subject. It is certainly not the *perceived object*, but through the conception it is added to the perception by thought, as something corresponding to it; and now the perception is experience, and has value and truth, which it thus only receives through the relation to a conception (in diametrical opposition to my exposition, according to which the conception only receives value and truth from the perception). It is then the proper function of the categories to add on in thought to the perception this directly non-perceptible object. "The object is given only through perception, and is afterwards thought in accordance with the category" (Critique of Pure Reason, first edition, p. 399). This is made specially clear by a passage on p. 125 of the fifth edition : "Now the question arises whether conceptions *a priori* do not also come first as conditions under which alone a thing can be, not perceived certainly, but yet *thought* as an *object* in general," which he answers in the affirmative. Here the source of the error and the confusion in which it is involved shows itself distinctly. For the *object* as such exists always only for *perception* and in it; it may now be completed through the senses, or, when it is absent, through the imagination. What is thought, on the contrary, is always an universal non-perceptible *conception*, which certainly can be the conception of an object in general; but only indirectly by means of conceptions does thought relate itself to *objects*, which always are and remain *perceptible*. For our thinking is not able to impart reality to perceptions ; this they have, so far as they are capable of it (empirical reality) of themselves ; but it serves to bring together the common element and the results of perceptions, in order to preserve them, and to be able to use them more easily. But Kant ascribes the objects themselves to thought, in order to make experience and the objective world dependent upon *under-standing*, yet without allowing understanding to be a faculty of *perception*. In this relation he certainly distinguishes perception from thought, but he makes particular things sometimes the object of perception and sometimes the object of thought. In reality, however, they are only the object of the former; our empirical perception is at once *objective*, just because it proceeds from the causal nexus. Things, not ideas different from them, are directly its object. Particular things as such are perceived in the understanding and through the senses; the one-sided impression upon the latter is at once completed by the imagination. But, on the contrary, as soon as we pass over to thought, we leave the particular things, and have to do with general conceptions, which cannot be presented in perception, although we afterwards apply the results of our thought to particular things. If we hold firmly to this, the inadmissibleness of the assumption becomes evident that the perception of things only obtains reality and becomes experience through the thought of these very things applying its twelve categories. Rather in perception itself the empirical reality, and consequently experience, is already given; but the perception itself can only come into existence by the application to sensation of the knowledge of the causal nexus, which is the one function of the understanding. Perception is accordingly in reality intellectual, which is just what Kant denies.

Besides in the passages quoted, the assumption of Kant here criticised will be found expressed with admirable clearness in the "Critique of Judgment," § 36, just at the beginning; also in the "Metaphysical Principles of Natural Science," in the note to the first explanation of "Phenomenology." But with a *naïveté* which Kant ventured upon least of all with reference to this doubtful point, it is to be found most distinctly laid down in the book of a Kantian, Kiesewetter's "*Grundriss einer allgemeinen Logik*," third edition, part i., p. 434 of the exposition, and part ii., § 52 and 53 of the exposition; similarly in Tieftrunk's "*Denklehre in rein Deutschem Gewande*" (1825). It there appears so clearly how those disciples who do not themselves think become a magnifying mirror of the errors of every thinker. Once having determined his doctrine of the categories, Kant was always cautious when expounding it, but his disciples on the contrary were quite bold, and thus exposed its falseness.

According to what has been said, the object of the categories is for Kant, not indeed the thing in itself, but yet most closely akin to it. It is the *object in itself;* it is an object that requires no subject; it is a particular thing, and yet not in space and time, because not perceptible ; it is an object of thought, and yet not an abstract conception. Accordingly Kant really makes a triple division : (1.) the idea; (2.) the object of the idea; (3.) the thing in itself. The first belongs to the sensibility, which in its case, as in that of sensation, includes the pure forms of perception, space and time. The second belongs to the understanding, which thinks it through its twelve categories. The third lies beyond the possibility of all knowledge. (In support of this, *cf.* Critique of Pure Reason, first edition, p. 108 and 109.) The distinction of the idea from the object of the idea is however unfounded ; this had already been proved by Berkeley, and it appears from my whole exposition in the first book, especially chap. i. of the supplements; nay, even from Kant's own completely idealistic point of view in the first edition. But if we should not wish to count the object of the idea as belonging to the idea and identify it with the idea, it would be necessary to attribute it to the thing in itself: this ultimately depends on the sense which is attached to the word object. This, however, always remains certain, that, when we think clearly, nothing more can be found than idea and thing in itself. The illicit introduction of that hybrid, the object of the idea, is the source of Kant's errors ; yet when it is taken away, the doctrine of the categories as conceptions *a priori* also falls to the ground; for they bring nothing to the perception, and are not supposed to hold good of the thing in itself, but by means of them we only think those " objects of the ideas," and thereby change ideas into experience. For every empirical perception is already experience; but every perception which proceeds from sensation is empirical: this sensation is related by the understanding, by means of its sole function (knowledge *a priori* of the law of causality), to its cause, which just on this account presents itself in space and time (forms of pure perception) as object of experience, material object, enduring in space through all time, yet as such always remains idea, as do space and time themselves. If we desire to go beyond this idea, then we arrive at the question as to the thing in itself, the answer to which is the theme of my whole work, as of all metaphysics in general. Kant's error here explained is connected with his mistake, which we condemned before, that he gives no theory of the origin of empirical perception, but, without saying more, treats it as *given*, identifying it with the mere sensation, to which he only adds the forms of intuition or perception, space and time, comprehending both under the name sensibility. But from these materials no objective idea arises : this absolutely demands the relation of the idea to its cause, thus the application of the law of causality, and thus understanding; for without this the sensation still remains always subjective, and does not take the form of an object in space, even if space is given with it. But according to Kant, the understanding must not be assigned to perception ; it is supposed merely to *think*, so as to remain within the transcendental logic. With this again is connected another mistake of Kant's : that he left it to me to adduce the only valid proof of the *a priori* nature of the law of causality which he rightly recognised, the proof from the possibility of objective empirical perception itself, and instead of it gives a palpably false one, as I have already shown in my essay on the principle of sufficient reason, § 23. From the above it is clear that Kant's "object of the idea" (2) is made up of what he has stolen partly from the idea (1), and partly from the thing in itself (3). If, in reality, experience were only brought about by the understanding applying its twelve different functions in order to *think* through as many conceptions *a priori*, the objects which were previously merely perceived, then every real thing would necessarily as such have a number of determinations, which, as given *a priori*, absolutely could not be thought away, just like space and time, but would belong quite essentially to the existence of the thing, and yet could not be deduced from the properties of space and time. But only one such determination is to be found—that of causality. Upon this rests materiality, for the essence of matter consists in action, and it is through and through causality (*cf.* Bk. II. ch. iv.) But it is materiality alone that distinguishes the real thing from the picture of the imagination, which is then only idea. For matter, as permanent, gives to the thing permanence through all time, in respect of its matter, while the forms change in conformity with causality. Everything else in the thing consists either of determinations of space or of time, or of its empirical properties, which are all referable to its activity, and are thus fuller determinations of causality. But causality enters already as a condition into the empirical perception, and this is accordingly a thing of the understanding, which makes even perception possible, and yet apart from the law of causality contributes nothing to experience and its possibilty. What fills the old ontologies is, with the exception of what is given here, nothing more than relations of things to each other, or to our reflection, and a farrago of nonsense.

The language in which the doctrine of the categories is expressed affords an evidence of its baselessness. What a difference in this respect between the Transcendental Æsthetic and the Transcendental Analytic! In the former, what clearness, definiteness, certainty, firm conviction which is freely expressed and infallibly communicates itself! All is full of light, no dark lurking-places are left: Kant knows what he wants and knows that he is right. In the latter, on the other hand, all is obscure, confused, indefinite, wavering, uncertain, the language anxious, full of excuses and appeals to what is coming, or indeed of suppression. Moreover, the whole second and third sections of the Deduction of the Pure Conceptions of the Understanding are completely changed in the second edition, because they did not satisfy Kant himself, and they have become quite different from the first edition, though not clearer. We actually see Kant in conflict with the truth in order to carry out his hypothesis which he has once fixed upon. In the Transcendental Æsthetic all his propositions are really proved from undeniable facts of consciousness, in the Transcendental Analytic, on the contrary, we find, if we consider it closely, mere assertions that thus it is and must be. Here, then, as everywhere, the language bears the stamp of the thought from which it has proceeded, for style is the physiognomy of the mind. We have still to remark, that whenever Kant wishes to give an example for the purpose of fuller explanation, he almost always takes for this end the category of causality, and then what he has said turns out correct; for the law of causality is indeed the real form of the understanding, but it is also its only form, and the remaining eleven categories are merely blind windows. The deduction of the categories is simpler and less involved in the first edition than in the second. He labours to explain how, according to the perception given by sensibility, the understanding produces experience by means of thinking the categories. In doing so, the words recognition, reproduction, association, apprehension, transcendental unity of apperception, are repeated to weariness, and yet no distinctness is attained. It is well worth noticing, however, that in this explanation he does not once touch upon what must nevertheless first occur to every one—the relation of the sensation to its external cause. If he did not intend this relation to hold good, he ought to have expressly denied it; but neither does he do this. Thus in this way he evades the point, and all the Kantians have in like manner evaded it. The secret motive of this is, that he reserves the causal nexus, under the name "ground of the phenomenon," for his false deduction of the thing in itself; and also that perception would become intellectual through the relation to the cause, which he dare not admit. Besides this, he seems to have been afraid that if the causal nexus were allowed to hold good between sensation and object, the latter would at once become the thing in itself, and introduce the empiricism of Locke. But this difficulty is removed by reflection, which shows us that the law of causality is of subjective origin, as well as the sensation itself; and besides this, our own body also, inasmuch as it appears in space, already belongs to ideas. But Kant was hindered from confessing this by his fear of the Berkeleian idealism.

"The combination of the manifold of perception" is repeatedly given as the essential operation of the understanding, by means of its twelve categories. Yet this is never adequately explained, nor is it shown what this manifold of perception is before it is combined by the understanding. But time and space, the latter in all its three dimensions, are *continua*, *i.e.*, all their parts are originally not separate but combined. Thus, then, everything that exhibits itself in them (is given) appears originally as a *continuum*, *i.e.*, its parts appear already combined and require no adventitious combination of a manifold. If, however, some one should seek to interpret that combining of the manifold of perception by saying that I refer the different sense-impressions of one object to this one only—thus, for example, perceiving a bell, I recognise that what affects my eye as yellow, my hand as smooth and hard, my ear as sounding, is yet only one and the same body,—then I reply that this is rather a consequence of the knowledge *a priori* of the causal nexus (this actual and only function of the understanding), by virtue of which all those different effects upon my different organs of sense yet lead me only to one common cause of them, the nature of the body standing before me, so that my understanding, in spite of the difference and multiplicity of the effects, still apprehends the unity of the cause as a single object, which just on that account exhibits itself in perception.   In the beautiful recapitulation of his doctrine which Kant gives at p. 719-726 or V. 747-754 of the "Critique of Pure Reason," he explains the categories, perhaps more distinctly than anywhere else, as "the mere rule of the synthesis of that which empirical apprehension has given *a posteriori*." It seems as if here he had something in his mind, such as that, in the construction of the triangle, the angles give the rule for the composition of the lines; at least by this image one can best explain to oneself what he says of the function of the categories.   The preface to the "Metaphysical First Principles of Natural Science" contains a long note which likewise gives an explanation of the categories, and says that they "differ in no respect from the formal acts of the understanding in judging," except that in the latter subject and predicate can always change places; then the judgment in general is defined in the same passage as "an act through which given ideas first become knowledge of an object." According to this, the brutes, since they do not judge, must also have no knowledge of objects.   In general, according to Kant, there are only conceptions of objects, no perceptions.   I, on the contrary, say : Objects exist primarily only for perception, and conceptions are always abstractions from this perception.   Therefore abstract thinking must be conducted exactly according to the world present in perception, for it is only their relation to this that gives content to conceptions ; and we must assume for the conceptions no other *a priori* determined form than the faculty of reflection in general, the nature of which is the construction of conceptions, *i.e.*, of abstract non-perceptible ideas, which constitutes the sole function of the *reason*, as I have shown in the first book. I therefore require that we should reject eleven of the categories, and only retain that of causality, and yet that we should see clearly that its activity is indeed the condition of empirical perception, which accordingly is not merely sensuous but intellectual, and that the object so perceived, the object of experience, is one with the idea, from which there remains nothing to distinguish except the thing in itself.

After repeated study of the "Critique of Pure Reason" at different periods of my life, a conviction has forced itself upon me with regard to the origin of the Transcendental Logic, which I now impart as very helpful to an understanding of it. Kant's only discovery, which is based upon objective comprehension and the highest human thought, is the *apperçu* that time and space are known by us *a priori*. Gratified by this happy hit, he wished to pursue the same vein further, and his love of architectonic symmetry afforded him the clue. As he had found that a pure intuition or perception *a priori* underlay the empirical *perception* as its condition, he thought that in the same way certain *pure conceptions* as presuppositions in our faculty of knowledge must lie at the foundation of the. empirically obtained *conceptions*, and that real empirical thought must be only possible through a pure thought *a priori*, which, however, would have no objects in itself, but would be obliged to take them from perception. So that as the *Transcendental Æsthetic* establishes an *a priori* basis of mathematics, there must, he supposed, also be a similar basis for logic; and thus, then for the sake of symmetry, the former received a pendant in a *Transcendental Logic*. From this point onwards Kant was no more free, no more in the position of purely, investigating and observing what is present in consciousness; but he was guided by an assumption and pursued a purpose—the purpose of finding what he assumed, in order to add to the Transcendental Æsthetic so happily discovered a Transcendental Logic analogous to it, and thus symmetrically corresponding to it, as a second storey. Now for this purpose he hit upon the table of judgments, out of which he constructed, as well as he could, the table of categories, the doctrine of twelve pure *a priori* conceptions, which are supposed to be the conditions of our *thinking* those very *things* the *perception* of which is conditioned by the two *a priori* forms of sensibility: thus a *pure understanding* now corresponded symmetrically to a *pure sensibility.* Then another consideration occurred to him, which offered a means of increasing the plausibility of the thing, by the assumption of the *schematism* of the pure conceptions of the understanding. But just through this the way in which his procedure had, unconsciously indeed, originated betrayed itself most distinctly. For because he aimed at finding something *a priori* analogous to every empirical function of the faculty of knowledge, he remarked that between our empirical perception and our empirical thinking, conducted in abstract non-perceptible conceptions, a connection very frequently, though not always, takes place, because every now and then we try to go back from abstract thinking to perception; but try to do so merely in order really to convince ourselves that our abstract thought has not strayed far from the safe ground of perception, and perhaps become exaggeration, or, it may be, mere empty talk; much in the same way as, when we are walking in the dark, we stretch out our hand every now and then to the guiding wall. We go back, then, to the perception only tentatively and for the moment, by calling up in imagination a perception corresponding to the conceptions which are occupying us at the time—a perception which can yet never be quite adequate to the conception, but is merely a temporary *representative* of it. I have already adduced what is needful on this point in my essay on the principle of sufficient reason, § 28. Kant calls a fleeting phantasy of this kind a schema, in opposition to the perfected picture of the imagination. He says it is like a monogram of the imagination, and asserts that just as such a schema stands midway between our abstract thinking of empirically obtained conceptions, and our clear perception which comes to us through the senses, so there are *a priori schemata of the pure conceptions of the understanding* between the faculty of perception *a priori* of pure sensibility and the faculty of thinking *a priori* of the pure understanding (thus the categories). These schemata, as monograms of the pure imagination *a priori*, he describes one by one, and assigns to each of them its corresponding category, in the wonderful "Chapter on the Schematism of the Pure Conceptions of the Understanding," which is noted as exceedingly obscure, because no man has ever been able to make anything out of it. Its obscurity, however, vanishes if it is considered from the point of view here indicated, but there also comes out more clearly in it than anywhere else the intentional nature of Kant's procedure, and of the determination formed beforehand of finding what would correspond to the analogy, and could assist the architectonic symmetry; indeed this is here the case to such a degree as to be almost comical. For when he assumes schemata of the pure (empty) *a priori* conceptions of the understanding (categories) analogous to the empirical schemata (or representatives through the fancy of our actual conceptions), he overlooks the fact that the end of such schemata is here entirely wanting. For the end of the schemata in the case of empirical (real) thinking is entirely connected with the *material content* of such conceptions. For since these conceptions are drawn from empirical perception, we assist and guide ourselves when engaged in abstract thinking by now and then casting a momentary glance back at the perception out of which the conceptions are framed, in order to assure ourselves that our thought has still real content. This, however, necessarily presupposes that the conceptions which occupy us are sprung from perception, and it is merely a glance back at their material content, indeed a mere aid to our weakness. But in the case of *a priori* conceptions which as yet have no content at all, clearly this is necessarily omitted. For these conceptions are not sprung from perception, but come to it from within, in order to receive a content first from it. Thus they have as yet nothing on which they could look back. I speak fully upon this point, because it is just this that throws light upon the secret origin of the Kantian philosophising, which accordingly consists in this, tha Kant, after the happy discovery of the two forms of intuition or perception *a priori*, exerted himself, under the guidance of the analogy, to prove that for every determination of our empirical knowledge there is an *a priori* analogue, and this finally extended, in the schemata, even to a mere psychological fact. Here the apparent depth and the difficulty of the exposition just serve to conceal from the reader that its content remains a wholly undemonstrable and merely arbitrary assumption. But he who has penetrated at last to the meaning of such an exposition is then easily induced to mistake this understanding so painfully attained for a conviction of the truth of the matter. If, on the contrary, Kant had kept himself here as unprejudiced and purely observant as in the discovery of *a priori* intuition or perception, he must have found that what is added to the pure intuition or perception of space and time, if an empirical perception arises from it, is on the one hand the sensation, and on the other hand the knowledge of causality, which changes the mere sensation into objective empirical perception, but just on this account is not first derived and learned from sensation, but exists *a priori*, and is indeed the form and function of the pure understanding. It is also, however, its sole form and function, yet one so rich in results that all our empirical knowledge rests upon it. If, as has often been said, the refutation of an error is only complete when the way it originated has been psychologically demonstrated, I believe I have achieved this, with regard to Kant's doctrine of the categories and their schemata, in what I have said above.

After Kant had thus introduced such great errors into the first simple outlines of a theory of the faculty of perception, he adopted a variety of very complicated assumptions. To these belongs first of all the synthetic unity of apperception: a very strange thing, very strangely explained. "The *I think* must be able to accompany all my ideas." Must—be able: this is a problematic-apodictic enunciation; in plain English, a proposition which takes with one hand what it gives with the other. And what is the meaning of this carefully balanced proposition? That all knowledge of ideas is thinking? That is not the case: and it would be dreadful; there would then be nothing but abstract conceptions, or at any rate a pure perception free from reflection and will, such as that of the beautiful, the deepest comprehension of the true nature of things, *i.e.*, of their Platonic Ideas. And besides, the brutes would then either think also, or else they would not even have ideas. Or is the proposition perhaps intended to mean: no object without a subject? That would be very badly expressed by it, and would come too late. If we collect Kant's utterances on the subject, we shall find that what he understands by the synthetic unity of apperception is, as it were, the extensionless centre of the sphere of all our ideas, whose radii converge to it. It is what I call the subject of knowing, the correlative of all ideas, and it is also that which I have fully described and explained in the 22d chapter of the Supplements, as the focus in which the rays of the activity of the brain converge. Therefore, to avoid repetition, I now refer to that chapter.

That I reject the whole doctrine of the categories, and reckon it among the groundless assumptions with which Kant burdened the theory of knowledge, results from the criticism given above; and also from the proof of the contradictions in the Transcendental Logic, which had their ground in the confusion of perception and abstract knowledge; also further from the proof of the want of a distinct and definite conception of the nature of the understanding and of the reason, instead of which we found in Kant's writings only incoherent, inconsistent, insufficient, and incorrect utterances with regard to these two faculties of the mind. Finally, it results from the explanations which I myself have given of these faculties of the mind in the first book and its Supplements, and more fully in the essay on the principle of sufficient reason, § 21, 26, and 34,—explanations which are very definite and distinct, which clearly follow from the consideration of the nature of our knowledge, and which completely agree with the conceptions of those two faculties of knowledge that appear in the language and writings of all ages and all nations, but were not brought to distinctness. Their defence against the very different exposition of Kant has, for the most part, been given already along with the exposure of the errors of that exposition. Since, however, the table of judgments, which Kant makes the foundation of his theory of thinking, and indeed of his whole philosophy, has, in itself, as a whole, its correctness, it is still incumbent upon me to show how these universal forms of all judgment arise in our faculty of knowledge, and to reconcile them with my exposition of it. In this discussion I shall always attach to the concepts understanding and reason the sense given them in my explanation, which I therefore assume the reader is familiar with.

An essential difference between Kant's method and that which I follow lies in this, that he starts from indirect, reflected knowledge, while I start from direct or intuitive knowledge. He may be compared to a man who measures the height of a tower by its shadow, while I am like him who applies the measuring-rule directly to the tower itself. Therefore, for him philosophy is a science *of* conceptions, but for me it is a science *in* conceptions, drawn from knowledge of perception, the one source of all evidence, and comprehended and made permanent in general conceptions. He passes over this whole world of perception which surrounds us, so multifarious and rich in significance, and confines himself to the forms of abstract thinking; and, although he never expressly says so, this procedure is founded on the assumption that reflection is the ectype of all perception, that, therefore, all that is essential in perception must be expressed in reflection, and expressed in very contracted forms and outlines, which are thus easily surveyed. According to this, what is essential and conformable to law in abstract knowledge would, as it were, place in our hands all the threads by which the varied puppet-show of the world of perception is set in motion before our eyes. If Kant had only distinctly expressed this first principle of his method, and then followed it consistently, he would at least have been obliged to separate clearly the intuitive from the abstract, and we would not have had to contend with inextricable contradictions and confusions. But from the way in which he solves his problem we see that that fundamental principle of his method was only very indistinctly present to his mind, and thus we have still to arrive at it by conjecture even after a thorough study of his philosophy.

Now as concerns the specified method and fundamental maxim itself, there is much to be said for it, and it is a brilliant thought. The nature of all science indeed consists in this, that we comprehend the endless manifold of perceptible phenomena under comparatively few abstract conceptions, and out of these construct a system by means of which we have all those phenomena completely in the power of our knowledge, can explain the past and determine the future. The sciences, however, divide the wide sphere of phenomena among them according to the special and manifold classes of the latter. Now it was a bold and happy thought to isolate what is absolutely essential to the conceptions as such and apart from their content, in order to discover from these forms of all thought found in this way what is essential to all intuitive knowledge also, and consequently to the world as phenomenon in general; and because this would be found *a priori* on account of the necessity of those forms of thought, it would be of subjective origin, and would just lead to the ends Kant had in view. Here, however, before going further, the relation of reflection to knowledge of perception ought to have been investigated (which certainly presupposes the clear separation of the two, which was neglected by Kant). He ought to have inquired in what way the former really repeats and represents the latter, whether quite pure, or changed and to some extent disguised by being taken up into its special forms (forms of reflection); whether the form of abstract reflective knowledge becomes more determined through the form of knowledge of perception, or through the nature or constitution which unalterably belongs to itself, *i.e.*, to reflective knowledge, so that even what is very heterogeneous in intuitive knowledge can no longer be distinguished when it has entered reflective knowledge, and conversely many distinctions of which we are conscious in the reflective method of knowledge have also sprung from this knowledge itself, and by no means point to corresponding differences in intuitive knowledge. As the result of this investigation, however, it would have appeared that knowledge of perception suffers very nearly as much change when it is taken up into reflection as food when it is taken into the animal organism whose forms and compounds are determined by itself, so that the nature of the food can no longer be recognised from the result they produce. Or (for this is going a little too far) at least it would have appeared that reflection is by no means related to knowledge of perception as the reflection in water is related to the reflected objects, but scarcely even as the mere shadow of these objects stands to the objects themselves; which shadow repeats only a few external outlines, but also unites the most manifold in the same form and presents the most diverse through the same outline; so that it is by no means possible, starting from it, to construe the forms of things with completeness and certainty.

The whole of reflective knowledge, or the reason, has only one chief form, and that is the abstract conception. It is proper to the reason itself, and has no direct necessary connection with the world of perception, which therefore exists for the brutes entirely without conceptions, and indeed, even if it were quite another world from what it is, that form of reflection would suit it just as well. But the combination of conceptions for the purpose of judging has certain definite and normal forms, which have been found by induction, and constitute the table of judgments. These forms are for the most part deducible from the nature of reflective knowledge itself, thus directly from the reason, because they spring from the four laws of thought (called by me metalogical truths) and the *dictum de omni et nullo*. Certain others of these forms, however, have their ground in the nature of knowledge of perception, thus in the understanding; yet they by no means point to a like number of special forms of the understanding, but can all be fully deduced from the sole function which the understanding has—the direct knowledge of cause and effect. Lastly, still others of these forms have sprung from the concurrence and combination of the reflective and intuitive modes of knowledge, or more properly from the assumption of the latter into the former. I shall now go through the moments of the judgment one by one, and point out the origin of each of them in the sources referred to; and from this it follows of itself that a deduction of categories from them is wanting, and the assumption of this is just as groundless as its exposition was found to be entangled and self-conflicting.

1. The so-called *Quantity* of judgments springs from the nature of concepts as such. It thus has its ground in the reason alone, and has absolutely no direct connection with the understanding and with knowledge of perception. It is indeed, as is explained at length in the first book, essential to concepts, as such, that they should have an extent, a sphere, and the wider, less determined concept includes the narrower and more determined. The latter can therefore be separated from the former, and this may happen in two ways,—either the narrower concept may be indicated as an indefinite part of the wider concept in general, or it may be defined and completely separated by means of the addition of a special name. The judgment which carries out this operation is in the first case called a particular, and in the second case an universal judgment. For example, one and the same part of the sphere of the concept tree may be isolated through a particular and through an universal judgment, thus—"Some trees bear gall-nuts," or "All oaks bear gall-nuts." One sees that the difference of the two operations is very slight; indeed, that the possibility of it depends upon the richness of the language. Nevertheless, Kant has explained this difference as disclosing two fundamentally different actions, functions, categories of the pure understanding which determines experience *a priori* through them.

Finally, a concept may also be used in order to arrive by means of it at a definite particular idea of perception, from which, as well as from many others, this concept itself is drawn; this happens in the singular judgment. Such a judgment merely indicates the boundary-line between abstract knowledge and knowledge of perception, and passes directly to the latter, "This tree here bears gall-nuts." Kant has made of this also a special category.

After all that has been said there is no need of further polemic here.

2. In the same way the *Quality* of the judgment lies entirely within the province of reason, and is not an adumbration of any law of that understanding which makes perception possible, *i.e.*, it does not point to it. The nature of abstract concepts, which is just the nature of the reason itself objectively comprehended, carries with it the possibility of uniting and separating their spheres, as was already explained in the first book, and upon this possibility, as their presupposition, rest the universal laws of thought of identity and contradiction, to which I have given the name of *metalogical* truths, because they spring purely from the reason, and cannot be further explained. They determine that what is united must remain united, and what is separated must remain separate, thus that what is established cannot at the same time be also abolished, and thus they presuppose the possibility of the combination and separation of spheres, *i.e.*, of judgment. This, however, lies, according to its *form*, simply and solely in the reason, and this *form* has not, like the *content* of the judgments, been brought over from the perceptible knowledge of the understanding, and therefore there is no correlative or analogue of it to be looked for there. After the perception has been brought about through the understanding and for the understanding, it exists complete, subject to no doubt nor error, and therefore knows neither assertion nor denial; for it expresses itself, and has not, like the abstract knowledge of the reason, its value and content in its mere relation to something outside of it, according to the principle of the ground of knowing. It is, therefore, pure reality; all negation is foreign to its nature, can only be added on through reflection, and **just**

on this account remains always in the province of abstract thought.

To the affirmative and negative Kant adds the infinite judgment, making use of a crotchet of the old scholastics, an ingeniously invented stop-gap, which does not even require to be explained, a blind window, such as many others he made for the sake of his architectonic symmetry.

3. Under the very wide conception of *Relation* Kant has brought three entirely different properties of judgments, which we must, therefore, examine singly, in order to recognise their origin.

(a.) The *hypothetical judgment* in general is the abstract expression of that most universal form of all our knowledge, the principle of sufficient reason. In my essay on this principle, I already showed in 1813 that it has four entirely different meanings, and in each of these originally originates in a different faculty of knowledge, and also concerns a different class of ideas. It clearly follows from this, that the source of the hypothetical judgment in general, of that universal form of thought, cannot be, as Kant wishes to make it, merely the understanding and its category of causality; but that the law of causality which, according to my exposition, is the one form of knowledge of the pure understanding, is only one of the forms of that principle which embraces all pure or *a priori* knowledge—the principle of sufficient reason—which, on the other hand, in each of its meanings has this hypothetical form of judgment as its expression. We see here, however, very distinctly how kinds of knowledge which are quite different in their origin and significance yet appear, if thought *in abstracto* by the reason, in one and the same form of combination of concepts and judgments, and then in this form can no longer be distinguished, but, in order to distinguish them, we must go back to knowledge of perception, leaving abstract knowledge altogether. Therefore the path which was followed by Kant, starting from the point of view of abstract knowledge, to find the elements and the inmost spring of intuitive knowledge also, was quite a wrong one. For the rest, my whole introductory essay on the principle of sufficient reason is, to a certain extent, to be regarded merely as a thorough exposition of the significance of the hypothetical form of judgment; therefore I do not dwell upon it longer here.

(b.) The form of the *categorical judgment* is nothing but the form of judgment in general, in its strictest sense. For, strictly speaking, judging merely means thinking, the combination of, or the impossibility of combining, the spheres of the concepts. Therefore the hypothetical and the disjunctive combination are properly no special forms of the judgment; for they are only applied to already completed judgments, in which the combination of the concepts remains unchanged the categorical. But they again connect these judgments, for the hypothetical form expresses their dependence upon each other, and the disjunctive their incompatibility. Mere concepts, however, have only *one* class of relations to each other, those which are expressed in the categorical judgment. The fuller determination, or the sub-species of this relation, are the intersection and the complete separateness of the concept-spheres, *i.e.*, thus affirmation and negation; out of which Kant has made special categories, under quite a different title, that of *quality*. Intersection and separateness have again sub-species, according as the spheres lie within each other entirely, or only in part, a determination which constitutes the *quantity* of the judgments; out of which Kant has again made a quite special class of categories. Thus he separates what is very closely related, and even identical, the easily surveyed modifications of the one possible relation of mere concepts to each other, and, on the other hand, unites what is very different under this title of relation.

Categorical judgments have as their metalogical principle the laws of thought of identity and contradiction.

But the *ground* of the connection of the concept-spheres which gives *truth* to the judgment, which is nothing but this connection, may be of very different kinds; and, according to this, the truth of the judgment is either logical, or empirical, or metaphysical, or metalogical, as is explained in the introductory essay, § 30–33, and does not require to be repeated here. But it is apparent from this how very various the direct cognitions may be, all of which exhibit themselves in the abstract, through the combination of the spheres of two concepts, as subject and predicate, and that we can by no means set up the sole function of the understanding as corresponding to them and producing them. For example, the judgments, "Water boils, the sine measures the angle, the will resolves, business distracts, distinction is difficult," express through the same logical form the most different kinds of relations; but from this we obtain the right, however irregular the beginning may be, of placing ourselves at the standpoint of abstract knowledge to analyse direct intuitive knowledge. For the rest, the categorical judgment springs from knowledge of the understanding proper, in my sense, only when causation is expressed by it; this is, however, the case in all judgments which refer to a physical quality. For if I say, "This body is heavy, hard, fluid, green, sour, alkaline, organic, &c., &c.," this always refers to its effect, and thus is knowledge which is only possible through the pure understanding. Now, after this, like much which is quite different from it (for example, the subordination of very abstract concepts), has been expressed in the abstract through subject and predicate, these mere relations of concepts have been transferred back to knowledge of perception, and it has been supposed that the subject and predicate of the judgment must have a peculiar and special correlative in perception, substance and accident. But I shall show clearly further on that the conception substance has no other true content than that of the conception matter. Accidents, however, are quite synonymous with

kinds of effects, so that the supposed knowledge of substance and accident is never anything more than the
knowledge of cause and effect by the understanding. But
the special manner in which the idea of matter arises is
explained partly in § 4 of the first book, and still more
clearly in the essay on the principle of sufficient reason
at the end of § 21, p. 77 (3d ed., p. 82), and in some
respects we shall see it still more closely when we investigate the principle of the permanence of substance.

(c.) *Disjunctive judgments* spring from the law of
thought of excluded third, which is a metalogical truth;
they are, therefore, entirely the property of the reason,
and have not their origin in the understanding. The
deduction of the category of community or *reciprocity*
from them is, however, a glaring example of the violence
which Kant sometimes allowed to be done to truth,
merely in order to satisfy his love of architectonic symmetry. The illegitimacy of that deduction has already
often been justly condemned and proved upon various
grounds, especially by G. E. Schulze in his "*Kritik der
theoretischen Philosophie,*" and by Berg in his "*Epikritik
der Philosophie.*" What real analogy is there, indeed,
between the problematical determination of a concept by
disjunctive predicates and the thought of reciprocity?
The two are indeed absolutely opposed, for in the disjunctive judgment the actual affirmation of one of the two
alternative propositions is also necessarily the negation of
the other; if, on the other hand, we think two things in
the relation of reciprocity, the affirmation of one is also
necessarily the affirmation of the other, and *vice versa.*
Therefore, unquestionably, the real logical analogue of
reciprocity is the vicious circle, for in it, as nominally in
the case of reciprocity, what is proved is also the proof,
and conversely. And just as logic rejects the vicious
circle, so the conception of reciprocity ought to be banished from metaphysics. For I now intend, quite seriously, to prove that there is no reciprocity in the strict

sense, and this conception, which people are so fond of using, just on account of the indefiniteness of the thought, is seen, if more closely considered, to be empty, false, and invalid. First of all, the reader must call to mind what causality really is, and to assist my exposition, see upon this subject § 20 of the introductory essay, also my prize-essay on the freedom of the will, chap. iii. p. *27 seq.*, and lastly the fourth chapter of the second book of this work. Causality is the law according to which the conditions or states of matter which appear determine their position in time. Causality has to do merely with conditions **or** states, indeed, properly, only with *changes,* and neither with matter as such, nor with permanence without change. *Matter,* as such, does not come under the law of causality, for it neither comes into being nor passes away; thus neither does the whole *thing,* as we commonly express ourselves, come under this law, but only the *conditions* or *states* of matter. Further, the law of causality has nothing to do with *permanence,* for where nothing changes there is no producing of *effects* and no causality, but a continuing quiet condition or state. But if, now, such a state is changed, then the new state is either again permanent or it is not, but immediately introduces a third state, and the necessity with which this happens is just the law of causality, which is a form of the principle of sufficient reason, and therefore cannot be further explained, because the principle of sufficient reason is the principle of all explanation and of all necessity. From this it is clear that cause and effect stand in intimate connection with, and necessary relation to, the *course of time.* Only because the state A. precedes in time the state B., and their succession is necessary and not accidental, *i.e.,* no mere sequence but a consequence—only because of this is the state A. cause and the state B. effect. The conception *reciprocity,* however, contains this, that both are cause and both are effect of each other; but this really amounts to saying that each of the two is the earlier and also the later; thus it is an absurdity. For that both states are simultaneous, and indeed necessarily simultaneous, cannot be admitted , because, as necessarily belonging to each other and existing at the same time, they constitute only *one* state. For the permanence of this state there is certainly required the continued exis-tence of all its determinations, but we are then no longer concerned with change and causality, but with duration and rest, and nothing further is said than that if *one* determination of the whole state be changed, the new state which then appears cannot continue, but becomes the cause of the change of all the other determinations of the first state, so that a new third state appears; which all happens merely in accordance with the simple law of causality, and does not establish a *new* law, that of reci-procity.

I also definitely assert that the conception *reciprocity* cannot be supported by a single example. Everything that one seeks to pass off as such is either a state of rest, to which the conception of causality, which has only sig-nificance with reference to changes, finds no application at all, or else it is an alternating succession of states of the same name which condition each other, for the explanation of which simple causality is quite sufficient. An example of the first class is afforded by a pair of scales brought to rest by equal weights. Here there is no effect produced, for there is no change; it is a state of rest; gravity acts, equally divided, as in every body which is supported at its centre of gravity, but it cannot show its force by any effect. That the taking away of one weight produces a second state, which at once be-comes the cause of the third, the sinking of the other scale, happens according to the simple law of cause and effect, and requires no special category of the under-standing, and not even a special name. An example of the second class is the continuous burning of a fire. The combination of oxygen with the combustible body is the cause of heat, and heat, again, is the cause of the renewed occurrence of the chemical combination. But this is nothing more than a chain of causes and effects, the links of which have alternately *the same name.* The burning, A., produces free heat, B., this produces new burning, C. (*i.e.*, a new effect which has the same name as the cause A., but is not individually identical with it), this produces new heat, D. (which is not really identical with the effect B., but only according to the concept, *i.e.*, it has the same name), and so on indefinitely. A good example of what in ordinary life is called reciprocity is afforded by a theory about deserts given by Humboldt (*Ansichten der Natur,* 2d ed., vol. ii. p. 79). In the sandy deserts it does not rain, but it rains upon the wooded mountains surrounding them. The cause is not the attraction of the clouds by the mountains; but it is the column of heated air rising from the sandy plain which prevents the particles of vapour from condensing, and drives the clouds high into the heavens. On the mountains the perpendicular rising stream of air is weaker, the clouds descend, and the rainfall ensues in the cooler air. Thus, want of rain and the absence of plants in the desert stand in the relation of reciprocity; it does not rain because the heated sand-plain sends out more heat; the desert does not become a steppe or prairie because it does not rain. But clearly we have here again, as in the example given above, only a succession of causes and effects of the same names, and throughout nothing essentially different from simple causality. This is also the case with the swinging of the pendulum, and indeed also with the self-conservation of the organised body, in which case likewise every state introduces a new one, which is of the same kind as that by which it was itself brought about, but individually is new. Only here the matter is complicated, because the chain no longer consists of links of two kinds, but of many kinds, so that a link of the same name only recurs after several others have intervened. But we always see before us only an application of the single and simple law of causality which gives the rule to the sequence of states, but never anything which must be comprehended by means of a new and special function of the understanding.

Or is it perhaps advanced in support of the conception of reciprocity that action and reaction are equal? But the reason of this is what I urge so strongly and have fully explained in the essay on the principle of sufficient reason, that the cause and the effect are not two bodies, but two successive states of bodies, consequently each of the two states implicates all bodies concerned; thus the effect, *i.e.*, the newly appearing state, for example, in the case of an impulse, extends to both bodies in the same proportion; therefore the body impelled produces just as great a change in the body impelling as it itself sustains (each in proportion to its mass and velocity). If one pleases to call this reciprocity, then absolutely every effect is a reciprocal effect, and no new conception is introduced on this account, still less does it require a new function of the understanding, but we only have a superfluous synonym for causality. But Kant himself, in a moment of thoughtlessness, exactly expressed this view in the "Metaphysical First Principles of Natural Science," at the beginning of the proof of the fourth principle of mechanics: "All external effect in the world is reciprocal effect." How then should different functions lie *a priori* in the understanding for simple causality and for reciprocity, and, indeed, how should the real succession of things only be possible and knowable by means of the first, and their co-existence by means of the second? According to this, if all effect is reciprocal effect, succession and simultaneity would be the same thing, and therefore everything in the world would take place at the same moment. If there were true reciprocity, then perpetual motion would also be possible, and indeed *a priori* certain; but it is rather the case that the *a priori* conviction that there is no true reciprocity,

and no corresponding form of the understanding, is
the ground of the assertion that perpetual motion is
impossible.

Aristotle also denies reciprocity in the strict sense; for
he remarks that two things may certainly be reciprocal
causes of each other, but only if this is understood in a
different sense of each of them; for example, that one
acts upon the other as the motive, but the latter acts
upon the former as the cause of its movement. We find
in two passages the same words: Physic., lib. ii. c. 3, and
Metaph., lib. v. c. 2. *Εστι δε τινα και αλληλων αιτια· οίον
το πονειν αιτιον της ευεξιας, και αυτη του πονειν· αλλ' ου
τον αυτον τροπον, αλλα το μεν ως τελος, το δε ως αρχη
κινησεως.* (*Sunt præterea quæ sibi sunt mutuo causæ, ut
exercitium bonæ habitudinis, et hæc exercitii: at non eodem
modo, sed hæc ut finis, aliud ut principium motus.*) If,
besides this, he had accepted a reciprocity proper, he
would have introduced it here, for in both passages he is
concerned with enumerating all the possible kinds of
causes. In the *Analyt. post.*, lib. ii. c. 11, he speaks of a
circle of causes and effects, but not of reciprocity.

4. The categories of *Modality* have this advantage over
all others, that what is expressed through each of them
really corresponds to the form of judgment from which it
is derived; which with the other categories is scarcely
ever the case, because for the most part they are deduced
from the forms of judgment with the most capricious
violence.

Thus that it is the conceptions of the possible, the actual,
and the necessary which occasion the problematic, assertatory, and apodictic forms of judgment, is perfectly true;
but that those conceptions are special, original forms of
knowledge of the understanding which cannot be further
deduced is not true. On the contrary, they spring from
the single original form of all knowledge, which is, therefore, known to us *a priori*, the principle of sufficient reason; and indeed out of this the knowledge of *necessity*

springs directly. On the other hand, it is only because reflection is applied to this that the conceptions of contingency, possibility, impossibility, and actuality arise. Therefore all these do not by any means spring from *one* faculty of the mind, the understanding, but arise through the conflict of abstract and intuitive knowledge, as will be seen directly.

I hold that to be necessary and to be the consequent of a given reason are absolutely interchangeable notions, and completely identical. We can never know, nor even think, anything as necessary, except so far as we regard it as the consequent of a given reason ; and the conception of necessity contains absolutely nothing more than this dependence, this being established through something else, and this inevitable following from it. Thus it arises and exists simply and solely through the application of the principle of sufficient reason. Therefore, there is, according to the different forms of this principle, a physical necessity (the effect from the cause), a logical (through the ground of knowing, in analytical judgments, syllogisms, &c.), a mathematical (according to the ground of being in time and space), and finally a practical necessity, by which we intend to signify not determination through a pretended categorical imperative, but the necessary occurrence of an action according to the motives presented, in the case of a given empirical character. But everything necessary is only so relatively, that is, under the presupposition of the reason from which it follows; therefore absolute necessity is a contradiction. With regard to the rest, I refer to § 49 of the essay on the principle of sufficient reason.

The contradictory opposite, *i.e.*, the denial of necessity, is *contingency*. The content of this conception is, therefore, negative—nothing more than this : absence of the connection expressed by the principle of sufficient reason. Consequently the contingent is also always merely relative. It is contingent in relation to something which is not its reason. Every object, of whatever kind it may be —for example, every event in the actual world—is always at once necessary and contingent, *necessary* in relation to the *one* condition which is its cause: *contingent* in relation to everything else. For its contact in time and space with everything else is a mere coincidence without necessary connection: hence also the words chance, σύμπτωμα, *contingens.* Therefore an absolute contingency is just as inconceivable as an absolute necessity. For the former would be simply an object which stood to no other in the relation of consequent to its reason. But the inconceivability of such a thing is just the content of the principle of sufficient reason negatively expressed, and therefore this principle must first be upset before we can think an absolute contingency; and even then it itself would have lost all significance, for the conception of contingency has meaning only in relation to that principle, and signifies that two objects do not stand to each other in the relation of reason and consequent.

In nature, which consists of ideas of perception, everything that happens is necessary; for it proceeds from its cause. If, however, we consider this individual with reference to everything else which is not its cause, we know it as contingent; but this is already an abstract reflection. Now, further, let us abstract entirely from a natural object its causal relation to everything else, thus its necessity and its contingency; then this kind of knowledge comprehends the conception of the *actual,* in which one only considers the *effect,* without looking for the cause, in relation to which one would otherwise have to call it *necessary,* and in relation to everything else *contingent.* All this rests ultimately upon the fact that the *modality* of the judgment does not indicate so much the objective nature of things as the relation of our knowledge to them. Since, however, in nature everything proceeds from a cause, everything *actual* is also *necessary,* yet only so far as it is *at this time, in this place;* for only so far does determination by the law of causality extend. Let us leave, however, concrete nature and pass over to abstract thinking; then we can present to ourselves in reflection all the natural laws which are known to us partly *a priori*, partly only *a posteriori*, and this abstract idea contains all that is in nature at *any* time, in *any* place, but with abstraction from every definite time and place; and just in this way, through such reflection, we have entered the wide kingdom of *the possible*. But what finds no place even here is the *impossible*. It is clear that possibility and impossibility exist only for reflection, for abstract knowledge of the reason, not for knowledge of perception; although it is the pure forms of perception which supply the reason with the determination of the possible and impossible. According as the laws of nature, from which we start in the thought of the possible and impossible, are known *a priori* or *a posteriori*, is the possibility or impossibility metaphysical or physical.

From this exposition, which requires no proof because it rests directly upon the knowledge of the principle of sufficient reason and upon the development of the conceptions of the necessary, the actual, and the possible, it is sufficiently evident how entirely groundless is Kant's assumption of three special functions of the understanding for these three conceptions, and that here again he has allowed himself to be disturbed by no reflection in the carrying out of his architectonic symmetry.

To this, however, we have to add the other great mistake, that, certainly according to the procedure of earlier philosophy, he has confounded the conceptions of necessity and contingency with each other. That earlier philosophy has applied abstraction to the following mistaken use. It was clear that that of which the reason is given inevitably follows, *i.e.*, cannot not be, and thus necessarily is. But that philosophy held to this last determination alone, and said that is necessary which cannot be otherwise, or the opposite of which is impossible. It left, however, the

ground and root of such necessity out of account, overlooked the relativity of all necessity which follows from
it, and thereby made the quite unthinkable fiction of an
absolute necessity, i.e., of something the existence of which
would be as inevitable as the consequent of a reason, but
which yet was not the consequent of a reason, and
therefore depended upon nothing; an addition which is
an absurd *petitio,* for it conflicts with the principle of
sufficient reason. Now, starting from this fiction, it explained, in diametrical opposition to the truth, all that
is established by a reason as contingent, because it looked
at the relative nature of its necessity and compared this
with that entirely imaginary *absolute* necessity, which
is self-contradictory in its conception.[1] Now Kant adheres to this fundamentally perverse definition of the
contingent and gives it as explanation. (Critique of Pure
Reason, V. p. 289–291, 243. V. 301, 419. V. 447, 486,
488.) He falls indeed into the most evident contradiction with himself upon this point, for on p. 301 he
says: "Everything contingent has a cause," and adds,
"That is contingent which might possibly not be." But
whatever has a cause cannot possibly not be: thus it is
necessary. For the rest, the source of the whole of this
false explanation of the necessary and the contingent is
to be found in Aristotle in *"De Generatione et Corruptione,"*
lib. ii. c. 9 et 11, where the necessary is explained as
that which cannot possibly not be: there stands in opposi-

[1] Cf. Christian Wolf's *"Vernün-
ftige Gedanken von Gott, Welt und
Seele,"* § 577–579. It is strange
that he only explains as contingent
what is necessary according to the
principle of sufficient reason of becoming, *i.e.,* what takes place from
causes, and on the contrary recognises as necessary that which is so
according to the other forms of the
principle of sufficient reason; for
example, what follows from the
essentia (definition), thus analytical
judgments, and further also mathematical truths. The reason he assigns for this is, that only the law
of causality gives infinite series,
while the other kinds of grounds
give only finite series. Yet this is
by no means the case with the forms
of the principle of sufficient reason
in pure space and time, but only
holds good of the logical ground of
knowledge; but he held mathematical necessity to be such also.
Compare the essay on the principle
of sufficient reason, § 50.

tion to it that which cannot possibly be, and between these two lies that which can both be and not be,—thus that which comes into being and passes away, and this would then be the contingent. In accordance with what has been said above, it is clear that this explanation, like so many of Aristotle's, has resulted from sticking to abstract conceptions without going back to the concrete and perceptible, in which, however, the source of all abstract conceptions lies, and by which therefore they must always be controlled. "Something which cannot possibly not be" can certainly be thought in the abstract, but if we go with it to the concrete, the real, the perceptible, we find nothing to support the thought, even as possible, —as even merely the asserted consequent of a given reason, whose necessity is yet relative and conditioned.

I take this opportunity of adding a few further remarks on these conceptions of modality. Since all necessity rests upon the principle of sufficient reason, and is on this account relative, all *apodictic* judgments are originally, and according to their ultimate significance, *hypothetical.* They become *categorical* only through the addition of an *assertatory* minor, thus in the conclusion. If this minor is still undecided, and this indecision is expressed, this gives the problematical judgment.

What in general (as a rule) is apodictic (a law of nature), is in reference to a particular case only problematical, because the condition must actually appear which brings the case under the rule. And conversely, what in the particular as such is necessary (apodictic) (every particular change necessary through the cause), is again in general, and predicated universally, only problematical; because the causes which appear only concern the particular case, and the apodictic, always hypothetical judgment, always expresses merely the general law, not the particular case directly. All this has its ground in the fact that possibility exists only in the province of reflection and for the reason; the actual, in the province of perception and for the understanding; the necessary, for both. Indeed, the distinction between necessary, actual, and possible really exists only in the abstract and according to the conception; in the real world, on the other hand, all three fall into one. For all that happens, happens *necessarily*, because it happens from causes; but these themselves have again causes, so that the whole of the events of the world, great and small, are a strict concatenation of necessary occurrences. Accordingly everything actual is also necessary, and in the real world there is no difference between actuality and necessity, and in the same way no difference between actuality and possibility; for what has not happened, *i.e.*, has not become actual, was also not possible, because the causes without which it could never appear have not themselves appeared, nor could appear, in the great concatenation of causes; thus it was an impossibility. Every event is therefore either necessary or impossible. All this holds good only of the empirically real world, *i.e.*, the complex of individual things, thus of the whole particular as such. If, on the other hand, we consider things generally, comprehending them *in abstracto*, necessity, actuality, and possibility are again separated; we then know everything which is in accordance with the *a priori* laws which belong to our intellect as possible in general; that which corresponds to the empirical laws of nature as possible in this world, even if it has never become actual; thus we distinguish clearly the possible from the actual. The actual is in itself always also necessary, but is only comprehended as such by him who knows its cause; regarded apart from this, it is and is called contingent. This consideration also gives us the key to that *contentio* περι δυνατων between the Megaric Diodorus and Chrysippus the Stoic which Cicero refers to in his book *De Fato*. Diodorus says: "Only what becomes actual was possible, and all that is actual is also necessary." Chrysippus on the other hand says: "Much that is possible never becomes actual; for only the necessary becomes actual." We may explain this thus: Actuality is the conclusion of a syllogism to which possibility gives the premises. But for this is required not only the major but also the minor; only the two give complete possibility. The major gives a merely theoretical, general possibility *in abstracto*, but this of itself does not make anything possible, *i.e.*, capable of becoming actual. For this the minor also is needed, which gives the possibility for the particular case, because it brings it under the rule, and thereby it becomes at once actual. For example:

Maj. All houses (consequently also my house) can be destroyed by fire.

Min. My house is on fire.

Concl. My house is being destroyed by fire.

For every general proposition, thus every major, always determines things with reference to actuality only under a presupposition, therefore hypothetically ; for example, the capability of being burnt down has as a presupposition the catching fire. This presupposition is produced in the minor. The major always loads the cannon, but only if the minor brings the match does the shot, *i.e.*, the conclusion, follow. This holds good throughout of the relation of possibility to actuality. Since now the conclusion, which is the assertion of actuality, always follows *necessarily*, it is evident from this that all that is actual is also necessary, which can also be seen from the fact that necessity only means being the consequent of a given reason : this is in the case of the actual a cause : thus everything actual is necessary. Accordingly, we see here the conceptions of the possible, the actual, and the necessary unite, and not merely the last presuppose the first, but also the converse. What keeps them apart is the limitation of our intellect through the form of time ; for time is the mediator between possibility and actuality. The necessity of the particular event may be fully seen from the knowledge of all its causes ; but the concurrence of the whole of these different and independent causes seems to us *contingent;* indeed their independence of each other is just the conception of contingency. Since, however, each of them was the necessary effect of *its* causes, the chain of which has no beginning, it is evident that contingency is merely a subjective phenomenon, arising from the limitation of the horizon of our understanding, and just as subjective as the optical horizon at which the heavens touch the earth.

Since necessity is the same thing as following from given grounds, it must appear in a special way in the case of every form of the principle of sufficient reason, and also have its opposite in the possibility and impossibility which always arises only through the application of the abstract reflection of the reason to the object. Therefore the four kinds of necessity mentioned above stand opposed to as many kinds of impossibility, physical, logical, mathematical, and practical. It may further be remarked that if one remains entirely within the province of abstract concepts, possibility is always connected with the more general, and necessity with the more limited concept; for example, " An animal *may* be a bird, a fish, an amphibious creature, &c." " A nightingale *must* be a bird, a bird *must* be an animal, an animal *must* be an organism, an organism *must* be a body." This is because logical necessity, the expression of which is the syllogism, proceeds from the general to the particular, and never conversely. In the concrete world of nature (ideas of the first class), on the contrary, everything is really necessary through the law of causality ; only added reflection can conceive it as also contingent, comparing it with that which is not its cause, and also as merely and purely actual, by disregarding all causal connection. Only in this class of ideas does the conception of the *actual* properly occur, as is also shown by the derivation of the word from the conception of causality. In the third class of ideas, that of pure mathematical perception or intuition, if we confine ourselves strictly to it, there is only necessity. Possibility occurs here also only through relation to the concepts of reflection: for example, " A triangle *may* be right-angled, obtuse-angled, or equi-angular; its three angles *must* be equal to two right-angles." Thus here we only arrive at the possible through the tran-sition from the perceptible to the abstract.

After this exposition, which presupposes the recollec-tion of what was said both in the essay on the principle of sufficient reason and in the first book of the present work, there will, it is hoped, be no further doubt as to the true and very heterogeneous source of those forms which the table of judgments lays before us, nor as to the inadmissibility and utter groundlessness of the assump-tion of twelve special functions of the understanding for the explanation of them. The latter point is also sup-ported by a number of special circumstances very easily noted. Thus, for example, it requires great love of sym-metry and much trust in a clue derived from it, to lead one to assume that an affirmative, a categorical, and an assertatory judgment are three such different things that they justify the assumption of an entirely special function of the understanding for each of them.

Kant himself betrays his consciousness of the unten-able nature of his doctrine of the categories by the fact that in the third chapter of the Analytic of Principles (*phœnomena et noumena*) several long passages of the first edition (p. 241, 242, 244–246, 248–253) are omitted in the second—passages which displayed the weakness of that doctrine too openly. So, for example, he says there (p. 241) that he has not defined the individual categories, because he could not define them even if he had wished to do so, inasmuch as they were susceptible of no defini-tion. In saying this he forgot that at p. 82 of the same first edition he had said: " I purposely dispense with the definition of the categories although I may be in possession of it." This then was, *sit venia verbo*, wind. But this last passage he has allowed to stand. And so all those passages wisely omitted afterwards betray the fact that nothing distinct can be thought in connection with the categories, and this whole doctrine stands upon a weak foundation.

This table of the categories is now made the guiding clue according to which every metaphysical, and indeed every scientific inquiry is to be conducted (Prolegomena, § 39). And, in fact, it is not only the foundation of the whole Kantian philosophy and the type according to which its symmetry is everywhere carried out, as I have already shown above, but it has also really become the procrustean bed into which Kant forces every possible inquiry, by means of a violence which I shall now consider somewhat more closely. But with such an opportunity what must not the *imitatores servum pecus* have done! We have seen. That violence then is applied in this way. The meaning of the expressions denoted by the titles, forms of judgment and categories, is entirely set aside and forgotten, and the expressions alone are retained. These have their source partly in Aristotle's *Analyt. priora,* i. 23 (περι ποιοτητος και ποσοτητος των του συλλογισμου ορων: *de qualitate et quantitate terminorum syllogismi*), but are arbitrarily chosen; for the extent of the concepts might certainly have been otherwise expressed than through the word *quantity*, though this word is more suited to its object than the rest of the titles of the categories. Even the word *quality* has obviously been chosen on account of the custom of opposing quality to quantity; for the name quality is certainly taken arbitrarily enough for affirmation and negation. But now in every inquiry instituted by Kant, every quantity in time and space, and every possible quality of things, physical, moral, &c., is brought by him under those category titles, although between these things and those titles of the forms of judgment and of thought there is absolutely nothing in common except the accidental and arbitrary nomenclature. It is needful to keep in mind all the respect which in other regards is due to Kant to enable one to refrain from expressing in hard terms one's repugnance to this procedure. The nearest example is afforded us at once by the pure physiological table of the general principles of natural science. What in all the world has the quantity of judgments to do with the fact that every perception has an extensive magnitude ? What has the quality of judgments to do with the fact that every sensation has a degree ? The former rests rather on the fact that space is the form of our external perception, and the latter is nothing more than an empirical, and, moreover, entirely subjective feeling, drawn merely from the consideration of the nature of our organs of sense. Further, in the table which gives the basis of rational psychology (Critique of Pure Reason, p. 344; V. 402), the *simplicity* of the soul is cited under quality; but this is just a quantitative property, and has absolutely no relation to the affirmation or negation in the judgment. But quantity had to be completed by the *unity* of the soul, which is, however, already included in its simplicity. Then modality is forced in in an absurd way; the soul stands in connection with *possible* objects; but connection belongs to relation, only this is already taken possession of by substance. Then the four cosmological Ideas, which are the material of the antinomies, are referred to the titles of the categories; but of this we shall speak more fully further on, when we come to the examination of these antinomies. Several, if possible, still more glaring examples are to be found in the table of the *Categories of Freedom !* in the " Critique of Practical Reason ; " also in the first book of the " Critique of Judgment," which goes through the judgment of taste according to the four titles of the categories ; and, finally, in the " Metaphysical First Principles of Natural Science," which are entirely adapted to the table of the categories, whereby the false that is mingled here and there with what is true and excellent in this important work is for the most part introduced. See, for example, at the end of the first chapter how the unity, the multiplicity, and the

totality of the directions of lines are supposed to correspond to the categories, which are so named according to
the quantity of judgments.

The principle of the *Permanence of Substance* is deduced
from the category of subsistence and inherence. This,
however, we know only from the form of the categorical
judgment, *i.e.*, from the connection of two concepts as
subject and predicate. With what violence then is that
great metaphysical principle made dependent upon this
simple, purely logical form! Yet this is only done *pro
forma*, and for the sake of symmetry. The proof of this
principle, which is given here, sets entirely aside its supposed origin in the understanding and in the category, and
is based upon the pure intuition or perception of time.
But this proof also is quite incorrect. It is false that in
mere time there is *simultaneity* and *duration;* these ideas
only arise from the union of *space* with time, as I have
already shown in the essay on the principle of sufficient
reason, § 18, and worked out more fully in § 4 of
the present work. I must assume a knowledge of both
these expositions for the understanding of what follows.
It is false that time *remains* the same through all change;
on the contrary, it is just time itself that is fleeting; a
permanent time is a contradiction. Kant's proof is untenable, strenuously as he has supported it with sophisms;
indeed, he falls into the most palpable contradictions.
Thus, after he has falsely set up co-existence as a mode of
time (p. 177; V. 219), he says, quite rightly (p. 183; V. 226),
" Co-existence is not a mode of time, for in time there are
absolutely no parts together, but all in succession." In
truth, space is quite as much implicated in co-existence as
time. For if two things are co-existent and yet not one,
they are different in respect of space; if two states of one
thing are co-existent (*e.g.*, the glow and the heat of iron),
then they are two contemporaneous effects of *one* thing,

therefore presuppose matter, and matter presupposes space. Strictly speaking, co-existence is a negative determination, which merely signifies that two things or states are not different in respect of time; thus their difference is to be sought for elsewhere. But in any case, our knowledge of the permanence of substance, i.e., of matter, must be based upon insight a priori; for it is raised above all doubt, and therefore cannot be drawn from experience. I deduce it from the fact that the principle of all becoming and passing away, the law of causality, of which we are conscious a priori, is essentially concerned only with the changes, i.e., the successive states of matter, is thus limited to the form, and leaves the matter untouched, which therefore exists in our consciousness as the foundation of all things, which is not subject to becoming or passing away, which has therefore always been and will always continue to be. A deeper proof of the permanence of substance, drawn from the analysis of our perception of the empirical world in general, is to be found in the first book of this work, § 4, where it is shown that the nature of matter consists in the absolute union of space and time, a union which is only possible by means of the idea of causality, consequently only for the understanding, which is nothing but the subjective correlative of causality. Hence, also, matter is never known otherwise than as producing effects, i.e., as through and through causality; to be and to act are with it one, which is indeed signified by the word actuality. Intimate union of space and time—causality, matter, actuality—are thus one, and the subjective correlative of this one is the understanding. Matter must bear in itself the conflicting properties of both factors from which it proceeds, and it is the idea of causality which abolishes what is contradictory in both, and makes their co-existence conceivable by the understanding, through which and for which alone matter is, and whose whole faculty consists in the knowledge of cause and effect. Thus for the understanding there is united in matter the inconstant flux of time, appearing as change of the accidents, with the rigid immobility of space, which exhibits itself as the permanence of substance. For if the substance passed away like the accidents, the phenomenon would be torn away from space altogether, and would only belong to time; the world of experience would be destroyed by the abolition of matter, annihilation. Thus from the share which space has in matter, *i.e.*, in all phenomena of the actual—in that it is the opposite and counterpart of time, and therefore in itself and apart from the union with the latter knows absolutely no change—the principle of the permanence of substance, which recognises everything as *a priori* certain, had to be deduced and explained; but not from mere time, to which for this purpose and quite erroneously Kant has attributed *permanence.*

In the essay on the principle of sufficient reason, § 23, I have fully explained the incorrectness of the following proof of the *a priori* nature and of the necessity of the law of causality from the mere succession of events in time; I must, therefore, content myself here by referring to that passage.[1] This is precisely the case with the proof of reciprocity also, the concept of which I was obliged to explain above as invalid. What is necessary has also been said of modality, the working out of the principles of which now follows.

There are still a few points in the further course of the transcendental analytic which I should have to refute were it not that I am afraid of trying the patience of the reader; I therefore leave them to his own reflection. But ever anew in the "Critique of Pure Reason" we meet that principal and fundamental error of Kant's, which I have copiously denounced above, the complete failure to distinguish abstract, discursive knowledge from intuitive. It is this that throws a constant obscurity over Kant's whole

---

[1] With my refutation of the Kantian proof may be compared the earlier attacks upon it by Feder, *Ueber Zeit, Raum und Kausalität,* § 28; and by G. E. Schulze, *Kritik der theoretischen Philosophie,* Bd. ii. S. 422-442

theory of the faculty of knowledge, and never allows the reader to know what he is really speaking about at any time, so that instead of understanding, he always merely conjectures, for he alternately tries to understand what is said as referring to thought and to perception, and remains always in suspense. In the chapter "On the Division of all Objects into Phenomena and Noumena," Kant carries that incredible want of reflection as to the nature of the idea of perception and the abstract idea, as I shall explain more fully immediately, so far as to make the monstrous assertion that without thought, that is, without abstract conceptions, there is no knowledge of an object; and that perception, because it is not thought, is also not knowledge, and, in general, is nothing but a mere affection of sensibility, mere sensation! Nay, more, that perception without conception is absolutely void; but conception without perception is yet always something (p. 253; V. 309). Now this is exactly the opposite of the truth; for concepts obtain all significance, all content, only from their relation to ideas of perception, from which they have been abstracted, derived, that is, constructed through the omission of all that is unessential: therefore if the foundation of perception is taken away from them, they are empty and void. Perceptions, on the contrary, have in themselves immediate and very great significance (in them, indeed, the thing in itself objectifies itself); they represent themselves, express themselves, have no mere borrowed content like concepts. For the principle of sufficient reason governs them only as the law of causality, and determines as such only their position in space and time; it does not, however, condition their content and their significance, as is the case with concepts, in which it appears as the principle of the ground of knowing. For the rest, it looks as if Kant really wished here to set about distinguishing the idea of perception and the abstract idea. He objects to Leibnitz and Locke that the former reduced everything to abstract ideas, and the latter everything to ideas of perception. But yet he arrives at **no** distinction; and although Locke and Leibnitz really committed these errors, Kant himself is burdened with a third error which includes them both—the error of having so mixed up knowledge of perception and abstract knowledge that a monstrous hybrid of the two resulted, a chimera of which no distinct idea is possible, and which therefore necessarily only confused and stupefied students, and set them at variance.

Certainly thought and perception are separated more in the chapter referred to "On the Division of all Objects into Phenomena and Noumena" than anywhere else, but the nature of this distinction is here a fundamentally false one. On p. 253; V. 309, it is said: "If I take away all thought (through the categories) from empirical knowledge, there remains absolutely no knowledge of an object, for through mere perception nothing at all is thought, and that this affection of sensibility is in me establishes really no relation of such ideas to any object." This sentence contains, in some degree, all the errors of Kant in a nutshell ; for it brings out clearly that he has falsely conceived the relation between sensation, perception, and thought, and accordingly identifies the perception, whose form he yet supposes to be space, and indeed space in all its three dimensions, with the mere subjective sensation in the organs of sense, but only allows the knowledge of an object to be given through thought, which is different from perception. I, on the contrary, say : Objects are first of all objects of perception, not of thought, and all knowledge of *objects* is originally and in itself perception. Perception, however, is by no means mere sensation, but the understanding is already active in it. The thought, which is added only in the case of men, not in the case of the brutes, is mere abstraction from perception, gives no fundamentally new knowledge, does not itself establish objects which were not before, but merely changes the form of the knowledge already won through perception, makes it abstract knowledge in concepts, whereby its concrete or perceptible character is lost, but, on the other hand, combination of it becomes possible, which immeasurably extends the range of its applicability.   The material of our thought is, on the other hand, nothing else than our perceptions themselves, and not something which the perceptions did not contain, and which was added by the thought; therefore the material of everything that appears in our thought must be capable of verification in our perception, for otherwise it would be an empty thought. Although this material is variously manipulated and transformed by thought, it must yet be capable of being reduced to perception, and the thought traced back to this—just as a piece of gold can be reduced from all its solutions, oxides, sublimates, and combinations, and presented pure and undiminished. This could not happen if thought itself had added something, and, indeed, the principal thing, to the object.

The whole of the chapter on the Amphiboly, which follows this, is merely a criticism of the Leibnitzian philosophy, and as such is on the whole correct, though the form or pattern on which it is constructed is chosen merely for the sake of architectonic symmetry, which here also is the guiding clue. Thus, to carry out the analogy with the Aristotelian Organon, a transcendental Topic is set up, which consists in this, that every conception is to be considered from four points of view, in order to make out to which faculty of knowledge it belongs. But these four points of view are quite arbitrarily selected, and ten others might be added to them with just as much right; but their fourfold number corresponds to the titles of the categories, and therefore the chief doctrine of Leibnitz is divided among them as best it may be. By this critique, also, to some extent, certain errors are stamped as natural to the reason, whereas they were merely false abstractions of Leibnitz's, who, rather than learn from his great philosophical contemporaries, Spinoza and Locke, preferred to serve up his own strange inventions. In the chapter on the Amphiboly of Reflection it is finally said that there may possibly be a kind of perception entirely different from ours, to which, however, our categories are applicable ; therefore the objects of that supposed perception would be *noumena*, things which can only be *thought* by us ; but since the perception which would give that thought meaning is wanting to us, and indeed is altogether quite problematical, the object of that thought would also merely be a wholly indefinite possibility. I have shown above by quotations that Kant, in utter contradiction with himself, sets up the categories now as the condition of knowledge of perception, now as the function of merely abstract thought. Here they appear exclusively in the latter sense, and it seems quite as if he wished to attribute them merely to discursive thought. But if this is really his opinion, then necessarily at the beginning of the Transcendental Logic, before specifying the different functions of thought at such length, he was necessarily bound to characterise thought in general, and consequently to distinguish it from perception ; he ought to have shown what knowledge is given by mere perception, and what that is new is added by thought. Then we would have known what he was really speaking about ; or rather, he would then have spoken quite differently, first of perception, and then of thought ; instead of which, as it is, he is always dealing with something between the two, which is a mere delusion. There would not then be that great gap between the transcendental Æsthetic and the transcendental Logic, where, after the exposition of the mere form of perception, he simply dismisses its content, all that is empirically apprehended, with the phrase " It is given," and does not ask how it came about, *whether with or without understanding ;* but, with one spring, passes over to abstract thought ; and not even to thought in general, but at once to certain forms of thought, and does not say a word about what thought is, what the concept is, what is the relation of abstract and discursive to concrete and intuitive, what is the difference between the knowledge of men and that of brutes, and what is reason.

Yet it was just this distinction between abstract knowledge and knowledge of perception, entirely overlooked by Kant, which the ancients denoted by φαινομενα and νοουμενα,[1] and whose opposition and incommensurability occupied them so much in the philosophemes of the Eleatics, in Plato's doctrine of Ideas, in the dialectic of the Megarics, and later the Scholastics in the controversy between Nominalism and Realism, the seed of which, so late in developing, was already contained in the opposite mental tendencies of Plato and Aristotle. But Kant, who, in an inexcusable manner, entirely neglected the thing to denote which the words φαινομενα and νοουμενα had already been taken, took possession of the words, as if they were still unappropriated, in order to denote by them his thing in itself and his phenomenon.

Since I have been obliged to reject Kant's doctrine of the categories, just as he rejected that of Aristotle, I wish here to indicate as a suggestion a third way of reaching what is aimed at. What both Kant and Aristotle sought for under the name of the categories were the most general conceptions under which all things, however different, must be subsumed, and through which therefore everything that exists would ultimately be thought. Just on this account Kant conceived them as the *forms* of all thought.

Grammar is related to logic as clothes to the body. Should not, therefore, these primary conceptions, the groundbass of the reason, which is the foundation of all special thought, without whose application, therefore, no thought can take place, ultimately lie in those conceptions which

---

[1] See *Sext. Empir. Pyrrhon. hypotyp.*, lib. i. c. 13, νοουμενα φαινομε- νοις αντετιθη Αναξαγορας (*intelligibilia apparentibus opposuit Anaxagoras.*

just on account of their exceeding generality (transcendentalism) have their expression not in single words, but in whole classes of words, because one of them is thought along with every word whatever it may be, whose designation would therefore have to be looked for, not in the lexicon but in the grammar? In fact, should they not be those distinctions of conceptions on account of which the word which expresses them is either a substantive or an adjective, a verb or an adverb, a pronoun, a preposition, or some other particle—in short, the parts of speech? For undoubtedly these denote the forms which all thought primarily assumes, and in which it directly moves; accordingly they are the essential forms of speech, the fundamental constituent elements of every language, so that we cannot imagine any language which would not consist of at least substantives, adjectives, and verbs. These fundamental forms would then have subordinated to them those forms of thought which are expressed through their inflections, that is, through declension and conjugation, and it is unessential to the chief concern whether in denoting them we call in the assistance of the article and the pronoun. We will examine the thing, however, somewhat more closely, and ask the question anew: What are the forms of thought?

(1.) Thought consists throughout of judging; judgments are the threads of its whole web, for without making use of a verb our thought does not move, and as often as we use a verb we judge.

(2.) Every judgment consists in the recognition of the relation between subject and predicate, which it separates or unites with various restrictions. It unites them from the recognition of the actual identity of the two, which can only happen in the case of synonyms; then in the recognition that the one is always thought along with the other, though the converse does not hold—in the universal affirmative proposition; up to the recognition that the one is sometimes thought along with the other, in the particular affirmative proposition. The negative propositions take the opposite course. Accordingly in every judgment the subject, the predicate, and the copula, the latter affirmative or negative, must be to be found; even although each of these is not denoted by a word of its own, as is however generally the case. The predicate and the copula are often denoted by *one* word, as " Caius ages;" sometimes one word denotes all three, as *concurritur, i.e.,* "the armies engage." From this it is evident that the forms of thought are not to be sought for precisely and directly in words, nor even in the parts of speech, for even in the same language the same judgment may be expressed in different words, and indeed in different parts of speech, yet the thought remains the same, and consequently also its form; for the thought could not be the same if the form of thought itself were different. But with the same thought and the same form of thought the form of words may very well be different, for it is merely the outward clothing of the thought, which, on the other hand, is inseparable from *its* form. Thus grammar only explains the clothing of the forms of thought. The parts of speech can therefore be deduced from the original forms of thought themselves which are independent of all language; their work is to express these forms of thought in all their modifications. They are the instrument and the clothing of the forms of thought, and must be accurately adapted to the structure of the latter, so that it may be recognised in them.

(3.) These real, unalterable, original forms of thought are certainly *those of Kant's logical table of judgments ;* only that in this table are to be found blind windows for the sake of symmetry and the table of the categories; these must all be omitted, and also a false arrangement. Thus :—

(*a.*) *Quality :* affirmation and negation, *i.e.,* combination and separation of concepts: two forms. It depends on the copula.

(*b.*) *Quantity :* the subject-concept is taken either in

whole or in part: totality or multiplicity. To the first belong also individual subjects: Socrates means "all Socrateses." Thus two forms. It depends on the subject.

(*c.*) *Modality :* has really three forms. It determines the quality as necessary, actual, or contingent. It consequently depends also on the copula.

These three forms of thought spring from the laws of thought of contradiction and identity. But from the principle of sufficient reason and the law of excluded middle springs—

(*d.*) *Relation.* It only appears if we judge concerning completed judgments, and can only consist in this, that it either asserts the dependence of one judgment upon another (also in the plurality of both), and therefore combines them in the *hypothetical* proposition; or else asserts that judgments exclude each other, and therefore separates them in the *disjunctive* proposition. It depends on the copula, which here separates or combines the completed judgments.

The *parts of speech* and grammatical forms are ways of expressing the three constituent parts of the judgment, the subject, the predicate, and the copula, and also of the possible relations of these; thus of the forms of thought just enumerated, and the fuller determinations and modifications of these. Substantive, adjective, and verb are therefore essential fundamental constituent elements of language in general; therefore they must be found in all languages. Yet it is possible to conceive a language in which adjective and verb would always be fused together, as is sometimes the case in all languages. Provisionally it may be said, for the expression of the *subject* are intended the substantive, the article, and the pronoun; for the expression of the *predicate*, the adjective, the adverb, and the preposition ; for the expression of the *copula*, the verb, which, however, with the exception of the verb to be, also contains the predicate. It is the task of the philosophy of grammar to teach the precise mechanism of

the expression of the forms of thought, as it is the task of
logic to teach the operations with the forms of thought
themselves.

Note.—As a warning against a false path and to illustrate the above, I mention S. Stern's " *Vorläufige Grund-
lage zur Sprachphilosophie,*" 1835, which is an utterly
abortive attempt to construct the categories out of the
grammatical forms. He has entirely confused thought
with perception, and therefore, instead of the categories of
thought, he has tried to deduce the supposed categories
of perception from the grammatical forms, and consequently has placed the grammatical forms in direct relation to perception. He is involved in the great error that
language is immediately related to *perception,* instead of
being directly related only to thought as such, thus to
the *abstract concepts,* and only by means of these to perception, to which they, however, have a relation which
introduces an entire change of the form. What exists
in perception, thus also the relations which proceed
from time and space, certainly becomes an object of
thought ; thus there must also be forms of speech to
express it, yet always merely in the abstract, as concepts.
Concepts are always the primary material of thought, and
the forms of logic are always related to these, never
directly to perception. Perception always determines only
the material, never the formal truth of the proposition,
for the formal truth is determined according to the logical
rules alone.

———————

I return to the Kantian philosophy, and come now to
the *Transcendental Dialectic.* Kant opens it with the
explanation of *reason,* the faculty which is to play the
principal part in it, for hitherto only sensibility and
understanding were on the scene. When considering his
different explanations of reason, I have already spoken
above of the explanation he gives here that " it is the

faculty of principles." It is now taught here that all the *a priori* knowledge hitherto considered, which makes pure mathematics and pure natural science possible, affords only *rules*, and no *principles;* because it proceeds from perceptions and forms of knowledge, and not from mere conceptions, which is demanded if it is to be called a principle. Such a principle must accordingly be knowledge *from pure conceptions* and yet *synthetical.* But this is absolutely impossible. From pure conceptions nothing but *analytical* propositions can ever proceed. If conceptions are to be synthetically and yet *a priori* combined, this combination must necessarily be accomplished by some third thing, through a pure perception of the formal possibility of experience, just as synthetic judgments *a posteriori* are brought about through empirical perception; consequently a synthetic proposition *a priori* can never proceed from pure conceptions. In general, however, we are *a priori* conscious of nothing more than the principle of sufficient reason in its different forms, and therefore no other synthetic judgments *a priori* are possible than those which proceed from that which receives its content from that principle.

However, Kant finally comes forward with a pretended principle of the reason answering to his demand, yet only with this *one*, from which others afterwards follow as corollaries. It is the principle which Chr. Wolf set up and explained in his *"Cosmologia,"* sect. i. c. 2, § 93, and in his *"Ontologia,"* § 178. As now above, under the title of the Amphiboly, mere Leibnitzian philosophemes were taken for natural and necessary aberrations of the reason, and were criticised as such, so here precisely the same thing happens with the philosophemes of Wolf. Kant still presents this principle of the reason in an obscure light, through indistinctness, indefiniteness, and breaking of it up (p. 307; V. 361, and 322; V. 379). Clearly expressed, however, it is as follows: "If the conditioned is given, the totality of its conditions must also be given, and therefore also the *unconditioned,* through which alone that totality becomes complete." We become most vividly aware of the apparent truth of this proposition if we imagine the conditions and the conditioned as the links of a suspended chain, the upper end of which, however, is not visible, so that it might extend *ad infinitum;* since, however, the chain does not fall, but hangs, there must be above *one* link which is the first, and in some way is fixed. Or, more briefly: the reason desires to have a point of attachment for the causal chain which reaches back to infinity; it would be convenient for it. But we will examine the proposition, not in figures, but in itself. Synthetic it certainly is; for, analytically, nothing more follows from the conception of the conditioned than that of the condition. It has not, however, *a priori* truth, nor even *a posteriori,* but it surreptitiously obtains its appearance of truth in a very subtle way, which I must now point out. Immediately, and *a priori,* we have the knowledge which the principle of sufficient reason in its four forms expresses. From this immediate knowledge all abstract expressions of the principle of sufficient reason are derived, and they are thus indirect; still more, however, is this the case with inferences or corollaries from them. I have already explained above how *abstract* knowledge often unites a variety of *intuitive* cognitions in *one* form or *one* concept in such a way that they can no longer be distinguished; therefore abstract knowledge stands to intuitive knowledge as the shadow to the real objects, the great multiplicity of which it presents through one outline comprehending them all. Now the pretended principle of the reason makes use of this shadow. In order to deduce from the principle of sufficient reason the unconditioned, which directly contradicts it, it prudently abandons the immediate concrete knowledge of the content of the principle of sufficient reason in its particular forms, and only makes use of abstract concepts which are derived from it, and have value and significance only through it, in order to smuggle its unconditioned somehow or other into the wide sphere of those concepts. Its procedure becomes most distinct when clothed in dialectical form; for example, thus: " If the conditioned exists, its condition must also be given, and indeed all given, thus completely, thus the totality of its conditions ; consequently, if they constitute a series, the whole series, consequently also its first beginning, thus the unconditioned." Here it is false that the conditions of a conditioned can constitute a *series*. Rather must the totality of the conditions of everything conditioned be contained in its *nearest* ground or reason from which it directly proceeds, and which is only thus a *sufficient* ground or reason. For example, the different determinations of the state which is the cause, all of which must be present together before the effect can take place. But the series, for example, the chain of causes, arises merely from the fact that we regard what immediately before was the condition as now a conditioned; but then at once the whole operation begins again from the beginning, and the principle of sufficient reason appears anew with its claim. But there can never be for a conditioned a properly successive *series* of conditions, which exist merely as such, and on account of that which is at last conditioned; it is always an alternating series of conditioneds and conditions ; as each link is laid aside the chain is broken, and the claim of the principle of sufficient reason entirely satisfied, it arises anew because the condition becomes the conditioned. Thus the principle of *sufficient* reason always demands only the completeness of the *immediate or next condition*, never the completeness of a *series*. But just this conception of the completeness of the condition leaves it undetermined whether this completeness should be simultaneous or successive ; and since the latter is chosen, the demand now arises for a complete series of conditions following each other. Only through an arbitrary abstraction is a series of causes and effects regarded as a series of causes alone, which exists merely on account of the last effect, and is therefore demanded as its *sufficient* reason. From closer and more intelligent consideration, and by rising from the indefinite generality of abstraction to the particular definite reality, it appears, on the contrary, that the demand for a *sufficient* reason extends only to the completeness of the determinations of the *immediate* cause, not to the completeness of a series. The demand of the principle of sufficient reason is completely extinguished in each sufficient reason given. It arises, however, immediately anew, because this reason is again regarded as a consequent; but it never demands directly a series of reasons. If, on the other hand, instead of going to the thing itself, we confine ourselves to the abstract concepts, these distinctions vanish. Then a chain of alternating causes and effects, or of alternating logical reasons and consequents, is given out as simply a chain of causes of the last effect, or reasons of the last consequent, and the *completeness of the conditions*, through which alone a reason becomes *sufficient*, appears as the completeness of that assumed *series* of reasons alone, which only exist on account of the last consequent. There then appears the abstract principle of the reason very boldly with its demand for the unconditioned. But, in order to recognise the invalidity of this claim, there is no need of a critique of reason by means of antinomies and their solution, but only of a critique of reason understood in my sense, an examination of the relation of abstract knowledge to direct intuitive knowledge, by means of ascending from the indefinite generality of the former to the fixed definiteness of the latter. From such a critique, then, it here appears that the nature of the reason by no means consists in the demand for an unconditioned; for, whenever it proceeds with full deliberation, it must itself find that an unconditioned is an absurdity. The reason as a faculty of knowledge can always have to do only with objects; but every object for the subject is necessarily and irrevocably subordinated to the principle of sufficient

reason, both *a parte ante* and *a parte post.* The validity of
the principle of sufficient reason is so involved in the
form of consciousness that we absolutely cannot imagine
anything objective of which no *why* could further be demanded ; thus we cannot imagine an absolute absolute,
like a blind wall in front of us. That his convenience
should lead this or that person to stop at some point, and
assume such an absolute at pleasure, is of no avail against
that incontestable certainty *a priori,* even if he should put
on an air of great importance in doing so. In fact, the
whole talk about the absolute, almost the sole theme of
philosophies since Kant, is nothing but the cosmological
proof *incognito.* This proof, in consequence of the case
brought against it by Kant, deprived of all right and
declared outlawed, dare no longer show itself in its true
form, and therefore appears in all kinds of disguises—now
in distinguished form, concealed under intellectual intuition or pure thought; now as a suspicious vagabond, half
begging, half demanding what it wants in more unpre-
tending philosophemes. If an absolute must absolutely
be had, then I will give one which is far better fitted to
meet all the demands which are made on such a thing
than these visionary phantoms; it is matter. It has no
beginning, and it is imperishable ; thus it is really independent, and *quod per se est et per se concipitur ;* from its
womb all proceeds, and to it all returns; what more can
be desired of an absolute ? But to those with whom no
critique of reason has succeeded, we should rather say—

> " Are not ye like unto women, who ever
> Return to the point from which they set out,
> Though reason should have been talked by the hour ? "

That the return to an unconditioned cause, to a first
beginning, by no means lies in the nature of reason, is,
moreover, practically proved by the fact that the primitive religions of our race, which even yet have the
greatest number of followers upon earth, Brahmanism and

Buddhaism, neither know nor admit such assumptions, but carry the series of phenomena conditioning each other into infinity. Upon this point, I refer to the note appended to the criticism of the first antinomy, which occurs further on ; and the reader may also see Upham's "Doctrine of Buddhaism" (p. 9), and in general all genuine accounts of the religions of Asia. Judaism and reason ought not to be identified.

Kant, who by no means desires to maintain his pretended principle of reason as objectively valid, but merely as subjectively necessary, deduces it even as such only by means of a shallow sophism, p. 307; V. 364. He says that because we seek to subsume every truth known to us under a more general truth, as far as this process can be carried, this is nothing else than the pursuit of the unconditioned, which we already presuppose. But, in truth, in this endeavour we do nothing more than apply reason, and intentionally make use of it to simplify our knowledge by enabling us to survey it—reason, which is that faculty of abstract, general knowledge that distinguishes the reflective, thinking man, endowed with speech, from the brute, which is the slave of the present. For the use of reason just consists in this, that we know the particular through the universal, the case through the rule, the rule through the more general rule ; thus that we seek the most general points of view. Through such survey or general view our knowledge is so facilitated and perfected that from it arises the great difference between the life of the brutes and that of men, and again between the life of educated and that of uneducated men. Now, certainly the series of *grounds of knowledge*, which exist only in the sphere of the abstract, thus of reason, always finds an end in what is indemonstrable, *i.e.*, in an idea which is not further conditioned according to this form of the principle of sufficient reason, thus in the *a priori* or *a posteriori* directly perceptible ground of the first proposition of the train of reasoning. I have already shown in the essay on the principle of sufficient reason, § 50, that here the series of grounds of knowledge really passes over into grounds of becoming or of being. But one can only desire to make this circumstance hold good as a proof of an unconditioned according to the law of causality, or even of the mere demand for such an unconditioned, if one has not yet distinguished the forms of the principle of sufficient reason at all, but, holding to the abstract expression, has confounded them all. Kant, however, seeks to establish that confusion, through a mere play upon words, with *Universalitas* and *Universitas*, p. 322; V. 379. Thus it is fundamentally false that our search for higher grounds of knowledge, more general truths, springs from the presupposition of an object unconditioned in its being, or has anything whatever in common with this. Moreover, how should it be essential to the reason to presuppose something which it must know to be an absurdity as soon as it reflects? The source of that conception of the unconditioned is rather to be found only in the indolence of the individual who wishes by means of it to get rid of all further questions, whether his own or of others, though entirely without justification.

Now Kant himself denies objective validity to this pretended principle of reason; he gives it, however, as a necessary subjective assumption, and thus introduces an irremediable split into our knowledge, which he soon allows to appear more clearly. With this purpose he unfolds that principle of reason further, p. 322; V, 379, in accordance with the method of architectonic symmetry of which he is so fond. From the three categories of relation spring three kinds of syllogisms, each of which gives the clue for the discovery of a special unconditioned, of which again there are three: the soul, the world (as an object in itself and absolute totality), and God. Now here we must at once note a great contradiction, of which Kant, however, takes no notice, because it would be very dangerous to the symmetry. Two of these unconditioneds are themselves conditioned by the third, the soul and the world by God, who is the cause of their existence. Thus the two former have by no means the predicate of unconditionedness in common with the latter, though this is really the point here, but only that of inferred being according to the principles of experience, beyond the sphere of the possibility of experience.

Setting this aside, we recognise in the three unconditioneds, to which, according to Kant, reason, following its essential laws, must come, the three principal subjects round which the whole of philosophy under the influence of Christianity, from the Scholastics down to Christian Wolf, has turned. Accessible and familiar as these conceptions have become through all these philosophers, and now also through the philosophers of pure reason, this by no means shows that, without revelation, they would necessarily have proceeded from the development of all reason as a production peculiar to its very nature. In order to prove this it would be necessary to call in the aid of historical criticism, and to examine whether the ancient and non-European nations, especially the peoples of Hindostan and many of the oldest Greek philosophers, really attained to those conceptions, or whether it is only we who, by quite falsely translating the Brahma of the Hindus and the Tien of the Chinese as "God," good-naturedly attribute such conceptions to them, just as the Greeks recognised their gods everywhere; whether it is not rather the case that theism proper is only to be found in the religion of the Jews, and in the two religions which have proceeded from it, whose followers just on this account comprise the adherents of all other religions on earth under the name of heathen, which, by the way, is a most absurd and crude expression, and ought to be banished at least from the writings of the learned, because it identifies and jumbles together Brahmanists, Buddhists, Egyptians, Greeks, Romans, Germans, Gauls, Iroquois, Patagonians, Caribbeans, Otaheiteans, Australians, and many others. Such an expression is all very well for priests, but in the learned world it must at once be shown the door: it can go to England and take up its abode at Oxford. It is a thoroughly established fact that Buddhism, the religion which numbers more followers than any other on earth, contains absolutely no theism, indeed rejects it. As regards Plato, it is my opinion that he owes to the Jews the theism with which he is periodically seized. On this account Numenius (according to Clem. Alex., *Strom.*, i. c. 22, Euseb. *præp. evang.*, xiii. 12, and Suidas under Numenius) called him the *Moses græcisans*: Τι γαρ εστι Πλατων, η Μωσης αττικιζων; and he accuses him of having stolen (αποσυλησας) his doctrine of God and the creation from the Mosaical writings. Clemens often repeats that Plato knew and made use of Moses, *e.g.*, *Strom.*, i. 25.—v. c. 14, § 90, &c., &c.; *Pædagog.*, ii. 10, and iii. 11; also in the *Cohortatio ad gentes*, c. 6, where, after he has bitterly censured and derided the whole of the Greek philosophers in the preceding chapter because they were not Jews, he bestows on Plato nothing but praise, and breaks out into pure exultation that as Plato had learnt his geometry from the Egyptians, his astronomy from the Babylonians, magic from the Thracians, and much also from the Assyrians, so he had learnt his theism from the Jews: Οιδα σου τους διδασκαλους, κἀν αποκρυπτειν εθελῆς, . . . δοξαν την του θεου παρ' αυτων ωφελησει των Εβραιων (*Tuos magistros novi, licet eos celare velis*, . . . *illa de Deo sententia suppeditata tibi est ab Hebræis*). A pathetic scene of recognition. But I see a remarkable confirmation of the matter in what follows. According to Plutarch (*in Mario*), and, better, according to Lactantius (i. 3, 19), Plato thanked Nature that he had been born a human being and not a brute, a man and not a woman, a Greek and not a barbarian. Now in Isaac Euchel's "Prayers of the Jews," from the Hebrew, second edition, 1799, p. 7, there is a morning prayer in which God is thanked and praised that the worshipper was born a Jew and not a heathen, a free man and not a slave, a man and not a woman. Such an historical investigation would have spared Kant an unfortunate necessity in which he now becomes involved, in that he makes these three conceptions spring necessarily from the nature of reason, and yet explains that they are untenable and unverifiable by the reason, and thus makes the reason itself a sophisticator; for he says, p. 339; V. 397: "There are sophistications, not of man, but of pure reason itself, from which even the wisest cannot free himself, and although after much trouble he may be able to avoid error, yet he never can escape from the illusion which unceasingly torments and mocks him." Therefore these Kantian "Ideas of the Reason" might be compared to the focus in which the converging reflected rays from a concave mirror meet several inches before its surface, in consequence of which, by an inevitable process of the understanding, an object presents itself to us there which is a thing without reality. *96 / 99*

But the name "Idea" is very unfortunately chosen for these pretended necessary productions of the pure theoretical reason, and violently appropriated from Plato, who used it to denote the eternal forms which, multiplied through space and time, become partially visible in the innumerable individual fleeting things. Plato's "Ideas" are accordingly throughout perceptible, as indeed the word which he chose so definitely signifies, for it could only be adequately translated by means of perceptible or visible things; and Kant has appropriated it to denote that which lies so far from all possibility of perception that even abstract thought can only half attain to it. The word "Idea," which Plato first introduced, has, moreover, since then, through two-and-twenty centuries, always retained the significance in which he used it; for not only all ancient philosophers, but also all the Scholastics, and indeed the Church Fathers and the theologians of the Middle Ages, used it only in that Platonic sense, the sense of the Latin word *exemplar*, as Suarez expressly mentions in his twenty-fifth Disputation, sect. 1. That Englishmen and Frenchmen were later induced by the poverty of their languages to misuse this word is bad enough, but not of importance. Kant's misuse of the word idea, by the substitution of a new significance introduced by means of the slender clue of not being object of experience, which it has in common with Plato's ideas, but also in common with every possible chimera, is thus altogether unjustifiable. Now, since the misuse of a few years is not to be considered against the authority of many centuries, I have always used the word in its old, original, Platonic significance.

The refutation of *rational psychology* is much fuller and more thorough in the first edition of the "Critique of Pure Reason" than in the second and following editions, and therefore upon this point we must make use of the first edition exclusively. This refutation has as a whole very great merit and much truth. Yet I am clearly of opinion that it was merely from his love of symmetry that Kant deduced as necessary the conception of the soul from the paralogism of substantiality by applying the demand for the unconditioned to the conception *substance*, which is the first category of relation, and accordingly maintained that the conception of a soul arose in this way in every speculative reason. If this conception really had its origin in the presupposition of a final subject of all predicates of a thing, one would have assumed a soul not in men alone, but also just as necessarily in every lifeless thing, for such a thing also requires a final subject of all its predicates. Speaking generally, however, Kant makes use of a quite inadmissible expression when he talks of something which can exist only as subject and not as predicate (*e.g.*, Critique of Pure Reason, p. 323; V. 412; Prolegomena, § 4 and

47); though a precedent for this is to be found in Aristotle's "Metaphysics," iv. ch. 8. Nothing whatever exists as subject and predicate, for these expressions belong exclusively to logic, and denote the relations of abstract conceptions to each other. Now their correlative or representative in the world of perception must be substance and accident. But then we need not look further for that which exists always as substance and never as accident, but have it directly in matter. It is the substance corresponding to all properties of things which are their accidents. It is, in fact, if one wishes to retain the expression of Kant which has just been condemned, the final subject of all predicates of that empirically given thing, that which remains after the abstraction of all its properties of every kind. And this holds good of man as of a brute, a plant, or a stone, and is so evident, that in order not to see it a determined desire not to see is required. That it is really the prototype of the conception substance, I will show soon. But subject and predicate are related to substance and accident rather as the principle of sufficient reason in logic to the law of causality in nature, and the substitution or identification of the former is just as inadmissible as that of the latter. Yet in the "Prolegomena," § 46, Kant carries this substitution and identification to its fullest extent in order to make the conception of the soul arise from that of the final subject of all predicates and from the form of the categorical syllogism. In order to discover the sophistical nature of this paragraph, one only needs to reflect that subject and predicate are purely logical determinations, which concern abstract conceptions solely and alone, and that according to their relation in the judgment. Substance and accident, on the other hand, belong to the world of perception and its apprehension in the understanding, and are even there only as identical with matter and form or quality. Of this more shortly.

The antithesis which has given occasion for the assumption of two fundamentally different substances, body and soul, is in truth that of objective and subjective. If a man apprehends himself objectively in external perception, he finds a being extended in space and in general merely corporeal; but if, on the other hand, he apprehends himself in mere self-consciousness, thus purely subjectively, he finds himself a merely willing and perceiving being, free from all forms of perception, thus also without a single one of the properties which belong to bodies. Now he forms the conception of the soul, like all the transcendental conceptions called by Kant Ideas, by applying the principle of sufficient reason, the form of all objects, to that which is not an object, and in this case indeed to the subject of knowing and willing. He treats, in fact, knowing, thinking, and willing as effects of which he seeks the cause, and as he cannot accept the body as their cause, he assumes a cause of them entirely different from the body. In this manner the first and the last of the dogmatists proves the existence of the soul: Plato in the "Phædrus" and also Wolf: from thinking and willing as the effects which lead to that cause. Only after in this way, by hypostatising a cause corresponding to the effect, the conception of an immaterial, simple, indestructible being had arisen, the school developed and demonstrated this from the conception of *substance*. But this conception itself they had previously constructed specially for this purpose by the following artifice, which is worthy of notice.

With the first class of ideas, *i.e.*, the real world of perception, the idea of matter is also given; because the law governing this class of ideas, the law of causality, determines the change of the states or conditions, and these conditions themselves presuppose something permanent, whose changes they are. When speaking above of the principle of the permanence of substance, I showed, by reference to earlier passages, that this idea of matter arises because in the understanding, for which alone it exists, time and space are intimately united, and the share of space in this product exhibits itself as the permanence of matter, while the share of time appears as the change of states. Purely in itself, matter can only be thought *in abstracto*, and not perceived; for to perception it always appears already in form and quality. From this conception of *matter, substance* is again an abstraction, consequently a higher *genus*, and arose in this way. Of the conception of matter, only the predicate of permanence was allowed to remain, while all its other essential properties, extension, impenetrability, divisibility, &c., were thought away. Like every higher *genus*, then, the concept *substance* contains *less in itself* than the concept *matter*, but, unlike every other higher *genus*, it does not contain *more under it*, because it does not include several lower *genera* besides matter; but this remains the one true species of the concept substance, the only assignable thing by which its content is realised and receives a proof. Thus the aim with which in other cases the reason produces by abstraction a higher conception, in order that in it several subordinate species may be thought at once through common determinations, has here no place; consequently that abstraction is either undertaken idly and entirely without aim, or it has a secret secondary purpose. This secret purpose is now brought to light; for under the conception substance, along with its true sub-species matter, a second species is co-ordinated—the immaterial, simple, indestructible substance, soul. But the surreptitious introduction of this last concept arose from the fact that the higher concept *substance* was framed illogically, and in a manner contrary to law. In its legitimate procedure the reason always frames the concept of a higher genus by placing together the concepts of several species, and now comparing them, proceeds discursively, and by omitting their differences and retaining the qualities in which they agree, obtains the generic concept which includes them all but has a smaller content. From this it follows that the concepts of the species must always precede the concept of the genus. But, in the present case, the converse is true. Only the concept matter existed before the generic concept *substance.* The latter was without occasion, and consequently without justification, as it were aimlessly framed from the former by the arbitrary omission of all its determinations except one. Not till afterwards was the second ungenuine species placed beside the concept matter, and so foisted in. But for the framing of this second concept nothing more was now required than an express denial of what had already been tacitly omitted in the higher generic concept, extension, impenetrability, and divisibility. Thus the concept *substance* was framed merely to be the vehicle for the surreptitious introduction of the concept of the immaterial substance. Consequently, it is very far from being capable of holding good as a category or necessary function of the understanding; rather is it an exceedingly superfluous concept, because its only true content lies already in the concept of matter, besides which it contains only a great void, which can be filled up by nothing but the illicitly introduced species *immaterial substance;* and, indeed, it was solely for the purpose of containing this that it was framed. Accordingly, in strictness, the concept substance must be entirely rejected, and the concept matter everywhere put in its place.

The categories were a procrustean bed for every possible thing, but the three kinds of syllogisms are so only for the three so-called Ideas. The Idea of the soul was compelled to find its origin in the form of the categorical syllogism. It is now the turn of the dogmatic ideas concerning the universe, so far as it is thought as an object in itself, between two limits—that of the smallest (atom), and that of the largest (limits of the universe in time and space). These must now proceed from the form of the hypothetical syllogism. Nor for this in itself is any special violence necessary. For the hypothetical judgment has its form from the principle of sufficient reason, and not the cosmological alone but all those so-called Ideas really have their origin in the inconsiderate and unrestricted application of that principle, and the laying aside of it at pleasure. For, in accordance with that principle, the mere dependence of an object upon another is ever sought for, till finally the exhaustion of the imagination puts an end to the journey; and thus it is lost sight of that every object, and indeed the whole chain of objects and the principle of sufficient reason itself, stand in a far closer and greater dependence, the dependence upon the knowing subject, for whose objects alone, *i.e.*, ideas, that principle is valid, for their mere position in space and time is determined by it. Thus, since the form of knowledge from which here merely the cosmological Ideas are derived, the principle of sufficient reason, is the source of all subtle hypostases, in this case no sophisms need be resorted to; but so much the more is sophistry required in order to classify those Ideas according to the four titles of the categories.

(1.) The cosmological Ideas with regard to time and space, thus of the limits of the world in both, are boldly regarded as determined through the category of *quantity*, with which they clearly have nothing in common, except the accidental denotation in logic of the extent of the concept of the subject in the judgment by the word *quantity*, a pictorial expression instead of which some other might just as well have been chosen. But for Kant's love of symmetry this is enough. He takes advantage of the fortunate accident of this nomenclature, and links to it the transcendent dogmas of the world's extension.

(2.) Yet more boldly does Kant link to *quality*, *i.e.*, the affirmation or negation in a judgment, the transcendent Ideas concerning matter; a procedure which has not even an accidental similarity of words as a basis. For it is just to the *quantity*, and not to the *quality* of matter that its mechanical (not chemical) divisibility is related. But, what is more, this whole idea of divisibility by no means belongs to those inferences according to the principle of sufficient reason, from which, however, as the content of the hypothetical form, all cosmological Ideas ought to flow. For the assertion upon which Kant there relies, that the relation of the parts to the whole is that of the condition to the conditioned, thus a relation according to the principle of sufficient reason, is certainly an ingenious but yet a groundless sophism. That relation is rather based upon the principle of contradiction; for the whole is not through the part, nor the parts through the whole, but both are necessarily together because they are one, and their separation is only an arbitrary act. It depends upon this, according to the principle of contradiction, that if the parts are thought away, the whole is also thought away, and conversely; and by no means upon the fact that the parts as the *reason* conditioned the whole as the *consequent*, and that therefore, in accordance with the principle of sufficient reason, we were necessarily led to seek the ultimate parts, in order, as its reason, to understand from them the whole. Such great difficulties are here overcome by the love of symmetry.

(3.) The Idea of the first cause of the world would now quite properly come under the title of *relation ;* but Kant must reserve this for the fourth title, that of *modality*, for which otherwise nothing would remain, and under which he forces this idea to come by saying that the contingent (*i.e.*, according to his explanation, which is diametrically opposed to the truth, every consequent of its reason) becomes the necessary through the first cause. Therefore, for the sake of symmetry, the conception of *freedom* appears here as the third Idea. By this conception, however, as is distinctly stated in the observations on the thesis of the third conflict, what is really meant is only that Idea of the cause of the world which alone is admissible here. The third and fourth conflicts are at bottom tauto-logical.

About all this, however, I find and assert that the whole antinomy is a mere delusion, a sham fight. Only the assertions of the antitheses really rest upon the forms of our faculty of knowledge, *i.e.*, if we express it objectively, on the necessary, *a priori* certain, most universal laws of nature. Their proofs alone are therefore drawn from objective grounds. On the other hand, the assertions and proofs of the theses have no other than a subjective ground, rest solely on the weakness of the reasoning individual; for his imagination becomes tired with an endless regression, and therefore he puts an end to it by arbitrary assumptions, which he tries to smooth over as well as he can; and his judgment, moreover, is in this case paralysed by early and deeply imprinted prejudices. On this account the proof of the thesis in all the four conflicts is throughout a mere sophism, while that of the antithesis is a necessary inference of the reason from the laws of the world as idea known to us *a priori.* It is, moreover, only with great pains and skill that Kant is able to sustain the thesis, and make it appear to attack its opponent, which is endowed with native power. Now in this regard his first and constant artifice is, that he does not render prominent the *nervus argumentationis,* and thus present it in as isolated, naked, and distinct a manner as he possibly can; but rather introduces the same argument on both sides, concealed under and mixed up with a mass of superfluous and prolix sentences.

The theses and antitheses which here appear in such conflict remind one of the δικαιος and αδικος λογος which Socrates, in the "Clouds" of Aristophanes, brings forward as contending. Yet this resemblance extends only to the form and not to the content, though this would gladly be asserted by those who ascribe to these most speculative of all questions of theoretical philosophy an influence upon morality, and therefore seriously regard the thesis as the

δίκαιος, and the antithesis as the ἄδικος λόγος. I shall
not, however, accommodate myself here with reference
to such small, narrow, and perverse minds; and, giving
honour not to them, but to the truth, I shall show that
the proofs which Kant adduced of the individual theses
are sophisms, while those of the antitheses are quite fairly
and correctly drawn from objective grounds. I assume
that in this examination the reader has always before him
the Kantian antinomy itself.

If the proof of the thesis in the first conflict is to be
held as valid, then it proves too much, for it would be
just as applicable to time itself as to change in time, and
would therefore prove that time itself must have had a
beginning, which is absurd. Besides, the sophism consists
in this, that instead of the beginninglessness of the series
of states, which was at first the question, suddenly the
endlessness (infinity) of the series is substituted; and now
it is proved that this is logically contradicted by completeness, and yet every present is the end of the past,
which no one doubted. The end of a beginningless series
can, however, always be *thought*, without prejudice to the
fact that it has no beginning; just as, conversely, the beginning of an endless series can also be *thought*. But
against the real, true argument of the antithesis, that the
changes of the world necessarily presuppose an infinite
series of changes *backwards*, absolutely nothing is advanced. We can think the possibility that the causal
chain will some day end in an absolute standstill, but
we can by no means think the possibility of an absolute
beginning.[1]

[1] That the assumption of a limit
of the world in time is certainly not
a necessary thought of the reason
may be also proved historically, for
the Hindus teach nothing of the
kind, even in the religion of the
people, much less in the Vedas, but
try to express mythologically by
means of a monstrous chronology the
infinity of this phenomenal world,
this fleeting and baseless web of
Mâyâ, for they at once bring out
very ingeniously the relativity of all
periods of time in the following my-
thus (Polier, *Mythologie des Indous*,
vol. ii. p. 585). The four ages, in
the last of which we live, embrace
together 4,320,000 years. Each day
of the creating Brahma has 1000
such periods of four ages, and his

With reference to the spatial limits of the world, it is proved that, if it is to be regarded as a *given whole*, it must necessarily have limits. The reasoning is correct, only it was just the first link of it that was to be proved, and that remains unproved. Totality presupposes limits, and limits presuppose totality; but here both together are arbitrarily presupposed. For this second point, however, the antithesis affords no such satisfactory proof as for the first, because the law of causality provides us with necessary determinations only with reference to time, not to space, and affords us *a priori* the certainty that no occupied time can ever be bounded by a previous empty time, and that no change can be the first change, but not that an occupied space can have no empty space beside it. So far no *a priori* decision on the latter point would be possible; yet the difficulty of conceiving the world in space as limited lies in the fact that space itself is necessarily infinite, and therefore a limited finite world in space, however large it may be, becomes an infinitely small magnitude; and in this incongruity the imagination finds an insuperable stumbling-block, because there remains for it only the choice of thinking the world either as infinitely large or infinitely small. This was already seen by the ancient philosophers: Μητροδωρος, ὁ καθηγητης Επικουρου, φησιν ατοπον ειναι εν μεγαλῳ πεδιῳ ἑνα σταχυν γεννηθηναι, και ἑνα κοσμον εν τῳ απειρῳ (*Metrodorus, caput scholæ Epicuri, absurdum ait, in magno campo spicam unam produci, et unum in infinito mundum*) Stob. Ecl., i. c. 23. Therefore many of them taught (as immediately follows), απειρους κοσμους εν τῳ απειρῳ (*infinitos mundos in infinito*). This is also the sense of the Kantian argument for the

nights have also 1000. His year has 365 days and as many nights. He lives 100 of his years, always creating; and if he dies, at once a new Brahma is born, and so on from eternity to eternity. The same relativity of time is also expressed in the special myth which is quoted in Polier's work, vol. ii. p. 594, from the Puranas. In it a Rajah, after a visit of a few seconds to Vishnu in his heaven, finds on his return to earth that several millions of years have elapsed, and a new age has begun; for every day of Vishnu is 100 recurrences of the four ages.

antithesis, only he has disfigured it by a scholastic and ambiguous expression. The same argument might be used against the limitation of the world in time, only we have a far better one under the guidance of causality. In the case of the assumption of a world limited in space, there arises further the unanswerable question, What advantage has the filled part of space enjoyed over the infinite space that has remained empty? In the fifth dialogue of his book, "*Del Infinito, Universo e Mondi,*" Giordano Bruno gives a full account of the arguments for and against the finiteness of the world, which is very well worth reading. For the rest, Kant himself asserts seriously, and upon objective grounds, the infinity of the world in space in his "Natural History of the Theory of the Heavens," part ii. ch. 7. Aristotle also acknowledges the same, "Phys.," iii. ch. 4, a chapter which, together with the following one, is very well worth reading with reference to this antinomy.

In the second conflict the thesis is at once guilty of a very palpable *petitio principii,* for it commences, "Every *compound* substance consists of simple parts." From the compoundness here arbitrarily assumed, no doubt it afterwards very easily proves the simple parts. But the proposition, "All matter is compound," which is just the point, remains unproved, because it is simply a groundless assumption. The opposite of simple is not compound, but extended, that which has parts and is divisible. Here, however, it is really tacitly assumed that the parts existed before the whole, and were brought together, whence the whole has arisen; for this is the meaning of the word "compound." Yet this can just as little be asserted as the opposite. Divisibility means merely the possibility of separating the whole into parts, and not that the whole is compounded out of parts and thus came into being. Divisibility merely asserts the parts *a parte post;* compoundness asserts them *a parte ante.* For there is essentially no temporal relation between the parts and the whole; they rather condition each other reciprocally, and thus always exist at the same time, for only so far as both are there is there anything extended in space. Therefore what Kant says in the observations on the thesis, "Space ought not to be called a *compositum*, but a *totum*," &c., holds good absolutely of matter also, which is simply space become perceptible. On the other hand, the infinite divisibility of matter, which the antithesis asserts, follows *a priori* and incontrovertibly from that of space, which it fills. This proposition has absolutely nothing against it; and therefore Kant also (p. 513; V. 541), when he speaks seriously and in his own person, no longer as the mouth-piece of the αδικος λογος, presents it as objective truth; and also in the "Metaphysical First Principles of Natural Science" (p. 108, first edition), the proposition, "Matter is infinitely divisible," is placed at the beginning of the proof of the first proposition of mechanics as established truth, having appeared and been proved as the fourth proposition in the Dynamics. But here Kant spoils the proof of the antithesis by the greatest obscurity of style and useless accumulation of words, with the cunning intention that the evidence of the antithesis shall not throw the sophisms of the thesis too much into the shade. Atoms are no necessary thought of the reason, but merely an hypothesis for the explanation of the difference of the specific gravity of bodies. But Kant himself has shown, in the dynamics of his "Metaphysical First Principles of Natural Science," that this can be otherwise, and indeed better and more simply explained than by atomism. In this, however, he was anticipated by Priestley, "On Matter and Spirit," sect. 1. Indeed, even in Aristotle, "Phys." iv. 9, the fundamental thought of this is to be found.

The argument for the third thesis is a very fine sophism, and is really Kant's pretended principle of pure reason itself entirely unadulterated and unchanged. It tries to prove the finiteness of the series of causes by saying that, in order to be *sufficient*, a cause must contain the complete sum of the conditions from which the succeeding state, the effect, proceeds. For the completeness of the determinations present *together* in the state which is the cause, the argument now substitutes the completeness of the series of causes by which that state itself was brought to actuality; and because completeness presupposes the condition of being rounded off or closed in, and this again presupposes finiteness, the argument infers from this a first cause, closing the series and therefore unconditioned. But the juggling is obvious. In order to conceive the state A. as the sufficient cause of the state B., I assume that it contains the sum of the necessary determinations from the co-existence of which the estate B. inevitably follows. Now by this my demand upon it as a *sufficient* cause is entirely satisfied, and has no direct connection with the question how the state A. itself came to be; this rather belongs to an entirely different consideration, in which I regard the said state A. no more as cause, but as itself an effect; in which case another state again must be related to it, just as it was related to B. The assumption of the finiteness of the series of causes and effects, and accordingly of a first beginning, appears nowhere in this as necessary, any more than the presentness of the present moment requires us to assume a beginning of time itself. It only comes to be added on account of the laziness of the speculating individual. That this assumption lies in the acceptance of a cause as a *sufficient reason* is thus unfairly arrived at and false, as I have shown at length above when considering the Kantian principle of pure reason which coincides with this thesis. In illustration of the assertion of this false thesis, Kant is bold enough in his observations upon it to give as an example of an unconditioned beginning his rising from his chair; as if it were not just as impossible for him to rise without a motive as for a ball to roll without a cause. I certainly do not need to prove the baselessness of the appeal which, induced by a sense of weakness, he makes to the philosophers of antiquity, by quoting from Ocellus Lucanus, the Eleatics, &c., not to speak of the Hindus. Against the proof of this anti-thesis, as in the case of the previous ones, there is nothing to advance.

The fourth conflict is, as I have already remarked, really tautological with the third; and the proof of the thesis is also essentially the same as that of the preceding one. His assertion that every conditioned presupposes a complete series of conditions, and therefore a series which ends with an unconditioned, is a *petitio principii*, which must simply be denied. Everything conditioned presupposes nothing but its condition; that this is again conditioned raises a new consideration which is not directly contained in the first.

A certain appearance of probability cannot be denied to the antinomy; yet it is remarkable that no part of the Kantian philosophy has met so little contradiction, indeed has found so much acceptance, as this exceed-ingly paradoxical doctrine. Almost all philosophical parties and text-books have regarded it as valid, and have also repeatedly reconstructed it; while nearly all Kant's other doctrines have been contested, and indeed there have never been wanting some perverse minds which rejected even the transcendental æsthetic. The undivided assent which the antinomy, on the other hand, has met with may ultimately arise from the fact that certain persons regard with inward satisfaction the point at which the understanding is so thoroughly brought to a standstill, having hit upon something which at once is and is not, so that they actually have before them here the sixth trick of Philadelphia in Lichtenberg's broadsheet.

If we examine the real meaning of Kant's *Critical Solu-tion* of the cosmological problem which now follows, we find that it is not what he gives it out to be, the solution of the problem by the disclosure that both sides, starting from false assumptions, are wrong in the first and second conflicts, and that in the third and fourth both are right. It is really the confirmation of the antitheses by the explanation of their assertions.

First Kant asserts, in this solution, obviously wrongly, that both sides started from the assumption, as their first principle, that with the conditioned the completed (thus rounded off) *series* of its conditions is given. Only the thesis laid down this proposition, Kant's principle of pure reason, as the ground of its assertions; the antithesis, on the other hand, expressly denied it throughout, and asserted the contrary. Further, Kant charges both sides with this assumption, that the world exists in itself, *i.e.*, independently of being known and of the forms of this knowledge, but this assumption also is only made by the thesis; indeed, it is so far from forming the ground of the assertions of the antithesis that it is absolutely inconsistent with them. For that it should all be given is absolutely contradictory of the conception of an infinite series. It is therefore essential to it that it should always exist only with reference to the process of going through it, and not independently of this. On the other hand, in the assumption of definite limits also lies that of a whole which exists absolutely and independently of the process of completely measuring it. Thus it is only the thesis that makes the false assumption of a self-existent universe, *i.e.*, a universe given prior to all knowledge, and to which knowledge came as to something external to itself. The antithesis from the outset combats this assumption absolutely; for the infinity of the series which it asserts merely under the guidance of the principle of sufficient reason can only exist if the regressus is fully carried out, but not independently of it. As the object in general presupposes the subject, so also the object which is determined as an *endless* chain of conditions necessarily presupposes in the subject the kind of knowledge corresponding to this, that is, the *constant following* of the links of that chain. But this is just what Kant gives as the solution of the problem, and so often repeats: "The infinity of the world is only *through* the regressus, not *before* it." This his solution of the conflict is thus really only the decision in favour of the antithesis in the assertion of which this truth already lies, while it is altogether inconsistent with the assertions of the thesis. If the antithesis had asserted that the world consisted of infinite series of reasons and consequents, and yet existed independently of the idea and its regressive series, thus in itself, and therefore constituted a given whole, it would have contradicted not only the thesis but also itself. For an infinite can never be given as a whole, nor an *endless* series exist, except as an endless progress; nor can what is boundless constitute a whole. Thus this assumption, of which Kant asserts that it led both sides into error, belongs only to the thesis.

It is already a doctrine of Aristotle's that an infinity can never be *actu*, *i.e.*, actual and given, but only *potentiâ*. Ουκ εστιν ενεργεια ειναι το απειρον . . . αλλ' αδυνατον το εντελεχεια ον απειρον (*infinitum non potest esse actu:* . . . *sed impossibile, actu esse infinitum*), Metaph. K. 10. Further: κατ' ενεργειαν μεν γαρ ουδεν εστιν απειρον, δυναμει δε επι την διαιρεσιν (*nihil enim actu infinitum est, sed potentia tantum, nempe divisione ipsa*). *De generat. et corrupt.*, i., 3. He develops this fully in the "Physics," iii. 5 and 6, where to a certain extent he gives the perfectly correct solution of the whole of the antinomies. He expounds the antinomies in his short way, and then says, "A mediator (διαιτητου) is required;" upon which he gives the solution that the infinite, both of the world in space and in time and in division, is never *before* the regressus, or progressus, but in it. This truth lies then in the rightly apprehended conception of the infinite. Thus one misunderstands himself if he imagines that he can think the infinite, of whatever kind it may be, as something objectively present and complete, and independent of the regressus.

Indeed if, reversing the procedure, we take as the

starting-point what Kant gives as the solution of the conflict, the assertion of the antithesis follows exactly from it. Thus: if the world is not an unconditioned whole and does not exist absolutely but only in the idea, and if its series of reasons and consequents do not exist *before* the regressus of the ideas of them but only *through* this regressus, then the world cannot contain determined and finite series, because their determination and limitation would necessarily be independent of the idea, which would then only come afterwards; but all its series must be infinite, *i.e.*, inexhaustible by any idea.

On p. 506; V. 534, Kant tries to prove from the falseness of both sides the transcendental ideality of the phenomenon, and begins, " If the world is a whole existing by itself, it is either finite or infinite." But this is false; a whole existing of itself cannot possibly be infinite. That ideality may rather be concluded from the infinity of the series in the world in the following manner: — If the series of reasons and consequents in the world are absolutely without end, the world cannot be a given whole independent of the idea; for such a world always presupposes definite limits, just as on the contrary infinite series presuppose an infinite regressus. Therefore, the presupposed infinity of the series must be determined through the form of reason and consequent, and this again through the form of knowledge of the subject; thus the world as it is known must exist only in the idea of the subject.

Now whether Kant himself was aware or not that his critical solution of the problem is really a decision in favour of the antithesis, I am unable to decide. For it depends upon whether what Schelling has somewhere very happily called Kant's system of accommodation extended so far; or whether Kant's mind was here already involved in an unconscious accommodation to the influence of his time and surroundings.

The solution of the third antinomy, the subject of which was the Idea of freedom, deserves a special consideration, because it is for us very well worth notice that it is just here in connection with *the Idea of freedom* that Kant is obliged to speak more fully of the *thing in itself*, which was hitherto only seen in the background. This is very explicable to us since we have recognised the thing in itself as the *will*. Speaking generally, this is the point at which the Kantian philosophy leads to mine, or at which mine springs out of his as its parent stem. One will be convinced of this if one reads with attention pp. 536 and 537; V. 564 and 565, of the "Critique of Pure Reason," and, further, compares these passages with the introduction to the "Critique of Judgment," pp. xviii. and xix. of the third edition, or p. 13 of Rosenkranz's edition, where indeed it is said: "The conception of freedom can in its object (that is then the will) present to the mind a thing in itself, but not in perception; the conception of nature, on the other hand, can present its object to the mind in perception, but not as a thing in itself." But specially let any one read concerning the solution of the antinomies the fifty-third paragraph of the Prolegomena, and then honestly answer the question whether all that is said there does not sound like a riddle to which my doctrine is the answer. Kant never completed his thought; I have merely carried out his work. Accordingly, what Kant says only of the human phenomenon I have extended to all phenomena in general, as differing from the human phenomenon only in degree, that their true being is something absolutely free, *i.e.*, a will. It appears from my work how fruitful this insight is in connection with Kant's doctrine of the ideality of space, time, and causality.

Kant has nowhere made the thing in itself the subject of a special exposition or distinct deduction; but, whenever he wants it, he introduces it at once by means of the conclusion that the phenomenon, thus the visible world, must have a reason, an intelligible cause, which is not a phenomenon, and therefore belongs to no possible experience. He does this after having assiduously insisted that the categories, and thus causality also, had a use which was absolutely confined to possible experience; that they were merely forms of the understanding, which served to spell out the phenomena of the world of sense, beyond which, on the other hand, they had no significance, &c., &c. Therefore, he denies in the most uncompromising manner their application to things beyond experience, and rightly explains and at once rejects all earlier dogmatism as based upon the neglect of this law. The incredible inconsistency which Kant here fell into was soon noticed, and used by his first opponents to make attacks on his philosophy to which it could offer no resistance. For certainly we apply the law of causality entirely *a priori* and before all experience to the changes felt in our organs of sense. But, on this very account, this law is just as much of subjective origin as these sensations themselves, and thus does not lead to a thing in itself. The truth is, that upon the path of the idea one can never get beyond the idea; it is a rounded-off whole, and has in its own resources no clue leading to the nature of the thing in itself, which is *toto genere* different from it. If we were merely perceiving beings, the way to the thing in itself would be absolutely cut off from us. Only the other side of our own being can disclose to us the other side of the inner being of things. This path I have followed. But Kant's inference to the thing in itself, contrary as it is to his own teaching, obtains some excuse from the following circumstance. He does not say, as truth required, simply and absolutely that the object is conditioned by the subject, and conversely ; but only that the manner of the appearance of the object is conditioned by the forms of knowledge of the subject, which, therefore, also come *a priori* to consciousness. But that now which in opposition to this is only known *a posteriori* is for him the immediate effect of the thing in itself, which becomes phenomenon only in its passage through these forms which are given *a priori*. From this point of view it is to some extent explicable how it could escape him that objectivity in general belongs to the form of the phenomenon, and is just as much conditioned by subjectivity in general as the mode of appearing of the object is conditioned by the forms of knowledge of the subject; that thus if a thing in itself must be assumed, it absolutely cannot be an object, which however he always assumes it to be, but such a thing in itself must necessarily lie in a sphere *toto genere* different from the idea (from knowing and being known), and therefore could least of all be arrived at through the laws of the combination of objects among themselves.

With the proof of the thing in itself it has happened to Kant precisely as with that of the *a priori* nature of the law of causality. Both doctrines are true, but their proof is false. They thus belong to the class of true conclusions from false premises. I have retained them both, but have proved them in an entirely different way, and with certainty.

The thing in itself I have neither introduced surreptitiously nor inferred according to laws which exclude it, because they really belong to its phenomenal appearance; nor, in general, have I arrived at it by roundabout ways. On the contrary, I have shown it directly, there where it lies immediately, in the will, which reveals itself to every one directly as the in-itself of his own phenomenal being.

And it is also this immediate knowledge of his own will out of which in human consciousness the conception of *freedom* springs; for certainly the will, as world-creating, as thing in itself, is free from the principle of sufficient reason, and therewith from all necessity, thus is completely independent, free, and indeed almighty. Yet, in truth, this only holds good of the will in itself, not of its manifestations, the individuals, who, just through the will itself, are unalterably determined as its manifestations in time. But in the ordinary consciousness, unenlightened by philosophy, the will is at once confused with its manifestation, and what belongs only to the former is attributed to the latter, whence arises the illusion of the unconditioned freedom of the individual. Therefore Spinoza says rightly that if the projected stone had consciousness, it would believe that it flew of its own free will. For certainly the in-itself of the stone also is the will, which alone is free ; but, as in all its manifestations, here also, where it appears as a stone, it is already fully determined. But of all this enough has already been said in the text of this work.

Kant fails to understand and overlooks this immediate origin of the conception of freedom in every human consciousness, and therefore he now places (p. 533 ; V. 561) the source of that conception in a very subtle speculation, through which the unconditioned, to which the reason must always tend, leads us to hypostatise the conception of freedom, and it is only upon this transcendent Idea of freedom that the practical conception of it is supposed to be founded. In the " Critique of Practical Reason," § 6, and p. 158 of the fourth and 235 of Rosenkranz's edition, he yet deduces this last conception differently by saying that the categorical imperative presupposes it. The speculative Idea is accordingly only the primary source of the conception of freedom for the sake of this presupposition, but here it obtains both significance and application. Neither, however, is the case. For the delusion of a perfect freedom of the individual in his particular actions is most lively in the conviction of the least cultivated man who has never reflected, and it is thus founded on no speculation, although often assumed by speculation from without. Thus only philosophers, and indeed only the most profound of them, are free from it, and also the most thoughtful and enlightened of the writers of the Church.

It follows, then, from all that has been said, that the

true source of the conception of freedom is in no way essentially an inference, either from the speculative Idea of an unconditioned cause, nor from the fact that it is presupposed by the categorical imperative. But it springs directly from the consciousness in which each one recognises himself at once as the *will*, *i.e.*, as that which, as the thing in itself, has not the principle of sufficient reason for its form, and which itself depends upon nothing, but on which everything else rather depends. Every one, however, does not recognise himself at once with the critical and reflective insight of philosophy as a determined manifestation of this will which has already entered time, as we might say, an act of will distinguished from that will to live itself; and, therefore, instead of recognising his whole existence as an act of his freedom, he rather seeks for freedom in his individual actions. Upon this point I refer the reader to my prize-essay on the freedom of the will.

Now if Kant, as he here pretends, and also apparently did in earlier cases, had merely inferred the thing in itself, and that with the great inconsistency of an inference absolutely forbidden by himself, what a remarkable accident would it then be that here, where for the first time he approaches the thing in itself more closely and explains it, he should recognise in it at once the *will*, the free will showing itself in the world only in temporal manifestations! I therefore really assume, though it cannot be proved, that whenever Kant spoke of the thing in itself, in the obscure depths of his mind he already always indistinctly thought of the will. This receives support from a passage in the preface to the second edition of the " Critique of Pure Reason," pp. xxvii. and xxviii., in Rosenkranz's edition, p. 677 of the Supplement.

For the rest, it is just this predetermined solution of the sham third conflict that affords Kant the opportunity of expressing very beautifully the deepest thoughts of his whole philosophy. This is the case in the whole of the

"Sixth Section of the Antinomy of Pure Reason;" but, above all, in the exposition of the opposition between the empirical and the intelligible character, p. 534–550; V. 562–578, which I number among the most admirable things that have ever been said by man. (As a supplemental explanation of this passage, compare a parallel passage in the Critique of Practical Reason, p. 169–179 of the fourth edition, or p. 224–231 of Rosenkranz's edition.) It is yet all the more to be regretted that this is here not in its right place, partly because it is not found in the way which the exposition states, and therefore could be otherwise deduced than it is, partly because it does not fulfil the end for which it is there—the solution of the sham antinomy. The intelligible character, the thing in itself, is inferred from the phenomenon by the inconsistent use of the category of causality beyond the sphere of all phenomena, which has already been sufficiently condemned. In this case the will of man (which Kant entitles reason, most improperly, and with an unpardonable breach of all use of language) is set up as the thing in itself, with an appeal to an unconditioned ought, the categorical imperative, which is postulated without more ado.

Now, instead of all this, the plain open procedure would have been to start directly from the will, and prove it to be the in-itself of our own phenomenal being, recognised without any mediation ; and then to give that exposition of the empirical and the intelligible character to explain how all actions, although necessitated by motives, yet, both by their author and by the disinterested judge, are necessarily and absolutely ascribed to the former himself and alone, as depending solely upon him, to whom therefore guilt and merit are attributed in respect of them. This alone was the straight path to the knowledge of that which is not phenomenon, and therefore will not be found by the help of the laws of the phenomenon, but is that which reveals itself through the phenomenon, becomes knowable, objectifies itself—the will to live. It would then have had to be exhibited merely by analogy as the inner nature of every phenomenon. Then, however, it certainly could not have been said that in lifeless or even animal nature no faculty can be thought except as sensuously conditioned (p. 546; V. 574), which in Kant's language is simply saying that the explanation, according to the law of causality, exhausts the inner nature of these phenomena, and thus in their case, very inconsistently, the thing in itself disappears. Through the false position and the roundabout deduction according with it which the exposition of the thing in itself has received from Kant, the whole conception of it has also become falsified. For the will or the thing in itself, found through the investigation of an unconditioned cause, appears here related to the phenomenon as cause to effect. But this relation exists only within the phenomenal world, therefore presupposes it, and cannot connect the phenomenal world itself with what lies outside it, and is *toto genere* different from it.

Further, the intended end, the solution of the third antinomy by the decision that both sides, each in a different sense, are right, is not reached at all. For neither the thesis nor the antithesis have anything to do with the thing in itself, but entirely with the phenomenon, the objective world, the world as idea. This it is, and absolutely nothing else, of which the thesis tries to show, by means of the sophistry we have laid bare, that it contains unconditioned causes, and it is also this of which the antithesis rightly denies that it contains such causes. Therefore the whole exposition of the transcendental freedom of the will, so far as it is a thing in itself, which is given here in justification of the thesis, excellent as it is in itself, is yet here entirely a μεταβασις εισ αλλο γενος. For the transcendental freedom of the will which is expounded is by no means the unconditioned causality of a cause, which the thesis asserts, because it is of the essence of a cause that it must be a phenomenon, and not something which lies beyond all phenomena and is *toto genere* different.

If what is spoken of is cause and effect, the relation of the will to the manifestation (or of the intelligible character to the empirical) must never be introduced, as happens here: for it is entirely different from causal relation. However, here also, in this solution of the antinomy, it is said with truth that the empirical character of man, like that of every other cause in nature, is unalterably determined, and therefore that his actions necessarily take place in accordance with the external influences; therefore also, in spite of all transcendental freedom (*i.e.*, independence of the will in itself of the laws of the connection of its manifestation), no man has the power of himself to begin a series of actions, which, however, was asserted by the thesis. Thus also freedom has no causality; for only the will is free, and it lies outside nature or the phenomenon, which is just its objectification, but does not stand in a causal relation to it, for this relation is only found within the sphere of the phenomenon, thus presupposes it, and cannot embrace the phenomenon itself and connect it with what is expressly not a phenomenon. The world itself can only be explained through the will (for it is the will itself, so far as it manifests itself), and not through causality. But *in the world* causality is the sole principle of explanation, and everything happens simply according to the laws of nature. Thus the right lies entirely on the side of the antithesis, which sticks to the question in hand, and uses that principle of explanation which is valid with regard to it; therefore it needs no apology. The thesis, on the other hand, is supposed to be got out of the matter by an apology, which first passes over to something quite different from the question at issue, and then assumes a principle of explanation which is inapplicable to it.

The fourth conflict is, as has already been said, in its real meaning tautological with the third. In its solution

Kant develops still more the untenable nature of the thesis; while for its truth, on the other hand, and its pretended consistency with the antithesis, he advances no reason, as conversely he is able to bring no reason against the antithesis. The assumption of the thesis he introduces quite apologetically, and yet calls it himself (p. 562; V. 590) an arbitrary presupposition, the object of which might well in itself be impossible, and shows merely an utterly impotent endeavour to find a corner for it somewhere where it will be safe from the prevailing might of the antithesis, only to avoid disclosing the emptiness of the whole of his once-loved assertion of the necessary antinomy in human reason.

Now follows the chapter on the transcendental ideal, which carries us back at once to the rigid Scholasticism of the Middle Ages. One imagines one is listening to Anselm of Canterbury himself. The *ens realissimum*, the essence of all realities, the content of all affirmative propositions, appears, and indeed claims to be a necessary thought of the reason. I for my part must confess that to my reason such a thought is impossible, and that I am not able to think anything definite in connection with the words which denote it.

Moreover, I do not doubt that Kant was compelled to write this extraordinary chapter, so unworthy of him, simply by his fondness for architectonic symmetry. The three principal objects of the Scholastic philosophy (which, as we have said, if understood in the wider sense, may be regarded as continuing down to Kant), the soul, the world, and God, are supposed to be deduced from the three possible major propositions of syllogisms, though it is plain that they have arisen, and can arise, simply and solely through the unconditioned application of the principle of sufficient reason. Now, after the soul had been forced into the categorical judgment, and the hypothetical was set apart for the world, there remained for the third Idea nothing but the disjunctive major. Fortunately there existed a previous work in this direction, the *ens realissimum* of the Scholastics, together with the onto-logical proof of the existence of God set up in a rudi-mentary form by Anselm of Canterbury and then per-fected by Descartes. This was joyfully made use of by Kant, with some reminiscence also of an earlier Latin work of his youth. However, the sacrifice which Kant makes to his love of architectonic symmetry in this chapter is exceedingly great. In defiance of all truth, what one must regard as the grotesque idea of an essence of all possible realities is made an essential and necessary thought of the reason. For the deduction of this Kant makes use of the false assertion that our knowledge of particular things arises from a progressive limitation of general conceptions ; thus also of a most general concep-tion of all which contains all reality *in itself*. In this he stands just as much in contradiction with his own teach-ing as with the truth, for exactly the converse is the case. Our knowledge starts with the particular and is extended to the general, and all general conceptions arise by abstrac-tion from real, particular things known by perception, and this can be carried on to the most general of all concep-tions, which includes everything under it, but almost nothing *in it*. Thus Kant has here placed the procedure of our faculty of knowledge just upside down, and thus might well be accused of having given occasion to a philo-sophical charletanism that has become famous in our day, which, instead of recognising that conceptions are thoughts abstracted from things, makes, on the contrary the conceptions first, and sees in things only concrete conceptions, thus bringing to market the world turned upside down as a philosophical buffoonery, which of course necessarily found great acceptance.

Even if we assume that every reason must, or at least can, attain to the conception of God, even without revelation, this clearly takes place only under the guidance of causality. This is so evident that it requires no proof. Therefore Chr. Wolf says (*Cosmologia Generalis, præf.,* p. 1): *Sane in theologia naturali existentiam Numinis e principiis cosmologicis demonstramus. Contingentia universi et ordinis naturæ, una cum impossibilitate casus, sunt scala, per quam a mundo hoc adspectabili ad Deum ascenditur.* And, before him, Leibnitz said, in connection with the law of causality: *Sans ce grand principe on ne saurait venir à la preuve de l'existence de Dieu.* On the other hand, the thought which is worked out in this chapter is so far from being essential and necessary to reason, that it is rather to be regarded as a veritable masterpiece of the monstrous productions of an age which, through strange circumstances, fell into the most singular aberrations and perversities, such as the age of the Scholastics was—an age which is unparalleled in the history of the world, and can never return again. This Scholasticism, as it advanced to its final form, certainly derived the principal proof of the existence of God from the conception of the *ens realissimum,* and only then used the other proofs as accessory. This, however, is mere methodology, and proves nothing as to the origin of theology in the human mind. Kant has here taken the procedure of Scholasticism for that of reason—a mistake which indeed he has made more than once. If it were true that according to the essential laws of reason the Idea of God proceeds from the disjunctive syllogism under the form of an Idea of the most real being, this Idea would also have existed in the philosophy of antiquity; but of the *ens realissimum* there is nowhere a trace in any of the ancient philosophers, although some of them certainly teach that there is a Creator of the world, yet only as the giver of form to the matter which exists without him, δεμιουργος, a being whom they yet infer simply and solely in accordance with the law of causality. It is true that Sextus Empiricus (*adv. Math.,* ix. § 88) quotes an argu-

ment of Cleanthes, which some have held to be the
ontological proof. This, however, it is not, but merely an
inference from analogy; because experience teaches that
upon earth one being is always better than another, and
man, indeed, as the best, closes the series, but yet has
many faults; therefore there must exist beings who are still
better, and finally one being who is best of all (κρατιστον,
αριστον), and this would be God.

On the detailed refutation of speculative theology which
now follows I have only briefly to remark that it, and in
general the whole criticism of the three so-called Ideas of
reason, thus the whole Dialectic of Pure Reason, is indeed
to a certain extent the goal and end of the whole work;
yet this polemical part has not really an absolutely universal, permanent, and purely philosophical interest, such
as is possessed by the preceding doctrinal part, *i.e.*, the
æsthetic and analytic; but rather a temporary and local
interest, because it stands in a special relation to the
leading points of the philosophy which prevailed in Europe
up till the time of Kant, the complete overthrow of which
was yet, to his immortal credit, achieved by him through
this polemic. He has eliminated theism from philosophy;
for in it, as a science and not a system of faith, only that
can find a place which is either empirically given or established by valid proofs. Naturally we only mean here the
real seriously understood philosophy which is concerned
with the truth, and nothing else; and by no means the
jest of philosophy taught in the universities, in which, after
Kant as before him, speculative theology plays the principal
part, and where, also, after as before him, the soul appears
without ceremony as a familiar person. For it is the philosophy endowed with salaries and fees, and, indeed, also
with titles of Hofrath, which, looking proudly down from
its height, remains for forty years entirely unaware of the
existence of little people like me, and would be thoroughly

glad to be rid of the old Kant with his Critiques, that they might drink the health of Leibnitz with all their hearts. It is further to be remarked here, that as Kant was confessedly led to his doctrine of the *a priori* nature of the conception of causality by Hume's scepticism with regard to that conception, it may be that in the same way Kant's criticism of all speculative theology had its occasion in Hume's criticism of all popular theology, which he had given in his "Natural History of Religion," a book so well worth reading, and in the "Dialogues on Natural Religion." Indeed, it may be that Kant wished to a certain extent to supplement this. For the first-named work of Hume is really a critique of popular theology, the pitiable condition of which it seeks to show; while, on the other hand, it points to rational or speculative theology as the genuine, and that which is worthy of respect. But Kant now discloses the groundlessness of the latter, and leaves, on the other hand, popular theology untouched, nay, even establishes it in a nobler form as a faith based upon moral feeling. This was afterwards distorted by the philosophasters into rational apprehensions, consciousness of God, or intellectual intuitions of the supersensible, of the divine, &c., &c.; while Kant, as he demolished old and revered errors, and knew the danger of doing so, rather wished through the moral theology merely to substitute a few weak temporary supports, so that the ruin might not fall on him, but that he might have time to escape.

Now, as regards the performance of the task, no critique of reason was necessary for the refutation of the *ontological* proof of the existence of God; for without presupposing the æsthetic and analytic, it is quite easy to make clear that that ontological proof is nothing but a subtle playing with conceptions which is quite powerless to produce conviction. There is a chapter in the "*Organon*" of Aristotle which suffices as fully for the refutation of the ontological proof as if it had been written intentionally with that purpose. It is the seventh chapter of the second book of the "*Analyt. Post.*"   Among other things, it is expressly said there: "το δε ειναι ουκ ουσια ουδενι," i.e., *existentia nunquam ad essentiam rei pertinet.*

The refutation of the *cosmological* proof is an application to a given case of the doctrine of the Critique as expounded up to that point, and there is nothing to be said against it.   The *physico-theological* proof is a mere amplification of the cosmological, which it presupposes, and it finds its full refutation only in the " Critique of Judgment."   I refer the reader in this connection to the rubric, " Comparative Anatomy," in my work on the Will in Nature.

In the criticism of this proof Kant has only to do, as we have already said, with speculative theology, and limits himself to the School.   If, on the contrary, he had had life and popular theology also in view, he would have been obliged to add a fourth proof to the three he has considered—that proof which is really the effective one with the great mass of men, and which in Kant's technical language might best be called the *keraunological.*   It is the proof which is founded upon the needy, impotent, and dependent condition of man as opposed to natural forces, which are infinitely superior, inscrutable, and for the most part threatening evil; to which is added man's natural inclination to personify everything, and finally the hope of effecting something by prayers and flattery, and even by gifts.   In every human undertaking there is something which is not in our power and does not come within our calculations; the wish to win this for oneself is the origin of the gods.   "*Primus in orbe Deos fecit timor*" is an old and true saying of Petronius.   It is principally this proof which is criticised by Hume, who throughout appears as Kant's forerunner in the writings referred to above.   But those whom Kant has placed in a position of permanent embarrassment by his criticism of speculative theology are the professors of philosophy.   Salaried by Christian governments, they dare not give up the chief article of faith.[1] Now, how do these gentlemen help themselves ? They simply declare that the existence of God is self-evident. Indeed! After the ancient world, at the expense of its conscience, had worked miracles to prove it, and the modern world, at the expense of its understanding, had brought into the field ontological, cosmological, and physico-theological proofs—to these gentlemen it is self-evident. And from this self-evident God they then explain the world : that is their philosophy.

Till Kant came there was a real dilemma between materialism and theism, *i.e.*, between the assumption that a blind chance, or that an intelligence working from without in accordance with purposes and conceptions, had brought about the world, *neque dabatur tertium.* Therefore atheism and materialism were the same; hence the doubt whether there really could be an atheist, *i.e.*, a man who really could attribute to blind chance the disposition of nature, so full of design, especially organised nature. See, for example, Bacon's Essays (*sermones fideles*), Essay 16, on Atheism. In the opinion of the great mass of men, and of the English, who in such things belong entirely to the great mass (the mob), this is still the case, even with their most celebrated men of learning. One has only to look at Owen's " *Ostéologie Comparée*," of 1855, preface, p. 11, 12, where he stands always before the old dilemma between Democritus and Epicurus on the one side, and an intelligence on the other, in which *la con-*

---

[1] Kant said, "It is very absurd to expect enlightenment from reason, and yet to prescribe to her beforehand which side she must necessarily take" ("Critique of Pure Reason," p. 747; V. 775). On the other hand, the following is the naive assertion of a professor of philosophy in our own time : "If a philosophy denies the reality of the fundamental ideas of Christianity, it is either false, or, *even if true, it is yet useless.*" That is to say, for professors of philosophy. It was the late Professor Bachmann who, in the Jena *Litteraturzeitung* for July 1840, No. 126, so indiscreetly blurted out the maxim of all his colleagues. However, it is worth noticing, as regards the characteristics of the University philosophy, how here the truth, if it will not suit and adapt itself, is shown the door without ceremony, with, "Be off, truth! we cannot make *use* of you. Do we owe you anything? Do you pay us? Then be off!"

naissance d'un être tel que l'homme a existé avant que l'homme fît son apparition. All design must have proceeded from an *intelligence;* he has never even dreamt of doubting this. Yet in the lecture based upon this now modified preface, delivered in the *Académie des Sciences* on the 5th September 1853, he says, with childish naivete: "*La téléologie, ou la théologie scientifique*" (*Comptes Rendus,* Sept. 1853), that is for him precisely the same thing! Is anything in nature designed? then it is a work of intention, of reflection, of intelligence. Yet, certainly, what has such an Englishman and the *Académie des Sciences* to do with the " Critique of Judgment," or, indeed, with my book upon the Will in Nature ? These gentlemen do not see so far below them. These *illustres confrères* disdain metaphysics and the *philosophie allemande:* they confine themselves to the old woman's philosophy. The validity of that disjunctive major, that dilemma between materialism and theism, rests, however, upon the assumption that the present given world is the world of things in themselves; that consequently there is no other order of things than the empirical. But after the world and its order had through Kant become mere phenomenon, the laws of which rest principally upon the forms of our intellect, the existence and nature of things and of the world no longer required to be explained according to the analogy of the changes perceived or effected by us in the world ; nor must that which we comprehend as means and end have necessarily arisen as the consequence of a similar knowledge Thus, inasmuch as Kant, through his important distinction between phenomenon and thing in itself, withdrew the foundation from theism, he opened, on the other hand, the way to entirely different and more profound explanations of existence.

In the chapter on the ultimate aim of the natural dialectic of reason it is asserted that the three transcendent Ideas are of value as regulative principles for the advancement of the knowledge of nature. But Kant can barely have been serious in making this assertion. At least its opposite, that these assumptions are restrictive and fatal to all investigation of nature, is to every natural philosopher beyond doubt. To test this by an example, let any one consider whether the assumption of the soul as an immaterial, simple, thinking substance would have been necessarily advantageous or in the highest degree impeding to the truths which Cabanis has so beautifully expounded, or to the discoveries of Flourens, Marshall Hall, and Ch. Bell. Indeed Kant himself says (*Prolegomena*, § 44), "The Ideas of the reason are opposed and hindering to the maxims of the rational knowlege of nature."

It is certainly not the least merit of Frederick the Great, that under his Government Kant could develop himself, and dared to publish the "Critique of Pure Reason." Hardly under any other Government would a salaried professor have ventured such a thing. Kant was obliged to promise the immediate successor of the great king that he would write no more.

I might consider that I could dispense with the criticism of the ethical part of the Kantian philosophy here because I have given a detailed and thorough criticism of it twenty-two years later than the present work in the "*Beiden Grundproblemen der Ethik.*" However, what is here retained from the first edition, and for the sake of completeness must not be omitted, may serve as a suitable introduction to that later and much more thorough criticism, to which in the main I therefore refer the reader.

On account of Kant's love of architectonic symmetry, the theoretical reason had also to have a *pendant*. The *intellectus practicus* of the Scholastics, which again springs from the νους πρακτικος of Aristotle (*De Anima*, iii. 10, and *Polit.*, vii. c. 14 : ὁ μεν γαρ πρακτικος εστι λογος, ὁ δε θεωρητικος), provides the word ready made. Yet here something quite different is denoted by it—not as there, the reason directed to technical skill. Here the practical reason appears as the source and origin of the undeniable ethical significance of human action, and of all virtue, all nobleness, and every attainable degree of holiness. All this accordingly should come from mere *reason*, and demand nothing but this. To act rationally and to act virtuously, nobly, holily, would be one and the same; and to act selfishly, wickedly, viciously, would be merely to act irrationally. However, all times and peoples and languages have distinguished the two, and held them to be quite different things; and so does every one even at the present day who knows nothing of the language of the new school, *i.e.*, the whole world, with the exception of a small company of German *savants*. Every one but these last understands by virtuous conduct and a rational course of life two entirely different things. To say that the sublime founder of the Christian religion, whose life is presented to us as the pattern of all virtue, was *the most rational* of all men would be called a very unbecoming and even a blasphemous way of speaking; and almost as much so if it were said that His precepts contained all the best directions for a perfectly *rational life*. Further, that he who, in accordance with these precepts, instead of taking thought for his own future needs, always relieves the greater present wants of others, without further motive, nay, gives all his goods to the poor, in order then, destitute of all means of subsistence, to go and preach to others also the virtue which he practises himself; this every one rightly honours; but who ventures to extol it as the highest pitch of *reasonableness?* And finally, who praises it as a *rational* deed that Arnold von Winkelried, with surpassing courage, clasped the hostile spears against his own body in order to gain victory and deliverance for his countrymen? On the other hand, if we see a man who from his youth upwards deliberates with exceptional foresight how he may procure for himself an easy competence, the means for the support of wife and children, a good name among men, outward honour and distinction, and in doing so never allows himself to be led astray or induced to lose sight of his end by the charm of present pleasures or the satisfaction of defying the arrogance of the powerful, or the desire of revenging insults and undeserved humiliations he has suffered, or the attractions of useless aesthetic or philosophical occupations of the mind, or travels in interesting lands, but with great consistency works towards his one end,—who ventures to deny that such a philistine is in quite an extraordinary degree *rational*, even if he has made use of some means which are not praiseworthy but are yet without danger ? Nay, more, if a bad man, with deliberate shrewdness, through a well-thought-out plan attains to riches and honours, and even to thrones and crowns, and then with the acutest cunning gets the better of neighbouring states, overcomes them one by one, and now becomes a conqueror of the world, and in doing so is not led astray by any respect for right, any sense of humanity, but with sharp consistency tramples down and dashes to pieces everything that opposes his plan, without compassion plunges millions into misery of every kind, condemns millions to bleed and die, yet royally rewards and always protects his adherents and helpers, never forgetting anything, and thus reaches his end,—who does not see that such a man must go to work in a most rational manner ?—that, as a powerful understanding was needed to form the plans, their execution demanded the complete command of the *reason*, and indeed properly of *practical reason ?* Or are the precepts which the prudent and consistent, the thoughtful and far-seeing Machiavelli prescribes to the prince *irrational ?* [1]

---

[1] By the way, Machiavelli's problem was the solution of the question how the prince, *as a prince*, was to keep himself on the throne in spite of internal and external enemies. His problem was thus by no means the ethical problem whether a prince, as a man, ought to will such things, but purely the political one how, if he so wills, he can carry it out. And the solution of this problem he gives just as one writes directions for playing chess, with which it would be folly to mix up the answer to the question whether from an ethical point of view it is advisable to play chess

As wickedness is quite consistent with reason, and indeed only becomes really terrible in this conjunction, so, conversely, nobleness is sometimes joined with want of reason. To this may be attributed the action of Coriolanus, who, after he had applied all his strength for years to the accomplishment of his revenge upon the Romans, when at length the time came, allowed himself to be softened by the prayers of the Senate and the tears of his mother and wife, gave up the revenge he had so long and so painfully prepared, and indeed, by thus bringing on himself the just anger of the Volscians, died for those very Romans whose thanklessness he knew and desired so intensely to punish. Finally, for the sake of completeness, it may be mentioned that reason may very well exist along with want of understanding. This is the case when a foolish maxim is chosen, but is followed out consistently. An example of this is afforded by the case of the Princess Isabella, daughter of Philip II., who vowed that she would not put on a clean chemise so long as Ostend remained unconquered, and kept her word through three years. In general all vows are of this class, whose origin is a want of insight as regards the law of causality, *i.e.*, want of understanding; nevertheless it is rational to fulfil them if one is of such narrow understanding as to make them.

In agreement with what we have said, we see the writers who appeared just before Kant place the conscience, as the seat of the moral impulses, in opposition to the reason. Thus Rousseau, in the fourth book of "*Emile*," says: "*La raison nous trompe, mais la conscience ne trompe jamais;*" and further on: "*Il est impossible d'expliquer par les conséquences de notre nature le principe immédiat de la conscience indépendant de la raison même.*" Still further: "*Mes sentimens naturels parlaient pour l'intérêt commun, ma raison rapportait tout a moi. . . . On a beau vouloir etablir la vertu*

at all. To reproach Machiavelli with the immorality of his writing is just the same as to reproach a fencing-master because he does not begin his instructions with a moral lecture against murder and slaughter.

par la raison seul, quelle solide base peut-on lui donner ?" In
the " *Rêveries du Promeneur,*" prom. 4 ême, he says : " *Dans
toutes les questions de morale difficiles je me suis toujours bien
trouvé de les résoudre par le dictamen de la conscience, plutôt
que par les lumières de la raison.*" Indeed Aristotle already
says expressly (*Eth. Magna,* i. 5) that the virtues have
their seat in the αλογω μοριω της ψυχης (*in parte irra-
tionali animi*), and not in the λογον εχοντι (*in parte
rationali*). In accordance with this, Stobæus says (*Ecl.,*
ii., c. 7), speaking of the Peripatetics : " Την ηθικην αρετην
ὑπολαμβανουσι περι το αλογον μερος γιγνεσθαι της ψυχης,
επειδη διμερη προς την παρουσαν θεωριαν ὑπεθεντο την
ψυχην, το μεν λογικον εχουσαν, το δ' αλογον. Και περι
μεν το λογικον την καλοκαγαθιαν γιγνεσθαν, και την φρονη-
σιν, και την αγχινοιαν, και σοφιαν, και ευμαθειαν, και
μνημην, και τας ὁμοιους· περι δε το αλογον, σωφροσυνην,
και δικαιοσυνην, και ανδρειαν, και τας αλλας τας ηθικας
καλουμενας αρετας." (*Ethicam virtutem circa partem animæ
ratione carentem versari putant, cum duplicem, ad hanc
disquisitionem, animam ponant, ratione prœditam, et ea
carentem. In parte vero ratione prœdita collocant ingenui-
tatem, prudentiam, perspicacitatem, sapientiam, docilitatem,
memoriam et reliqua ; in parte vero ratione destituta tem-
perantiam, justitiam, fortitudinem, et reliquas virtutes, quas
ethicas vocant.*) And Cicero (*De Nat. Deor.,* iii., c. 26–31)
explains at length that reason is the necessary means, the
tool, of all crime.

I have explained *reason* to be the *faculty of framing
concepts.* It is this quite special class of general non-
perceptible ideas, which are symbolised and fixed only
by words, that distinguishes man from the brutes and
gives him the pre-eminence upon earth. While the brute
is the slave of the present, and knows only immediate
sensible motives, and therefore when they present themselves to it is necessarily attracted or repelled by them,
as iron is by the magnet, in man, on the contrary, deliberation has been introduced through the gift of reason.

This enables him easily to survey as a whole his life and
the course of the world, looking before and after; it makes
him independent of the present, enables him to go to
work deliberately, systematically, and with foresight, to
do evil as well as to do good. But what he does he does
with complete self-consciousness; he knows exactly how
his will decides, what in each case he chooses, and what
other choice was in the nature of the case possible; and
from this self-conscious willing he comes to know himself
and mirrors himself in his actions. In all these relations
to the conduct of men reason is to be called *practical;*
it is only theoretical so far as the objects with which
it is concerned have no relation to the action of the
thinker, but have purely a theoretical interest, which
very few men are capable of feeling. What in this sense
is called *practical reason* is very nearly what is signified by the Latin word *prudentia,* which, according to
Cicero (*De Nat. Deor.* ii., 22), is a contraction of *provi-
dentia;* while, on the other hand, *ratio,* if used of a faculty
of the mind, signifies for the most part theoretical reason
proper, though the ancients did not observe the distinction
strictly. In nearly all men reason has an almost exclusively
practical tendency; but if this also is abandoned thought
loses the control of action, so that it is then said, "*Scio
meliora, proboque, deteriora sequor,*" or "*Le matin je fais
des projets, et le soir je fais des sottises.*" Thus the man does
not allow his conduct to be guided by his thought, but by
the impression of the moment, after the manner of the
brute; and so he is called irrational (without thereby im-
puting to him moral turpitude), although he is not really
wanting in reason, but in the power of applying it to his
action; and one might to a certain extent say his reason is
theoretical and not practical. He may at the same time
be a really good man, like many a one who can never see
any one in misfortune without helping him, even making
sacrifices to do so, and yet leaves his debts unpaid. Such an
irrational character is quite incapable of committing great

crimes, because the systematic planning, the discrimination and self-control, which this always requires are quite impossible to him. Yet, on the other hand, he will hardly attain to a very high degree of virtue, for, however much inclined to good he may be by nature, those single vicious and wicked emotions to which every one is subject cannot be wanting; and where reason does not manifest itself practically, and oppose to them unalterable maxims and firm principles, they must become deeds.

Finally, *reason* manifests itself very specially as *practical* in those exceedingly rational characters who on this account are called in ordinary life practical philosophers, and who are distinguished by an unusual equanimity in disagreeable as in pleasing circumstances, an equable disposition, and a determined perseverance in resolves once made. In fact, it is the predominance of reason in them, *i.e.*, the more abstract than intuitive knowledge, and therefore the survey of life by means of conceptions, in general and as a whole, which has enabled them once for all to recognise the deception of the momentary impression, the fleeting nature of all things, the shortness of life, the emptiness of pleasures, the fickleness of fortune, and the great and little tricks of chance. Therefore nothing comes to them unexpectedly, and what they know in the abstract does not surprise nor disturb them when it meets them in the actual and in the particular case, though it does so in the case of those less reasonable characters upon whom the present, the perceptible, the actual, exerts such an influence that the cold, colourless conceptions are thrown quite into the background of consciousness, and forgetting principles and maxims, they are abandoned to emotions and passions of every kind. I have already explained at the end of the first book that in my opinion the ethics of Stoicism were simply a guide to a truly reasonable life, in this sense. Such a life is also repeatedly praised by Horace in very many passages. This is the significance of his *nil admirari*, and also of the

Delphic *Μηδεν αγαν*. To translate *nil admirari* "to admire nothing" is quite wrong. This Horatian maxim does not concern the theoretical so much as the practical, and its real meaning is : " Prize no object unconditionally. Do not fall in love with anything; do not believe that the possession of anything can give you happiness. Every intense longing for an object is only a delusive chimera, which one may just as well, and much more easily, get quit of by fuller knowledge as by attained possession." Cicero also uses *admirari* in this sense (*De Divinatione*, ii. 2). What Horace means is thus the *αθαμβια* and *ακαταπληξις*, also *αθανμασια*, which Democritus before him prized as the highest good (see *Clem. Alex. Strom.*, ii. 21, and cf. *Strabo*, i. p. 98 and 105). Such reasonableness of conduct has properly nothing to do with virtue and vice ; but this practical use of reason is what gives man his pre-eminence over the brute, and only in this sense has it any meaning and is it permissible to speak of a dignity of man.

In all the cases given, and indeed in all conceivable cases, the distinction between rational and irrational action runs back to the question whether the motives are abstract conceptions or ideas of perception. Therefore the explanation which I have given of reason agrees exactly with the use of language at all times and among all peoples—a circumstance which will not be regarded as merely accidental or arbitrary, but will be seen to arise from the distinction of which every man is conscious, of the different faculties of the mind, in accordance with which consciousness he speaks, though certainly he does not raise it to the distinctness of an abstract definition. Our ancestors did not make the words without attaching to them a definite meaning, in order, perhaps, that they might lie ready for philosophers who might possibly come centuries after and determine what ought to be thought in connection with them ; but they denoted by them quite definite conceptions. Thus the words are no longer unclaimed, and to attribute to them an entirely different sense from that which they have hitherto had means to misuse them, means to introduce a licence in accordance with which every one might use any word in any sense he chose, and thus endless confusion would necessarily arise. Locke has already shown at length that most disagreements in philosophy arise from a false use of words. For the sake of illustration just glance for a moment at the shameful misuse which philosophers destitute of thoughts make at the present day of the words substance, consciousness, truth, and many others. Moreover, the utterances and explanations concerning reason of all philosophers of all ages, with the exception of the most modern, agree no less with my explanation of it than the conceptions which prevail among all nations of that prerogative of man. Observe what Plato, in the fourth book of the Republic, and in innumerable scattered passages, calls the λογιμον, or λογιστικον της ψυχης, what Cicero says (*De Nat. Deor.*, iii. 26–31), what Leibnitz and Locke say upon this in the passages already quoted in the first book. There would be no end to the quotations here if one sought to show how all philosophers before Kant have spoken of reason in general in my sense, although they did not know how to explain its nature with complete definiteness and distinctness by reducing it to one point. What was understood by reason shortly before Kant's appearance is shown in general by two essays of Sulzer in the first volume of his miscellaneous philosophical writings, the one entitled "Analysis of the Conception of Reason," the other, " On the Reciprocal Influence of Reason and Language." If, on the other hand, we read how reason is spoken about in the most recent times, through the influence of the Kantian error, which after him increased like an avalanche, we are obliged to assume that the whole of the wise men of antiquity, and also all philosophers before Kant, had absolutely no reason at all; for the immediate perceptions, intuitions, apprehensions, presentiments of the reason now discovered were as utterly unknown to them as the sixth sense of the bat is to us. And as far as I am concerned, I must confess that I also, in my weakness, cannot comprehend or imagine that reason which directly perceives or apprehends, or has an intellectual intuition of the super-sensible, the absolute, together with long yarns that accompany it, in any other way than as the sixth sense of the bat. This, however, must be said in favour of the invention or discovery of such a reason, which at once directly perceives whatever you choose, that it is an incomparable expedient for withdrawing oneself from the affair in the easiest manner in the world, along with one's favourite ideas, in spite of all Kants, with their Critiques of Reason. The invention and the reception it has met with do honour to the age.

Thus, although what is essential in reason (το λογιμον, ή φρονησις, *ratio, raison,* Vernunft) was, on the whole and in general, rightly understood by all philosophers of all ages, though not sharply enough defined nor reduced to one point, yet it was not so clear to them what the understanding (νους, διανοια, *intellectus, esprit,* Verstand) is. Therefore they often confuse it with reason, and just on this account they did not attain to a thoroughly complete, pure, and simple explanation of the nature of the latter. With the Christian philosophers the conception of reason received an entirely extraneous, subsidiary meaning through the opposition of it to revelation. Starting, then, from this, many are justly of opinion that the knowledge of the duty of virtue is possible from mere reason, *i.e.,* without revelation. Indeed this aspect of the matter certainly had influence upon Kant's exposition and language. But this opposition is properly of positive, historical significance, and is therefore for philosophy a foreign element, from which it must keep itself free.

We might have expected that in his critiques of theoretical and practical reason Kant would have started with an exposition of the nature of reason in general, and, after he had thus defined the *genus,* would have gone on to the explanation of the two *species,* showing how one and the same reason manifests itself in two such different ways, and yet, by retaining its principal characteristic, proves itself to be the same. But we find nothing of all this. I have already shown how inadequate, vacillating, and inconsistent are the explanations of the faculty he is criticising, which he gives here and there by the way in the " Critique of Pure Reason." The *practical* reason appears in the " Critique of Pure Reason " without any introduction, and afterwards stands in the " Critique " specially devoted to itself as something already established. No further account of it is given, and the use of language of all times and peoples, which is treated with contempt, and the definitions of the conception given by the greatest of earlier philosophers, dare not lift up their voices. In general, we may conclude from particular passages that Kant's opinion amounts to this : the knowledge of principles *a priori* is the essential characteristic of reason : since now the knowledge of the ethical significance of action is not of empirical origin, it also is an *a priori* principle, and accordingly proceeds from the reason, and therefore thus far the reason is *practical.* I have already spoken enough of the incorrectness of this explanation of reason. But, independently of this, how superficial it is, and what a want of thoroughness it shows, to make use here of the single quality of being independent of experience in order to combine the most heterogeneous things, while overlooking their most essential and immeasurable difference in other respects. For, even assuming, though we do not admit it, that the knowledge of the ethical significance of action springs from an imperative lying in us, an unconditioned *ought,* yet how fundamentally different would such an imperative be from those universal *forms of knowledge* of which, in the " Critique of Pure Reason," Kant proves that we are conscious *a priori,* and by virtue of which consciousness we can assert beforehand an unconditioned *must,* valid for all experience possible for us. But the difference between this *must,* this necessary form of all objects which is already determined in the subject, and that *ought* of morality is so infinitely great and palpable that the mere fact that they agree in the one particular that neither of them is empirically known may indeed be made use of for the purpose of a witty comparison, but not as a philosophical justification for regarding their origin as the same.

Moreover, the birthplace of this child of practical reason, the *absolute ought* or the categorical imperative, is not in the " Critique of Practical Reason," but in that of " Pure Reason," p. 802 ; V. 830. The birth is violent, and is only accomplished by means of the forceps of a *therefore,* which stands boldly and audaciously, indeed one might say shamelessly, between two propositions which are utterly foreign to each other and have no connection, in order to combine them as reason and consequent. Thus, that not merely perceptible but also abstract motives determine us, is the proposition from which Kant starts, expressing it in the following manner : " Not merely what excites, *i.e.,* what affects the senses directly, determines human will, but we have a power of overcoming the impressions made upon our sensuous appetitive faculty through ideas of that which is itself in a more remote manner useful or hurtful. These deliberations as to what is worthy of desire, with reference to our whole condition, *i.e.,* as to what is good and useful, rest upon reason." (Perfectly right; would that he only always spoke so rationally of reason !) " Reason *therefore* gives ! also laws, which are imperatives, *i.e.,* objective laws of freedom, and say what ought to take place, though perhaps it never does take place " ! Thus, without further authentication, the categorical imperative comes into the world, in order to rule there with its unconditioned *ought*—a sceptre of wooden iron. For in the conception " *ought* " there lies always and essentially the reference to threatened punishment, or promised reward, as a necessary condition, and cannot be separated from it without abolishing the conception itself and taking all meaning from it. Therefore an *unconditioned ought* is a *contradictio in adjecto.* It was necessary to censure this mistake, closely as it is otherwise connected with Kant's great service to ethics, which consists in this, that he has freed ethics from all principles of the world of experience, that is, from all direct or indirect doctrines of happiness, and has shown in a quite special manner that the kingdom of virtue is not of this world. This service is all the greater because all ancient philosophers, with the single exception of Plato, thus the Peripatetics, the Stoics, and the Epicureans, sought by very different devices either to make virtue and happiness dependent on each other in accordance with the principle of sufficient reason, or to identify them in accordance with the principle of contradiction. This charge applies with equal force to all modern philosophers down to Kant. His merit in this respect is therefore very great; yet justice demands that we should also remember here first that his exposition and elaboration often does not correspond with the tendency and spirit of his ethics, and secondly that, even so, he is not really the first who separated virtue from all principles of happiness. For Plato, especially in the "Republic," the principal tendency of which is just this, expressly teaches that virtue is to be chosen for itself alone, even if unhappiness and ignominy are inevitably connected with it. Still more, however, Christianity preaches a perfectly unselfish virtue, which is practised not on account of the reward in a life after death, but quite disinterestedly from love to God, for works do not justify, but only faith, which accompanies virtue, so to speak, as its symptom, and therefore appears quite irrespective of reward and of its own accord. See Luther's "*De Libertate Christiana.*" I will not take into account at all the Indians, in whose sacred books the hope of a reward for our works is everywhere described as the way of darkness, which can never lead to blessedness. Kant's doctrine of virtue, however, we do not find so pure; or rather the exposition remains far behind the spirit of it, and indeed falls into inconsistency. In his *highest good,* which he afterwards discussed, we find virtue united to happiness. The ought originally so unconditioned does yet afterwards postulate one condition, in order to escape from the inner contradiction with which it is affected and with which it cannot live. Happiness in the highest good is not indeed really meant to be the motive for virtue; yet there it is, like a secret article, the existence of which reduces all the rest to a mere sham contract. It is not really the reward of virtue, but yet it is a voluntary gift for which virtue, after work accomplished, stealthily opens the hand. One may convince oneself of this from the "Critique of Practical Reason" (p. 223–266 of the fourth, or p. 264–295 of Rosenkranz's, edition). The whole of Kant's moral theology has also the same tendency, and just on this account morality really destroys itself through moral theology. For I repeat that all virtue which in any way is practised for the sake of a reward is based upon a prudent, methodical, far-seeing egoism.

The content of the absolute ought, the fundamental principle of the practical reason, is the famous: "So act that the maxim of your will might always be also valid as the principle of a universal legislation." This principle presents to him who desires a rule for his own will the task of seeking such a rule for the wills of all. Then the question arises how such a rule is to be found. Clearly, in order to discover the rule of my conduct, I ought not to have regard to myself alone, but to the sum of all individuals. Then, instead of my own well-being, the well-being of all without distinction becomes my aim. Yet the aim still always remains well-being. I find, then, that all can be equally well off only if each limits his own egoism by that of others. From this it certainly follows that I must injure no one, because, since this principle is assumed to be universal, I also will not be injured. This, however, is the sole ground on account of which I, who do not yet possess a moral principle, but am only seeking one, can wish this to be a universal law. But clearly in this way the desire of well-being, *i.e.*, egoism, remains the source of this ethical principle. As the basis of politics it would be excellent, as the basis of ethics it is worthless. For he who seeks to establish a rule for the wills of all, as is demanded by that moral principle, necessarily stands in need of a rule himself; otherwise everything would be alike to him. But this rule can only be his own egoism, since it is only this that is affected by the conduct of others; and therefore it is only by means of this egoism, and with reference to it, that each one can have a will concerning the conduct of others, and that it is not a matter of indifference to him. Kant himself very naively intimates this (p. 123 of the "Critique of Practical Reason; ' Rosenkranz's edition, p. 192), where he thus prosecutes the search for maxims for the will: " If every one regarded the need of others with complete indifference, *and thou also didst belong* to such an order of things, wouldst thou consent thereto?" *Quam temere in nosmet legem sancimus iniquam!* would be the rule of the consent inquired after. So also in the "Fundamental Principles of the Metaphysic of Morals" (p. 56 of the third, and p. 50 of Rosenkranz's, edition) : "A will which resolved to assist no one in distress would contradict itself, for cases might arise in which *it required the love and sympathy of others*," &c. &c. This principle of ethics, which when light is thrown upon it is therefore nothing else than an indirect and disguised expression of the old, simple principle, " *Quod tibi fieri non vis, alteri ne feceris*," is related first and directly to passivity, suffering, and then only by means of this to action. Therefore, as we have said, it would be thoroughly serviceable as a guide for the constitution of the State, which aims at the prevention of *the suffering of wrong*, and also desires to procure for all and each the greatest sum of well-being. But in ethics, where the object of investigation is *action* as *action*, and in its direct significance for the *actor*—not its consequences, suffering, or its relation to others—in this reference, I say, it is altogether inadmissible, because at bottom it really amounts to a principle of happiness, thus to egoism.

We cannot, therefore, share Kant's satisfaction that his principle of ethics is not a material one, *i.e.*, one which sets up an object as a motive, but merely formal, whereby it corresponds symmetrically to the formal laws with which the " Critique of Pure Reason " has made us familiar. Certainly it is, instead of a law, merely a formula for finding such a law. But, in the first place, we had this formula already more briefly and clearly in the " *Quod tibi fieri non vis, alteri ne feceris ;* " and, secondly, the analysis of this formula shows that it is simply and solely the reference to one's own happiness that gives it content, and therefore it can only be serviceable to a rational egoism, to which also every legal constitution owes its origin.

Another mistake which, because it offends the feelings of every one, has often been condemned, and was satirised by Schiller in an epigram, is the pedantic rule that for an act to be really good and meritorious it must be done simply and solely out of respect for the known law and the conception of duty, and in accordance with a maxim known to the reason *in abstracto*, and not from any inclination, not from benevolence felt towards others, not from tender-hearted compassion, sympathy, or emotion of the heart, which (according to the " Critique of Practical Reason," p. 213 ; Rosenkranz's edition, p. 257) to right-thinking persons are indeed very burdensome, as confusing their deliberate maxims. The act must be performed unwillingly and with self-compulsion. Remember that nevertheless the hope of reward is not allowed to enter, and estimate the great absurdity of the demand. But, what is saying more, this is directly opposed to the true spirit of virtue ; not the act, but the willingness to do it, the love from which it proceeds, and without which it is a dead work, constitutes its merit. Therefore Christianity rightly teaches that all outward works are worthless if they do not proceed from that genuine disposition which consists in true goodwill and pure love, and that what makes blessed and saves is not the works done (*opera operata*), but the faith, the genuine disposition, which is the gift of the Holy Ghost alone, and which the free, deliberative will, having only the law in view, does not produce. This demand of Kant's, that all virtuous conduct shall proceed from pure, deliberate respect for the law and in accordance with its abstract maxims, coldly and without inclination, nay, opposed to all inclination, is just the same thing as if he asserted that every work of art must be accomplished by a well-considered application of æsthetical rules. The one is just as perverse as the other. The question, already handled by Plato and Seneca, whether virtue can be taught, is to be answered in the negative. We must finally make up our minds to see, what indeed was the source of the Christian doctrine of election by grace, that as regards its chief characteristic and its inner nature, virtue, like genius, is to a certain extent inborn; and that just as little as all the professors of æsthetics could impart to any one the power of producing works of genius, *i.e.*, genuine works of art, so little could all the professors of ethics and preachers of virtue transform an ignoble into a virtuous and noble character, the impossibility of which is very much more apparent than that of turning lead into gold. The search for a system of ethics and a first principle of the same, which would have practical influence and would actually transform and better the human race, is just like the search for the philosopher's stone. Yet I have spoken at length at the end of the fourth book of the possibility of an entire change of mind or conversion of man (new birth), not by means of abstract (ethics) but of intuitive knowledge (the work of grace). The contents of that book relieve me generally of the necessity of dwelling longer upon this point.

That Kant by no means penetrated to the real significance of the ethical content of actions is shown finally by his doctrine of the highest good as the necessary combination of virtue and happiness, a combination indeed in which virtue would be that which merits happiness. He is here involved in the logical fallacy that the conception of merit, which is here the measure or test, already presupposes a theory of ethics as its own measure, and thus could not be deducible from it. It appeared in our fourth book that all genuine virtue, after it has attained to its highest grade, at last leads to a complete renunciation in which all willing finds an end. Happiness, on the other hand, is a satisfied wish; thus the two are essentially incapable of being combined. He who has been enlightened by my exposition requires no further explanation of the complete perverseness of this Kantian view of the highest good. And, independent of my positive exposition, I have no further negative exposition to give.

Kant's love of architectonic symmetry meets us also in the " Critique of Practical Reason," for he has given it the shape of the " Critique of Pure Reason," and has again introduced the same titles and forms with manifest intention, which becomes specially apparent in the table of the categories of freedom.

The " Philosophy of Law " is one of Kant's latest works, and is so poor that, although I entirely disagree with it, I think a polemic against it is superfluous, since of its own weakness it must die a natural death, just as if it were not the work of this great man, but the production of an ordinary mortal. Therefore, as regards the " Philosophy of Law," I give up the negative mode of procedure and refer to the positive, that is, to the short outline of it given in the fourth book. Just one or two general remarks on

Kant's " Philosophy of Law" may be made here. The errors which I have condemned in considering the " Critique of Pure Reason," as clinging to Kant throughout, appear in the " Philosophy of Law" in such excess that one often believes he is reading a satirical parody of the Kantian style, or at least that he is listening to a Kantian. Two principal errors, however, are these. He desires (and many have since then desired) to separate the Philosophy of Law sharply from ethics, and yet not to make the former dependent upon positive legislation, *i.e.*, upon arbitrary sanction, but to let the conception of law exist for itself pure and *a priori.* But this is not possible; because conduct, apart from its ethical significance, and apart from the physical relation to others, and thereby from external sanction, does not admit even of the possibility of any third view. Consequently, when he says, " Legal obligation is that which *can* be enforced," this *can* is either to be understood physically, and then all law is positive and arbitrary, and again all arbitrariness that achieves its end is law; or the *can* is to be understood ethically, and we are again in the province of ethics. With Kant the conception of legal right hovers between heaven and earth, and has no ground on which to stand; with me it belongs to ethics. Secondly, his definition of the conception law is entirely negative, and thereby inadequate.[1] Legal right is that which is consistent with the compatibility of the respective freedom of individuals together, according to a general law." Freedom (here the empirical, *i.e.*, physical, not the moral freedom of the will) signifies not being hindered or interfered with, and is thus a mere negation; compatibility, again, has exactly the same significance. Thus we remain with mere negations and obtain no positive conception, indeed do not learn at all, what is really being spoken about, unless we know it already from some other source.

[1] Although the conception of legal right is properly negative in opposition to that of wrong, which is the positive starting-point, yet the explanation of these conceptions must not on this account be entirely negative.

In the course of the exposition the most perverse views afterwards develop themselves, such as that in the state of nature, *i.e.*, outside the State, there is no right to property at all, which really means that all right or law is positive, and involves that natural law is based upon positive law, instead of which the case ought to be reversed. Further, the founding of legal acquisition on possession; the ethical obligation to establish the civil constitution; the ground of the right of punishment, &c., &c., all of which, as I have said, I do not regard as worth a special refutation. However, these Kantian errors have exercised a very injurious influence. They have confused and obscured truths long known and expressed, and have occasioned strange theories and much writing and controversy. This certainly cannot last, and we see already how truth and sound reason again make way for themselves. Of the latter, the " *Naturrecht* " of J. C. F. Meister specially bears evidence, and is thus a contrast to many a preposterous theory, though I do not regard it as on this account a pattern of perfection.

On the " Critique of Judgment" also, after what has been said, I must be very short. We cannot but be surprised that Kant, to whom art certainly was very foreign, and who to all appearance had little susceptibility for the beautiful, indeed probably never had the opportunity of seeing an important work of art, and who seems, finally, to have had no knowledge of Goethe, the only man of his century and nation who was fit to be placed by his side as his giant equal,—it is, I say, surprising how, notwithstanding all this, Kant was able to render a great and permanent service to the philosophical consideration of art and the beautiful. His merit lies in this, that much as men had reflected upon the beautiful and upon art, they had yet really always considered it only from the empirical point of view, and had investigated upon a basis of facts what quality distinguished the object of any kind which was called beautiful from other objects of the same kind. On this path they first arrived at quite special principles, and then at more general ones. They sought to separate true artistic beauty from false, and to discover marks of this genuineness, which could then serve again as rules. What gives pleasure as beautiful and what does not, what therefore is to be imitated, what is to be striven against, what is to be avoided, what rules, at least negative rules, are to be established, in short, what are the means of exciting æsthetic satisfaction, *i.e.*, what are the conditions of this residing in the object—this was almost exclusively the theme of all treatises upon art. This path was followed by Aristotle, and in the most recent times we find it chosen by Home, Burke, Winckelmann, Lessing, Herder, and many others. It is true that the universality of the æsthetical principles discovered finally led back to the subject, and it was observed that if the effect upon the subject were adequately known we would then also be able to determine *a priori* the causes of this which lie in the object, and thus alone this method of treatment could attain to the certainty of a science. This occasioned once and again psychological disquisitions. Specially however, Alexander Baumgarten produced with this intention a general æsthetic of all beauty, in which he started from the conception of the perfection of sensuous knowledge, that is, of knowledge of perception. With him also, however, the subjective part is done with as soon as this conception has been established, and he passes on to the objective part and to the practical, which is connected with it. But here also the merit was reserved for Kant of investigating seriously and profoundly *the feeling itself*, in consequence of which we call the object occasioning it beautiful, in order to discover, wherever it was possible, the constituent elements and conditions of it in our nature. His investigation, therefore, took an entirely subjective direction. This path was clearly the right one, for in order to explain a phenomenon which is given in its effects, one must know accurately this effect itself, if one is to determine thoroughly the nature of the cause. Yet Kant's merit in this regard does not really extend much further than this, that he has indicated the right path, and by a provisional attempt has given an example of how, more or less, it is to be followed. For what he gave cannot be regarded as objective truth and as a real gain. He gave the method for this investigation, he broke ground in the right direction, but otherwise he missed the mark.

In the " Critique of Æsthetical Judgment" the observation first of all forces itself upon us that Kant retains the method which is peculiar to his whole philosophy, and which I have considered at length above—I mean the method of starting from abstract knowledge in order to establish knowledge of perception, so that the former serves him, so to speak, as a *camera obscura* in which to receive and survey the latter. As in the "Critique of Pure Reason" the forms of judgment are supposed to unfold to him the knowledge of our whole world of perception, so in this " Critique of Æsthetical Judgment" he does not start from the beautiful itself, from the perceptible and immediately beautiful, but from the *judgment* of the beautiful, the so-called, and very badly so-called, judgment of taste. This is his problem. His attention is especially aroused by the circumstance that such a judgment is clearly the expression of something that takes place in the subject, but yet is just as universally valid as if it concerned a quality of the object. It is this that struck him, not the beautiful itself. He starts always merely from the assertions of others, from the judgment of the beautiful, not from the beautiful itself. It is therefore as if he knew it simply from hearsay, not directly. A blind man of high understanding could almost in the same way make up a theory of colours from very accurate reports which he had heard concerning them. And really we can only venture to regard Kant's philosophemes concerning the beautiful as in almost the same position. Then we shall find that his theory is very ingenious indeed, that here and there telling and true observations are made; but his real solution of the problem is so very insufficient, remains so far below the dignity of the subject, that it can never occur to us to accept it as objective truth. Therefore I consider myself relieved from the necessity of refuting it; and here also I refer to the positive part of my work.

With regard to the form of his whole book, it is to be observed that it originated in the idea of finding in the teleological conception the key to the problem of the beautiful. This inspiration is deduced, which is always a matter of no difficulty, as we have learnt from Kant's successors. Thus there now arises the strange combination of the knowledge of the beautiful with that of the teleology of natural bodies in *one* faculty of knowledge called *judgment*, and the treatment of these two heterogeneous subjects in one book. With these three powers of knowledge, reason, judgment, and understanding, a variety of symmetrical-architectonic amusements are afterwards undertaken, the general inclination to which shows itself in many ways in this book; for example, in the forcible adaptation of the whole of it to the pattern of the " Critique of Pure Reason," and very specially in the antinomy of the æsthetical judgment, which is dragged in by the hair. One might also extract a charge of great inconsistency from the fact that after it has been incessantly repeated in the " Critique of Pure Reason " that the understanding is the faculty of judgment, and after the forms of its judgment have been made the foundation-stone of all philosophy, a quite special faculty of judgment now appears, which is completely different from the former. For the rest, what I call the faculty of judgment, the capacity for translating knowledge of perception into abstract knowledge, and again of applying the latter correctly to the former, is explained in the positive part of my work.

By far the best part of the " Critique of Æsthetical Judgment" is the theory of the sublime. It is incomparably more successful than that of the beautiful, and does not only give, as that does, the general method of investigation, but also a part of the right way to it—so much so that even though it does not give the real solution of the problem, it yet touches very closely upon it.

In the " Critique of the Teleological Judgment," on account of the simplicity of the matter, we can recognise perhaps more than anywhere else Kant's rare talent of turning a thought this way and that way, and expressing it in a multitude of different ways, until out of it there grows a book. The whole book is intended to say this alone : although organised bodies necessarily appear to us as if they were constructed in accordance with a conceived design of an end which preceded them, yet we are not justified in assuming that this is objectively the case. For our intellect, to which things are given from without and indirectly, which thus never knows their inner nature through which they arise and exist, but merely their outward side, cannot otherwise comprehend a certain quality peculiar to organised productions of nature than by analogy, for it compares it with the intentionally accomplished works of man, the nature of which is determined by a design and the conception of this design. This analogy is sufficient to enable us to comprehend the agreement of all the parts with the whole, and thus indeed to give us the clue to their investigation ; but it must by no means on this account be made the actual ground of explanation of the origin and existence of such bodies. For the necessity of so conceiving them is of subjective origin. Somewhat in this way I would epitomise Kant's doctrine on this question. In its most important aspect he had expounded it already in the " Critique of Pure Reason," p. 692–702 ; V., 720–730. But in the knowledge of *this* truth also we find David Hume to be Kant's worthy forerunner. He also had keenly controverted that assumption in the second part of his " Dialogues concerning Natural

Religion." The difference between Hume's criticism of
that assumption and Kant's is principally this, that Hume
criticised it as an assumption based upon experience, while
Kant, on the other hand, criticised it as an *a priori* assumption. Both are right, and their expositions supplement each
other. Indeed what is really essential in the Kantian
doctrine on this point we find already expressed in the
commentary of Simplicius on Aristotle's Physics: " ἡ δε
πλανη γεγονεν αυτοις απο του ἡγεισθαι, παντα τα ἑνεκα
του γινομενα κατα προαιρεσιν γενεσθαι και λογισμον, τα
δε φυσει μη ὁυτως ὁραν γινομενα." (*Error iis ortus est ex eo,
quod credebant, omnia, quœ propter finem aliquem fierent, ex
proposito et ratiocinio fieri, dum videbant, naturœ opera non
ita fieri.*) *Schol. in Arist., ex edit. Berol.,* p. 354. Kant
is perfectly right in the matter; and it was necessary that
after it had been shown that the conception of cause and
effect is inapplicable to the whole of nature in general, in
respect of its existence, it should also be shown that in
respect of its qualities it is not to be thought of as the
effect of a cause guided by motives (designs). If we consider the great plausibility of the physico-theological proof,
which even Voltaire held to be irrefragable, it was clearly
of the greatest importance to show that what is subjective
in our comprehension, to which Kant had relegated space,
time, and causality, extends also to our judgment of
natural bodies; and accordingly the compulsion which we
feel to think of them as having arisen as the result of premeditation, according to designs, thus in such a way that
the idea of them preceded their existence, is just as much of
subjective origin as the perception of space, which presents
itself so objectively, and that therefore it must not be set
up as objective truth. Kant's exposition of the matter,
apart from its tedious prolixity and repetitions, is excellent. He rightly asserts that we can never succeed in
explaining the nature of organised bodies from merely
mechanical causes, by which he understands the unde-
signed and regular effect of all the universal forces of

nature. Yet I find here another flaw. He denies the possibility of such an explanation merely with regard to the teleology and apparent adaptation of *organised* bodies. But we find that even where there is no organisation the grounds of explanation which apply to *one* province of nature cannot be transferred to another, but forsake us as soon as we enter a new province, and new fundamental laws appear instead of them, the explanation of which is by no means to be expected from the laws of the former province. Thus in the province of the mechanical, properly so called, the laws of gravitation, cohesion, rigidity, fluidity, and elasticity prevail, which in themselves (apart from my explanation of all natural forces as lower grades of the objectification of will) exist as manifestations of forces which cannot be further explained, but themselves constitute the principles of all further explanation, which merely consists in reduction to them. If we leave this province and come to the phenomena of chemistry, of electricity, magnetism, crystallisation, the former principles are absolutely of no use, indeed the former laws are no longer valid, the former forces are overcome by others, and the phenomena take place in direct contradiction to them, according to new laws, which, just like the former ones, are original and inexplicable, *i.e.*, cannot be reduced to more general ones. Thus, for example, no one will ever succeed in explaining even the dissolving of a salt in water in accordance with the laws proper to mechanics, much less the more complicated phenomena of chemistry. All this has already been explained at length in the second book of the present work. An exposition of this kind would, as it seems to me, have been of great use in the "Critique of the Teleological Judgment," and would have thrown much light upon what is said there. Such an exposition would have been especially favourable to his excellent remark that a more profound knowledge of the real being, of which the things of nature are the manifestation, would recognise both in the mechanical (according to law) and the apparently intentional effects of nature one and the same ultimate principle, which might serve as the more general ground of explanation of them both. Such a principle I hope I have given by establishing the will as the real thing in itself; and in accordance with it generally in the second book and the supplements to it, but especially in my work "On the Will in Nature," the insight into the inner nature of the apparent design and of the harmony and agreement of the whole of nature has perhaps become clearer and deeper. Therefore I have nothing more to say about it here.

The reader whom this criticism of the Kantian philosophy interests should not neglect to read the supplement to it which is given in the second essay of the first volume of my "Parerga and Paralipomena," under the title "*Noch einige Erläuterungen zur Kantischen Philosophie*" (Some Further Explanations of the Kantian Philosophy). For it must be borne in mind that my writings, few as they are, were not composed all at once, but successively, in the course of a long life, and with long intervals between them. Accordingly, it must not be expected that all I have said upon one subject should stand together in one place.

Supplements to the First Book.

" 'Warum willst du dich von uns Allen
Und unsrer Meinung entfernen ?'
Ich schreibe nicht euch zu gefallen,
Ihr sollt was lernen."
—GOETHE.

SUPPLEMENTS TO THE FIRST BOOK

FIRST HALF

THE DOCTRINE OF THE IDEA OF PERCEPTION.

(To § 1–7 of the First Volume.)

CHAPTER I.

THE STANDPOINT OF IDEALISM.

IN boundless space countless shining spheres, about each of which, and illuminated by its light, there revolve a dozen or so of smaller ones, hot at the core and covered with a hard, cold crust, upon whose surface there have been generated from a mouldy film beings which live and know—this is what presents itself to us in experience as the truth, the real, the world. Yet for a thinking being it is a precarious position to stand upon one of those numberless spheres moving freely in boundless space without knowing whence or whither, and to be only one of innumerable similar beings who throng and press and toil, ceaselessly and quickly arising and passing away in time, which has no beginning and no end; moreover, nothing permanent but matter alone and the recurrence of the same varied organised forms, by means of certain ways and channels which are there once for all. All that empirical science can teach is only the more exact nature and law of these events. But now at last modern philosophy especially through Berkeley and Kant, has called

to mind that all this is first of all merely a *phenomenon
of the brain*, and is affected with such great, so many,
and such different *subjective* conditions that its supposed
absolute reality vanishes away, and leaves room for an
entirely different scheme of the world, which consists of
what lies at the foundation of that phenomenon, *i.e.*, what
is related to it as the thing in itself is related to its mere
manifestation.

" The world is my idea " is, like the axioms of Euclid,
a proposition which every one must recognise as true as
soon as he understands it ; although it is not a proposition which every one understands as soon as he hears
it. To have brought this proposition to clear consciousness, and in it the problem of the relation of the ideal
and the real, *i.e.*, of the world in the head to the world
outside the head, together with the problem of moral
freedom, is the distinctive feature of modern philosophy.
For it was only after men had spent their labour for
thousands of years upon a mere philosophy of the object
that they discovered that among the many things that
make the world so obscure and doubtful the first and
chiefest is this, that however immeasurable and massive
it may be, its existence yet hangs by a single thread ; and
this is the actual consciousness in which it exists. This
condition, to which the existence of the world is irrevocably
subject, marks it, in spite of all *empirical* reality, with
the stamp of *ideality*, and therefore of mere *phenomenal
appearance*. Thus on one side at least the world must be
recognised as akin to dreams, and indeed to be classified
along with them. For the same function of the brain
which. during sleep, conjures up before us a completely
objective, perceptible, and even palpable world must have
just as large a share in the presentation of the objective
world of waking life. Both worlds, although different as
regards their matter, are yet clearly moulded in the one
form. This form is the intellect, the function of the brain.
Descartes was probably the first who attained to the

degree of reflection which this fundamental truth demands, and consequently he made it the starting-point
of his philosophy, though provisionally only in the
form of a sceptical doubt. When he took his *cogito
ergo sum* as alone certain, and provisionally regarded the
existence of the world as problematical, he really discovered the essential and only right starting-point of all
philosophy, and at the same time its *true* foundation.
This foundation is essentially and inevitably the *subjective*,
the *individual consciousness.* For this alone is and remains
immediate; everything else, whatever it may be, is medi-
ated and conditioned through it, and is therefore dependent upon it. Therefore modern philosophy is rightly
regarded as starting with Descartes, who was the father
of it. Not long afterwards Berkeley followed the same
path further, and attained to *idealism* proper, *i.e.*, to the
knowledge that the world which is extended in space,
thus the objective, material world in general, exists as
such simply and solely in our *idea*, and that it is false,
and indeed absurd, to attribute to it, *as such*, an existence
apart from all idea and independent of the knowing subject, thus to assume matter as something absolute and
possessed of real being in itself. But his correct and profound insight into this truth really constitutes Berkeley's
whole philosophy; in it he had exhausted himself.

Thus true philosophy must always be idealistic; indeed,
it must be so in order to be merely honest. For nothing
is more certain than that no man ever came out of himself in order to identify himself directly with things
which are different from him; but everything of which
he has certain, and therefore immediate, knowledge lies
within his own consciousness. Beyond this consciousness,
therefore, there can be no *immediate* certainty; but the
first principles of a science must have such certainty.
For the empirical standpoint of the other sciences it is
quite right to assume the objective world as something
absolutely given; but not so for the standpoint of philo-

sophy, which has to go back to what is first and original.
Only consciousness is immediately given; therefore the
basis of philosophy is limited to facts of consciousness, *i.e.*,
it is essentially *idealistic*. Realism which commends itself to the crude understanding, by the appearance which
it assumes of being matter-of-fact, really starts from an
arbitrary assumption, and is therefore an empty castle in
the air, for it ignores or denies the first of all facts, that
all that we know lies within consciousness. For that
the *objective existence* of things is conditioned through a
subject whose ideas they are, and consequently that the
objective world exists only as *idea*, is no hypothesis, and
still less a dogma, or even a paradox set up for the sake
of discussion; but it is the most certain and the simplest
truth; and the knowledge of it is only made difficult by
the fact that it is indeed so simple, and that it is not
every one who has sufficient power of reflection to go back
to the first elements of his consciousness of things. There
can never be an absolute and independent objective existence; indeed such an existence is quite unintelligible.
For the objective, as such, always and essentially has its
existence in the consciousness of a subject, is thus the
idea of this subject, and consequently is conditioned by it,
and also by its forms, the forms of the idea, which depend
upon the subject and not on the object.

That *the objective world would exist* even if there existed
no conscious being certainly seems at the first blush to
be unquestionable, because it can be thought in the abstract, without bringing to light the contradiction which
it carries within it. But if we desire to *realise* this abstract
thought, that is, to reduce it to ideas of perception, from
which alone (like everything abstract) it can have content and truth, and if accordingly we try *to imagine an
objective world without a knowing subject,* we become aware
that what we then imagine is in truth the opposite of
what we intended, is in fact nothing else than the process
in the intellect of a knowing subject who perceives an

objective world, is thus exactly what we desired to exclude. For this perceptible and real world is clearly a phenomenon of the brain; therefore there lies a contradiction in the assumption that as such it ought also to exist independently of all brains.

The principal objection to the inevitable and essential *ideality of all objects*, the objection which, distinctly or indistinctly, arises in every one, is certainly this: My own person also is an object for some one else, is thus his idea, and yet I know certainly that I would continue to exist even if he no longer perceived me. But all other objects also stand in the same relation to his intellect as I do; consequently they also would continue to exist without being perceived by him. The answer to this is: That other being as whose object I now regard my person is not absolutely *the subject*, but primarily is a knowing individual. Therefore, if he no longer existed, nay, even if there existed no other conscious being except myself, yet the subject, in whose idea alone all objects exist, would by no means be on that account abolished. For I myself indeed am this subject, as every conscious being is. Consequently, in the case assumed, my person would certainly continue to exist, but still as idea, in my own knowledge. For even by me myself it is always known only indirectly, never immediately; because all existence as idea is indirect. As *object, i.e.*, as extended, occupying space and acting, I know my body only in the perception of my brain. This takes place by means of the senses, upon data supplied by which the percipient understanding performs its function of passing from effect to cause, and thereby, in that the eye sees the body or the hands touch it, it constructs that extended figure which presents itself in space as my body. By no means, however, is there directly given me, either in some general feeling of bodily existence or in inner self-consciousness, any extension, form, or activity, which would then coincide with my nature itself, which accordingly, in order so to exist, would require no other being in whose knowledge it might exhibit itself. On the contrary, that general feeling of bodily existence, and also self-consciousness, exists directly only in relation to the *will*, that is, as agreeable or disagreeable, and as active in the acts of will, which for external perception exhibit themselves as actions of the body. From this it follows that the existence of my person or body as *something extended and acting* always presupposes a *knowing being* distinct from it; because it is essentially an existence in apprehension, in the idea, thus an existence *for another*. In fact, it is a phenomenon of brain, just as much whether the brain in which it exhibits itself is my own or belongs to another person. In the first case one's own person divides itself into the knowing and the known, into object and subject, which here as everywhere stand opposed to each other, inseparable and irreconcilable. If, then, my own person, in order to exist as such, always requires a knowing subject, this will at least as much hold good of the other objects for which it was the aim of the above objection to vindicate an existence independent of knowledge and its subject.

However, it is evident that the existence which is conditioned through a knowing subject is only the existence in space, and therefore that of an extended and active being. This alone is always something known, and consequently *an existence for another*. On the other hand, every being that exists in this way may yet have *an existence for itself*, for which it requires no subject. Yet this existence for itself cannot be extension and activity (together space-occupation), but is necessarily a being of another kind, that of a thing in itself, which, as such, can never be an *object*. This, then, would be the answer to the leading objection set forth above, which accordingly does not overthrow the fundamental truth that the objectively given world can only exist in the idea, thus only for a subject.

We have further to remark here that Kant also, so long at least as he remained consistent, can have thought no *objects* among his things in themselves. For this follows from the fact that he proves that space, and also time, are mere forms of our perception, which consequently do not belong to things in themselves. What is neither in space nor in time can be no *object;* thus the being of *things in themselves* cannot be objective, but of quite a different kind, a metaphysical being. Consequently that Kantian principle already involves this principle also, that the *objective* world exists only as *idea.*

In spite of all that one may say, nothing is so persistently and ever anew misunderstood as *Idealism,* because it is interpreted as meaning that one denies the *empirical* reality of the external world. Upon this rests the perpetual return to the appeal to common sense, which appears in many forms and guises; for example, as an "irresistible conviction" in the Scotch school, or as Jacobi's *faith* in the reality of the external world. The external world by no means presents itself, as Jacobi declares, upon credit, and is accepted by us upon trust and faith. It presents itself as that which it is, and performs directly what it promises. It must be remembered that Jacobi, who set up such a credit or faith theory of the world, and had the fortune to impose it upon a few professors of philosophy, who for thirty years have philosophised upon the same lines lengthily and at their ease, is the same man who once denounced Lessing as a Spinozist, and afterwards denounced Schelling as an atheist, and who received from the latter the well-known and well-deserved castigation. In keeping with such zeal, when he reduced the external world to a mere matter of faith he only wished to open the door to faith in general, and to prepare belief for that which was afterwards really to be made a matter of belief; as if, in order to introduce a paper currency, one should seek to appeal to the fact that the value of the ringing coin also depends merely on the stamp which the State has set upon it. Jacobi, in his doctrine that the reality of the external world is assumed upon faith, is just exactly " the transcendental realist who plays the empirical idealist" censured by Kant in the " Critique of Pure Reason," first edition, p. 369.

The true idealism, on the contrary, is not the empirical but the transcendental. This leaves the empirical reality of the world untouched, but holds fast to the fact that every *object*, thus the empirically real in general, is conditioned in a twofold manner by the subject; in the first place *materially* or as *object* generally, because an objective existence is only conceivable as opposed to a subject, and as its idea; in the second place *formally*, because the mode of existence of an object, *i.e.*, its being perceived (space, time, causality), proceeds from the subject, is pre-arranged in the subject. Therefore with the simple or Berkeleian idealism, which concerns the object in general, there stands in immediate connection the Kantian idealism, which concerns the specially given *mode or manner* of objective existence. This proves that the whole material world, with its bodies, which are extended in space and, by means of time, have causal relations to each other, and everything that depends upon this—that all this is not something which is there *independently* of our head, but essentially presupposes the functions of our brain *by means of which* and *in* which alone *such* an objective arrangement of things is possible. For time, space, and causality, upon which all those real and objective events rest, are themselves nothing more than functions of the brain; so that thus the unchangeable *order* of things which affords the criterion and clue to their empirical reality itself proceeds only from the brain, and has its credentials from this alone. All this Kant has expounded fully and thoroughly; only he does not speak of the brain, but calls it "the faculty of knowledge." Indeed he has attempted to prove that when that objective order in time, space, causality, matter, &c., upon which all the events of the real world ultimately rest, is properly considered, it cannot even be conceived as a self-existing order, *i.e.*, an order of the thing in itself, or as something absolutely objective and unconditionally given, for if one tries to think this out it leads to contradictions. To accomplish this was the object of the antinomies, but in the appendix to my work I have proved the failure of the attempt. On the other hand, the Kantian doctrine, even without the antinomies, leads to the insight that things and the whole mode of their existence are inseparably bound up with our consciousness of them. Therefore whoever has distinctly grasped this soon attains to the conviction that the assumption that things also exist as such, apart from and independently of our consciousness, is really absurd. That we are so deeply involved in time, space, causality, and the whole regular process of experience which rests upon them, that we (and indeed the brutes) are so perfectly at home, and know how to find our way from the first—this would not be possible if our intellect were one thing and things another, but can only be explained from the fact that both constitute one whole, the intellect itself creates that order, and exists only for things, while they, on the other hand, exist only for it.

But even apart from the deep insight, which only the Kantian philosophy gives, the inadmissibility of the assumption of absolute realism which is so obstinately clung to may be directly shown, or at least made capable of being felt, by the simple exhibition of its meaning in the light of such considerations as the following. According to realism, the world is supposed to exist, as we know it, independently of this knowledge. Let us once, then, remove all percipient beings from it, and leave only unorganised and vegetable nature. Rock, tree, and brook are there, and the blue heaven; sun, moon, and stars light this world, as before; yet certainly in vain, for there is no eye to see it. Let us now in addition place in it a percipient being. Now that world presents itself *again* in his brain, and repeats itself within it precisely as it was formerly without it. Thus to the *first* world a *second* has been added, which, although completely separated from it, resembles it to a nicety. And now the *subjective* world of this perception is precisely so constituted in *subjective*, known space as the *objective* world in *objective*, infinite space. But the subjective world has this advantage over the objective, the knowledge that that space, outside there, is infinite ; indeed it can also give beforehand most minutely and accurately the whole constitution or necessary properties of all relations which are possible, though not yet actual, in that space, and does not require to examine them. It can tell just as much with regard to the course of time, and also with regard to the relation of cause and effect which governs the changes in that external world. I think all this, when closely considered, turns out absurd enough, and hence leads to the conviction that that absolute objective world outside the head, independent of it and prior to all knowledge, which at first we imagined ourselves to conceive, is really no other than the second, the world which is known *subjectively*, the world of idea, as which alone we are actually able to conceive it. Thus of its own accord the assumption forces itself upon us, that the world, as we know it, exists also only for our knowledge, therefore in the *idea* alone, and not a second time outside of it.[1] In accordance, then, with this assumption, the thing in itself, *i.e.*, that which exists independently of our knowledge and of every knowledge, is to be regarded as something completely different from the *idea* and all its attributes, thus from objectivity in general. What this is will be the subject of our second book.

On the other hand, the controversy concerning the reality of the external world considered in § 5 of the first

[1] I specially recommend here the passage in Lichtenberg's "Miscellaneous Writings" (Göthingen, 1801, vol. ii. p. 12) : "Euler says, in his letters upon various subjects in connection with natural science (vol. ii. p. 228), that it would thunder and lighten just as well if there were no man present whom the lightning might strike. It is a very common expression, but I must confess that it has never been easy for me completely to comprehend it. It always seems to me as if the conception *being* were something derived from our thought, and thus, if there are no longer any sentient and thinking creatures, then there is nothing more whatever."

volume rests upon the assumption, which has just been criticised, of an objective and a subjective world both in *space*, and upon the impossibility which arises in connection with this presupposition of a transition from one to the other, a bridge between the two. Upon this controversy I have still to add the following remarks.

The subjective and the objective do not constitute a continuous whole. That of which we are immediately conscious is bounded by the skin, or rather by the extreme ends of the nerves which proceed from the cerebral system. Beyond this lies a world of which we have no knowledge except through pictures in our head. Now the question is, whether and how far there is a world independent of us which corresponds to these pictures. The relation between the two could only be brought about by means of the law of causality ; for this law alone leads from what is given to something quite different from it. But this law itself has first of all to prove its validity. Now it must either be of *objective* or of *subjective* origin ; but in either case it lies upon one or the other side, and therefore cannot supply the bridge between them. If, as Locke and Hume assume, it is *a posteriori*, thus drawn from experience, it is of *objective* origin, and belongs then itself to the external world which is in question. Therefore it cannot attest the reality of this world, for then, according to Locke's method, causality would be proved from experience, and the reality of experience from causality. If, on the contrary, it is given *a priori*, as Kant has more correctly taught us, then it is of *subjective* origin, and in that case it is clear that with it we remain always in the *subjective* sphere. For all that is actually given *empirically* in perception is the occurrence of a sensation in the organ of sense ; and the assumption that this, even in general, must have a cause rests upon a law which is rooted in the form of our knowledge, *i.e.*, in the functions of our brain. The origin of this law is therefore just as subjective as that of the sensation itself. The cause of the given sensation, which is assumed in consequence of this law, presents itself at once in perception as an *object*, which has space and time for the form of its manifestation. But *these forms* themselves again are entirely of subjective origin ; for they are the mode or method of our faculty of perception. That transition from the sensation to its cause which, as I have repeatedly pointed out, lies at the foundation of all sense-perception is certainly sufficient to give us the empirical presence in space and time of an empirical object, and is therefore quite enough for the practical purposes of life ; but it is by no means sufficient to afford us any conclusion as to the existence and real nature, or rather as to the intelligible substratum, of the phenomena which in this way arise for us. Thus that on the occasion of certain sensations occurring in my organs of sense there arises in my head a perception of things which are extended in space, permanent in time, and causally efficient by no means justifies the assumption that they also exist in themselves, *i.e.*, that such things with these properties belonging absolutely to themselves exist independently and outside of my head. This is the true outcome of the Kantian philosophy. It coincides with an earlier result of Locke's, which is just as true, but far more easily understood. For although, as Locke's doctrine permits, external things are absolutely assumed as the causes of sensations, yet there can be no *resemblance* between the sensation in which the *effect* consists and the objective nature of the *cause* which occasions it. For the sensation, as organic function, is primarily determined by the highly artificial and complicated nature of our organs of sense. It is therefore merely excited by the external cause, but is then perfected entirely in accordance with its own laws, and thus is completely subjective. Locke's philosophy was the criticism of the functions of sense ; Kant has given us the criticism of the functions of the brain. But to all this we have yet to add the Berkeleian result, which has been revised by me, that every object, whatever its origin may be, is *as object* already conditioned by the subject, is in fact merely its *idea*. The aim of realism is indeed the object without subject; but it is impossible even to conceive such an object distinctly.

From this whole inquiry it follows with certainty and distinctness that it is absolutely impossible to attain to the comprehension of the inner nature of things upon the path of mere *knowledge* and *perception*. For knowledge always comes to things from without, and therefore must for ever remain outside them. This end would only be reached if we could find *ourselves* in the inside of things, so that their inner nature would be known to us directly. Now, how far this is actually the case is considered in my second book. But so long as we are concerned, as in this first book, with objective comprehension, that is, with *knowledge*, the world is, and remains for us, a mere *idea*, for here there is no possible path by which we can cross over to it.

But, besides this, a firm grasp of the point of view of *idealism* is a necessary counterpoise to that of *materialism.* The controversy concerning the *real* and the *ideal* may also be regarded as a controversy concerning the existence of *matter.* For it is the reality or ideality of this that is ultimately in question. Does matter, as such, exist only in our *idea*, or does it also exist independently of it? In the latter case it would be the thing in itself; and whoever assumes a self-existent matter must also, consistently, be a materialist, *i.e.*, he must make matter the principle of explanation of all things. Whoever, on the contrary, denies its existence as a thing in itself is *eo ipso* an idealist. Among the moderns only Locke has definitely and without ambiguity asserted the reality of matter; and therefore his teaching led, in the hands of Condillac, to the sensualism and materialism of the French. Only Berkeley directly and without modifications denies matter. The complete antithesis is thus that of idealism and materialism, represented in its extremes by Berkeley and the

French materialists (Hollbach). Fichte is not to be mentioned here: he deserves no place among true philosophers; among those elect of mankind who, with deep earnestness, seek not their own things but the *truth*, and therefore must not be confused with those who, under this pretence, have only their personal advancement in view. Fichte is the father of the *sham philosophy*, of the *disingenuous* method which, through ambiguity in the use of words, incomprehensible language, and sophistry, seeks to deceive, and tries, moreover, to make a deep impression by assuming an air of importance—in a word, the philosophy which seeks to bamboozle and humbug those who desire to learn. After this method had been applied by Schelling, it reached its height, as every one knows, in Hegel, in whose hands it developed into pure charlatanism. But whoever even names this Fichte seriously along with Kant shows that he has not even a dim notion of what Kant is. On the other hand, materialism also has its warrant. It is just as true that the knower is a product of matter as that matter is merely the idea of the knower; but it is also just as one-sided. For materialism is the philosophy of the subject that forgets to take account of itself. And, accordingly, as against the assertion that I am a mere modification of matter, this must be insisted upon, that all matter exists merely in my idea; and it is no less right. A knowledge, as yet obscure, of these relations seems to have been the origin of the saying of Plato, " ὕλη ἀληθινον ψευδος " (*materia mendacium verax*).

Realism necessarily leads, as we have said, to *materialism.* For if empirical perception gives us things in themselves, as they exist independently of our knowledge, experience also gives us the *order* of things in themselves, *i.e.*, the true and sole order of the world. But this path leads to the assumption that there is only *one* thing in itself, matter; of which all other things are modifications; for the course of nature is here the absolute and only order of the world. To escape from these consequences, while realism remained in undisputed acceptance, spiritualism was set up, that is, the assumption of a second substance outside of and along with matter, an *immaterial substance.* This dualism and spiritualism, equally unsupported by experience and destitute of proof and comprehensibility, was denied by Spinoza, and was proved to be false by Kant, who dared to do so because at the same time he established idealism in its rights. For with realism materialism, as the counterpoise of which spiritualism had been devised, falls to the ground of its own accord, because then matter and the course of nature become mere phenomena, which are conditioned by the intellect, as they have their existence only in its *idea.* Accordingly spiritualism is the delusive and false safeguard against materialism, while the real and true safeguard is idealism, which, by making the objective world dependent upon us, gives the needed counterpoise to the position of dependence upon the objective world, in which we are placed by the course of nature. The world from which I part at death is, in another aspect, only my idea. The centre of gravity of existence falls back into the *subject.* What is proved is not, as in spiritualism, that the knower is independent of matter, but that all matter is dependent on him. Certainly this is not so easy to comprehend or so convenient to handle as spiritualism, with its two substances; but χαλεπα τα καλα.

In opposition to the *subjective* starting-point, " the world is my idea," there certainly stands provisionally with equal justification the *objective* starting-point, " the world is matter," or " matter alone is absolute " (since it alone is not subject to becoming and passing away), or " all that exists is matter." This is the starting-point of Democritus, Leucippus, and Epicurus. But, more closely considered, the departure from the subject retains a real advantage; it has the start by one perfectly justified step. For con sciousness alone is the *immediate:* but we pass over this if we go at once to matter and make it our starting-point.

On the other hand, it would certainly be possible to con•
struct the world from matter and its properties if these
were correctly, completely, and exhaustively known to us
(which is far from being the case as yet).   For all that
has come to be has become actual through *causes*, which
could operate and come together only by virtue of the
fundamental forces of matter.   But these must be perfectly
capable of demonstration at least objectively, even if subjectively we never attain to a knowledge of them.   But
such an explanation and construction of the world would
not only have at its foundation the assumption of an existence in itself of matter (while in truth it is conditioned
by the subject), but it would also be obliged to allow all
the *original qualities* in this matter to pass current and
remain absolutely inexplicable, thus as *qualitates occultœ*.
(Cf. § 26, 27 of the first volume.)   For matter is only the
vehicle of these forces, just as the law of causality is only
the arranger of their manifestations.   Therefore such an
explanation of the world would always remain merely
relative and conditioned, properly the work of a *physical
science*, which at every step longed for a *metaphysic*.   On
the other hand, there is also something inadequate about
the subjective starting-point and first principle, " the world
is my idea," partly because it is one-sided, since the world
is far more than that (the thing in itself, will), and indeed
its existence as idea is to a certain extent only accidental
to it ; but partly also because it merely expresses the fact
that the object is conditioned by the subject, without at
the same time saying that the subject, as such, is also conditioned by the object.   For the assertion, " the subject
would still remain a knowing being if it had no object, *i.e.*,
if it had absolutely no idea," is just as false as the assertion of the crude understanding, " the world, the object,
would still exist, even if there were no subject."   A consciousness without an object is no consciousness.   A thinking subject has conceptions for its object ; a subject of
sense perception has objects with the qualities correspond-

ing to its organisation. If we rob the subject of all special characteristics and forms of its knowledge, all the properties of the object vanish also, and nothing remains but *matter without form and quality*, which can just as little occur in experience as a subject without the forms of its knowledge, but which remains opposed to the naked subject as such, as its reflex, which can only disappear along with it. Although materialism pretends to postulate nothing more than this matter—for instance, atoms—yet it unconsciously adds to it not only the subject, but also space, time, and causality, which depend upon special properties of the subject.

The world as idea, the objective world, has thus, as it were, two poles; the simple knowing subject without the forms of its knowledge, and crude matter without form and quality. Both are completely unknowable; the subject because it is that which knows, matter because without form and quality it cannot be perceived. Yet both are fundamental conditions of all empirical perception. Thus the knowing subject, merely as such, which is a presupposition of all experience, stands opposed as its pure counterpart to the crude, formless, and utterly dead (*i.e.*, will-less) matter, which is given in no experience, but which all experience presupposes. This subject is not in time, for time is only the more definite form of all its ideas. The matter which stands over against it is, like it, eternal and imperishable, endures through all time, but is, properly speaking, not extended, for extension gives form, thus it has no spatial properties. Everything else is involved in a constant process of coming into being and passing away, while these two represent the unmoved poles of the world as idea. The permanence of matter may therefore be regarded as the reflex of the timelessness of the pure subject, which is simply assumed as the condition of all objects. Both belong to phenomena, not to the thing in itself, but they are the framework of the phenomenon. Both are arrived at only by abstraction, and are not given immediately, pure and for themselves.

The fundamental error of all systems is the failure to understand this truth. *Intelligence and matter are correlates, i.e.,* the one exists only for the other, both stand and fall together, the one is only the reflex of the other. Indeed they are really *one and the same thing* regarded from two opposite points of view; and this one thing, I am here anticipating, is the manifestation of the will, or the thing in itself. Consequently both are secondary, and therefore the origin of the world is not to be sought in either of the two. But because of their failure to understand this, all systems (with the exception perhaps of that of Spinoza) sought the origin of all things in one of these two. Some of them, on the one hand, suppose an intelligence, νους, as the absolutely First and δημιουργος, and accordingly in this allow an idea of things and of the world to precede their actual existence; consequently they distinguish the real world from the world of idea ; which is false. Therefore matter now appears as that through which the two are distinguished, as the thing in itself. Hence arises the difficulty of procuring this matter, the ὑλη, so that when added to the mere idea of the world it may impart reality to it. That original intelligence must now either find it ready to hand, in which case it is just as much an absolute First as that intelligence itself, and we have then two absolute Firsts, the δημιουργος and the ὑλη ; or the absolute intelligence must create this matter out of nothing, an assumption which our understanding refuses to make, for it is only capable of comprehending changes in matter, and not that matter itself should come into being or pass away. This rests ultimately upon the fact that matter is essential, the correlate of the understanding. On the other hand, the systems opposed to these, which make the other of the two correlates, that is, matter, the absolute First, suppose a matter which would exist without being perceived ; and it has been made sufficiently clear by all that has been said above that this is a direct contradiction, for by the existence of matter we always mean simply its being perceived. But here they encounter the difficulty of bringing to this matter, which alone is their absolute First, the intelligence which is finally to experience it. I have shown this weak side of materialism in § 7 of the first volume. For me, on the contrary, matter and intelligence are inseparable correlates, which exist only for each other, and therefore merely relatively. Matter is the idea of the intelligence; the intelligence is that in whose idea alone matter exists. The two together constitute *the world as idea*, which is just Kant's *phenomenon*, and consequently something secondary. What is primary is that which manifests itself, *the thing in itself*, which we shall afterwards discover is the will. This is in itself neither the perceiver nor the perceived, but is entirely different from the mode of its manifestation.

As a forcible conclusion of this important and difficult discussion I shall now personify these two abstractions, and present them in a dialogue after the fashion of Prabodha Tschandro Daya. It may also be compared with a similar dialogue between matter and form in the "*Duodecim Principia Philosophiæ*" of Raymund Lully, c. 1 and 2.

The Subject.

I am, and besides me there is nothing. For the world is my idea.

Matter.

Presumptuous delusion! I, I am, and besides me there is nothing, for the world is my fleeting form. Thou art a mere result of a part of this form and altogether accidental.

The Subject.

What insane arrogance! Neither thou nor thy form would exist without me; ye are conditioned by me. Whosoever thinks me away, and believes he can still think ye there, is involved in gross delusion, for your existence apart from my idea is a direct contradiction, a meaningless form of words. *Ye are* simply means ye are perceived by me. My idea is the sphere of your existence; therefore I am its first condition.

Matter.

Fortunately the audacity of your assertion will soon be put to silence in reality and not by mere words. Yet a few moments and thou actually art no more. With all thy boasting thou hast sunk into nothing, vanished like a shadow, and shared the fate of all my transitory forms. But I, I remain, unscathed and undiminished, from age to age, through infinite time, and behold unshaken the play of my changing form.

The Subject.

This infinite time through which thou boastest that thou livest, like the infinite space which thou fillest, exists only in my idea. Indeed it is merely the form of my idea which I bear complete in myself, and in which thou exhibitest thyself, which receives thee, and through which thou first of all existest. But the annihilation with which thou threatenest me touches me not; were it so, then wouldst thou also be annihilated. It merely affects the individual, which for a short time is my vehicle, and which, like everything else, is my idea.

Matter.

And if I concede this, and go so far as to regard thy existence, which is yet inseparably linked to that of these fleeting individuals, as something absolute, it yet remains dependent upon mine. For thou art subject only so far as thou hast an object; and this object I am. I am its kernel and content, that which is permanent in it, that which holds it together, and without which it would be as disconnected, as wavering, and unsubstantial as the dreams and fancies of thy individuals, which have yet borrowed from me even the illusive content they possess.

The Subject.

Thou dost well to refrain from contesting my existence on the ground that it is linked to individuals; for, as inseparably as I am joined to them, thou art joined to thy sister, Form, and hast never appeared without her. No eye hath yet seen either thee or me naked and isolated; for we are both mere abstractions. It is in reality *one* being that perceives itself and is perceived by itself, but whose real being cannot consist either in perceiving or in being perceived, since these are divided between us two.

Both.

We are, then, inseparably joined together as necessary parts of one whole, which includes us both and exists through us. Only a misunderstanding can oppose us two hostilely to each other, and hence draw the false conclusion that the one contests the existence of the other, with which its own existence stands or falls.

This whole, which comprehends both, is the world as idea, or the world of phenomena. When this is taken away there remains only what is purely metaphysical, the thing in itself, which in the second book we shall recognise as the will.

CHAPTER II.

WITH all *transcendental* ideality the objective world re-tains *empirical* reality; the object is indeed not the thing in itself, but as an empirical object it is real. It is true that space is only in my head; but empirically my head is in space. The law of causality can certainly never enable us to get quit of idealism by building a bridge between things in themselves and our knowledge of them, and thus certifying the absolute reality of the world, which exhibits itself in consequence of its applica-tion; but this by no means does away with the causal relation of objects to each other, thus it does not abolish the causal relation which unquestionably exists between the body of each knowing person and all other material objects. But the law of causality binds together only phenomena, and does not lead beyond them. With that law we are and remain in the world of objects, *i.e.*, the world of phenomena, or more properly the world of ideas. Yet the whole of such a world of experience is primarily conditioned by the knowledge of a subject in general as its necessary presupposition, and then by the special forms of our perception and apprehension, thus necessarily be-longs to the merely *phenomenal*, and has no claim to pass for the world of things in themselves. Indeed the subject itself (so far as it is merely the *knowing* subject) belongs to the merely phenomenal, of which it constitutes the complementary half.

Without application of the law of causality, however, perception of an *objective* world could never be arrived at;

for this perception is, as I have often explained, essentially matter of the *intellect*, and not merely of the *senses*. The senses afford us mere *sensation*, which is far from being *perception*. The part played by sensations of the senses in perception was distinguished by Locke under the name *secondary qualities*, which he rightly refused to ascribe to things in themselves. But Kant, carrying Locke's method further, distinguished also, and refused to ascribe to things in themselves what belongs to the working up of this material (the sensations) by the brain. The result was, that in this was included all that Locke had left to things in themselves as *primary* qualities —extension, form, solidity, &c.—so that with Kant the thing in itself was reduced to a completely unknown quantity $= x$. With Locke accordingly the thing in itself is certainly without colour, sound, smell, taste, neither warm nor cold, neither soft nor hard, neither smooth nor rough; yet it has still extension and form, it is impenetrable, at rest or in motion, and has mass and number. With Kant, on the other hand, it has laid aside all these latter qualities also, because they are only possible by means of time, space, and causality, and these spring from an intellect (brain), just as colours, tones, smells, &c., originate in the nerves of the organs of sense. The thing in itself has with Kant become spaceless, unextended, and incorporeal. Thus what the mere senses bring to the perception, in which the objective world exists, stands to what is supplied by the *functions of the brain* (space, time, causality) as the mass of the nerves of sense stand to the mass of the brain, after subtracting that part of the latter which is further applied to thinking proper, *i.e.*, to abstract ideas, and is therefore not possessed by the brutes. For as the nerves of the organs of sense impart to the phenomenal objects colour, sound, taste, smell, temperature, &c., so the brain imparts to them extension, form, impenetrability, the power of movement, &c., in short all that can only be presented in perception by means of time, space, and causality. How small is the share of the senses in perception, compared with that of the intellect, is also shown by a comparison of the nerve apparatus for receiving impressions with that for working them up. The mass of the nerves of sensation of the whole of the organs of sense is very small compared with that of the brain, even in the case of the brutes, whose brain, since they do not, properly speaking, *i.e.*, in the abstract, think, is merely used for effecting perception, and yet when this is complete, thus in the case of mammals, has a very considerable mass, even after the cerebellum, whose function is the systematic guidance of movements, has been taken away.

That excellent book by Thomas Reid, the "Inquiry into the Human Mind" (first edition, 1764; 6th edition, 1810), as a *negative* proof of the Kantian truths, affords us a very thorough conviction of the inadequacy of the senses to produce the objective perception of things, and also of the non-empirical origin of the perception of space and time. Reid refutes Locke's doctrine that perception is a product of the senses, by a thorough and acute demonstration that the collective sensations of the senses do not bear the least resemblance to the world as known in perception, and especially that the five primary qualities of Locke (extension, form, solidity, movement, and number) absolutely could not be afforded us by any sensation of the senses. Accordingly he gives up the question as to the mode of origination and the source of perception as completely insoluble; and although altogether unacquainted with Kant, he gives us, as it were, according to the *regula falsi*, a thorough proof of the intellectual nature of perception (really first explained by me as a consequence of the Kantian doctrine), and also of the *a priori* source, discovered by Kant, of its constituent elements, space, time, and causality, from which those primary qualities of Locke first proceed, but by means of which they are easily constructed. Thomas Reid's book is very instructive and well worth reading— ten times more so than all the philosophy together that has

been written since Kant. Another indirect proof of the
same doctrine, though in the way of error, is afforded by
the French sensational philosophers, who, since Condillac
trod in the footsteps of Locke, have laboured to show
once for all that the whole of our perception and thinking
can be referred to mere sensations (*penser c'est sentir*),
which, after Locke's example, they call *idées simples*, and
through the mere coming together and comparison of which
the whole objective world is supposed to build itself up
in our heads. These gentlemen certainly have *des idées
bien simples*. It is amusing to see how, lacking alike
the profundity of the German and the honesty of the
English philosopher, they turn the poor material of sensation this way and that way, and try to increase its importance, in order to construct out of it the deeply significant
phenomena of the world of perception and thought. But
the man constructed by them would necessarily be an
Anencephalus, a *Tête de crapaud*, with only organs of sense
and without a brain. To take only a couple of the better
attempts of this sort out of a multitude of others, I may
mention as examples Condorcet at the beginning of his
book, " *Des Progrès de l'Esprit Humain*," and Tourtual
on Sight, in the second volume of the " *Scriptores Ophthalmologici Minores*," *edidit Justus Radius* (1828).

The feeling of the insufficiency of a purely sensational-
istic explanation of perception is in like manner shown in
the assertion which was made shortly before the appearance of the Kantian philosophy, that we not only have
ideas of things called forth by sensation, but apprehend
the *things themselves* directly, although they lie outside us
—which is certainly inconceivable. And this was not
meant in some idealistic sense, but was said from the
point of view of common realism. This assertion is well
and pointedly put by the celebrated Euler in his " Letters
to a German Princess," vol. ii. p. 68. He says: " I therefore believe that the sensations (of the senses) contain
something more than philosophers imagine. They are not

merely empty perceptions of certain impressions made in
the brain.   They do not give the soul mere *ideas* of things,
but actually place before it objects which exist outside
it, although we cannot conceive how this really happens." This opinion is explained by the following facts.
Although, as I have fully proved, perception is brought
about by application of the law of causality, of which we
are conscious *a priori*, yet in sight the act of the understanding, by means of which we pass from the effect to
the cause, by no means appears distinctly in consciousness ; and therefore the sensation does not separate itself
clearly from the idea which is constructed out of it, as the
raw material, by the understanding.   Still less can a distinction between object and idea, which in general does
not exist, appear in consciousness ; but we feel the *things
themselves* quite directly, and indeed as lying *outside us*,
although it is certain that what is immediate can only be
the sensation, and this is confined to the sphere of the body
enclosed by our skin.   This can be explained from the fact
that *outside us* is exclusively a *spatial* determination.   But
space itself is a form of our faculty of perception, *i.e.*, a
function of our brain.   Therefore that externality to us to
which we refer objects, on the occasion of sensations of
sight, is itself really within our heads ; for that is its
whole sphere of activity.   Much as in the theatre we see
the mountains, the woods, and the sea, but yet everything
is inside the house.   From this it becomes intelligible that
we perceive things in the relation of externality, and yet
in every respect immediately, but have not within us an
idea of the things which lie outside us, different from these
things.   For things are in space, and consequently also
external to us only in so far as we *perceive* them.   Therefore those things which to this extent we perceive directly,
and not mere images of them, are themselves only *our
ideas*, and as such exist only in our heads.   Therefore we
do not, as Euler says, directly perceive the things themselves which are external to us, but rather the things

which are perceived by us as external to us are only our ideas, and consequently are apprehended by us immediately. The whole observation given above in Euler's words, and which is quite correct, affords a fresh proof of Kant's Transcendental Æsthetic, and of my theory of perception which is founded upon it, as also of idealism in general. The directness and unconsciousness referred to above, with which in perception we make *the transition from the sensation to its cause,* may be illustrated by an analogous procedure in the use of abstract ideas or thinking. When we read or hear we receive mere words, but we pass from these so immediately to the conceptions denoted by them, that it is as if we *received the conceptions directly ;* for we are absolutely unconscious of the transition from the words to the conceptions. Therefore it sometimes happens that we do not know in what language it was that we read something yesterday which we now remember. Yet that such a transition always takes place becomes apparent if it is once omitted, that is, if in a fit of abstraction we read without thinking, and then become aware that we certainly have taken in all the words but no conceptions. Only when we pass from abstract conceptions to pictures of the imagination do we become conscious of the transposition we have made.

Further, it is really only in perception in the narrowest sense, that is, in *sight*, that in empirical apprehension the transition from the sensation to its cause takes place quite unconsciously. In every other kind of sense perception, on the contrary, the transition takes place with more or less distinct consciousness; therefore, in the case of apprehension through the four coarser senses, its reality is capable of being established as an immediate fact. Thus in the dark we feel a thing for a long time on all sides until from the different effects upon our hands we are able to construct its definite form as their cause. Further, if something feels smooth we sometimes reflect whether we may not have fat or oil upon our hands; and

again, if something feels cold we ask ourselves whether it
may not be that we have very warm hands.   When we
hear a sound we sometimes doubt whether it was really
an affection of our sense of hearing from without or merely
an inner affection of it; then whether it sounded near and
weak or far off and strong, then from what direction it
came, and finally whether it was the voice of a man or of
a brute, or the sound of an instrument; thus we investigate the cause of each effect we experience.   In the case
of smell and taste uncertainty as to the objective nature
of the cause of the effect felt is of the commonest occurrence, so distinctly are the two separated here.   The
fact that *in sight* the transition from the effect to the
cause occurs quite unconsciously, and hence the illusion
arises that this kind of perception is perfectly direct, and
consists simply in the sensation alone without any operation of the understanding—this has its explanation partly
in the great perfection of the organ of vision, and partly
in the exclusively rectilineal action of light.   On account
of the latter circumstance the impression itself leads
directly to the place of the cause, and since the eye is
capable of perceiving with the greatest exactness and at a
glance all the fine distinctions of light and shade, colour
and outline, and also the data in accordance with which
the understanding estimates distance, it thus happens that
in the case of impressions of this sense the operation of
the understanding takes place with such rapidity and
certainty that we are just as little conscious of it as of
spelling when we read.   Hence arises the delusion that
the sensation itself presents us directly with the objects.
Yet it is just in sight that the operation of the *understanding*, consisting in the knowledge of the cause from
the effect, is most significant.   By means of it what is felt
doubly, with two eyes, is perceived as single; by means of
it the impression which strikes the retina upside down, in
consequence of the crossing of the rays in the pupils, is
put right by following back the cause of this in the same

direction, or as we express ourselves, we see things upright although their image in the eye is reversed; and finally by means of the operation of the understanding magni tude and distance are estimated by us in direct perception from five different data, which are very clearly and beautifully described by Dr. Thomas Reid. I expounded all this, and also the proofs which irrefutably establish the *intellectual nature of perception*, as long ago as 1816, in my essay "On Sight and Colour" (second edition, 1854; third edition, 1870), and with important additions fifteen years later in the revised Latin version of it which is given under the title, " *Theoria Colorum Physiologica Eademque Primaria*," in the third volume of the "*Scriptores Ophthalmologici Minores*," published by Justus Radius in 1830; yet most fully and thoroughly in the second (and third) edition of my essay "On the Principle of Sufficient Reason," § 21. Therefore on this important subject I refer to these works, so as not to extend unduly the present exposition.

On the other hand, an observation which trenches on the province of æsthetics may find its place here. It follows from the proved intellectual nature of perception that the sight of beautiful objects—for example, of a beautiful view—is also a *phenomenon of the brain*. Its purity and completeness, therefore, depends not merely on the object, but also upon the quality of the brain, its form and size, the fineness of its texture, and the stimulation of its activity by the strength of the pulse of the arteries which supply it. Accordingly the same view appears in different heads, even when the eyes are equally acute, as different as, for example, the first and last impressions of a copper plate that has been much used. This is the explanation of the difference of capacity for enjoying natural beauty, and consequently also for reproducing it, *i.e.*, for occasioning a similar phenomenon of the brain by means of an entirely different kind of cause, the arrangement of colours on a canvas.

The apparent immediacy of perception, depending on

its entire intellectuality, by virtue of which, as Euler says, we apprehend the thing itself, and as external to us, finds an analogy in the way in which we feel the parts of our own bodies, especially when they suffer pain, which when we do feel them is generally the case.   Just as we imagine that we perceive things where they are, while the perception really takes place in the brain, we believe that we feel the pain of a limb in the limb itself, while in reality it also is felt in the brain, to which it is conducted by the nerve of the affected part.   Therefore, only the affections of those parts whose nerves go to the brain are felt, and not those of the parts whose nerves belong to the sympathetic system, unless it be that an unusually strong affection of these parts penetrates by some roundabout way to the brain, where yet for the most part it only makes itself known as a dull sense of discomfort, and always without definite determination of its locality. Hence, also, it is that we do not feel injuries to a limb whose nerve-trunk has been severed or ligatured.   And hence, finally, the man who has lost a limb still sometimes feels pain in it, because the nerves which go to the brain are still there.   Thus, in the two phenomena here compared, what goes on in the brain is apprehended as outside of it; in the case of perception, by means of the understanding, which extends its feelers into the outer world; in the case of the feeling of our limbs, by means of the nerves.

CHAPTER III.

IT is not the object of my writings to repeat what has been said by others, and therefore I only make here some special remarks of my own on the subject of the senses.

The senses are merely the channels through which the brain receives from without (in the form of sensations) the materials which it works up into ideas of perception. Those sensations which principally serve for the objective comprehension of the external world must in themselves be neither agreeable nor disagreeable. This really means that they must leave the will entirely unaffected. Otherwise the sensation *itself* would attract our attention, and we would remain at the *effect* instead of passing to the *cause*, which is what is aimed at here. For it would bring with it that marked superiority, as regards our consideration, which the will always has over the mere idea, to which we only turn when the will is silent. Therefore colours and sounds are in themselves, and so long as their impression does not pass the normal degree, neither painful nor pleasurable sensations, but appear with the indifference that fits them to be the material of pure objective perception. This is as far the case as was possible in a body which is in itself through and through will; and just in this respect it is worthy of admiration. Physiologically it rests upon the fact that in the organs of the nobler senses, thus in sight and hearing, the nerves which have to receive the specific outward impression are quite insusceptible to any sensation of pain, and know no other sensation than that which is specifically peculiar to them, and which serves the purpose of mere apprehension. Thus the retina, as also the optic nerve, is insensible to every injury; and this is also the case with the nerve of hearing. In both organs pain is only felt in their other parts, the surroundings of the nerve of sense which is peculiar to them, never in this nerve itself. In the case of the eye such pain is felt principally in the *conjunctiva;* in the case of the ear, in the *meatus auditorius.* Even with the brain this is the case, for if it is cut into directly, thus from above, it has no feeling. Thus only on account of this indifference with regard to the will which is peculiar to them are the sensations of the eye capable of supplying the understanding with such multifarious and finely distinguished data, out of which it constructs in our head the marvellous objective world, by the application of the law of causality upon the foundation of the pure perceptions of space and time. Just that freedom from affecting the will which is characteristic of sensations of colour enables them, when their energy is heightened by transparency, as in the glow of an evening sky, in painted glass, and the like, to raise us very easily into the state of pure objective will-less perception, which, as I have shown in my third book, is one of the chief constituent elements of the æsthetic impression. Just this indifference with regard to the will fits sounds to supply the material for denoting the infinite multiplicity of the conceptions of the reason.

Outer sense, that is, receptivity for external impressions as pure data for the understanding, is divided into *five senses,* and these accommodate themselves to the four elements, *i.e.,* the four states of aggregation, together with that of imponderability. Thus the sense for what is firm (earth) is touch; for what is fluid (water), taste; for what is in the form of vapour, *i.e.,* volatile (vapour, exhalation), smell; for what is permanently elastic (air), hearing; for what is imponderable (fire, light), sight. The second imponderable, heat, is not properly an object of the senses, but of general feeling, and therefore always affects the *will* directly, as agreeable or disagreeable. From this classification there also follows the relative dignity of the senses. Sight has the highest rank, because its sphere is the widest and its susceptibility the finest. This rests upon the fact that what affects it is an imponderable, that is, something which is scarcely corporeal, but is *quasi* spiritual. Hearing has the second place, corresponding to air. However, touch is a more thorough and well-informed sense. For while each of the other senses gives us only an entirely one-sided relation to the object, as its sound, or its relation to light, touch, which is closely bound up with general feeling and muscular power, supplies the understanding with the data at once for the form, magnitude, hardness, softness, texture, firmness, temperature, and weight of bodies, and all this with the least possibility of illusion and deception, to which all the other senses are far more subject. The two lowest senses, smell and taste, are no longer free from a direct affection of the will, that is, they are always agreeably or disagreeably affected, and are therefore more subjective than objective.

Sensations of hearing are exclusively in *time*, and therefore the whole nature of music consists in degrees of time, upon which depends both the quality or pitch of tones, by means of vibrations, and also their quantity or duration, by means of time. The sensations of sight, on the other hand, are primarily and principally in *space;* but secondarily, by reason of their duration, they are also in time.

Sight is the sense of the understanding which perceives; hearing is the sense of the reason which thinks and apprehends. Words are only imperfectly represented by visible signs; and therefore I doubt whether a deaf and dumb man, who can read, but has no idea of the sound of the words, works as quickly in thinking with the mere visible signs of conceptions as we do with the real, *i.e.,* the audible words. ff he cannot read, it is well known that he is almost like an irrational animal, while the man born blind is from the first a thoroughly rational being.

Sight is an *active*, hearing a *passive* sense. Therefore sounds affect our mind in a disturbing and hostile manner, and indeed they do so the more in proportion as the mind is active and developed; they distract all thoughts and instantly destroy the power of thinking. On the other hand, there is no analogous disturbance through the eye, no direct effect of what is seen, *as such*, upon the activity of thought (for naturally we are not speaking here of the influence which the objects looked at have upon the will); but the most varied multitude of things before our eyes admits of entirely unhindered and quiet thought. Therefore the thinking mind lives at peace with the eye, but is always at war with the ear. This opposition of the two senses is also confirmed by the fact that if deaf and dumb persons are cured by galvanism they become deadly pale with terror at the first sounds they hear (Gilbert's " *Annalen der Physik*," vol. x. p. 382), while blind persons, on the contrary, who have been operated upon, behold with ecstasy the first light, and unwillingly allow the bandages to be put over their eyes again. All that has been said, however, can be explained from the fact that hearing takes place by means of a mechanical vibration of the nerve of hearing which is at once transmitted to the brain, while seeing, on the other hand, is a real *action* of the retina which is merely stimulated and called forth by light and its modifications; as I have shown at length in my physiological theory of colours. But this whole opposition stands in direct conflict with that coloured-ether, drum-beating theory which is now everywhere unblushingly served up, and which seeks to degrade the eye's sensation of light to a mechanical vibration, such as primarily that of hearing actually is, while nothing can be more different than the still, gentle effect of light and the alarm-drum of hearing. If we add to this the remarkable circumstance that although we hear with two ears, the sensibility of which is often very different, yet we never hear a sound double, as we often see things double with our two eyes, we are led to the conjecture that the sensation of hearing does not arise in the labyrinth or in the cochlea, but deep in the brain where the two nerves of hearing meet, and thus the impression becomes simple. But this is where the *pons Varolii* encloses the *medulla oblongata*, thus at the absolutely lethal spot, by the injury of which every animal is instantly killed, and from which the nerve of hearing has only a short course to the labyrinth, the seat of acoustic vibration. Now it is just because its source is here, in this dangerous place, in which also all movement of the limbs originates, that we start at a sudden noise; which does not occur in the least degree when we suddenly see a light; for example, a flash of lightning. The optic nerve, on the contrary, proceeds from its *thalami* much further forward (though perhaps its source lies behind them), and throughout its course is covered by the anterior lobes of the brain, although always separated from them till, having extended quite out of the brain, it is spread out in the retina, upon which, on stimulation by light, the sensation first arises, and where it is really localised. This is shown in my essay upon sight and colour. This origin of the auditory nerve explains, then, the great disturbance which the power of thinking suffers from sound, on account of which thinking men, and in general all people of much intellect, are without exception absolutely incapable of enduring any noise. For it disturbs the constant stream of their thoughts, interrupts and paralyses their thinking, just because the vibration of the auditory nerve extends so deep into the brain, the whole mass of which feels the oscillations set up through this nerve, and vibrates along with them, and because the brains of such persons are more easily moved than those of ordinary men. On the same readiness to be set in

motion, and capacity for transmission, which characterises
their brains depends the fact that in the case of persons
like these every thought calls forth so readily all those
analogous or related to it whereby the similarities, analogies, and relations of things in general come so quickly
and easily into their minds; that the same occasion which
millions of ordinary minds have experienced before brings
them to *the* thought, to *the* discovery, that other people
are subsequently surprised they did not reach themselves,
for they certainly can think afterwards, but they cannot
think before. Thus the sun shone on all statues, but
only the statue of Memnon gave forth a sound. For
this reason Kant, Gœthe, and Jean Paul were highly
sensitive to every noise, as their biographers bear witness.[1] Gœthe in his last years bought a house which had
fallen into disrepair close to his own, simply in order that
he might not have to endure the noise that would be
made in repairing it. Thus it was in vain that in his
youth he followed the drum in order to harden himself
against noise. It is not a matter of custom. On the
other hand, the truly stoical indifference to noise of
ordinary minds is astonishing. No noise disturbs them
in their thinking, reading, writing, or other occupations,
while the finer mind is rendered quite incapable by it.
But just that which makes them so insensible to noise of
every kind makes them also insensible to the beautiful
in plastic art, and to deep thought or fine expression in
literary art; in short, to all that does not touch their
personal interests. The following remark of Lichtenberg's
applies to the paralysing effect which noise has upon
highly intellectual persons: "It is always a good sign
when an artist can be hindered by trifles from exercising
his art. F——— used to stick his fingers into sulphur if
he wished to play the piano. . . . Such things do not

---

[1] Lichtenberg says in his "*Nach-richten und Bemerkungen von und über sich selbst*" (*Vermischte Schriften, Göttingen*, 1800, vol. i. p. 43): "I am extremely sensitive to all noise, but it entirely loses its disagreeable character as soon as it is associated with a rational purpose."

interfere with the average mind ; . . . it acts like a coarse sieve" (*Vermischte Schriften*, vol. i. p. 398). I have long really held the opinion that the amount of noise which any one can bear undisturbed stands in inverse proportion to his mental capacity, and therefore may be regarded as a pretty fair measure of it. Therefore, if I hear the dogs barking for hours together in the court of a house without being stopped, I know what to think of the intellectual capacity of the inhabitants. The man who habitually slams the door of a room, instead of shutting it with his hand, or allows this to go on in his house, is not only ill-bred, but is also a coarse and dull-minded fellow. That in English "sensible" also means gifted with understanding is based upon accurate and fine observation. We shall only become quite civilised when the ears are no longer unprotected, and when it shall no longer be the right of everybody to sever the consciousness of each thinking being, in its course of a thousand steps, with whistling, howling, bellowing, hammering, whip-cracking, barking, &c. &c. The Sybarites banished all noisy trades without the town; the honourable sect of the Shakers in North America permit no unnecessary noise in their villages, and the Moravians have a similar rule. Something more is said upon this subject in the thirtieth chapter of the second volume of the " Parerga."

The effect of music upon the mind, so penetrating, so direct, so unfailing, may be explained from the *passive* nature of hearing which has been discussed; also the after effect which sometimes follows it, and which consists in a specially elevated frame of mind. The vibrations of the tones following in rationally combined numerical relations set the fibre of the brain itself in similar vibration. On the other hand, the *active* nature of sight, opposed as it is to the passive nature of hearing, makes it intelligible why there can be nothing analogous to music for the eye, and the piano of colours was an absurd mistake. Further, it is just on account of the active nature of the sense of sight that it is remarkably acute in the case of beasts that hunt, *i.e.*, beasts of prey, while conversely the *passive* sense of hearing is specially acute in those beasts that are hunted, that flee, and are timid, so that it may give them timely warning of the pursuer that is rushing or creeping upon them.

Just as we have recognised in sight the sense of the understanding, and in hearing the sense of the reason, so we might call smell the sense of the memory, because it recalls to us more directly than any other the specific impression of an event or a scene even from the most distant past.

CHAPTER IV.

FROM the fact that we are able spontaneously to assign and determine the laws of relations in space without having recourse to experience, Plato concludes (*Meno,* p. 353, Bip.) that all learning is mere recollection. Kant, on the other hand, concludes that space is subjectively conditioned, and merely a form of the faculty of knowledge. How far, in this regard, does Kant stand above Plato!

Cogito, ergo sum, is an analytical judgment. Indeed Parmenides held it to be an identical judgment: " το γαρ αυτο νοειν εστι τε και ειναι" (*nam intelligere et esse idem est,* Clem. Alex. Strom., vi. 2, § 23). As such, however, or indeed even as an analytical judgment, it cannot contain any special wisdom; nor yet if, to go still deeper, we seek to deduce it as a conclusion from the major premise, *non-entis nulla sunt prædicata.* But with this proposition what Descartes really wished to express was the great truth that immediate certainty belongs only to self-consciousness, to what is subjective. To what is objective, on the other hand, thus to everything else, only indirect certainty belongs; for it is arrived at through self-consciousness; and being thus merely at second hand, it is to be regarded as problematical. Upon this depends the value of this celebrated proposition. As its opposite we may set up, in the sense of the Kantian philosophy, *cogito, ergo est,* that is, exactly as I think certain relations in things (the mathematical), they must always occur in all possible experience ;—this was an important, profound, and a late *apperçu*, which appeared in the form of the problem as to the *possibility of synthetic judgments a priori*, and has actually opened up the way to a deeper knowledge. This problem is the watchword of the Kantian philosophy, as the former proposition is that of the Cartesian, and shows εξ οἰων εις οἰα.

Kant very fitly places his investigations concerning time and space at the head of all the rest. For to the speculative mind these questions present themselves before all others : what is time ?—what is this that consists of mere movement, without anything that moves it ?—and what is space ? this omnipresent nothing, out of which nothing that exists can escape without ceasing to be anything at all ?

That time and space depend on the subject, are the mode in which the process of objective apperception is brought about in the brain, has already a sufficient proof in the absolute impossibility of thinking away time and space, while we can very easily think away everything that is presented in them. The hand can leave go of everything except itself. However, I wish here to illustrate by a few examples and deductions the more exact proofs of this truth which are given by Kant, not for the purpose of refuting stupid objections, but for the use of those who may have to expound Kant's doctrine in future.

" A right-angled equilateral triangle " contains no logical contradiction ; for the predicates do not by any means cancel the subject, nor are they inconsistent with each other. It is only when their object is constructed in pure perception that the impossibility of their union in it appears. Now if on this account we were to regard this as a contradiction, then so would every physical impossibility, only discovered to be such after the lapse of centuries, be a contradiction ; for example, the composition of a metal from its elements, or a mammal with more or fewer than seven cervical vertebra,[1] or horns and upper incisors in the same animal. But only *logical* impossibility is a contradiction, not physical, and just as little mathemathical. Equilateral and rectangled do not contradict each other (they coexist in the square), nor does either of them contradict a triangle. Therefore the incompatibility of the above conceptions can never be known by mere *thinking*, but is only discovered by perception—merely mental perception, however, which requires no experience, no real object. We should also refer here to the proposition of Giordano Bruno, which is also found in Aristotle : " An infinitely large body is necessarily immovable "—a proposition which cannot rest either upon experience or upon the principle of contradiction, since it speaks of things which cannot occur in any experience, and the conceptions " infinitely large " and " movable " do not contradict each other ; but it is only pure perception that informs us that motion demands a space outside the body, while its infinite size leaves no space over. Suppose, now, it should be objected to the first mathematical example that it is only a question of how complete a conception of a triangle the person judging has : if the conception is quite complete it will also contain the impossibility of a triangle being rectangular and also equilateral. The answer to this is : assume that his conception is not so complete, yet without recourse to experience he can, by the mere construction of the triangle in his imagination, extend his conception of it and convince himself for ever of the impossibility of this combination of these conceptions. This process, however, is a synthetic judgment *a priori*, that is, a judgment through which, independently of all experience, and yet with validity for all experience, we form and perfect our conceptions. For, in general, whether a given judgment is analytical or synthetical can only be determined in the particular case according as

---

[1] That the three-toed sloth has nine must be regarded as a mistake; yet Owen still states this, " *Ostéologie Comp.*," p. 405.

the conception of the subject in the mind of the person judging is more or less complete. The conception "cat" contains in the mind of a Cuvier a hundred times more than in that of his servant; therefore the same judgments about it will be synthetical for the latter, and only analytical for the former. But if we take the conceptions objectively, and now wish to decide whether a given judgment is analytical or synthetical, we must change the predicate into its contradictory opposite, and apply this to the subject without a cupola. If this gives a *contradictio in adjecto,* then the judgment was analytical; otherwise it was synthetical.

That Arithmetic rests on the pure intuition or perception of time is not so evident as that Geometry is based upon that of space.[1] It can be proved, however, in the following manner. All counting consists in the repeated affirmation of unity. Only for the purpose of always knowing how often we have already affirmed unity do we mark it each time with another word: these are the numerals. Now repetition is only possible through succession. But succession, that is, being after one another, depends directly upon the intuition or perception of *time.* It is a conception which can only be understood by means of this;

---

[1] This, however, does not excuse a professor of philosophy who, sitting in Kant's chair, expresses himself thus: "That mathematics as such contains arithmetic and geometry is correct. It is incorrect, however, to conceive arithmetic as the science of time, really for no other reason than to give a pendant (*sic*) to geometry as the science of space" (Rosenkranz in the "*Deutschen Museum,*" 1857, May 14, No. 20). This is the fruit of Hegelism. If the mind is once thoroughly debauched with its senseless jargon, serious Kantian philosophy will no longer enter it. The audacity to talk at random about what one does not understand has been inherited from the master, and one comes in the end to condemn without ceremony the fundamental teaching of a great genius in a tone of peremptory decision, just as if it were Hegelian foolery. We must not, however, fail to notice that these little people struggle to escape from the track of great thinkers. They would therefore have done better not to attack Kant, but to content themselves with giving their public full details about God, the soul, the actual freedom of the will, and whatever belongs to that sort of thing, and then to have indulged in a private luxury in their dark back-shop, the philosophical journal; there they may do whatever they like without constraint, for no one sees it.

and thus counting also is only possible by means of time. This dependence of all counting upon time is also betrayed by the fact that in all languages multiplication is expressed by "time," thus by a time-concept: *sexies, ἑξάκις, six fois, sex mal.* But simple counting is already a multiplication by one, and for this reason in Pestalozzi's educational establishment the children are always made to multiply thus: "Two times two is four times one." Aristotle already recognised the close relationship of number and time, and expounded it in the fourteenth chapter of the fourth book of the "Physics." Time is for him "the number of motion" ("ὁ χρονος αριθμος εστι κινησεως"). He very profoundly suggests the question whether time could be if the soul were not, and answers it in the negative. If arithmetic had not this pure intuition or perception of time at its foundation, it would be no science *a priori*, and therefore its propositions would not have infallible certainty.

Although time, like space, is the form of knowledge of the subject, yet, just like space, it presents itself as independent of the subject and completely objective. Against our will, or without our knowledge, it goes fast or slow. We ask what o'clock it is; we investigate time, as if it were something quite objective. And what is this objective existence? Not the progress of the stars, or of the clocks, which merely serve to measure the course of time itself, but it is something different from all things, and yet, like them, independent of our will and knowledge. It exists only in the heads of percipient beings, but the uniformity of its course and its independence of the will give it the authority of objectivity.

Time is primarily the form of inner sense. Anticipating the following book, I remark that the only object of inner sense is the individual will of the knowing subject. Time is therefore the form by means of which self-consciousness becomes possible for the individual will, which originally and in itself is without knowledge. In it the nature of the will, which in itself is simple and identical, appears drawn out into a course of life. But just on account of this original simplicity and identity of what thus exhibits itself, its *character* remains always precisely the same, and hence also the course of life itself retains throughout the same key-note, indeed its multifarious events and scenes are at bottom just like variations of one and the same theme.

The *a priori nature of the law of causality* has, by Englishmen and Frenchmen, sometimes not been seen at all, sometimes not rightly conceived of; and therefore some of them still prosecute the earlier attempts to find for it an *empirical* origin. Maine de Biran places this in the experience that the act of will as cause is followed by the movement of the body as effect. But this fact itself is untrue. We certainly do not recognise the really immediate act of will as something different from the action of the body, and the two as connected by the bond of causality; but both are one and indivisible. Between them there is no succession; they are simultaneous. They are one and the same thing, apprehended in a double manner. That which makes itself known to inner apprehension (self-consciousness) as the real *act of will* exhibits itself at once in external perception, in which the body exists objectively as an *action* of the body. That physiologically the action of the nerve precedes that of the muscle is here immaterial, for it does not come within self-consciousness; and we are not speaking here of the relation between muscle and nerve, but of that between the act of will and the action of the body. Now this does not present itself as a causal relation. If these two presented themselves to us as cause and effect their connection would not be so incomprehensible to us as it actually is; for what we understand from its cause we understand as far as there is an understanding of things generally. On the other hand, the movement of our limbs by means of mere acts of will is indeed a miracle of such common occurrence that we no longer observe it; but if we once turn our attention to it we become keenly conscious of the incomprehensibility of the matter, just because in this we have something before us which we do *not* understand as the effect of a cause. This apprehension, then, could never lead us to the idea of causality, for that never appears in it at all. Maine de Biran himself recognises the perfect simultaneousness of the act of will and the movement (*Nouvelles Considérations des Rapports du Physique au Moral*, p. 377, 378). In England Thomas Reid (On the First Principles of Contingent Truths, Essay IV. c. 5) already asserted that the knowledge of the causal relation has its ground in the nature of the faculty of knowledge itself. Quite recently Thomas Brown, in his very tediously composed book, "Inquiry into the Relation of Cause and Effect," 4th edit., 1835, says much the same thing, that that knowledge springs from an innate, intuitive, and instinctive conviction; thus he is at bottom upon the right path. Quite unpardonable, however, is the crass ignorance on account of which in this book of 476 pages, of which 130 are devoted to the refutation of Hume, absolutely no mention is made of Kant, who cleared up the question more than seventy years ago. If Latin had remained the exclusive language of science such a thing would not have occurred. In spite of Brown's exposition, which in the main is correct, a modification of the doctrine set up by Maine de Biran, of the empirical origin of the fundamental knowledge of the causal relation, has yet found acceptance in England; for it is not without a certain degree of plausibility. It is this, that we abstract the law of causality from the perceived effect of our own body upon other bodies. This was already refuted by Hume. I, however, have shown that it is untenable in my work, "*Ueber den Willen in der Natur*" (p. 75 of the second edition, p. 82 of the third), from the fact that since we apprehend both our own and other bodies objectively in spatial perception, the knowledge of causality must

already be there, because it is a condition of such perception. The one genuine proof that we are conscious of
the law of causality *before all experience* lies in the necessity of making a *transition* from the sensation, which is
only empirically given, to its *cause,* in order that it may
become perception of the external world. Therefore I
have substituted this proof for the Kantian, the incorrectness of which I have shown. A most full and thorough
exposition of the whole of this important subject, which
is only touched on here, the *a priori* nature of the law of
causality and the intellectual nature of empirical perception, will be found in my essay on the principle of sufficient reason, § 21, to which I refer, in order to avoid the
necessity of repeating here what is said there. I have
also shown there the enormous difference between the
mere sensation of the senses and the perception of an
objective world, and discovered the wide gulf that lies
between the two. The law of causality alone can bridge
across this gulf, and it presupposes for its application the
two other forms which are related to it, space and time.
Only by means of these three combined is the objective
idea attained to. Now whether the sensation from which
we start to arrive at apprehension arises through the
resistance which is suffered by our muscular exertion, or
through the impression of light upon the retina, or of
sound upon the nerves of the brain, &c. &c., is really a
matter of indifference. The *sensation* always remains a
mere *datum* for the *understanding,* which alone is capable
of apprehending it as the effect of a cause different from
itself, which the understanding now perceives as external,
i.e., as something occupying and filling space, which is
also a form inherent in the intellect prior to all experience. Without this intellectual operation, for which the
forms must lie ready in us, the perception of an *objective,
external world* could never arise from a mere *sensation*
within our skin. How can it ever be supposed that the
mere feeling of being hindered in intended motion, which

occurs also in lameness, could be sufficient for this? We may add to this that before I attempt to affect external things *they* must necessarily have affected me as motives. But this almost presupposes the apprehension of the external world. According to the theory in question (as I have remarked in the place referred to above), a man born without arms and legs could never attain to the idea of causality, and consequently could never arrive at the apprehension of the external world. But that this is not the case is proved by a fact communicated in Froriep's *Notizen,* July 1838, No. 133 — the detailed account, accompanied by a likeness, of an Esthonian girl, Eva Lauk, then fourteen years old, who was born entirely without arms or legs. The account concludes with these words: "According to the evidence of her mother, her mental development had been quite as quick as that of her brothers and sisters; she attained just as soon as they did to a correct judgment of size and distance, yet without the assistance of hands.—Dorpat, 1st March 1838, Dr. A. Hueck."

Hume's doctrine also, that the conception of causality arises from the custom of seeing two states constantly following each other, finds a practical refutation in the oldest of all successions, that of day and night, which no one has ever held to be cause and effect of each other. And the same succession also refutes Kant's false assertion that the *objective* reality of a succession is only known when we apprehend the two succeeding events as standing in the relation of cause and effect to each other. Indeed the converse of this doctrine of Kant's is true. We know which of the two connected events is the cause and which the effect, *empirically,* only in the succession. Again, on the other hand, the absurd assertion of several professors of philosophy in our own day that cause and effect are simultaneous can be refuted by the fact that in cases in which the succession cannot be perceived on account of its great rapidity, we yet assume it with

certainty *a priori*, and with it the lapse of a certain time.
Thus, for example, we know that a certain time must
elapse between the falling of the flint and the projection
of the bullet, although we cannot perceive it, and that
this time must further be divided between several events
that occur in a strictly determined succession—the falling of the flint, the striking of the spark, ignition, the
spread of the fire, the explosion, and the projection of the
bullet. No man ever perceived this succession of events;
but because we know which is the cause of the others, we
thereby also know which must *precede the others in time*,
and consequently also that during the course of the whole
series a certain time must elapse, although it is so short
that it escapes our empirical apprehension; for no one
will assert that the projection of the bullet is actually
simultaneous with the falling of the flint. Thus not only
the law of causality, but also its relation to *time*, and the
necessity of the *succession* of cause and effect, is known to
us *a priori*. If we know which of two events is the cause
and which is the effect, we also know which precedes the
other in time ; if, on the contrary, we do not know which
is cause and which effect, but only know in general that
they are causally connected, we seek to discover the succession empirically, and according to that we determine
which is the cause and which the effect. The falseness of
the assertion that cause and effect are simultaneous further
appears from the following consideration. An unbroken
chain of causes and effects fills the whole of time. (For
if this chain were broken the world would stand still, or
in order to set it in motion again an effect without a cause
would have to appear.) Now if every effect were simultaneous with its cause, then every effect would be moved
up into the time of its cause, and a chain of causes and
effects containing as many links as before would fill no
time at all, still less an infinite time, but would be all
together in one moment. Thus, under the assumption that
cause and effect are simultaneous, the course of the world

shrinks up into an affair of a moment. This proof is analogous to the proof that every sheet of paper must have a certain thickness, because otherwise the whole book would have none. To say *when* the cause ceases and the effect begins is in almost all cases difficult, and often impossible. For the *changes* (*i.e.*, the succession of states) are continuous, like the time which they fill, and therefore also, like it, they are infinitely divisible. But their succession is as necessarily determined and as unmistakable as that of the moments of time itself, and each of them is called, with reference to the one which precedes it, "effect," and with reference to the one which follows it, "cause."

Every change in the material world can only take place because another has immediately preceded it: this is the true and the whole content of the law of causality. But no conception has been more misused in philosophy than that of *cause*, by means of the favourite trick or blunder of conceiving it too widely, taking it too generally, through abstract thinking. Since Scholasticism, indeed properly since Plato and Aristotle, philosophy has been for the most part a *systematic misuse of general conceptions*. Such, for example, are substance, ground, cause, the good, perfection, necessity, and very many others. A tendency of the mind to work with such abstract and too widely comprehended conceptions has shown itself almost at all times. It may ultimately rest upon a certain indolence of the intellect, which finds it too difficult a task to be constantly controlling thought by perception. By degrees such unduly wide conceptions come to be used almost like algebraical symbols, and tossed about like them, and thus philosophy is reduced to a mere process of combination, a kind of reckoning which (like all calculations) employs and demands only the lower faculties. Indeed there finally results from this a mere juggling with words, of which the most shocking example is afforded us by the mind-destroying Hegelism, in which it is carried to the extent of pure nonsense. But Scholasticism also often degenerated into word-juggling. Nay even the "Topi" of Aristotle—very abstract principles, conceived with absolute generality, which one could apply to the most different kinds of subjects, and always bring into the field in arguing either *pro* or *contra*—have also their origin in this misuse of general conceptions. We find innumerable examples of the way the Schoolmen worked with such abstractions in their writings, especially in those of Thomas Aquinas. But philosophy really pursued the path which was entered on by the Schoolmen down to the time of Locke and Kant, who at last bethought themselves as to the origin of conceptions. Indeed we find Kant himself, in his earlier years, still upon that path, in his " Proof of the Existence of God" (p. 191 of the first volume of Rosenkranz's edition), where the conceptions substance, ground, reality, are used in such a way as would never have been possible if he had gone back to the *source* of these conceptions and to their *true content* which is determined thereby. For then he would have found as the source and content of *substance* simply matter, of ground (if things of the real world are in question) simply cause, that is, the prior change which brings about the later change, &c. It is true that in this case such an investigation would not have led to the intended result. But everywhere, as here, such unduly wide conceptions, under which, therefore, more was subsumed than their true content would have justified, there have arisen false principles, and from these false systems. Spinoza's whole method of demonstration rests upon such uninvestigated and too widely comprehended conceptions. Now here lies the great merit of Locke, who, in order to counteract all that dogmatic unreality, insisted upon the investigation of the *origin of the conceptions*, and thus led back to *perception and experience*. Bacon had worked in a similar frame of mind, yet more with reference to Physics than to Metaphysics. Kant followed the path entered upon by Locke, but in a higher sense and much further, as has already been mentioned above. To the men of mere show who succeeded in diverting the attention of the public from Kant to themselves the results obtained by Locke and Kant were inconvenient. But in such a case they know how to ignore both the dead and the living. Thus without hesitation they forsook the only right path which had at last been found by those wise men, and philosophised at random with all kinds of indiscriminately collected conceptions, unconcerned as to their origin and content, till at last the substance of the Hegelian philosophy, wise beyond measure, was that the conceptions had no origin at all, but were rather themselves the origin and source of things. But Kant has erred in this respect. He has too much neglected empirical perception for the sake of *pure* perception—a point which I have fully discussed in my criticism of his philosophy. With me perception is throughout the source of all knowledge. I early recognised the misleading and insidious nature of abstractions, and in 1813, in my essay on the principle of sufficient reason, I pointed out the difference of the relations which are thought under *this* conception. General conceptions must indeed be the material in which philosophy deposits and stores up its knowledge, but not the source from which it draws it; the *terminus ad quem*, not *a quo*. It is not, as Kant defines it, a science *drawn from* conceptions, but a science *in* conceptions. Thus the conception of causality also, with which we are here concerned, has always been taken far too widely by philosophers for the furtherance of their dogmatic ends, and much was imported into it which does not belong to it at all. Hence arose propositions such as the following: "All that is has its cause"—"the effect cannot contain more than the cause, thus nothing that was not also in the cause"—"*causa est nobilior suo effectu*," and many others just as unwarranted. The following subtilty of that insipid gossip Proclus affords an elaborate and specially lucid example of this. It occurs in his "*Institutio Theologica*," § 76: "Παν το απο ακινητου γιγνο-

μενον αιτιας, αμεταβλητον εχει την ὑπαρξιν· παν δε το απο
κινουμενης, μεταβλητην· ει γαρ ακινητον εστι παντη το
ποιουν, ου δια κινησεως, αλλ᾽ αυτῳ τῳ ειναι παραγει το
δευτερον αφ᾽ ἑαυτου." (*Quidquid ab immobili causa manat,
immutabilem habet essentiam [substantiam]. Quidquid vero
a mobili causa manat, essentiam habet mutabilem. Si enim
illud, quod aliquid facit, est prorsus immobile, non per
motum, sed per ipsum Esse producit ipsum secundum ex se
ipso.*) Excellent! But just show me a cause which is not
itself set in motion: it is simply impossible. But here,
as in so many cases, abstraction has thought away all
determinations down to that one which it is desired to
make use of without regard to the fact that the latter
cannot exist without the former. The only correct expression of the law of causality is this: *Every change has
its cause in another change which immediately precedes it.*
If something *happens, i.e.,* if a new state of things appears,
i.e., if something is *changed*, then something else must
have *changed* immediately before, and something else again
before this, and so on *ad infinitum,* for a *first* cause is as
impossible to conceive as a beginning of time or a limit
of space. More than this the law of causality does not
assert. Thus its claims only arise in the case of *changes.*
So long as nothing changes there can be no question of
a cause. For there is no *a priori* ground for inferring
from the existence of given things, *i.e.,* states of matter,
their previous non-existence, and from this again their
coming into being, that is to say, there is no *a priori*
ground for inferring a change. Therefore the mere existence of a thing does not justify us in inferring that it
has a cause. Yet there may be *a posteriori* reasons,
that is, reasons drawn from previous experience, for the
assumption that the present state or condition did not
always exist, but has only come into existence in consequence of another state, and therefore by means of a
change, the cause of which is then to be sought, and also
the cause of this cause. Here then we are involved in

the *infinite regressus* to which the application of the law
of causality always leads. We said above : " *Things,* i.e.,
states or conditions of matter," for *change* and *causality*
have only to do with states or conditions. It is these
states which we understand by *form,* in the wider sense;
and only the forms change, the matter is permanent.
Thus it is only the form which is subject to the law of
causality. But the form constitutes the *thing, i.e.,* it is
the ground of *the difference* of things ; while matter must
be thought as the same in all. Therefore the Schoolmen said, "*Forma dat esse rei;*" more accurately this
proposition would run : *Forma dat rei essentiam, materia
existentiam.* Therefore the question as to the cause of a
thing always concerns merely its form, *i.e.,* its state or
quality, and not its matter, and indeed only the former so
far as we have grounds for assuming that it has not *always*
existed, but has come into being by means of a *change.* The
union of *form* and *matter,* or of *essentia* and *existentia,* gives
the *concrete,* which is always particular ; thus, the *thing.*
And it is the *forms* whose union with *matter, i.e.,* whose
appearance in matter by means of a *change,* are subject to
the law of causality. By taking the conception *too widely*
in the abstract the mistake slipped in of extending causality
to the thing absolutely, that is, to its whole inner nature
and existence, thus also to matter, and ultimately it was
thought justifiable to ask for a cause of the world itself.
This is the origin of the *cosmological proof.* This proof
begins by inferring from the existence of the world its
non-existence, which preceded its existence, and such an
inference is quite unjustifiable ; it ends, however, with the
most fearful inconsistency, for it does away altogether with
the law of causality, from which alone it derives all its
evidencing power, for it stops at a first cause, and will not
go further ; thus ends, as it were, by committing parricide,
as the bees kill the drones after they have served their
end. All the talk about the *absolute* is referable to a
shamefast, and therefore disguised cosmological proof,

which, in the face of the "Critique of Pure Reason," has
passed for philosophy in Germany for the last sixty years.
What does the absolute mean ?   Something that is, and of
which (under pain of punishment) we dare not ask further
whence and why it is.   A precious rarity for professors of
philosophy !   In the case, however, of the honestly expressed cosmological proof, through the assumption of a
first cause, and therefore of a first beginning in a time
which has absolutely no beginning, this beginning is always
pushed further back by the question : Why not earlier ?
And so far back indeed that one never gets down from
it to the present, but is always marvelling that the present
itself did not occur already millions of years ago.   In
general, then, the law of causality applies to all things in
the world, but not to the world itself, for it is *immanent*
in the world, not *transcendent ; with* it it comes into
action, and *with* it it is abolished.   This depends ultimately
upon the fact that it belongs to the mere form of our
understanding, like the whole of the objective world,
which accordingly is merely phenomenal, and is conditioned by the understanding.   Thus the law of causality
has full application, without any exception, to all things in
the world, of course in respect of their form, to the variation
of these forms, and thus to their changes.   It is valid for
the actions of men as for the impact of a stone, yet, as we
have said always, merely with regard to events, to *changes.*
But if we abstract from its origin in the understanding
and try to look at it as purely objective, it will be found
in ultimate analysis to depend upon the fact that everything that acts does so by virtue of its original, and
therefore eternal or timeless, power ; therefore its present
effect would necessarily have occurred infinitely earlier,
that is, before all conceivable time, but that it lacked the
temporal condition.   This temporal condition is the occasion, *i.e.,* the cause, on account of which alone the effect
only takes place *now,* but now takes place necessarily ;
the cause assigns it its place in time.

But in consequence of that unduly wide view in abstract thought of the conception *cause*, which was considered above, it has been confounded with the conception of *force*. This is something completely different from the cause, but yet is that which imparts to every cause its causality, *i.e.*, the capability of producing an effect. I have explained this fully and thoroughly in the second book of the first volume, also in "The Will in Nature," and finally also in the second edition of the essay on the principle of sufficient reason, § 20, p. 44 (third edition, p. 45). This confusion is to be found in its most aggravated form in Maine de Biran's book mentioned above, and this is dealt with more fully in the place last referred to; but apart from this it is also very common; for example, when people seek for the cause of any original force, such as gravitation. Kant himself (*Über den Einzig Möglichen Beweisgrund*, vol. i. p. 211–215 of Rosenkranz's edition) calls the forces of nature "efficient causes," and says "gravity is a cause." Yet it is impossible to see to the bottom of his thought so long as force and cause are not distinctly recognised as completely different. But the use of abstract conceptions leads very easily to their confusion if the consideration of their origin is set aside. The knowledge of causes and effects, always *perceptive*, which rests on the form of the understanding, is neglected in order to stick to the abstraction *cause*. In this way alone is the conception of causality, with all its simplicity, so very frequently wrongly apprehended. Therefore even in Aristotle ("Metaph.," iv. 2) we find causes divided into four classes which are utterly falsely, and indeed crudely conceived. Compare with it my classification of causes as set forth for the first time in my essay on sight and colour, chap. 1, and touched upon briefly in the sixth paragraph of the first volume of the present work, but expounded at full length in my prize essay on the freedom of the will, p. 30–33. Two things in nature remain untouched by that chain of causality which stretches into infinity in both directions; these are matter and the forces of nature. They are both conditions of causality, while everything else is conditioned by it. For the one (matter) is that *in* which the states and their changes appear; the other (forces of nature) is that by virtue of which alone they can appear at all. Here, however, one must remember that in the second book, and later and more thoroughly in "The Will in Nature," the natural forces are shown to be identical with the will in us; but matter appears as the mere *visibility of the will;* so that ultimately it also may in a certain sense be regarded as identical with the will.

On the other hand, not less true and correct is what is explained in § 4 of the first book, and still better in the second edition of the essay on the principle of sufficient reason at the end of § 21, p. 77 (third edition, p. 82), that matter is causality itself objectively comprehended, for its entire nature consists in *acting in general*, so that it itself is thus the activity (ενεργεια = reality) of things generally, as it were the abstraction of all their different kinds of acting. Accordingly, since the essence, *essentia*, of matter consists in *action in general*, and the reality, *existentia*, of things consists in their materiality, which thus again is one with action in general, it may be asserted of matter that in it *existentia* and *essentia* unite and are one, for it has no other attribute than *existence itself* in general and independent of all fuller definitions of it. On the other hand, all *empirically* given matter, thus all material or matter in the special sense (which our ignorant materialists at the present day confound with matter), has already entered the framework of the *forms* and manifests itself only through their qualities and accidents, because in experience every action is of quite a definite and special kind, and is never merely general. Therefore pure matter is an object of *thought* alone, not of *perception*, which led Plotinus (*Enneas II.*, lib. iv., c. 8 & 9) and Giordano Bruno (*Della Causa*, dial. 4) to make the paradoxical assertion that

matter has no extension, for extension is inseparable from
the form, and that therefore it is *incorporeal.* Yet Aristotle
had already taught that it is not a body although it is
corporeal : *"σωμα μεν ουκ αν ειη, σωματικη δε"* (*Stob. Ecl.,*
lib. i., c. 12, § 5). In reality we think under *pure matter*
only action, in the abstract, quite independent of the *kind*
of action, thus *pure causality* itself; and as such it is not
an *object* but a *condition* of experience, just like space and
time. This is the reason why in the accompanying table
of our pure *a priori* knowledge matter is able to take the
place of causality, and therefore appears along with space
and time as the third pure form, and therefore as dependent on our intellect.

This table contains all the fundamental truths which
are rooted in our perceptive or intuitive knowledge *a priori,*
expressed as first principles independent of each other.
What is special, however, what forms the content of
arithmetic and geometry, is not given here, nor yet what
only results from the union and application of those
formal principles of knowledge. This is the subject of
the "Metaphysical First Principles of Natural Science"
expounded by Kant, to which this table in some measure
forms the propædutic and introduction, and with which it
therefore stands in direct connection. In this table I have
primarily had in view the very remarkable *parallelism* of
those *a priori* principles of knowledge which form the
framework of all experience, but specially also the fact
that, as I have explained in § 4 of the first volume, matter
(and also causality) is to be regarded as a combination, or
if it is preferred, an amalgamation, of space and time. In
agreement with this, we find that what geometry is for the
pure perception or intuition of space, and arithmetic for
that of time, Kant's *phoronomy* is for the pure perception
or intuition of the two *united.* For matter is primarily
that which is movable in space. The mathematical point
cannot even be conceived as movable, as Aristotle has
shown ("Physics," vi. 10). This philosopher also himself

provided the first example of such a science, for in the fifth and sixth books of his " Physics " he determined *a priori* the laws of rest and motion.

Now this table may be regarded at pleasure either as a collection of the eternal laws of the world, and therefore as the basis of our ontology, or as a chapter of the physiology of the brain, according as one assumes the realistic or the idealistic point of view; but the second is in the last instance right. On this point, indeed, we have already come to an understanding in the first chapter; yet I wish further to illustrate it specially by an example. Aristotle's book "*De Xenophane,*" &c., commences with these weighty words of Xenophanes: "*Αϊδιον ειναι φησιν, ει τι εστιν, ειπερ μη ενδεχεται γενεσθαι μηδεν εκ μηδενος.*" (*Æternum esse, inquit, quicquid est, siquidem fieri non potest, ut ex nihilo quippiam existat.*) Here, then, Xenophanes judges as to the origin of things, as regards its possibility, and of this origin he can have had no experience, even by analogy; nor indeed does he appeal to experience, but judges apodictically, and therefore *a priori.* How can he do this if as a stranger he looks from without into a world that exists purely objectively, that is, independently of his knowledge? How can he, an ephemeral being hurrying past, to whom only a hasty glance into such a world is permitted, judge apodictically, *a priori* and without experience concerning that world, the possibility of its existence and origin? The solution of this riddle is that the man has only to do with his own ideas, which as such are the work of his brain, and the constitution of which is merely the manner or mode in which alone the function of his brain can be fulfilled, *i.e.*, the form of his perception. He thus judges only as to the *phenomena of his own brain,* and declares what enters into its forms, time, space, and causality, and what does not. In this he is perfectly at home and speaks apodictically. In a like sense, then, the following table of the *Prædicabilia a priori* of time, space, and matter is to be taken :—

PRÆDICABILIA *A PRIORI.*

Of Time.	Of Space.	Of Matter.
(1) There is only *one* Time, and all different times are parts of it.	(1) There is only *one* Space, and all different spaces are parts of it.	(1) There is only *one* Matter, and all different materials are different states of matter ; as such it is called *Substance.*
(2) Different times are not simultaneous but successive.	(2) Different spaces are not successive but simultaneous.	(2) Different matters (materials) are not so through substance but through accidents.
(3) Time cannot be thought away, but everything can be thought away from it.	(3) Space cannot be thought away, but everything can be thought away from it.	(3) Annihilation of matter is inconceivable, but annihilation of all its forms and qualities is conceivable.
(4) Time has three divisions, the past, the present, and the future, which constitute two directions and a centre of indifference.	(4) Space has three dimensions — height, breadth, and length.	(4) Matter exists, *i.e.*, acts in all the dimensions of space and throughout the whole length of time, and thus these two are united and thereby filled. In this consists the true nature of matter ; thus it is through and through causality.
(5) Time is infinitely divisible.	(5) Space is infinitely divisible.	(5) Matter is infinitely divisible.
(6) Time is homogeneous and a *Continuum*, *i.e.*, no one of its parts is different from the rest, nor separated from it by anything that is not time.	(6) Space is homogeneous and a *Continuum*, *i.e.*, no one of its parts is different from the rest, nor separated from it by anything that is not space.	(6) Matter is homogeneous and a *Continuum*, *i.e.*, it does not consist of originally different (*homoiomeria*) or originally separated parts (atoms) ; it is therefore not composed of parts, which would necessarily be separated by something that was not matter.
(7) Time has no beginning and no end, but all beginning and end is in it.	(7) Space has no limits, but all limits are in it.	(7) Matter has no origin and no end, but all coming into being and passing away are in it.
(8) By reason of time we count.	(8) By reason of space we measure.	(8) By reason of matter we weigh.
(9) Rhythm is only in time.	(9) Symmetry is only in space.	(9) Equilibrium is only in matter.
(10) We know the laws of time *a priori.*	(10) We know the laws of space *a priori.*	(10) We know the laws of the substance of all accidents *a priori.*

Of Time.	Of Space.	Of Matter.
(11) Time can be perceived *a priori*, although only in the form of a line.	(11) Space is immediately perceptible *a priori*.	(11) Matter can only be thought *a priori*.
(12) Time has no permanence, but passes away as soon as it is there.	(12) Space can never pass away, but endures through all time.	(12) The accidents change; the substance remains.
(13) Time never rests.	(13) Space is immovable.	(13) Matter is indifferent to rest and motion ; *i.e.*, it is originally disposed towards neither of the two.
(14) Everything that exists in time has duration.	(14) Everything that exists in space has a position.	(14) Everything material has the capacity for action.
(15) Time has no duration, but all duration is in it, and is the persistence of what is permanent in contrast with its restless course.	(15) Space has no motion, but all motion is in it, and it is the change of position of what is moved, in contrast with its unbroken rest.	(15) Matter is what is permanent in time and movable in space ; by the comparison of what rests with what is moved we measure duration.
(16) All motion is only possible in time.	(16) All motion is only possible in space.	(16) All motion is only possible to matter.
(17) Velocity is, in equal spaces, in inverse proportion to the time.	(17) Velocity is, in equal times, in direct proportion to the space.	(17) The magnitude of the motion, the velocity being equal, is in direct geometrical proportion to the matter (mass).
(18) Time is not measurable directly through itself, but only indirectly through motion, which is in space and time together : thus the motion of the sun and of the clock measure time.	(18) Space is measurable directly through itself, and indirectly through motion, which is in time and space together : hence, for example, an hour's journey, and the distance of the fixed stars expressed as the travelling of light for so many years.	(18) Matter as such (mass) is measurable, *i.e.*, determinable as regards its quantity only indirectly, only through the amount of the motion which it receives and imparts when it is repelled or attracted.
(19) Time is omnipresent. Every part of time is everywhere, *i.e.*, in all space, at once.	(19) Space is eternal. Every part of it exists always.	(19) Matter is absolute. That is, it neither comes into being nor passes away, and thus its quantity can neither be increased nor diminished.

Of Time.	Of Space.	Of Matter.
(20) In time taken by itself everything would be in succession.	(20) In space taken by itself everything would be simultaneous.	(20, 21) Matter unites the ceaseless flight of time with the rigid immobility of space ; therefore it is the permanent substance of the changing accidents. Causality determines this change for every place at every time, and thereby combines time and space, and constitutes the whole nature of matter.
(21) Time makes the change of accidents possible.	(21) Space makes the permanence of substance possible.	
(22) Every part of time contains all parts of matter.	(22) No part of space contains the same matter as another.	(22) For matter is both permanent and impenetrable.
(23) Time is the *principium individuationis.*	(23) Space is the *principium individuationis.*	(23) Individuals are material.
(24) The now has no duration.	(24) The point has no extension.	(24) The **atom** has no reality.
(25) Time in itself is empty and without properties.	(25) Space in itself is empty and without properties.	(25) Matter in itself is without form and quality, and likewise inert, *i.e.,* indifferent to rest or motion, thus without properties.
(26) Every moment is conditioned by the preceding moment, and is only because the latter has ceased to be. (Principle of sufficient reason of existence in time.—See my essay on the principle of sufficient reason.)	(26) By the position of every limit in space with reference to any other limit, its position with reference to every possible limit is precisely determined. (Principle of sufficient reason of existence in space.)	(26) Every change in matter can take place only on account of another change which preceded it ; and therefore a first change, and thus also a first state of matter, is just as inconceivable as a beginning of time or a limit of space. (Principle of sufficient reason of becoming.)
(27) Time makes arithmetic possible.	(27) Space makes geometry possible.	(27) Matter, as that which is movable in space, makes phoronomy possible.
(28) The simple element in arithmetic is unity.	(28) The simple element in geometry is the point.	(28) The simple element in phoronomy is the atom.

NOTES TO THE ANNEXED TABLE.

(1) *To No. 4 of Matter.*

The essence of matter is acting, it is acting itself, in the abstract, thus acting in general apart from all difference of the kind of action : it is through and through causality. On this account it is itself, as regards its existence, not subject to the law of causality, and thus has neither come into being nor passes away, for otherwise the law of causality would be applied to itself. Since now causality is known to us *a priori*, the conception of matter, as the indestructible basis of all that exists, can so far take its place in the knowledge we possess *a priori*, inasmuch as it is only the realisation of an *a priori* form of our knowledge. For as soon as we see anything that acts or is causally efficient it presents itself *eo ipso* as material, and conversely anything material presents itself as necessarily active or causally efficient. They are in fact interchangeable conceptions. Therefore the word "actual" is used as synonymous with "material;" and also the Greek κατ᾽ ενεργειαν, in opposition to κατα δυναμιν, reveals the same source, for ενεργεια signifies action in general; so also with *actu* in opposition to *potentia*, and the English "actually" for "*wirklich.*" What is called space-occupation, or impenetrability, and regarded as the essential predicate of body (*i.e.* of what is material), is merely that *kind of action* which belongs to *all* bodies without exception, the mechanical. It is this universality alone, by virtue of which it belongs to the conception of body, and follows *a priori* from this conception, and therefore cannot be thought away from it without doing away with the conception itself—it is this, I say, that distinguishes it from any other kind of action, such as that of electricity or chemistry, or light or heat. Kant has very accurately analysed this space-occupation of the mechanical mode of activity into repulsive and attractive force, just as a given mechanical force is analysed into two others by means of the parallelogram of forces. But this is really only the thoughtful analysis of the phenomenon into its two constituent parts. The two forces in conjunction exhibit the body within its own limits, that is, in a definite volume, while the one alone would diffuse it into infinity, and the other alone would contract it to a point. Notwithstanding this reciprocal balancing or neutralisation, the body still acts upon other bodies which contest its space with the first force, repelling them, and with the other force, in gravitation, attracting all bodies in general. So that the two forces are not extinguished in their product, as, for instance, two equal forces acting in different directions, or + E and – E, or oxygen and hydrogen in water. That impenetrability and gravity really exactly coincide is shown by their empirical inseparableness. in that the one never appears without the other, although we can separate them in thought.

I must not, however, omit to mention that the doctrine of Kant referred to, which forms the fundamental thought of the second part of his "Metaphysical First Principles of Natural Science," thus of the Dynamics, was distinctly and fully expounded before Kant by Priestley, in his excellent "Disquisitions on Matter and Spirit," § 1 and 2, a book which appeared in 1777, and the second edition in 1782, while Kant's work was published in 1786. Unconscious recollection may certainly be assumed in the case of subsidiary thoughts, flashes of wit, comparisons, &c., but not in the case of the principal and fundamental thought. Shall we then believe that Kant silently appropriated such important thoughts of another man? and this from a book which at that time was new? Or that this book was unknown to him, and that the same thoughts sprang up in two minds within a short time? The explanation, also, which Kant gives, in the "Metaphysical First Principles of Natural Science" (first edition, p. 88; Rosenkranz's edition, p. 384), of the real difference between fluids and solids, is in substance already to be found in Kaspar Freidr. Wolff's "Theory of Generation," Berlin 1764, p. 132. But what are we to say if we find Kant's most important and brilliant doctrine, that of the ideality of space and the merely phenomenal existence of the corporeal world, already expressed by Maupertuis thirty years earlier? This will be found more fully referred to in Frauenstädt's letters on my philosophy, Letter 14. Maupertuis expresses this paradoxical doctrine so decidedly, and yet without adducing any proof of it, that one must suppose that he also took it from somewhere else. It is very desirable that the matter should be further investigated, and as this would demand tiresome and extensive researches, some German Academy might very well make the question the subject of a prize essay. Now in the same relation as that in which Kant here stands to Priestley, and perhaps also to Kaspar Wolff, and Maupertuis or his predecessor, Laplace stands to Kant. For the principal and fundamental thought of Laplace's admirable and certainly correct theory of the origin of the planetary system, which is set forth in his *"Exposition du Système du Monde,"* liv. v. c. 2, was expressed by Kant nearly fifty years before, in 1755, in his *"Naturgeschichte und Theorie des Himmels,"* and more fully in 1763 in his *"Einzig möglichen Beweisgrund des Daseyns Gottes,"* ch. 7. Moreover, in the later work he gives us to understand that Lambert in his *"Kosmologischen Briefen,"* 1761, tacitly adopted that doctrine from him, and these letters at the same time also appeared in French (*Lettres Cosmologiques sur la Constitution de l'Univers*). We are therefore obliged to assume that Laplace knew that Kantian doctrine. Certainly he expounds the matter more thoroughly, strikingly, and fully, and at the same time more simply than Kant, as is natural from his more profound astronomical knowledge; yet in the main it is to be found clearly expressed in Kant, and on account of the importance of the matter, would alone have been sufficient to make his name immortal. It cannot but disturb us very much if we find minds of the first order under suspicion of dishonesty, which would be a scandal to those of the lowest order. For we feel that theft is even more inexcusable in a rich man than in a poor one. We dare not, however, be silent; for here we are posterity, and must be just, as we hope that posterity will some day be just to us. Therefore, as a third example, I will add to these cases, that the fundamental thoughts of the "Metamorphosis of Plants," by Goethe, were already expressed by Kaspar Wolff in 1764 in his "Theory of Generation," p. 148, 229, 243, &c. Indeed, is it otherwise with the *system of gravitation?* the discovery of which is on the Continent of Europe always ascribed to Newton, while in England the learned at least know very well that it belongs to Robert Hooke, who in the year 1666, in a "Communication to the Royal Society," expounds it quite distinctly, although only as an hypothesis and without proof. The principal passage of this communication is quoted in Dugald Stewart's "Philosophy of the Human Mind," and is probably taken from Robert Hooke's Posthumous Works. The history of the matter, and how Newton got into difficulty by it, is also to be found in the "*Biographie Universelle*," article Newton. Hooke's priority is treated as an established fact in a short history of astronomy, *Quarterly Review*, August 1828. Further details on this subject are to be found in my "*Parerga*," vol. ii., § 86 (second edition, § 88). The story of the fall of an apple is a fable as groundless as it is popular, and is quite without authority.

(2) *To No.* 18 *of Matter.*

The *quantity of a motion* (*quantitas motus*, already in Descartes) is the product of the mass into the velocity.

This law is the basis not only of the doctrine of impact in mechanics, but also of that of equilibrium in statics. From the force of impact which two bodies with the same velocity exert the relation of their masses to each other may be determined. Thus of two hammers striking with the same velocity, the one which has the greater mass will drive the nail deeper into the wall or the post deeper into the earth. For example, a hammer weighing six pounds with a velocity = 6 effects as much as a hammer weighing three pounds with a velocity = 12, for in both cases the quantity of motion or the momentum = 36. Of two balls rolling at the same pace, the one which has the greater mass will impel a third ball at rest to a greater distance than the ball of less mass can. For the mass of the first multiplied by the same velocity gives a *greater quantity of motion,* or a *greater momentum.* The cannon carries further than the gun, because an equal velocity communicated to a much greater mass gives a much *greater quantity of motion,* which resists longer the retarding effect of gravity. For the same reason, the same arm will throw a lead bullet further than a stone one of equal magnitude, or a large stone further than quite a small one. And therefore also a case-shot does not carry so far as a ball-shot.

The same law lies at the foundation of the theory of the lever and of the balance. For here also the smaller mass, on the longer arm of the lever or beam of the balance, has a greater velocity in falling; and multiplied by this it may be equal to, or indeed exceed, the *quantity of motion* or the *momentum* of the greater mass at the shorter arm of the lever. In the state of *rest* brought about by *equilibrium* this velocity exists merely in intention or virtually, *potentiâ,* not *actu ;* but it acts just as well as *actu,* which is very remarkable.

The following explanation will be more easily understood now that these truths have been called to mind.

The quantity of a given matter can only be estimated in general according to its force, and its force can only be known in its *expression.* Now when we are considering matter only as regards its quantity, not its quality, this expression can only be mechanical, *i.e.,* it can only consist in motion which it imparts to other matter. For only in motion does the force of matter become, so to speak, *alive ;* hence the expression *vis viva* for the manifestation of force of matter in motion. Accordingly the only measure of the quantity of a given matter is the *quantity of its motion,* or its *momentum.* In this, however, if it is given, the *quantity* of matter still appears in conjunction and amalgamated with its other factor, *velocity*. Therefore if we want to know the quantity of matter (the mass) this other factor must be eliminated. Now the velocity is known directly ; for it is $\frac{S}{T}$. But the other factor, which remains when this is eliminated, can always be known only *relatively* in comparison with other masses, which again can only be known themselves by means of the *quantity of their motion*, or their *momentum*, thus in their combination with velocity. We must therefore compare one *quantity of motion* with the other, and then subtract the velocity from both, in order to see how much each of them owed to its mass. This is done by weighing the masses against each other, in which that *quantity of motion* is compared which, in each of the two masses, calls forth the attractive power of the earth that acts upon both only in proportion to their *quantity*. Therefore there are two kinds of weighing. Either we impart to the two masses to be compared *equal* velocity, in order to find out which of the two now *communicates* motion to the other, thus itself *has* a greater quantity of motion, which, since the velocity is the same on both sides, is to be ascribed to the other factor of the *quantity of motion* or the *momentum*, thus to the mass (common balance). Or we weigh, by investigating how much *more velocity* the one mass must receive than the other has, in order to be equal to the latter in *quantity of motion* or *momentum*, and therefore allow no more motion to be communicated to itself by the other ; for then in proportion as its velocity must exceed that of the other, its mass, *i.e.*, the quantity of its matter, is less than that of the other (steelyard). This estimation of masses by weighing depends upon the favourable circumstance that the moving force, in itself, acts upon both quite equally, and each of the two is in a position to *communicate* to the other directly its surplus *quantity of motion* or *momentum*, so that it becomes visible.

The substance of these doctrines has long ago been expressed by Newton and Kant, but through the connection and the clearness of this exposition I believe I have made it more intelligible, so that that insight is possible for all which I regarded as necessary for the justification of proposition No. 18.

THE DOCTRINE OF THE ABSTRACT IDEA, OR THINKING.

CHAPTER V.[1]

ON THE IRRATIONAL INTELLECT.

IT must be possible to arrive at a complete knowledge of the consciousness of the brutes, for we can construct it by abstracting certain properties of our own consciousness. On the other hand, there enters into the consciousness of the brute instinct, which is much more developed in all of them than in man, and in some of them extends to what we call mechanical instinct.

The brutes have understanding without having reason, and therefore they have knowledge of perception but no abstract knowledge. They apprehend correctly, and also grasp the immediate causal connection, in the case of the higher species even through several links of its chain, but they do not, properly speaking, *think.* For they lack *conceptions,* that is, abstract ideas. The first consequence of this, however, is the want of a proper memory, which applies even to the most sagacious of the brutes, and it is just this which constitutes the principal difference between their consciousness and that of men. Perfect intelligence depends upon the distinct consciousness of the

---

[1] This chapter, along with the one which follows it, is connected with § 8 and 9 of the first book.

past and of the eventual future, *as such*, and in connection with the present. The special memory which this demands is therefore an orderly, connected, and thinking retrospective recollection. This, however, is only possible by means of *general conceptions*, the assistance of which is required by what is entirely individual, in order that it may be recalled in its order and connection. For the boundless multitude of things and events of the same and similar kinds, in the course of our life, does not admit directly of a perceptible and individual recollection of each particular, for which neither the powers of the most comprehensive memory nor our time would be sufficient. Therefore all this can only be preserved by subsuming it under general conceptions, and the consequent reference to relatively few principles, by means of which we then have always at command an orderly and adequate survey of our past. We can only present to ourselves in perception particular scenes of the past, but the time that has passed since then and its content we are conscious of only in the abstract by means of conceptions of things and numbers which now represent days and years, together with their content. The memory of the brutes, on the contrary, like their whole intellect, is confined to what they *perceive*, and primarily consists merely in the fact that a recurring impression presents itself as having already been experienced, for the present perception revivifies the traces of an earlier one. Their memory is therefore always dependent upon what is now actually present. Just on this account, however, this excites anew the sensation and the mood which the earlier phenomenon produced. Thus the dog recognises acquaintances, distinguishes friends from enemies, easily finds again the path it has once travelled, the houses it has once visited, and at the sight of a plate or a stick is at once put into the mood associated with them. All kinds of training depend upon the use of this perceptive memory and on the force of habit, which in the case of animals is specially strong. It is therefore just as different from human education as perception is from thinking. We ourselves are in certain cases, in which memory proper refuses us its service, confined to that merely perceptive recollection, and thus we can measure the difference between the two from our own experience. For example, at the sight of a person whom it appears to us we know, although we are not able to remember when or where we saw him; or again, when we visit a place where we once were in early childhood, that is, while our reason was yet undeveloped, and which we have therefore entirely forgotten, and yet feel that the present impression is one which we have already experienced. This is the nature of all the recollections of the brutes. We have only to add that in the case of the most sagacious this merely perceptive memory rises to a certain degree of *phantasy*, which again assists it, and by virtue of which, for example, the image of its absent master floats before the mind of the dog and excites a longing after him, so that when he remains away long it seeks for him everywhere. Its dreams also depend upon this phantasy. The consciousness of the brutes is accordingly a mere succession of presents, none of which, however, exist as future before they appear, nor as past after they have vanished; which is the specific difference of human consciousness. Hence the brutes have infinitely less to *suffer* than we have, because they know no other pains but those which the *present* directly brings. But the present is without extension, while the future and the past, which contain most of the causes of our suffering, are widely extended, and to their actual content there is added that which is merely possible, which opens up an unlimited field for desire and aversion. The brutes, on the contrary, undisturbed by these, enjoy quietly and peacefully each present moment, even if it is only bearable. Human beings of very limited capacity perhaps approach them in this. Further, the sufferings which belong *purely* to the present can only be physical. Indeed the brutes do not properly speaking feel death: they can only know it when it appears, and then they are already no more. Thus then the life of the brute is a continuous present. It lives on without reflection, and exists wholly in the present; even the great majority of men live with very little reflection. Another consequence of the special nature of the intellect of the brutes, which we have explained is the perfect accordance of their consciousness with their environment. Between the brute and the external world there is nothing, but between us and the external world there is always our thought about it, which makes us often inapproachable to it, and it to us. Only in the case of children and very primitive men is this wall of partition so thin that in order to see what goes on in them we only need to see what goes on round about them. Therefore the brutes are incapable alike of purpose and dissimulation; they reserve nothing. In this respect the dog stands to the man in the same relation as a glass goblet to a metal one, and this helps greatly to endear the dog so much to us, for it affords us great pleasure to see all those inclinations and emotions which we so often conceal displayed simply and openly in him. In general, the brutes always play, as it were, with their hand exposed; and therefore we contemplate with so much pleasure their behaviour towards each other, both when they belong to the same and to different species. It is characterised by a certain stamp of innocence, in contrast to the conduct of men, which is withdrawn from the innocence of nature by the entrance of reason, and with it of prudence or deliberation. Hence human conduct has throughout the stamp of intention or deliberate purpose, the absence of which, and the consequent determination by the impulse of the moment, is the fundamental characteristic of all the action of the brutes. No brute is capable of a purpose properly so-called. To conceive and follow out a purpose is the prerogative of man, and it is a prerogative which is rich in consequences. Certainly an instinct like that of the bird of passage or the

bee, still more a permanent, persistent desire, a longing like
that of the dog for its absent master, may present the
appearance of a purpose, with which, however, it must
not be confounded.   Now all this has its ultimate ground
in the relation between the human and the brute intellect, which may also be thus expressed : The brutes
have only *direct* knowledge, while we, in addition to
this, have *indirect* knowledge ; and the advantage which
in many things—for example, in trigonometry and
analysis, in machine work instead of hand work, &c.—
indirect has over direct knowledge appears here also.
Thus again we may say : The brutes have only a *single*
intellect, we a *double* intellect, both perceptive and thinking,
and the operation of the two often go on independently of
each other.   We perceive one thing, and we think another.
Often, again, they act upon each other.   This way of putting the matter enables us specially to understand that
natural openness and naivete of the brutes, referred to
above, as contrasted with the concealment of man.

However, the law *natura non facit saltus* is not entirely
suspended even with regard to the intellect of the brutes,
though certainly the step from the brute to the human
intelligence is the greatest which nature has made in the
production of her creatures.   In the most favoured individuals of the highest species of the brutes there certainly
sometimes appears, always to our astonishment, a faint
trace of reflection, reason, the comprehension of words, of
thought, purpose, and deliberation.   The most striking
indications of this kind are afforded by the elephant, whose
highly developed intelligence is heightened and supported
by an experience of a lifetime which sometimes extends
to two hundred years.   He has often given unmistakable
signs, recorded in well-known anecdotes, of premeditation,
which, in the case of brutes, always astonishes us more
than anything else.   Such, for instance, is the story of the
tailor on whom an elephant revenged himself for pricking
him with a needle.   I wish, however, to rescue from

oblivion a parallel case to this, because it has the advantage of being authenticated by judicial investigation. On the 27th of August 1830 there was held at Morpeth, in England, a coroner's inquest on the keeper, Baptist Bernhard, who was killed by his elephant. It appeared from the evidence that two years before he had offended the elephant grossly, and now, without any occasion, but on a favourable opportunity, the elephant had seized him and crushed him. (See the *Spectator* and other English papers of that day.) For special information on the intelligence of brutes I recommend Leroy's excellent book, " *Sur l'Intelligence des Animaux,*" *nouv. éd.* 1802.

CHAPTER VI.

ON THE DOCTRINE OF ABSTRACT OR RATIONAL
KNOWLEDGE.

THE outward impression upon the senses, together with the mood which it alone awakens in us, vanishes with the presence of the thing. Therefore these two cannot of themselves constitute *experience* proper, whose teaching is to guide our conduct for the future. The image of that impression which the imagination preserves is originally weaker than the impression itself, and becomes weaker and weaker daily, until in time it disappears altogether. There is only one thing which is not subject either to the instantaneous vanishing of the impression or to the gradual disappearance of its image, and is therefore free from the power of time. This is the *conception*. In it, then, the teaching of experience must be stored up, and it alone is suited to be a safe guide to our steps in life. Therefore Seneca says rightly, " *Si vis tibi omnia subjicere, te subjice rationi* " (Ep. 37). And I add to this that the essential condition of surpassing others in actual life is that we should reflect or deliberate. Such an important tool of the intellect as the *concept* evidently cannot be identical with the *word*, this mere sound, which as an impression of sense passes with the moment, or as a phantasm of hearing dies away with time. Yet the concept is an idea, the distinct consciousness and preservation of which are bound up with the word. Hence the Greeks called word, concept, relation, thought, and reason by the name of the first, ὁ λόγος. Yet the concept is perfectly different both from the word, to which it is joined, and from the perceptions, from which it has originated. It is of an entirely different nature from these impressions of the senses. Yet it is able to take up into itself all the results of perception, and give them back again unchanged and undiminished after the longest period of time; thus alone does *experience* arise. But the concept preserves, not what is perceived nor what is then felt, but only what is essential in these, in an entirely altered form, and yet as an adequate representative of them. Just as flowers cannot be preserved, but their ethereal oil, their essence, with the same smell and the same virtues, can be. The action that has been guided by correct conceptions will, in the result, coincide with the real object aimed at. We may judge of the inestimable value of conceptions, and consequently of the reason, if we glance for a moment at the infinite multitude and variety of the things and conditions that coexist and succeed each other, and then consider that speech and writing (the signs of conceptions) are capable of affording us accurate information as to everything and every relation when and wherever it may have been; for comparatively *few* conceptions can contain and represent an infinite number of things and conditions. In our own reflection *abstraction* is a throwing off of useless baggage for the sake of more easily handling the knowledge which is to be compared, and has therefore to be turned about in all directions. We allow much that is unessential, and therefore only confusing, to fall away from the real things, and work with few but essential determinations thought in the abstract. But just because general conceptions are only formed by thinking away and leaving out existing qualities, and are therefore the emptier the more general they are, the use of this procedure is confined to the *working up* of knowledge which we have already acquired. This working up includes the drawing of conclusions from premisses contained in our knowledge. New insight, on the contrary, can only be obtained by the help of the faculty of judgment, from perception, which alone is complete and rich knowledge. Further, because the content and the extent of the concepts stand in inverse relation to each other, and thus the more is thought *under* a concept, the less is thought *in* it, concepts form a graduated series, a hierarchy, from the most special to the most general, at the lower end of which scholastic realism is almost right, and at the upper end nominalism. For the most special conception is almost the individual, thus almost real; and the most general conception, *e.g.*, being (*i.e.*, the infinitive of the copula), is scarcely anything but a word. Therefore philosophical systems which confine themselves to such very general conceptions, without going down to the real, are little more than mere juggling with words. For since all abstraction consists in thinking away, the further we push it the less we have left over. Therefore, if I read those modern philosophemes which move constantly in the widest abstractions, I am soon quite unable, in spite of all attention, to think almost anything more in connection with them; for I receive no material for thought, but am supposed to work with mere empty shells, which gives me a feeling like that which we experience when we try to throw very light bodies; the strength and also the exertion are there, but there is no object to receive them, so as to supply the other moment of motion. If any one wants to experience this let him read the writings of the disciples of Schelling, or still better of the Hegelians. *Simple conceptions* would necessarily be such as could not be broken up. Accordingly they could never be the subject of an analytical judgment. This I hold to be impossible, for if we think a conception we must also be able to give its content. What are commonly adduced as examples of simple conceptions are really not conceptions at all, but partly mere sensations—as, for instance, those of some special colour; partly the forms of perception which are known to us *a priori*, thus properly the ultimate elements of *perceptive knowledge*. But this itself is for the whole system of our thought what granite is for geology, the ultimate firm basis which supports all, and beyond which we cannot go. The *distinctness* of a conception demands not only that we should be able to separate its predicates, but also that we should be able to analyse these even if they are abstractions, and so on until we reach knowledge of *perception*, and thus refer to concrete things through the distinct perception of which the final abstractions are verified and reality guaranteed to them, as well as to all the higher abstractions which rest upon them. Therefore the ordinary explanation that the conception is distinct as soon as we can give its predicates is not sufficient. For the separating of these predicates may lead perhaps to more conceptions ; and so on again without there being that ultimate basis of perceptions which imparts reality to all those conceptions. Take, for example, the conception "spirit," and analyse it into its predicates : "A thinking, willing, immaterial, simple, indestructible being that does not occupy space." Nothing is yet distinctly thought about it, because the elements of these conceptions cannot be verified by means of perceptions, for a thinking being without a brain is like a digesting being without a stomach. Only perceptions are, properly speaking, *clear*, not conceptions ; these at the most can only be distinct. Hence also, absurd as it was, "clear and confused" were coupled together and used as synonymous when knowledge of perception was explained as merely a confused abstract knowledge, because the latter kind of knowledge alone was distinct. This was first done by Duns Scotus, but Leibnitz has substantially the same view, upon which his "*Identitas Indiscernibilium*" depends. (See Kant's refutation of this, p. 275 of the first edition of the Critique of Pure Reason.)

The close connection of the conception with the word, thus of speech with reason, which was touched on above, rests ultimately upon the following ground. *Time* is throughout the form of our whole consciousness, with its inward and outward apprehension. Conceptions, on the other hand, which originate through abstraction and are perfectly general ideas, different from all particular things, have in this property indeed a certain measure of objective existence, which does not, however, belong to any series of events in time. Therefore in order to enter the immediate present of an individual consciousness, and thus to admit of being introduced into a series of events in time, they must to a certain extent be reduced again to the nature of individual things, individualised, and therefore linked to an idea of sense. Such an idea is the *word.* It is accordingly the sensible sign of the conception, and as such the necessary means of *fixing* it, that is, of presenting it to the consciousness, which is bound up with the form of time, and thus establishing a connection between the reason, whose objects are merely general universals, knowing neither place nor time, and consciousness, which is bound up with time, is sensuous, and so far purely animal. Only by this means is the reproduction at pleasure, thus the recollection and preservation, of conceptions possible and open to us; and only by means of this, again, are the operations which are undertaken with conceptions possible—judgment, inference, comparison, limitation, &c. It is true it sometimes happens that conceptions occupy consciousness without their signs, as when we run through a train of reasoning so rapidly that we could not think the words in the time. But such cases are exceptions, which presuppose great exercise of the reason, which it could only have obtained by means of language. How much the use of reason is bound up with speech we see in the case of the deaf and dumb, who, if they have learnt no kind of language, show scarcely more intelligence than the ourang-outang or the elephant. For their reason is almost entirely potential, not actual.

Words and speech are thus the indispensable means of distinct thought. But as every means, every machine, at once burdens and hinders, so also does language; for it forces the fluid and modifiable thoughts, with their infinitely fine distinctions of difference, into certain rigid, permanent forms, and thus in fixing also fetters them. This hindrance is to some extent got rid of by learning several languages. For in these the thought is poured from one mould into another, and somewhat alters its form in each, so that it becomes more and more freed from all form and clothing, and thus its own proper nature comes more distinctly into consciousness, and it recovers again its original capacity for modification. The ancient languages render this service very much better than the modern, because, on account of their great difference from the latter, the same thoughts are expressed in them in quite another way, and must thus assume a very different form; besides which the more perfect grammar of the ancient languages renders a more artistic and more perfect construction of the thoughts and their connection possible. Thus a Greek or a Roman might perhaps content himself with his own language, but he who understands nothing but some single modern patois will soon betray this poverty in writing and speaking; for his thoughts, firmly bound to such narrow stereotyped forms, must appear awkward and monotonous. Genius certainly makes up for this as for everything else, for example in Shakespeare.

Burke, in his "Inquiry into the Sublime and Beautiful," p. 5, § 4 and 5, has given a perfectly correct and very elaborate exposition of what I laid down in § 9 of the first volume, that the words of a speech are perfectly understood without calling up ideas of perception, pictures in our heads. But he draws from this the entirely false conclusion that we hear, apprehend, and make use of words without connecting with them any idea whatever; whereas he ought to have drawn the conclusion that all ideas are not perceptible images, but that precisely those ideas which must be expressed by means of words are abstract notions or conceptions, and these from their very nature are not perceptible. Just because words impart only general conceptions, which are perfectly different from ideas of perception, when, for example, an event is recounted all the hearers will receive the same conceptions ; but if afterwards they wish to make the incident clear to themselves, each of them will call up in his imagination a different *image* of it, which differs considerably from the correct image that is possessed only by the eye-witness. This is the primary reason (which, however, is accompanied by others) why every fact is necessarily distorted by being repeatedly told. The second recounter communicates conceptions which he has abstracted from the image of *his own* imagination, and from these conceptions the third now forms another image differing still more widely from the truth, and this again he translates into conceptions, and so the process goes on. Whoever is sufficiently matter of fact to stick to the conceptions imparted to him, and repeat them, will prove the most truthful reporter.

The best and most intelligent exposition of the essence and nature of conceptions which I have been able to find is in Thomas Reid's "Essays on the Powers of Human Mind," vol. ii., Essay 5, ch. 6. This was afterwards condemned by Dugald Stewart in his "Philosophy of the Human Mind." Not to waste paper I will only briefly remark with regard to the latter that he belongs to that large class who have obtained an undeserved reputation through favour and friends, and therefore I can only advise that not an hour should be wasted over the scribbling of this shallow writer.

The princely scholastic Pico de Mirandula already saw that reason is the faculty of abstract ideas, and understanding the faculty of ideas of perception. For in his book, "*De Imaginatione*," ch. 11, he carefully distinguishes understanding and reason, and explains the latter as the discursive faculty peculiar to man, and the former as the intuitive faculty, allied to the kind of knowledge which is proper to the angels, and indeed to God. Spinoza also characterises reason quite correctly as the faculty of framing general conceptions (Eth., ii. prop. 40, schol. 2). Such facts would not need to be mentioned if it were not for the tricks that have been played in the last fifty years by the whole of the philosophasters of Germany with the conception *reason*. For they have tried, with shameless audacity, to smuggle in under this name an entirely spurious faculty of immediate, metaphysical, so-called super-sensuous knowledge. The reason proper, on the other hand, they call *understanding*, and the understanding proper, as something quite strange to them, they overlook altogether, and ascribe its intuitive functions to sensibility.

In the case of all things in this world new drawbacks or disadvantages cleave to every source of aid, to every gain, to every advantage; and thus reason also, which gives to man such great advantages over the brutes, carries with it its special disadvantages, and opens for him paths of error into which the brutes can never stray. Through it a new species of motives, to which the brute is not accessible, obtains power over his will. These are the *abstract* motives, the mere thoughts, which are by no means always drawn from his own experience, but often come to him only through the talk and example of others, through tradition and literature. Having become accessible to thought, he is at once exposed to error. But every error must sooner or later do harm, and the greater the error the greater the harm it will do. The individual error must be atoned for by him who cherishes it, and often he has to pay dearly for it. And the same thing holds good on a large scale of the common errors of whole nations. Therefore it cannot too often be repeated that every error wherever we meet it, is to be pursued and rooted out as an enemy of mankind, and that there can be no such thing as privileged or sanctioned error. The thinker ought to attack it, even if humanity should cry out with pain, like a sick man whose ulcer the physician touches. The brute can never stray far from the path of nature; for its motives lie only in the world of perception, where only the possible, indeed only the actual, finds room.   On the other hand, all that is only imaginable, and therefore also the false, the impossible, the absurd, and senseless, enters into abstract conceptions, into thoughts and words. Since now all partake of reason, but few of judgment, the consequence is that man is exposed to delusion, for he is abandoned to every conceivable chimera which any one talks him into, and which, acting on his will as a motive, may influence him to perversities and follies of every kind, to the most unheard-of extravagances, and also to actions most contrary to his animal nature.   True culture, in which knowledge and judgment go hand in hand, can only be brought to bear on a few; and still fewer are capable of receiving it.   For the great mass of men a kind of training everywhere takes its place.   It is effected by example, custom, and the very early and firm impression of certain conceptions, before any experience, understanding, or judgment were there to disturb the work.   Thus thoughts are implanted, which afterward cling as firmly, and are as incapable of being shaken by any instruction as if they were *inborn;* and indeed they have often been regarded, even by philosophers, as such.   In this way we can, with the same trouble, imbue men with what is right and rational, or with what is most absurd.   For example, we can accustom them to approach this or that idol with holy dread, and at the mention of its name to prostrate in the dust not only their bodies but their whole spirit ; to sacrifice their property and their lives willingly to words, to names, to the defence of the strangest whims ; to attach arbitrarily the greatest honour or the deepest disgrace to this or that, and to prize highly or disdain everything accordingly with full inward conviction ; to renounce all animal food, as in Hindustan, or to devour still warm and quivering pieces, cut from the living animal, as in Abyssinia; to eat men, as in New Zealand, or to sacrifice their children to Moloch; to castrate themselves, to fling themselves voluntarily on the funeral piles of the dead—in a word, to do anything we please. Hence the Crusades, the extravagances of fanatical sects; hence Chiliasts and Flagellants, persecutions, *autos da fe*, and all that is offered by the long register of human perversities. Lest it should be thought that only the dark ages afford such examples, I shall add a couple of more modern instances. In the year 1818 there went from Würtemberg 7000 Chiliasts to the neighbourhood of Ararat, because the new kingdom of God, specially announced by Jung Stilling, was to appear there.[1] Gall relates that in his time a mother killed her child and roasted it in order to cure her husband's rheumatism with its fat.[2] The tragical side of error lies in the practical, the comical is reserved for the theoretical. For example, if we could firmly persuade three men that the sun is not the cause of daylight, we might hope to see it soon established as the general conviction. In Germany it was possible to proclaim as the greatest philosopher of all ages Hegel, a repulsive, mindless charlatan, an unparalleled scribbler of nonsense, and for twenty years many thousands have believed it stubbornly and firmly; and indeed, outside Germany, the Danish Academy entered the lists against myself for his fame, and sought to have him regarded as a *summus philosophus*. (Upon this see the preface to my *Grundproblemen der Ethik.*) These, then, are the disadvantages which, on account of the rarity of judgment, attach to the existence of reason. We must add to them the possibility of madness. The brutes do not go mad, although the carnivora are subject to fury, and the ruminants to a sort of delirium.

---

[1] Illgen's "*Zeitschrift für Historische Theologie,*" 1839, part i. p. 182.

[2] *Gall et Spurzheim, "Des Dispositions Innées,"* 1811, p. 253.

CHAPTER VII.[1]

ON THE RELATION OF THE CONCRETE KNOWLEDGE OF PERCEPTION TO ABSTRACT KNOWLEDGE.

IT has been shown that conceptions derive their material from knowledge of perception, and therefore the entire structure of our world of thought rests upon the world of perception. We must therefore be able to go back from every conception, even if only indirectly through intermediate conceptions, to the perceptions from which it is either itself directly derived or those conceptions are derived of which it is again an abstraction. That is to say, we must be able to support it with perceptions which stand to the abstractions in the relation of examples. These perceptions thus afford the real content of all our thought, and whenever they are wanting we have not had conceptions but mere words in our heads. In this respect our intellect is like a bank, which, if it is to be sound, must have cash in its safe, so as to be able to meet all the notes it has issued, in case of demand; the perceptions are the cash, the conceptions are the notes. In this sense the perceptions might very appropriately be called *primary*, and the conceptions, on the other hand, *secondary* ideas. Not quite so aptly, the Schoolmen, following the example of Aristotle (*Metaph.*, vi. 11, xi. 1), called real things *substantiæ primæ*, and the conceptions *substantiæ secundæ*. Books impart only secondary ideas. Mere conceptions of a thing without perception give only a general knowledge of it. We only have a thorough understanding of things and their relations so far as we are able to represent them

<hr>

[1] This chapter is connected with § 12 of the first volume.

to ourselves in pure, distinct perceptions, without the aid of words. To explain words by words, to compare concepts with concepts, in which most philosophising consists, is a trivial shifting about of the concept-spheres in order to see which goes into the other and which does not. At the best we can in this way only arrive at conclusions; but even conclusions give no really new knowledge, but only show us all that lay in the knowledge we already possessed, and what part of it perhaps might be applicable to the particular case. On the other hand, to perceive, to allow the things themselves to speak to us, to apprehend new relations of them, and then to take up and deposit all this in conceptions, in order to possess it with certainty—that gives new knowledge. But, while almost every one is capable of comparing conceptions with conceptions, to compare conceptions with perceptions is a gift of the select few. It is the condition, according to the degree of its perfection, of wit, judgment, ingenuity, genius. The former faculty, on the contrary, results in little more than possibly rational reflections. The inmost kernel of all genuine and actual knowledge is a perception; and every new truth is the profit or gain yielded by a perception. All original thinking takes place in images, and this is why imagination is so necessary an instrument of thought, and minds that lack imagination will never accomplish much, unless it be in mathematics. On the other hand, merely abstract thoughts, which have no kernel of perception, are like cloud-structures, without reality. Even writing and speaking, whether didactic or poetical, has for its final aim to guide the reader to the same concrete knowledge from which the author started; if it has not this aim it is bad. This is why the contemplation and observing of every real thing, as soon as it presents something new to the observer, is more instructive than any reading or hearing. For indeed, if we go to the bottom of the matter, all truth and wisdom, nay, the ultimate secret of things, is contained in each real object, yet certainly only *in concreto*, just as gold lies hidden in the ore; the difficulty is to extract it. From a book, on the contrary, at the best we only receive the truth at second hand, and oftener not at all.

In most books, putting out of account those that are thoroughly bad, the author, when their content is not altogether empirical, has certainly *thought* but not *perceived;* he has written from reflection, not from intuition, and it is this that makes them commonplace and tedious. For what the author has thought could always have been thought by the reader also, if he had taken the same trouble; indeed it consists simply of intelligent thought, full exposition of what is *implicite* contained in the theme. But no actually new knowledge comes in this way into the world; this is only created in the moment of perception, of direct comprehension of a new side of the thing. When, therefore, on the contrary, *sight* has formed the foundation of an author's thought, it is as if he wrote from a land where the reader has never been, for all is fresh and new, because it is drawn directly from the original source of all knowledge. Let me illustrate the distinction here touched upon by a perfectly easy and simple example. Any commonplace writer might easily describe profound contemplation or petrifying astonishment by saying: "He stood like a statue;" but Cervantes says: "Like a clothed statue, for the wind moved his garments" (*Don Quixote*, book vi. ch. 19). It is thus that all great minds have ever *thought in presence of the perception*, and kept their gaze steadfastly upon it in their thought. We recognise this from this fact, among others, that even the most opposite of them so often agree and coincide in some particular; because they all speak of the same thing which they all had before their eyes, the world, the perceived reality; indeed in a certain degree they all say the same thing, and others never believe them. We recognise it further in the appropriateness and originality of the expression, which is always perfectly adapted to the subject because it has been inspired by perception, in the naivete of the language, the freshness of the imagery, and the impressiveness of the similes, all of which qualities, without exception, distinguish the works of great minds, and, on the contrary, are always wanting in the works of others. Accordingly only commonplace forms of expression and trite figures are at the service of the latter, and they never dare to allow themselves to be natural, under penalty of displaying their vulgarity in all its dreary barrenness; instead of this they are affected mannerists. Hence Buffon says: "*Le style est l'homme même.*" If men of commonplace mind write poetry they have certain traditional conventional opinions, passions, noble sentiments, &c., which they have received in the abstract, and attribute to the heroes of their poems, who are in this way reduced to mere personifications of those opinions, and are thus themselves to a certain extent abstractions, and therefore insipid and tiresome. If they philosophise, they have taken in a few wide abstract conceptions, which they turn about in all directions, as if they had to do with algebraical equations, and hope that something will come of it; at the most we see that they have all read the same things. Such a tossing to and fro of abstract conceptions, after the manner of algebraical equations, which is now-a-days called dialectic, does not, like real algebra, afford certain results; for here the conception which is represented by the word is not a fixed and perfectly definite quality, such as are symbolised by the letters in algebra, but is wavering and ambiguous, and capable of extension and contraction. Strictly speaking, all thinking, *i.e.*, combining of abstract conceptions, has at the most the *recollections* of earlier perceptions for its material, and this only indirectly, so far as it constitutes the foundation of all conceptions. Real knowledge, on the contrary, that is, immediate knowledge, is perception alone, new, fresh perception itself. Now the concepts which the reason has framed and the memory has preserved cannot all be present to consciousness at once, but

only a very small number of them at a time. On the other
hand, the energy with which we apprehend what is present
in perception, in which really all that is essential in all
things generally is virtually contained and represented, is
apprehended, fills the consciousness in one moment with
its whole power. Upon this depends the infinite superiority
of genius to learning ; they stand to each other as the text
of an ancient classic to its commentary. All truth and
all wisdom really lies ultimately in perception. But this
unfortunately can neither be retained nor communicated.
The *objective* conditions of such communication can certainly be presented to others purified and illustrated
through plastic and pictorial art, and even much more
directly through poetry ; but it depends so much upon *subjective* conditions, which are not at the command of every
one, and of no one at all times, nay, indeed in the higher
degrees of perfection, are only the gift of the favoured
few. Only the worst knowledge, abstract, secondary
knowledge, the conception, the mere shadow of true knowledge, is unconditionally communicable. If perceptions
were communicable, that would be a communication worth
the trouble ; but at last every one must remain in his own
skin and skull, and no one can help another. To enrich
the conception from perception is the unceasing endeavour
of poetry and philosophy. However, the aims of man are
essentially *practical ;* and for these it is sufficient that
what he has apprehended through perception should leave
traces in him, by virtue of which he will recognise it in
the next similar case; thus he becomes possessed of
worldly wisdom. Thus, as a rule, the man of the world
cannot teach his accumulated truth and wisdom, but
only make use of it ; he rightly comprehends each event
as it happens, and determines what is in conformity with
it. That books will not take the place of experience nor
learning of genius are two kindred phenomena. Their
common ground is that the abstract can never take the
place of the concrete. Books therefore do not take the

place of experience, because *conceptions* always remain
general, and consequently do not get down to the particular, which, however, is just what has to be dealt with
in life ; and, besides this, all conceptions are abstracted
from what is particular and perceived in experience, and
therefore one must have come to know these in order
adequately to understand even the general conceptions
which the books communicate. Learning cannot take the
place of genius, because it also affords merely conceptions,
but the knowledge of genius consists in the apprehension
of the (Platonic) Ideas of things, and therefore is essentially
intuitive. Thus in the first of these phenomena the
objective condition of perceptive or intuitive knowledge is
wanting ; in the second the *subjective ;* the former may
be attained, the latter cannot.

Wisdom and genius, these two summits of the Parnassus
of human knowledge, have their foundation not in the
abstract and discursive, but in the perceptive faculty.
Wisdom proper is something intuitive, not something
abstract. It does not consist in principles and thoughts,
which one can carry about ready in his mind, as results of
his own research or that of others ; but it is the whole
manner in which the world presents itself in his mind.
This varies so much that on account of it the wise man
lives in another world from the fool, and the genius sees
another world from the blockhead. That the works of the
man of genius immeasurably surpass those of all others
arises simply from the fact that the world which he sees,
and from which he takes his utterances, is so much clearer,
as it were more profoundly worked out, than that in the
minds of others, which certainly contains the same objects,
but is to the world of the man of genius as the Chinese
picture without shading and perspective is to the finished
oil-painting. The material is in all minds the same ; but
the difference lies in the perfection of the form which
it assumes in each, upon which the numerous grades
of intelligence ultimately depend. These grades thus

exist in the root, in the *perceptive* or *intuitive* apprehension, and do not first appear in the abstract. Hence original mental superiority shows itself so easily when the occasion arises, and is at once felt and hated by others.

In practical life the intuitive knowledge of the understanding is able to guide our action and behaviour directly, while the abstract knowledge of the reason can only do so by means of the memory. Hence arises the superiority of intuitive knowledge in all cases which admit of no time for reflection; thus for daily intercourse, in which, just on this account, women excel. Only those who intuitively know the nature of men as they are as a rule, and thus comprehend the individuality of the person before them, will understand how to manage him with certainty and rightly. Another may know by heart all the three hundred maxims of Gracian, but this will not save him from stupid mistakes and misconceptions if he lacks that intuitive knowledge. For all *abstract knowledge* affords us primarily mere general principles and rules; but the particular case is almost never to be carried out exactly according to the rule; then the rule itself has to be presented to us at the right time by the memory, which seldom punctually happens; then the *propositio minor* has to be formed out of the present case, and finally the conclusion drawn. Before all this is done the opportunity has generally turned its back upon us, and then those excellent principles and rules serve at the most to enable us to measure the magnitude of the error we have committed. Certainly with time we gain in this way experience and practice, which slowly grows to knowledge of the world, and thus, in connection with this, the abstract rules may certainly become fruitful. On the other hand, the *intuitive knowledge*, which always apprehends only the particular, stands in immediate relation to the present case. Rule, case, and application are for it one, and action follows immediately upon it. This explains why in real life the scholar, whose pre-eminence lies in the province of abstract knowledge, is so far surpassed by the man of the world, whose pre-eminence consists in perfect intuitive knowledge, which original disposition conferred on him, and a rich experience has developed. The two kinds of knowledge always stand to each other in the relation of paper money and hard cash; and as there are many cases and circumstances in which the former is to be preferred to the latter, so there are also things and situations for which abstract knowledge is more useful than intuitive. If, for example, it is a conception that in some case guides our action, when it is once grasped it has the advantage of being unalterable, and therefore under its guidance we go to work with perfect certainty and consistency. But this certainty which the conception confers on the subjective side is outweighed by the uncertainty which accompanies it on the objective side. The whole conception may be false and groundless, or the object to be dealt with may not come under it, for it may be either not at all or not altogether of the kind which belongs to it. Now if in the particular case we suddenly become conscious of something of this sort, we are put out altogether; if we do not become conscious of it, the result brings it to light. Therefore Vauvenargue says: "*Personne n'est sujet à plus de fautes, que ceux qui n'agissent que par réflexion.*" If, on the contrary, it is direct perception of the objects to be dealt with and their relations that guides our action, we easily hesitate at every step, for the perception is always modifiable, is ambiguous, has inexhaustible details in itself, and shows many sides in succession; we act therefore without full confidence. But the subjective uncertainty is compensated by the objective certainty, for here there is no conception between the object and us, we never lose sight of it; if therefore we only see correctly what we have before us and what we do, we shall hit the mark. Our action then is perfectly sure only when it is guided by a conception the right ground of which, its completeness, and applica-

bility to the given cause is perfectly certain. Action
in accordance with conceptions may pass into pedantry,
action in accordance with the perceived impression into
levity and folly.

Perception is not only the *source* of all knowledge, but
is itself knowledge κατ᾽ εξοχην, is the only unconditionally
true, genuine knowledge completely worthy of the name.
For it alone imparts *insight* properly so called, it alone is
actually assimilated by man, passes into his nature, and
can with full reason be called *his;* while the conceptions
merely cling to him. In the fourth book we see indeed
that true virtue proceeds from knowledge of perception or
intuitive knowledge; for only those actions which are
directly called forth by this, and therefore are performed
purely from the impulse of our own nature, are properly
symptoms of our true and unalterable character; not so
those which, resulting from reflection and its dogmas,
are often extorted from the character, and therefore have
no unalterable ground in us. But *wisdom* also, the true
view of life, the correct eye, and the searching judgment,
proceeds from the way in which the man apprehends the
perceptible world, but not from his mere abstract knowledge, *i.e.,* not from abstract conceptions. The basis or
ultimate content of every science consists, not in proofs,
nor in what is proved, but in the unproved foundation
of the proofs, which can finally be apprehended only
through perception. So also the basis of the true wisdom
and real insight of each man does not consist in conceptions and in abstract rational knowledge, but in what is
perceived, and in the degree of acuteness, accuracy, and
profundity with which he has apprehended it. He who
excels here knows the (Platonic) Ideas of the world and
life ; every case he has seen represents for him innumerable cases; he always apprehends each being according
to its true nature, and his action, like his judgment,
corresponds to his insight. By degrees also his coun-
tenance assumes the expression of penetration, of true

intelligence, and, if it goes far enough, of wisdom. For it is pre-eminence in knowledge of perception alone that stamps its impression upon the features also; while pre-eminence in abstract knowledge cannot do this. In accordance with what has been said, we find in all classes men of intellectual superiority, and often quite without learning. Natural understanding can take the place of almost every degree of culture, but no culture can take the place of natural understanding. The scholar has the advantage of such men in the possession of a wealth of cases and facts (historical knowledge) and of causal determinations (natural science), all in well-ordered connection, easily surveyed; but yet with all this he has not a more accurate and profound insight into what is truly essential in all these cases, facts, and causations. The unlearned man of acuteness and penetration knows how to dispense with this wealth; we can make use of much; we can do with little. One case in his own experience teaches him more than many a scholar is taught by a thousand cases which he *knows*, but does not, properly speaking, *understand*. For the little knowledge of that unlearned man is living, because every fact that is known to him is supported by accurate and well-apprehended perception, and thus represents for him a thousand similar facts. On the contrary, the much knowledge of the ordinary scholar is *dead*, because even if it does not consist, as is often the case, in mere words, it consists entirely in abstract knowledge. This, however, receives its value only through the *perceptive* knowledge of the individual with which it must connect itself, and which must ultimately realise all the conceptions. If now this perceptive knowledge is very scanty, such a mind is like a bank with liabilities tenfold in excess of its cash reserve, whereby in the end it becomes bankrupt. Therefore, while the right apprehension of the perceptible world has impressed the stamp of insight and wisdom on the brow of many an unlearned man, the face of many a scholar bears no other trace of his much study than that of exhaustion and weariness from excessive and forced straining of the memory in the unnatural accumulation of dead conceptions. Moreover, the insight of such a man is often so puerile, so weak and silly, that we must suppose that the excessive strain upon the faculty of indirect knowledge, which is concerned with abstractions, directly weakens the power of immediate perceptive knowledge, and the natural and clear vision is more and more blinded by the light of books. At any rate the constant streaming in of the thoughts of others must confine and suppress our own, and indeed in the long run paralyse the power of thought if it has not that high degree of elasticity which is able to withstand that unnatural stream. Therefore ceaseless reading and study directly injures the mind— the more so that completeness and constant connection of the system of our own thought and knowledge must pay the penalty if we so often arbitrarily interrupt it in order to gain room for a line of thought entirely strange to us. To banish my own thought in order to make room for that of a book would seem to me like what Shakespeare censures in the tourists of his time, that they sold their own land to see that of others. Yet the inclination for reading of most scholars is a kind of *fuga vacui*, from the poverty of their own minds, which forcibly draws in the thoughts of others. In order to have thoughts they must read something; just as lifeless bodies are only moved from without; while the man who thinks for himself is like a living body that moves of itself. Indeed it is dangerous to read about a subject before we have thought about it ourselves. For along with the new material the old point of view and treatment of it creeps into the mind, all the more so as laziness and apathy counsel us to accept what has already been thought, and allow it to pass for truth. This now insinuates itself, and henceforward our thought on the subject always takes the accustomed path, like brooks that are guided by ditches; to find a thought of our own, a new thought, is then doubly difficult. This contributes much to the want of originality on the part of scholars. Add to this that they suppose that, like other people, they must divide their time between pleasure and work. Now they regard reading as their work and special calling, and therefore they gorge themselves with it, beyond what they can digest. Then reading no longer plays the part of the mere initiator of thought, but takes its place altogether; for they think of the subject just as long as they are reading about it, thus with the mind of another, not with their own. But when the book is laid aside entirely different things make much more lively claims upon their interest; their private affairs, and then the theatre, card-playing, skittles, the news of the day, and gossip. The man of thought is so because such things have no interest for him. He is interested only in his problems, with which therefore he is always occupied, by himself and without a book. To give ourselves this interest, if we have not got it, is impossible. This is the crucial point. And upon this also depends the fact that the former always speak only of what they have read, while the latter, on the contrary, speaks of what he has thought, and that they are, as Pope says:

"For ever reading, never to be read."

The mind is naturally free, not a slave; only what it does willingly, of its own accord, succeeds. On the other hand, the compulsory exertion of a mind in studies for which it is not qualified, or when it has become tired, or in general too continuously and *invita Minerva*, dulls the brain, just as reading by moonlight dulls the eyes. This is especially the case with the straining of the immature brain in the earlier years of childhood. I believe that the learning of Latin and Greek grammar from the sixth to the twelfth year lays the foundation of the subsequent stupidity of most scholars. At any rate the mind requires the nourishment of materials from without. All that we eat is not at once incorporated in the organism, but only so much of it as is digested ; so that only a small part of it is assimilated, and the remainder passes away; and thus to eat more than we can assimilate is useless and injurious. It is precisely the same with what we read. Only so far as it gives food for thought does it increase our insight and true knowledge. Therefore Heracleitus says : " πολυ- μαθια νουν ου διδασκει " (*multiscitia non dat intellectum*). It seems, however, to me that learning may be compared to a heavy suit of armour, which certainly makes the strong man quite invincible, but to the weak man is a burden under which he sinks altogether.

The exposition given in our third book of the knowledge of the (Platonic) Ideas, as the highest attainable by man, and at the same time entirely *perceptive or intuitive* know- ledge, is a proof that the source of true wisdom does not lie in abstract rational knowledge, but in the clear and profound apprehension of the world in perception. There- fore wise men may live in any age, and those of the past remain wise men for all succeeding generations. Learn- ing, on the contrary, is relative ; the learned men of the past are for the most part children as compared with us, and require indulgence.

But to him who studies in order to gain *insight* books and studies are only steps of the ladder by which he climbs to the summit of knowledge. As soon as a round of the ladder has raised him a step, he leaves it behind him. The many, on the other hand, who study in order to fill their memory do not use the rounds of the ladder to mount by, but take them off, and load themselves with them to carry them away, rejoicing at the increasing weight of the burden. They remain always below, be- cause they bear what ought to have borne them.

Upon the truth set forth here, that the kernel of all knowledge is the *perceptive or intuitive* apprehension, de- pends the true and profound remark of Helvetius, that the really characteristic and original views of which a gifted individual is capable, and the working up, development, and manifold application of which is the material of all his works, even if written much later, can arise in him only up to the thirty-fifth or at the latest the fortieth year of his life, and are really the result of combinations he has made in his early youth. For they are not mere connections of abstract conceptions, but his own intuitive comprehension of the objective world and the nature of things. Now, that this intuitive apprehension must have completed its work by the age mentioned above depends partly on the fact that by that time the ectypes of all (Platonic) Ideas must have presented themselves to the man, and therefore cannot appear later with the strength of the first impression; partly on this, that the highest energy of brain activity is demanded for this quintessence of all knowledge, for this proof before the letter of the apprehension, and this highest energy of the brain is dependent on the freshness and flexibility of its fibres and the rapidity with which the arterial blood flows to the brain. But this again is at its strongest only as long as the arterial system has a decided predominance over the venous system, which begins to decline after the thirtieth year, until at last, after the forty-second year, the venous system obtains the upper hand, as Cabanis has admirably and instructively explained. Therefore the years between twenty and thirty and the first few years after thirty are for the intellect what May is for the trees; only then do the blossoms appear of which all the later fruits are the development. The world of perception has made its impression, and thereby laid the foundation of all the subsequent thoughts of the individual. He may by reflection make clearer what he has apprehended; he may yet acquire much knowledge as nourishment for the fruit which has once set; he may extend his views, correct his conceptions and judgments, it may be only through endless combinations that he becomes completely master of the materials he has gained; indeed he will generally produce his best works much later, as the greatest heat begins with the decline of the day, but he can no longer hope for new original knowledge from the one living fountain of perception. It is this that Byron feels when he breaks forth into his wonderfully beautiful lament:

> "No more—no more—oh! never more on me
>   The freshness of the heart can fall like dew,
> Which out of all the lovely things we see
>   Extracts emotions beautiful and new,
> Hived in our bosoms like the bag o' the bee:
>   Think'st thou the honey with those objects grew?
> Alas! 'twas not in them, but in thy power
> To double even the sweetness of a flower."

Through all that I have said hitherto I hope I have placed in a clear light the important truth that since all abstract knowledge springs from knowledge of perception, it obtains its whole value from its relation to the latter, thus from the fact that its conceptions, or the abstractions which they denote, can be realised, *i.e.*, proved, through perceptions; and, moreover, that most depends upon the quality of these perceptions. Conceptions and abstractions which do not ultimately refer to perceptions are like paths in the wood that end without leading out of it. The great value of conceptions lies in the fact that by means of them the original material of knowledge is more easily handled, surveyed, and arranged. But although many kinds of logical and dialectical operations are possible with them, yet no entirely original and new knowledge will result from these; that is to say, no knowledge whose material neither lay already in perception nor was drawn from self-consciousness. This is the true meaning of the doctrine attributed to Aristotle: *Nihil est in intellectu, nisi quod antea fuerit in sensu.* It is also the meaning of the Lockeian philosophy, which made for ever an epoch in philosophy, because it commenced at last the serious discussion of the question as to the origin of our knowledge. It is also principally what the " Critique of Pure Reason " teaches. It also desires that we should not

remain at the *conceptions,* but go back to their *source,* thus
to *perception ;* only with the true and important addition
that what holds good of the perception also extends to its
subjective conditions, thus to the forms which lie pre-
disposed in the perceiving and thinking brain as its
natural functions ; although these at least *virtualiter*
precede the actual sense-perception, *i.e.,* are *a priori,* and
therefore do not depend upon sense-perception, but it upon
them. For these forms themselves have indeed no other
end, nor service, than to produce the empirical perception
on the nerves of sense being excited, as other forms are
determined afterwards to construct thoughts in the abstract from the material of perception. The "Critique
of Pure Reason" is therefore related to the Lockeian
philosophy as the analysis of the infinite to elementary
geometry, but is yet throughout to be regarded as the
continuation of the Lockeian philosophy. The given material of every philosophy is accordingly nothing else than
the *empirical consciousness,* which divides itself into the
consciousness of one's own self (self-consciousness) and
the consciousness of other things (external perception).
For this alone is what is immediately and actually given.
Every philosophy which, instead of starting from this,
takes for its starting-point arbitrarily chosen abstract
conceptions, such as, for example, absolute, absolute substance, God, infinity, finitude, absolute identity, being,
essence, &c., &c., moves in the air without support, and
can therefore never lead to a real result. Yet in all ages
philosophers have attempted it with such materials ; and
hence even Kant sometimes, according to the common
usage, and more from custom than consistency, defines
philosophy as a science of mere conceptions. But such
a science would really undertake to extract from the
partial ideas (for that is what the abstractions are) what
is not to be found in the complete ideas (the perceptions),
from which the former were drawn by abstraction. The
possibility of the syllogism leads to this mistake, because

here the combination of the judgments gives a new result, although more apparent than real, for the syllogism only brings out what already lay in the given judgments; for it is true the conclusion cannot contain more than the premisses. Conceptions are certainly the material of philosophy, but only as marble is the material of the sculptor. It is not to work *out of* them but *in* them; that is to say, it is to deposit its results in them, but not to start from them as what is given. Whoever wishes to see a glaring example of such a false procedure from mere conceptions may look at the " *Institutio Theologica* " of Proclus in order to convince himself of the vanity of that whole method. There abstractions such as " ἐν, πληθος, αγαθον, παραγον και παραγομενον, αυταρκες, αιτιον, κρειττον, κινητον, ακινητον, κινουμενον " (*unum, multa, bonum, producens et productum, sibi sufficiens, causa, melius, mobile, immobile, motum*), &c., are indiscriminately collected, but the perceptions to which alone they owe their origin and content ignored and contemptuously disregarded. A theology is then constructed from these conceptions, but its goal, the θεος, is kept concealed; thus the whole procedure is apparently unprejudiced, as if the reader did not know at the first page, just as well as the author, what it is all to end in. I have already quoted a fragment of this above. This production of Proclus is really quite peculiarly adapted to make clear how utterly useless and illusory such combinations of abstract conceptions are, for we can make of them whatever we will, especially if we further take advantage of the ambiguity of many words, such, for example, as κρειττον. If such an architect of conceptions were present in person we would only have to ask naively where all the things are of which he has so much to tell us, and whence he knows the laws from which he draws his conclusions concerning them. He would then soon be obliged to turn to empirical perception, in which alone the real world exhibits itself, from which those conceptions are drawn. Then we would only have to ask further why he did not honestly start from the given perception of such a world, so that at every step his assertions could be proved by it, instead of operating with conceptions, which are yet drawn from perception alone, and therefore can have no further validity than that which it imparts to them. But of course this is just his trick. Through such conceptions, in which, by virtue of abstraction, what is inseparable is thought as separate, and what cannot be united as united, he goes far beyond the perception which was their source, and thus beyond the limits of their applicability, to an entirely different world from that which supplied the material for building, but just on this account to a world of chimeras. I have here referred to Proclus because in him this procedure becomes specially clear through the frank audacity with which he carries it out. But in Plato also we find some examples of this kind, though not so glaring; and in general the philosophical literature of all ages affords a multitude of instances of the same thing. That of our own time is rich in them. Consider, for example, the writings of the school of Schelling, and observe the constructions that are built up out of abstractions like finite and infinite—being, non-being, other being—activity, hindrance, product—determining, being determined, determinateness—limit, limiting, being limited—unity, plurality, multiplicity—identity, diversity, indifference—thinking, being, essence, &c. Not only does all that has been said above hold good of constructions out of such materials, but because an infinite amount can be thought *through* such wide abstractions, only very little indeed can be thought *in* them; they are empty husks. But thus the matter of the whole philosophising becomes astonishingly trifling and paltry, and hence arises that unutterable and excruciating tediousness which is characteristic of all such writings. If indeed I now chose to call to mind the way in which Hegel and his companions have abused such wide and empty abstractions, I should have to fear that both the reader and I myself would be ill; for the most nauseous tediousness hangs over the empty word-juggling of this loathsome philophaster.

That in *practical* philosophy also no wisdom is brought to light from mere abstract conceptions is the one thing to be learnt from the ethical dissertations of the theologian Schleiermacher, with the delivery of which he has wearied the Berlin Academy for a number of years, and which are shortly to appear in a collected form.   In them only abstract conceptions, such as duty, virtue, highest good, moral law, &c., are taken as the starting-point, without further introduction than that they commonly occur in ethical systems, and are now treated as given realities. He then discusses these from all sides with great subtilty, but, on the other hand, never makes for the source of these conceptions, for the thing itself, the actual human life, to which alone they are related, from which they ought to be drawn, and with which morality has, properly speaking, to do. On this account these diatribes are just as unfruitful and useless as they are tedious, which is saying a great deal.   At all times we find persons, like this theologian, who is too fond of philosophising, famous while they are alive, afterwards soon forgotten. My advice is rather to read those whose fate has been the opposite of this, for time is short and valuable.

Now although, in accordance with all that has been said, wide, abstract conceptions, which can be realised in no perception, must never be the source of knowledge, the starting-point or the proper material of philosophy, yet sometimes particular results of philosophy are such as can only be thought in the abstract, and cannot be proved by any perception. Knowledge of this kind will certainly only be half knowledge; it will, as it were, only point out the place where what is to be known lies; but this remains concealed.   Therefore we should only be satisfied with such conceptions in the most extreme case, and when we have reached the limit of the knowledge possible to our faculties. An example of this might perhaps be the conception of a being out of time; such as the proposition: the indestructibility of our true being by death is not a continued existence of it. With conceptions of this sort the firm ground which supports our whole knowledge, the perceptible, seems to waver. Therefore philosophy may certainly at times, and in case of necessity, extend to such knowledge, but it must never begin with it.

The working with wide abstractions, which is condemned above, to the entire neglect of the perceptive knowledge from which they are drawn, and which is therefore their permanent and natural controller, was at all times the principal source of the errors of dogmatic philosophy. A science constructed from the mere comparison of conceptions, that is, from general principles, could only be certain if all its principles were synthetical *a priori*, as is the case in mathematics: for only such admit of no exceptions. If, on the other hand, the principles have any empirical content, we must keep this constantly at hand, to control the general principles. For no truths which are in any way drawn from experience are ever unconditionally true. They have therefore only an approximately universal validity; for here there is no rule without an exception. If now I link these principles together by means of the intersection of their conceptspheres, one conception might very easily touch the other precisely where the exception lies. But if this happens even only once in the course of a long train of reasoning, the whole structure is loosed from its foundation and moves in the air. If, for example, I say, "The ruminants have no front incisors," and apply this and what follows from it to the camel, it all becomes false, for it only holds good of horned ruminants. What Kant calls *das Vernünfteln*, mere abstract reasoning, and so often condemns, is just of this sort. For it consists simply in subsuming conceptions under conceptions, without reference to their origin, and without proof of the correctness and exclusiveness of such subsumption—a method whereby we can arrive by longer or shorter circuits at almost any result we choose to set before us as our goal. Hence this mere abstract reasoning differs only in degree from sophistication strictly so called. But sophistication is in the theoretical sphere exactly what chicanery is in the practical. Yet even Plato himself has very frequently permitted such mere abstract reasoning; and Proclus, as we have already mentioned, has, after the manner of all imitators, carried this fault of his model much further. Dionysius the Areopagite, "*De Divinis Nominibus*," is also strongly affected with this. But even in the fragments of the Eleatic Melissus we already find distinct examples of such mere abstract reasoning (especially § 2–5 in Brandis' *Comment. Eleat.*) His procedure with the conceptions, which never touch the reality from which they have their content, but, moving in the atmosphere of abstact universality, pass away beyond it, resembles blows which never hit the mark. A good pattern of such mere abstract reasoning is the "*De Diis et Mundo*" of the philosopher Sallustius Büchelchen ; especially chaps. 7, 12, and 17. But a perfect gem of philosophical mere abstract reasoning passing into decided sophistication is the following reasoning of the Platonist, Maximus of Tyre, which I shall quote, as it is short: "Every injustice is the taking away of a good. There is no other good than virtue: but virtue cannot be taken away : thus it is not possible that the virtuous can suffer injustice from the wicked. It now remains either that no injustice can be suffered, or that it is suffered by the wicked from the wicked. But the wicked man possesses no good at all, for only virtue is a good ; therefore none can be taken from him. Thus he also can suffer no injustice. Thus injustice is an impossible thing." The original, which is less concise through repetitions, runs thus : "Αδικια εστι αφαιρεσις αγαθον· το δε αγαθον τι αν ειη αλλο η αρετη ;—ἡ δε αρετη αναφαιρετον. Ουκ αδικησεται τοινυν ὁ την αρετην εχων, η ουκ εστιν αδικια αφαιρεσις

αγαθον· ουδεν γαρ αγαθον αφαιρετον, ουδ'χαποβλητον, ουδ
ελετον, ουδε λη:στον. Ειεν ουν, ουδ' αδικειται ο χρησ-
τος, ουδ υπο του μοχθηρου· αναφαιρετος γαρ. ᾿ Λειπεται
τοινυν η μηδενα αδικεισθαι καθαπαξ, η τον μοχθηρον υπο
του ομοιου· αλλα τω μοχθηρω ουδενος μετεστιν αγαθου·
ή δε αδικια ην αγαθου αφαιρεσις· ο δε μη εχων ο, τι αφαι-
ρεσθη, ουδε εις ο, τι αδικησθη, εχει" (*Sermo* 2). I shall
add further a modern example of such proofs from
abstract conceptions, by means of which an obviously
absurd proposition is set up as the truth, and I shall take
it from the works of a great man, Giordano Bruno. In
his book, "*Del Infinito Universo e Mondi*" (p. 87 of the
edition of A. Wagner), he makes an Aristotelian prove
(with the assistance and exaggeration of the passage
of Aristotle's *De Cœlo*, i. 5) that there can be *no space*
beyond the world. The world is enclosed by the eight
spheres of Aristotle, and beyond these there can be
no space. For if beyond these there were still a body,
it must either be simple or compound. It is now
proved sophistically, from principles which are obviously
begged, that no *simple* body could be there; and therefore,
also, no compound body, for it would necessarily be composed of simple ones. Thus in general there can be no
body there—but if not, then *no space*. For space is defined
as "that in which bodies can be;" and it has just been
proved that no body can be there. Thus there is also
there no space. This last is the final stroke of this proof
from abstract conceptions. It ultimately rests on the
fact that the proposition, "Where no space is, there can
be no body" is taken as a universal negative, and therefore converted simply, "Where no body can be there is no
space." But the former proposition, when properly regarded, is a universal affirmative : "Everything that has
no space has no body," thus it must not be converted
simply. Yet it is not every proof from abstract conceptions, with a conclusion which clearly contradicts
perception (as here the finiteness of space), that can thus

be referred to a logical error. For the sophistry does not always lie in the form, but often in the matter, in the premisses, and in the indefiniteness of the conceptions and their extension. We find numerous examples of this in Spinoza, whose method indeed it is to prove from conceptions. See, for example, the miserable sophisms in his " Ethics," P. iv., prop. 29–31, by means of the ambiguity of the uncertain conceptions *convenire* and *commune habere.* Yet this does not prevent the neo-Spinozists of our own day from taking all that he has said for gospel. Of these the Hegelians, of whom there are actually still a few, are specially amusing on account of their traditional reverence for his principle, *omnis determinatio est negatio,* at which, according to the charlatan spirit of the school, they put on a face as if it was able to unhinge the world ; whereas it is of no use at all, for even the simplest can see for himself that if I limit anything by determinations, I thereby exclude and thus negate what lies beyond these limits.

Thus in all mere reasonings of the above kind it becomes very apparent what errors that algebra with mere conceptions, uncontrolled by perception, is exposed to, and that therefore perception is for our intellect what the firm ground upon which it stands is for our body : if we forsake perception everything is *instabilis tellus, innabilis unda.* The reader will pardon the fulness of these expositions and examples on account of their instructiveness. I have sought by means of them to bring forward and support the difference, indeed the opposition, between perceptive and abstract or reflected knowledge, which has hitherto been too little regarded, and the establishment of which is a fundamental characteristic of my philosophy. For many phenomena of our mental life are only explicable through this distinction. The connecting link between these two such different kinds of knowledge is the *faculty of judgment,* as I have shown in § 14 of the first volume. This faculty is certainly also active in the province of mere abstract knowledge, in which it compares conceptions only with conceptions; therefore every judgment, in the logical sense of the word, is certainly a work of the faculty of judgment, for it always consists in the subsumption of a narrower conception under a wider one. Yet this activity of the faculty of judgment, in which it merely compares conceptions with each other, is a simpler and easier task than when it makes the transition from what is quite particular, the perception, to the essentially general, the conception. For by the analysis of conceptions into their essential predicates it must be possible to decide upon purely logical grounds whether they are capable of being united or not, and for this the mere reason which every one possesses is sufficient. The faculty of judgment is therefore only active here in shortening this process, for he who is gifted with it sees at a glance what others only arrive at through a series of reflections. But its activity in the narrower sense really only appears when what is known through perception, thus the real experience, has to be carried over into distinct abstract knowledge, subsumed under accurately corresponding conceptions, and thus translated into reflected rational knowledge. It is therefore this faculty which has to establish the firm *basis* of all sciences, which always consists of what is known directly and cannot be further denied. Therefore here, in the fundamental judgments, lies the difficulty of the sciences, not in the inferences from these. To infer is easy, to judge is difficult. False inferences are rare, false judgments are always the order of the day. Not less in practical life has the faculty of judgment to give the decision in all fundamental conclusions and important determinations. Its office is in the main like that of the judicial sentence. As the burning-glass brings to a focus all the sun's rays, so when the understanding works, the intellect has to bring together all the data which it has upon the subject so closely that the understanding comprehends them at a glance, which it now rightly fixes, and then carefully makes the result distinct to itself.   Further, the great difficulty of judging in most cases depends upon the fact that we have to proceed from the consequent to the reason, a path which is always uncertain ; indeed I have shown that the source of all error lies here.   Yet in all the empirical sciences, and also in the affairs of real life, this way is for the most part the only one open to us.   The experiment is an attempt to go over it again the other way; therefore it is decisive, and at least brings out error clearly ; provided always that it is rightly chosen and honestly carried out; not like Newton's experiments in connection with the theory of colours.   But the experiment itself must also again be judged.   The complete certainty of the *a priori* sciences, logic and mathematics, depends principally upon the fact that in them the path from the reason to the consequent is open to us, and it is always certain.   This gives them the character of *purely objective* sciences, *i.e.*, sciences with regard to whose truths all who understand them must judge alike; and this is all the more remarkable as they are the very sciences which rest on the subjective forms of the intellect, while the empirical sciences alone have to do with what is palpably objective.

Wit and ingenuity are also manifestations of the faculty of judgment; in the former its activity is reflective, in the latter subsuming.   In most men the faculty of judgment is only nominally present; it is a kind of irony that it is reckoned with the normal faculties of the mind, instead of being only attributed to the *monstris per excessum.* Ordinary men show even in the smallest affairs want of confidence in their own judgment, just because they know from experience that it is of no service.   With them prejudice and imitation take its place; and thus they are kept in a state of continual non-age, from which scarcely one in many hundreds is delivered.   Certainly this is not avowed, for even to themselves they appear to judge; but all the time they are glancing stealthily at the opinion of others, which is their secret standard. While each one would be ashamed to go about in a borrowed coat, hat, or mantle, they all have nothing but borrowed opinions, which they eagerly collect wherever they can find them, and then strut about giving them out as their own. Others borrow them again from them and do the same thing. This explains the rapid and wide spread of errors, and also the fame of what is bad; for the professional purveyors of opinion, such as journalists and the like, give as a rule only false wares, as those who hire out masquerading dresses give only false jewels.

CHAPTER VIII.[1]

ON THE THEORY OF THE LUDICROUS.

MY theory of the ludicrous also depends upon the opposition explained in the preceding chapters between perceptible and abstract ideas, which I have brought into such marked prominence. Therefore what has still to be said in explanation of this theory finds its proper place here, although according to the order of the text it would have to come later.

The problem of the origin, which is everywhere the same, and hence of the peculiar significance of laughter, was already known to Cicero, but only to be at once dismissed as insoluble (*De Orat.*, ii. 58). The oldest attempt known to me at a psychological explanation of laughter is to be found in Hutcheson's "Introduction into Moral Philosophy," Bk. I., ch. i. § 14. A somewhat later anonymous work, "*Traité des Causes Physiques et Morals du Rire*," 1768, is not without merit as a ventilation of the subject. Platner, in his "Anthropology," § 894, has collected the opinions of the philosophers from Home to Kant who have attempted an explanation of this phenomenon peculiar to human nature. Kant's and Jean Paul's theories of the ludicrous are well known. I regard it as unnecessary to prove their incorrectness, for whoever tries to refer given cases of the ludicrous to them will in the great majority of instances be at once convinced of their insufficiency.

According to my explanation given in the first volume,

---

[1] This chapter is connected with § 13 of the first volume.

the source of the ludicrous is always the paradoxical, and
therefore unexpected, subsumption of an object under a
conception which in other respects is different from it,
and accordingly the phenomenon of laughter always
signifies the sudden apprehension of an incongruity
between such a conception and the real object thought
under it, thus between the abstract and the concrete
object of perception. The greater and more unexpected,
in the apprehension of the laugher, this incongruity is,
the more violent will be his laughter. Therefore in
everything that excites laughter it must always be
possible to show a conception and a particular, that is, a
thing or event, which certainly can be subsumed under
that conception, and therefore thought through it, yet
in another and more predominating aspect does not
belong to it at all, but is strikingly different from everything else that is thought through that conception. If,
as often occurs, especially in witticisms, instead of such
a real object of perception, the conception of a subordinate species is brought under the higher conception
of the genus, it will yet excite laughter only through
the fact that the imagination realises it, *i.e.*, makes a
perceptible representative stand for it, and thus the conflict between what is thought and what is perceived takes
place. Indeed if we wish to understand this perfectly
explicitly, it is possible to trace everything ludicrous to
a syllogism in the first figure, with an undisputed *major*
and an unexpected *minor*, which to a certain extent
is only sophistically valid, in consequence of which connection the conclusion partakes of the quality of the
ludicrous.

In the first volume I regarded it as superfluous to illustrate this theory by examples, for every one can do this
for himself by a little reflection upon cases of the ludicrous
which he remembers. Yet, in order to come to the assistance of the mental inertness of those readers who prefer
always to remain in a passive condition, I will accommodate

myself to them. Indeed in this third edition I wish to multiply and accumulate examples, so that it may be indisputable that here, after so many fruitless earlier attempts, the true theory of the ludicrous is given, and the problem which was proposed and also given up by Cicero is definitely solved.

If we consider that an angle requires two lines meeting so that if they are produced they will intersect each other; on the other hand, that the tangent of a circle only touches it at one point, but at this point is really parallel to it; and accordingly have present to our minds the abstract conviction of the impossibility of an angle between the circumference of a circle and its tangent; and if now such an angle lies visibly before us upon paper, this will easily excite a smile. The ludicrousness in this case is exceedingly weak; but yet the source of it in the incongruity of what is thought and perceived appears in it with exceptional distinctness. When we discover such an incongruity, the occasion for laughter that thereby arises is, according as we pass from the real, *i.e.*, the perceptible, to the conception, or conversely from the conception to the real, either a witticism or an absurdity, which in a higher degree, and especially in the practical sphere, is folly, as was explained in the text. Now to consider examples of the first case, thus of wit, we shall first of all take the familiar anecdote of the Gascon at whom the king laughed when he saw him in light summer clothing in the depth of winter, and who thereupon said to the king: "If your Majesty had put on what I have, you would find it very warm;" and on being asked what he had put on, replied: "My whole wardrobe!" Under this last conception we have to think both the unlimited wardrobe of a king and the single summer coat of a poor devil, the sight of which upon his freezing body shows its great incongruity with the conception. The audience in a theatre in Paris once called for the "Marseillaise" to be played, and as this was not done, began shrieking and howling, so that at last a commissary of police in uniform came upon the stage and explained that it was not allowed that anything should be given in the theatre except what was in the playbill. Upon this a voice cried: " *Et vous, Monsieur, êtes-vous aussi sur l'affiche?* "—a hit which was received with universal laughter. For here the subsumption of what is heterogeneous is at once distinct and unforced. The epigramme:

> " Bav is the true shepherd of whom the Bible spake :
> Though his flock be all asleep, he alone remains awake : "

subsumes, under the conception of a sleeping flock and a waking shepherd, the tedious preacher who still bellows on unheard when he has sent all the people to sleep. Analogous to this is the epitaph on a doctor : " Here lies he like a hero, and those he has slain lie around him; " it subsumes under the conception, honourable to the hero, of " lying surrounded by dead bodies," the doctor, who is supposed to preserve life. Very commonly the witticism consists in a single expression, through which only the conception is given, under which the case presented can be subsumed, though it is very different from everything else that is thought under it. So is it in " Romeo " when the vivacious Mercutio answers his friends who promise to visit him on the morrow : " Ask for me to-morrow, and you shall find me a grave man." Under this conception a dead man is here subsumed ; but in English there is also a play upon the words, for " a grave man " means both a serious man and a man of the grave. Of this kind is also the well-known anecdote of the actor Unzelmann. In the Berlin theatre he was strictly forbidden to improvise. Soon afterwards he had to appear on the stage on horseback, and just as he came on the stage the horse dunged, at which the audience began to laugh, but laughed much more when Unzelmann said to the horse : " What are you doing ? Don't you know we are forbidden to improvise ? " Here the subsumption of the heterogeneous under the more general conception is very distinct, but the witticism is exceedingly happy, and the ludicrous effect produced by it excessively strong. To this class also belongs the following announcement from Hall in a newspaper of March 1851 : " The band of Jewish swindlers to which we have referred were again delivered over to us with obligato accompaniment." This subsuming of a police escort under a musical term is very happy, though it approaches the mere play upon words. On the other hand, it is exactly a case of the kind we are considering when Saphir, in a paper-war with the actor Angeli, describes him as " Angeli, who is equally great in mind and body." The small statue of the actor was known to the whole town, and thus under the conception " great " unusual smallness was presented to the mind. Also when the same Saphir calls the airs of a new opera " good old friends," and so brings the quality which is most to be condemned under a conception which is usually employed to commend. Also, if we should say of a lady whose favour could be influenced by presents, that she knew how to combine the *utile* with the *dulci.* For here we bring the moral life under the conception of a rule which Horace has recommended in an æsthetical reference. Also if to signify a brothel we should call it the " modest abode of quiet joys." Good society, in order to be thoroughly insipid, has forbidden all decided utterances, and therefore all strong expressions. Therefore it is wont, when it has to signify scandalous or in any way indecent things, to mitigate or extenuate them by expressing them through general conceptions. But in this way it happens that they are more or less incongruously subsumed, and in a corresponding degree the effect of the ludicrous is produced. To this class belongs the use of *utile dulci* referred to above, and also such expressions as the following : " He had unpleasantness at the ball " when he was thrashed and kicked out ; or, " He has done too well " when he is drunk ; and also, " The woman has

weak moments " if she is unfaithful to her husband, &c.
Equivocal sayings also belong to the same class. They
are conceptions which in themselves contain nothing
improper, but yet the case brought under them leads to
an improper idea. They are very common in society.
But a perfect example of a full and magnificent equivocation is Shenstone's incomparable epitaph on a justice
of the peace, which, in its high-flown lapidary style, seems
to speak of noble and sublime things, while under each of
their conceptions something quite different is to be subsumed, which only appears in the very last word as the
unexpected key to the whole, and the reader discovers
with loud laughter that he has only read a very obscene
equivocation. In this smooth-combed age it is altogether
impossible to quote this here, not to speak of translating
it; it will be found in Shenstone's poetical works, under
the title "Inscription." Equivocations sometimes pass
over into mere puns, about which all that is necessary has
been said in the text.

Further, the ultimate subsumption, ludicrous to all, of
what in one respect is heterogeneous, under a conception
which in other respects agrees with it, may take place
contrary to our intention. For example, one of the free
negroes in North America, who take pains to imitate the
whites in everything, quite recently placed an epitaph
over his dead child which begins, "Lovely, early broken
lily." If, on the contrary, something real and perceptible
is, with direct intention, brought under the conception
of its opposite, the result is plain, common irony. For
example, if when it is raining hard we say, "Nice weather
we are having to-day;" or if we say of an ugly bride,
"That man has found a charming treasure;" or of a knave,
"This honest man," &c. &c. Only children and quite uneducated people will laugh at such things; for here the
incongruity between what is thought and what is perceived is total. Yet just in this direct exaggeration in
the production of the ludicrous its fundamental character,

incongruity, appears very distinctly. This species of the ludicrous is, on account of its exaggeration and distinct intention, in some respects related to *parody*. The procedure of the latter consists in this. It substitutes for the incidents and words of a serious poem or drama insignificant low persons or trifling motives and actions. It thus subsumes the commonplace realities which it sets forth under the lofty conceptions given in the theme, under which in a certain respect they must come, while in other respects they are very incongruous; and thereby the contrast between what is perceived and what is thought appears very glaring. There is no lack of familiar examples of this, and therefore I shall only give one, from the "Zobeide" of Carlo Gozzi, act iv., scene 3, where the famous stanza of Ariosto (*Orl. Fur.*, i. 22), "*Oh gran bontà de' cavalieri antichi*," &c., is put word for word into the mouth of two clowns who have just been thrashing each other, and tired with this, lie quietly side by side. This is also the nature of the application so popular in Germany of serious verses, especially of Schiller, to trivial events, which clearly contains a subsumption of heterogeneous things under the general conception which the verse expresses. Thus, for example, when any one has displayed a very characteristic trait, there will rarely be wanting some one to say, "From that I know with whom I have to do." But it was original and very witty of a man who was in love with a young bride to quote to the newly married couple (I know not how loudly) the concluding words of Schiller's ballad, "The Surety:"

> "Let me be, I pray you,
> In your bond the third."

The effect of the ludicrous is here strong and inevitable, because under the conceptions through which Schiller presents to the mind a moral and noble relation, a forbidden and immoral relation is subsumed, and yet correctly and without change, thus is thought through it.

In all the examples of wit given here we find that under a conception, or in general an abstract thought, a real thing is, directly, or by means of a narrower conception, subsumed, which indeed, strictly speaking, comes under it, and yet is as different as possible from the proper and original intention and tendency of the thought. Accordingly wit, as a mental capacity, consists entirely in a facility for finding for every object that appears a conception under which it certainly can be thought, though it is very different from all the other objects which come under this conception.

The second species of the ludicrous follows, as we have mentioned, the opposite path from the abstract conception to the real or perceptible things thought through it. But this now brings to light any incongruity with the conception which was overlooked, and hence arises an absurdity, and therefore in the practical sphere a foolish action. Since the play requires action, this species of the ludicrous is essential to comedy. Upon this depends the observation of Voltaire : "*J'ai cru remarquer aux spectacles, qu'il ne s'élève presque jamais de ces éclats de rire universels, qu'à l'occasion d'une* MÉPRISE" (*Preface de L'Enfant Prodigue*). The following may serve as examples of this species of the ludicrous. When some one had declared that he was fond of walking alone, an Austrian said to him : "You like walking alone ; so do I : therefore we can go together." He starts from the conception, "A pleasure which two love they can enjoy in common," and subsumes under it the very case which excludes community. Further, the servant who rubbed a worn sealskin in his master's box with Macassar oil, so that it might become covered with hair again ; in doing which he started from the conception, "Macassar oil makes hair grow." The soldiers in the guard-room who allowed a prisoner who was brought in to join in their game of cards, then quarrelled with him for cheating, and turned him out. They let themselves be led by the general conception, "Bad companions are turned out," and forget that he is also a prisoner, *i.e.*, one whom they ought to hold fast.   Two young peasants had loaded their gun with coarse shot, which they wished to extract, in order to substitute fine, without losing the powder.   So one of them put the mouth of the barrel in his hat, which he took between his legs, and said to the other: "Now you pull the trigger slowly, slowly, slowly ; then the shot will come first." He starts from the conception, " Prolonging the cause prolongs the effect." Most of the actions of Don Quixote are also cases in point, for he subsumes the realities he encounters under conceptions drawn from the romances of chivalry, from which they are very different.   For example, in order to support the oppressed he frees the galley slaves. Properly all Münch-hausenisms are also of this nature, only they are not actions which are performed, but impossibilities, which are passed off upon the hearer as having really happened. In them the fact is always so conceived that when it is thought merely in the abstract, and therefore compara-tively *a priori*, it appears possible and plausible ; but afterwards, if we come down to the perception of the parti-cular case, thus *a posteriori* the impossibility of the thing, indeed the absurdity of the assumption, is brought into prominence, and excites laughter through the evident incongruity of what is perceived and what is thought. For example, when the melodies frozen up in the post-horn are thawed in the warm room—when Münchhausen, sitting upon a tree during a hard frost, draws up his knife which has dropped to the ground by the frozen jet of his own water, &c.   Such is also the story of the two lions who broke down the partition between them during the night and devoured each other in their rage, so that in the morning there was nothing to be found but the two tails.

There are also cases of the ludicrous where the concep-tion under which the perceptible facts are brought does not require to be expressed or signified, but comes into consciousness itself through the association of ideas. The laughter into which Garrick burst in the middle of playing tragedy because a butcher in the front of the pit, who had taken off his wig to wipe the sweat from his head, placed the wig for a while upon his large dog, who stood facing the stage with his fore paws resting on the pit railings, was occasioned by the fact that Garrick started from the conception of a spectator, which was added in his own mind. This is the reason why certain animal forms, such as apes, kangaroos, jumping-hares, &c., sometimes appear to us ludicrous because something about them resembling man leads us to subsume them under the conception of the human form, and starting from this we perceive their incongruity with it.

Now the conceptions whose observed incongruity with the perceptions moves us to laughter are either those of others or our own. In the first case we laugh at others, in the second we feel a surprise, often agreeable, at the least amusing. Therefore children and uneducated people laugh at the most trifling things, even at misfortunes, if they were unexpected, and thus convicted their preconceived conception of error. As a rule laughing is a pleasant condition; accordingly the apprehension of the incongruity between what is thought and what is perceived, that is, the real, gives us pleasure, and we give ourselves up gladly to the spasmodic convulsions which this apprehension excites. The reason of this is as follows. In every suddenly appearing conflict between what is perceived and what is thought, what is perceived is always unquestionably right; for it is not subject to error at all, requires no confirmation from without, but answers for itself. Its conflict with what is thought springs ultimately from the fact that the latter, with its abstract conceptions, cannot get down to the infinite multifariousness and fine shades of difference of the concrete. This victory of knowledge of perception over thought affords us pleasure. For perception is the original kind of knowledge insepar-

able from animal nature, in which everything that gives
direct satisfaction to the will presents itself. It is the
medium of the present, of enjoyment and gaiety; moreover it is attended with no exertion. With thinking the
opposite is the case; it is the second power of knowledge,
the exercise of which always demands some, and often
considerable, exertion. Besides, it is the conceptions of
thought that often oppose the gratification of our immediate desires, for, as the medium of the past, the future, and
of seriousness, they are the vehicle of our fears, our repentance, and all our cares. It must therefore be diverting to us to see this strict, untiring, troublesome governess,
the reason, for once convicted of insufficiency. On this
account then the mien or appearance of laughter is very
closely related to that of joy.

On account of the want of reason, thus of general conceptions, the brute is incapable of laughter, as of speech.
This is therefore a prerogative and characteristic mark of
man. Yet it may be remarked in passing that his one
friend the dog has an analogous characteristic action
peculiar to him alone in distinction from all other brutes,
the very expressive, kindly, and thoroughly honest fawning
and wagging of its tail. But how favourably does this
salutation given him by nature compare with the bows
and simpering civilities of men. At least for the present,
it is a thousand times more reliable than their assurance
of inward friendship and devotion.

The opposite of laughing and joking is *seriousness*.
Accordingly it consists in the consciousness of the perfect
agreement and congruity of the conception, or thought,
with what is perceived, or the reality. The serious man
is convinced that he thinks the things as they are, and
that they are as he thinks them. This is just why the
transition from profound seriousness to laughter is so easy,
and can be effected by trifles. For the more perfect that
agreement assumed by seriousness may seem to be, the
more easily is it destroyed by the unexpected discovery

of even a slight incongruity. Therefore the more a man is capable of entire seriousness, the more heartily can he laugh. Men whose laughter is always affected and forced are intellectually and morally of little worth; and in general the way of laughing, and, on the other hand, the occasions of it, are very characteristic of the person. That the relations of the sexes afford the easiest materials for jokes always ready to hand and within the reach of the weakest wit, as is proved by the abundance of obscene jests, could not be if it were not that the deepest seriousness lies at their foundation.

That the laughter of others at what we do or say seriously offends us so keenly depends on the fact that it asserts that there is a great incongruity between our conceptions and the objective realities. For the same reason, the predicate "ludicrous" or "absurd" is insulting. The laugh of scorn announces with triumph to the baffled adversary how incongruous were the conceptions he cherished with the reality which is now revealing itself to him. Our own bitter laughter at the fearful disclosure of the truth through which our firmly cherished expectations are proved to be delusive is the active expression of the discovery now made of the incongruity between the thoughts which, in our foolish confidence in man or fate, we entertained, and the truth which is now unveiled.

The *intentionally* ludicrous is the *joke*. It is the effort to bring about a discrepancy between the conceptions of another and the reality by disarranging one of the two; while its opposite, *seriousness*, consists in the exact conformity of the two to each other, which is at least aimed at. But if now the joke is concealed behind seriousness, then we have *irony*. For example, if with apparent seriousness we acquiesce in the opinions of another which are the opposite of our own, and pretend to share them with him, till at last the result perplexes him both as to us and them. This is the attitude of Socrates as opposed to Hippias, Protagoras, Gorgias, and other sophists, and

indeed often to his collocutors in general. The converse
of irony is accordingly seriousness concealed behind a
joke, and this is *humour*. It might be called the double
counterpoint of irony. Explanations such as "Humour is
the interpenetration of the finite and the infinite" express
nothing more than the entire incapacity for thought of
those who are satisfied with such empty phrases. Irony
is objective, that is, intended for another; but humour is
subjective, that is, it primarily exists only for one's own
self. Accordingly we find the masterpieces of irony among
the ancients, but those of humour among the moderns.
For, more closely considered, humour depends upon a
subjective, yet serious and sublime mood, which is involuntarily in conflict with a common external world
very different from itself, which it cannot escape from and
to which it will not give itself up; therefore, as an accommodation, it tries to think its own point of view and that
external world through the same conceptions, and thus a
double incongruity arises, sometimes on the one side,
sometimes on the other, between these concepts and the
realities thought through them. Hence the impression of
the intentionally ludicrous, thus of the joke, is produced,
behind which, however, the deepest seriousness is concealed and shines through. Irony begins with a serious
air and ends with a smile; with humour the order is
reversed. The words of Mercutio quoted above may
serve as an example of humour. Also in "Hamlet"—
Polonius: "My honourable lord, I will most humbly take
my leave of you. *Hamlet:* You cannot, sir, take from
me anything that I will more willingly part withal, except
my life, except my life, except my life." Again, before
the introduction of the play at court, Hamlet says to
Ophelia: "What should a man do but be merry? for,
look you, how cheerfully my mother looks, and my father
died within these two hours. *Ophelia:* Nay, 'tis twice
two months, my lord. *Hamlet:* So long? Nay, then let
the devil wear black, for I'll have a suit of sables."

Again, in Jean Paul's "Titan," when Schoppe, melancholy and now brooding over himself, frequently looking at his hands, says to himself, "There sits a lord in bodily reality, and I in him ; but who is such ? " Heinrich Heine appears as a true humourist in his "*Romancero.*" Behind all his jokes and drollery we discern a profound seriousness, which is ashamed to appear unveiled. Accordingly humour depends upon a special kind of mood or temper (German, *Laune,* probably from *Luna*) through which conception in all its modifications, a decided predominance of the subjective over the objective in the apprehension of the external world, is thought. Moreover, every poetical or artistic presentation of a comical, or indeed even a farcical scene, through which a serious thought yet glimmers as its concealed background, is a production of humour, thus is humorous. Such, for example, is a coloured drawing of Tischbein's, which represents an empty room, lighted only by the blazing fire in the grate. Before the fire stands a man with his coat off, in such a position that his shadow, going out from his feet, stretches across the whole room. Tischbein comments thus on the drawing : "This is a man who has succeeded in nothing in the world, and who has made nothing of it; now he rejoices that he can throw such a large shadow." Now, if I had to express the seriousness that lies concealed behind this jest, I could best do so by means of the following verse taken from the Persian poem of Anwari Soheili :—

> "If thou hast lost possession of a world,
>   Be not distressed, for it is nought ;
> Or hast thou gained possession of a world,
>   Be not o'erjoyed, for it is nought.
> Our pains, our gains, all pass away ;
>   Get thee beyond the world, for it is nought."

That at the present day the word homorous is generally used in German literature in the sense of comical arises from the miserable desire to give things a more distinguished name than belongs to them, the name of a class that stands above them.   Thus every inn must be called a hotel, every money-changer a banker, every concert a musical academy, the merchant's counting-house a bureau, the potter an artist in clay, and therefore also every clown a humourist.   The word *humour* is borrowed from the English to denote a quite peculiar species of the ludicrous, which indeed, as was said above, is related to the sublime, and which was first remarked by them.   But it is not intended to be used as the title for all kinds of jokes and buffoonery, as is now universally the case in Germany, without opposition from men of letters and scholars; for the true conception of that modification, that tendency of the mind, that child of the sublime and the ridiculous, would be too subtle and too high for their public, to please which they take pains to make everything flat and vulgar.   Well, "high words and a low meaning" is in general the motto of the noble present, and accordingly now-a-days he is called a humourist who was formerly called a buffoon.

CHAPTER IX.[1]

LOGIC, Dialectic, and Rhetoric go together, because they make up the whole of a *technic of reason,* and under this title they ought also to be taught—Logic as the technic of our own thinking, Dialectic of disputing with others, and Rhetoric of speaking to many (*concionatio*); thus corresponding to the singular, dual, and plural, and to the monologue, the dialogue, and the panegyric.

Under Dialectic I understand, in agreement with Aristotle (*Metaph.,* iii. 2, and *Analyt. Post.,* i. 11), the art of conversation directed to the mutual investigation of truth, especially philosophical truth. But a conversation of this kind necessarily passes more or less into controversy; therefore dialectic may also be explained as the art of disputation. We have examples and patterns of dialectic in the Platonic dialogues; but for the special theory of it, thus for the technical rules of disputation, eristics, very little has hitherto been accomplished. I have worked out an attempt of the kind, and given an example of it, in the second volume of the "Parerga," therefore I shall pass over the exposition of this science altogether here.

In Rhetoric the rhetorical figures are very much what the syllogistic figures are in Logic; at all events they are worth considering. In Aristotle's time they seem to have not yet become the object of theoretical investigation, for he does not treat of them in any of his rhetorics, and in

---

[1] This chapter and the one which follows it are connected with § 9 of the first volume.

this reference we are referred to Rutilius Lupus, the epito-
miser of a later Gorgias.

All the three sciences have this in common, that without having learned them we follow their rules, which
indeed are themselves first abstracted from this natural
employment of them. Therefore, although they are of
great theoretical interest, they are of little practical use;
partly because, though they certainly give the rule, they
do not give the case of its application; partly because in
practice there is generally no time to recollect the rules.
Thus they teach only what every one already knows and
practises of his own accord; but yet the abstract knowledge of this is interesting and important. Logic will not
easily have a practical value, at least for our own thinking.
For the errors of our own reasoning scarcely ever lie in
the inferences nor otherwise in the form, but in the judgments, thus in the matter of thought. In controversy, on
the other hand, we can sometimes derive some practical
use from logic, by taking the more or less intentionally
deceptive argument of our opponent, which he advances
under the garb and cover of continuous speech, and
referring it to the strict form of regular syllogisms, and
thus convicting it of logical errors; for example, simple
conversion of universal affirmative judgments, syllogisms
with four terms, inferences from the consequent to the
reason, syllogisms in the second figure with merely affirmative premisses, and many such.

It seems to me that the doctrine of the laws of thought
might be simplified if we were only to set up two, the
law of excluded middle and that of sufficient reason. The
former thus : " Every predicate can either be affirmed or
denied of every subject." Here it is already contained in
the " either, or " that both cannot occur at once, and consequently just what is expressed by the laws of identity
and contradiction. Thus these would be added as corollaries of that principle which really says that every two
concept-spheres must be thought either as united or as

separated, but never as both at once; and therefore, even
although words are brought together which express the
latter, these words assert a process of thought which cannot be carried out. The consciousness of this infeasibility
is the feeling of contradiction. The second law of thought,
the principle of sufficient reason, would affirm that the
above attributing or denying must be determined by something different from the judgment itself, which may be a
(pure or empirical) perception, or merely another judgment. This other and different thing is then called the
ground or reason of the judgment. So far as a judgment
satisfies the first law of thought, it is thinkable; so far as
it satisfies the second, it is true, or at least in the case in
which the ground of a judgment is only another judgment
it is logically or formally true. But, finally, material or
absolute truth is always the relation between a judgment
and a perception, thus between the abstract and the concrete or perceptible idea. This is either an immediate
relation or it is brought about by means of other judgments, *i.e.*, through other abstract ideas. From this it is
easy to see that one truth can never overthrow another,
but all must ultimately agree; because in the concrete or
perceptible, which is their common foundation, no contradiction is possible. Therefore no truth has anything to
fear from other truths. Illusion and error have to fear
every truth, because through the logical connection of all
truths even the most distant must some time strike its
blow at every error. This second law of thought is therefore the connecting link between logic and what is no
longer logic, but the matter of thought. Consequently
the agreement of the conceptions, thus of the abstract
idea with what is given in the perceptible idea, is, on
the side of the object *truth*, and on the side of the subject
knowledge.

To express the union or separation of two concept-
spheres referred to above is the work of the copula, " **is**
—is not." Through this every verb can be expressed **by**

means of its participle. Therefore all judging consists in the use of a verb, and *vice versâ*. Accordingly the significance of the copula is that the predicate is to be thought in the subject, nothing more. Now, consider what the content of the infinitive of the copula "to be" amounts to. But this is a principal theme of the professors of philosophy of the present time. However, we must not be too strict with them; most of them wish to express by it nothing but material things, the corporeal world, to which, as perfectly innocent realists at the bottom of their hearts, they attribute the highest reality. To speak, however, of the bodies so directly appears to them too vulgar; and therefore they say "being," which they think sounds better, and think in connection with it the tables and chairs standing before them.

"For, because, why, therefore, thus, since, although, indeed, yet, but, if, then, either, or," and more like these, are properly *logical particles*, for their only end is to express the form of the thought processes. They are therefore a valuable possession of a language, and do not belong to all in equal numbers. Thus "*zwar*" (the contracted "*es ist wahr*") seems to belong exclusively to the German language. It is always connected with an "*aber*" which follows or is added in thought, as "if" is connected with "then."

The logical rule that, as regards quantity, singular judgments, that is, judgments which have a singular conception (*notio singularis*) for their subject, are to be treated as *universal judgments*, depends upon the circumstance that they are in fact universal judgments, which have merely the peculiarity that their subject is a conception which can only be supported by a single real object, and therefore only contains a single real object under it; as when the conception is denoted by a proper name. This, however, has really only to be considered when we proceed from the abstract idea to the concrete or perceptible, thus seek to realise the conceptions. In thinking itself, in operating with judgments, this makes no difference, simply because between singular and universal conceptions there is no logical difference. " Immanuel Kant" signifies logically, " *all* Immanuel Kant." Accordingly the quantity of judgments is really only of two kinds—universal and particular. An *individual idea* cannot be the subject of a judgment, because it is not an abstraction, it is not something thought, but something perceived. Every conception, on the other hand, is essentially universal, and every judgment must have a *conception* as its subject.

The difference between *particular judgments* (*propositiones particulares*) and *universal judgments* often depends merely on the external and contingent circumstance that the language has no word to express by itself the part that is here to be separated from the general conception which forms the subject of such a judgment. If there were such a word many a particular judgment would be universal. For example, the particular judgment, " Some trees bear gall-nuts," becomes a universal judgment, because for this part of the conception, " tree," we have a special word, " All oaks bear gall-nuts." In the same way is the judgment, " Some men are black," related to the judgment, " All negroes are black." Or else this difference depends upon the fact that in the mind of him who judges the conception which he makes the subject of the particular judgment has not become clearly separated from the general conception as a part of which he defines it ; otherwise he could have expressed a universal instead of a particular judgment. For example, instead of the judgment, " Some ruminants have upper incisors," this, " All unhorned ruminants have upper incisors."

The *hypothetical and disjunctive judgments* are assertions as to the relation of two (in the case of the disjunctive judgment even several) categorical judgments to each other. The *hypothetical judgment* asserts that the truth of the second of the two categorical judgments here linked together depends upon the truth of the first, and the falseness of the first depends upon the falseness of the second; thus that these two propositions stand in direct community as regards truth and falseness. The *disjunctive judgment,* on the other hand, asserts that upon the truth of one of the categorical judgments here linked together depends the falseness of the others, and conversely; thus that these propositions are in conflict as regards truth and falseness. The *question* is a judgment, one of whose three parts is left open : thus either the copula, "Is Caius a Roman—or not ?" or the predicate, "Is Caius a Roman—or something else ?" or the subject, "Is Caius a Roman—or is it some one else who is a Roman ?" The place of the conception which is left open may also remain quite empty; for example, "What is Caius ?"—"Who is a Roman ?"

The επαγωγη, *inductio,* is with Aristotle the opposite of the απαγωγη. The latter proves a proposition to be false by showing that what would follow from it is not true ; thus by the *instantia in contrarium.* The επαγωγη, on the other hand, proves the truth of a proposition by showing that what would follow from it is true. Thus it leads by means of examples to our accepting something while the απαγωγη leads to our rejecting it. Therefore the επαγωγη, or induction, is an inference from the consequents to the reason, and indeed *modo ponente ;* for from many cases it establishes the rule, from which these cases then in their turn follow. On this account it is never perfectly certain, but at the most arrives at very great probability. However, this *formal* uncertainty may yet leave room for *material* certainty through the number of the sequences observed ; in the same way as in mathematics the irrational relations are brought infinitely near to rationality by means of decimal fractions. The απαγωγη, on the contrary, is primarily an inference from the reason to the consequents, though it is afterwards carried out *modo tollente,* in that it proves the non-existence of a necessary consequent, and thereby destroys the truth of the assumed reason. On this account it is always perfectly certain, and accomplishes more by a single example *in contrarium* than the induction does by innumerable examples in favour of the proposition propounded. So much easier is it to refute than to prove, to overthrow than to establish.

CHAPTER X.

ON THE SYLLOGISM.

ALTHOUGH it is very hard to establish a new and correct view of a subject which for more than two thousand years has been handled by innumerable writers, and which, moreover, does not receive additions through the growth of experience, yet this must not deter me from presenting to the thinker for examination the following attempt of this kind.

An inference is that operation of our reason by virtue of which, through the comparison of two judgments a third judgment arises, without the assistance of any knowledge otherwise obtained. The condition of this is that these two judgments have *one* conception in common, for otherwise they are foreign to each other and have no community. But under this condition they become the father and mother of a child that contains in itself something of both. Moreover, this operation is no arbitrary act, but an act of the reason, which, when it has considered such judgments, performs it of itself according to its own Laws. So far it is objective, not subjective, and therefore subject to the strictest rules.

We may ask in passing whether he who draws an inference really learns something new from the new proposition, something previously unknown to him? Not absolutely; but yet to a certain extent he does. What he learns lay in what he knew: thus he knew it also, but he did not know that he knew it; which is as if he had something, but did not know that he had it, and this is just the same as if he had it not. He knew it only *implicite*, now he knows it *explicite ;* but this distinction may be so great that the conclusion appears to him a new truth. For example :

> All diamonds are stones ;
> All diamonds are combustible :
> Therefore some stones are combustible.

The nature of inference consequently consists in this, that we bring it to distinct consciousness that we have already thought in the premisses what is asserted in the conclusion. It is therefore a means of becoming more distinctly conscious of one's own knowledge, of learning more fully, or becoming aware of what one knows. The knowledge which is afforded by the conclusion was *latent*, and therefore had just as little effect as latent heat has on the thermometer. Whoever has salt has also chlorine ; but it is as if he had it not, for it can only act as chlorine if it is chemically evolved ; thus only, then, does he really possess it. It is the same with the gain which a mere conclusion from already known premisses affords : a previously *bound or latent knowledge* is thereby set *free*. These comparisons may indeed seem to be somewhat strained, but yet they really are not. For because we draw many of the possible inferences from our knowledge very soon, very rapidly, and without formality, and therefore have no distinct recollection of them, it seems to us as if no premisses for possible conclusions remained long stored up unused, but as if we already had also conclusions prepared for all the premisses within reach of our knowledge. But this is not always the case ; on the contrary, two premisses may have for a long time an isolated existence in the same mind, till at last some occasion brings them together, and then the conclusion suddenly appears, as the spark comes from the steel and the stone only when they are struck together. In reality the premisses assumed from without, both for theoretical insight and for motives, which bring about resolves, often lie for a long time in us, and become, partly through half-conscious, and even inarticulate, processes of thought, compared with the rest of our stock of knowledge, reflected upon, and, as it were, shaken up together, till at last the right major finds the right minor, and these immediately take up their proper places, and at once the conclusion exists as a light that has suddenly arisen for us, without any action on our part, as if it were an inspiration; for we cannot comprehend how we and others have so long been in ignorance of it. It is true that in a happily organised mind this process goes on more quickly and easily than in ordinary minds; and just because it is carried on spontaneously and without distinct consciousness it cannot be learned. Therefore Goethe says: "How easy anything is he knows who has discovered it, he knows who has attained to it." As an illustration of the process of thought here described we may compare it to those padlocks which consist of rings with letters; hanging on the box of a travelling carriage, they are shaken so long that at last the letters of the word come together in their order and the lock opens. For the rest, we must also remember that the syllogism consists in the process of thought itself, and the words and propositions through which it is expressed only indicate the traces it has left behind it—they are related to it as the sound-figures of sand are related to the notes whose vibrations they express. When we reflect upon something, we collect our data, reduce them to judgments, which are all quickly brought together and compared, and thereby the conclusions which it is possible to draw from them are instantly arrived at by means of the use of all the three syllogistic figures. Yet on account of the great rapidity of this operation only a few words are used, and sometimes none at all, and only the conclusion is formally expressed. Thus it sometimes happens that because in this way, or even merely intuitively, *i.e.*, by a happy *apperçu*, we have brought some new truth to consciousness, we now treat it as a conclusion and seek premisses for it, that is, we desire to prove it, for as a rule knowledge

exists earlier than its proofs. We then go through our
stock of knowledge in order to see whether we can find
some truth in it in which the newly discovered truth was
already implicitly contained, or two propositions which
would give this as a result if they were brought together
according to rule. On the other hand, every judicial
proceeding affords a most complete and imposing syllogism, a syllogism in the first figure. The civil or criminal
transgression complained of is the minor; it is established
by the prosecutor. The law applicable to the case is the
major. The judgment is the conclusion, which therefore,
as something necessary, is "merely recognised" by the
judge.

But now I shall attempt to give the simplest and most
correct exposition of the peculiar mechanism of inference.

Judging, this elementary and most important process
of thought, consists in the comparison of two *conceptions; inference* in the comparison of two *judgments*. Yet
ordinarily in text-books inference is also referred to
the comparison of conceptions, though of *three*, because
from the relation which two of these conceptions have
to a third their relation to each other may be known.
Truth cannot be denied to this view also; and since it
affords opportunity for the perceptible demonstration of
syllogistic relations by means of drawn concept-spheres,
a method approved of by me in the text, it has the
advantage of making the matter easily comprehensible.
But it seems to me that here, as in so many cases, comprehensibility is attained at the cost of thoroughness.
The real process of thought in inference, with which the
three syllogistic figures and their necessity precisely agree,
is not thus recognised. In inference we operate *not* with
mere *conceptions* but with whole *judgments*, to which
quality, which lies only in the copula and not in the
conceptions, and also quantity are absolutely essential,
and indeed we have further to add modality. That
exposition of inference as a relation of *three conceptions*

fails in this, that it at once resolves the judgments into their ultimate elements (the conceptions), and thus the means of combining these is lost, and that which is peculiar to the judgments as such and in their completeness, which is just what constitutes the necessity of the conclusion which follows from them, is lost sight of. It thus falls into an error analogous to that which organic chemistry would commit if, for example, in the analysis of plants it were at once to reduce them to their *ultimate* elements, when it would find in all plants carbon, hydrogen, and oxygen, but would lose the specific differences, to obtain which it is necessary to stop at their more special elements, the so-called alkaloids, and to take care to analyse these in their turn. From three given conceptions no conclusion can as yet be drawn. It may certainly be said: the relation of two of them to the third must be given with them. But it is just the *judgments* which combine these conceptions, that are the expression of this relation; thus *judgments*, not mere *conceptions*, are the material of the inference. Accordingly inference is essentially a comparison of two *judgments*. The process of thought in our mind is concerned with these and the thoughts expressed by them, not merely with three conceptions. This is the case even when this process is imperfectly or not at all expressed in words; and it is as such, as a bringing together of the complete and unanalysed judgments, that we must consider it in order properly to understand the technical procedure of inference. From this there will then also follow the necessity for three really rational syllogistic figures.

As in the exposition of syllogistic reasoning by means of *concept-spheres* these are presented to the mind under the form of circles, so in the exposition by means of entire judgments we have to think these under the form of rods, which, for the purpose of comparison, are held together now by one end, now by the other. The different ways in which this can take place give the three figures.

Since now every premiss contains its subject and its predicate, these two conceptions are to be imagined as situated at the two ends of each rod. The two judgments are now compared with reference to the two *different* conceptions in them; for, as has already been said, the third conception must be the same in both, and is therefore subject to no comparison, but is that *with which*, that is, in reference to which, the other two are compared; it is the *middle*. The latter is accordingly always only the means and not the chief concern. The two different conceptions, on the other hand, are the subject of reflection, and to find out their relation to each other by means of the judgments in which they are contained is the aim of the syllogism. Therefore the conclusion speaks only of them, not of the middle, which was only a means, a measuring rod, which we let fall as soon as it has served its end. Now if this conception which is *identical* in both propositions, thus the middle, is the subject of *one* premiss, the conception to be compared with it must be the predicate, and conversely. Here at once is established *a priori* the possibility of three cases; either the subject of one premiss is compared with the predicate of the other, or the subject of the one with the subject of the other, or, finally, the predicate of the one with the predicate of the other. Hence arise the three syllogistic figures of Aristotle; the fourth, which was added somewhat impertinently, is ungenuine and a spurious form. It is attributed to Galenus, but this rests only on Arabian authority. Each of the three figures exhibits a perfectly different, correct, and natural thought-process of the reason in inference.

If in the two judgments to be compared the relation between the *predicate of the one and the subject of the other* is the object of the comparison, the *first figure* appears. This figure alone has the advantage that the conceptions which in the conclusion are subject and predicate both appear already in the same character in the premisses; while in the two other figures one of them must always change its roll in the conclusion. But thus in the first figure the result is always less novel and surprising than in the other two. Now this advantage in the first figure is obtained by the fact that the predicate of the major is compared with the subject of the minor, but not conversely, which is therefore here essential, and involves that the middle should assume both the positions, *i.e.*, it is the subject in the major and the predicate in the minor. And from this again arises its subordinate significance, for it appears as a mere weight which we lay at pleasure now in one scale and now in the other. The course of thought in this figure is, that the predicate of the major is attributed to the subject of the minor, because the subject of the major is the predicate of the minor, or, in the negative case, the converse holds for the same reason. Thus here a property is attributed to the things thought through a conception, because it depends upon another property which we already know they possess; or conversely. Therefore here the guiding principle is: *Nota notæ est nota rei ipsius, et repugnans notæ repugnat rei ipsi.*

If, on the other hand, we compare two judgments with the intention of bringing out the relation which the *subjects of both* may have to each other, we must take as the common measure their predicate. This will accordingly be here the middle, and must therefore be the same in both judgments. Hence arises the *second figure.* In it the relation of two subjects to each other is determined by that which they have as their common predicate. But this relation can only have significance if the same predicate is attributed to the one subject and denied of the other, for thus it becomes an essential ground of distinction between the two. For if it were attributed to both the subjects this could decide nothing as to their relation to each other, for almost every predicate belongs to innumerable subjects. Still less would it decide this relation if the predicate were denied of both the subjects. From this follows the fundamental characteristic of the second figure, that the premisses must be of *opposite quality;* the one must affirm and the other deny. Therefore here the principal rule is: *Sit altera negans;* the corollary of which is: *E meris affirmativis nihil sequiter;* a rule which is sometimes transgressed in a loose argument obscured by many parenthetical propositions. The course of thought which this figure exhibits distinctly appears from what has been said. It is the investigation of two kinds of things with the view of distinguishing them, thus of establishing that they are *not* of the same species; which is here decided by showing that a certain property is essential to the one kind, which the other lacks. That this course of thought assumes the second figure of its own accord, and expresses itself clearly only in it, will be shown by an example:

> All fishes have cold blood;
> No whale has cold blood:
> Thus no whale is a fish.

In the first figure, on the other hand, this thought exhibits itself in a weak, forced, and ultimately patched-up form :

> Nothing that has cold blood is a whale;
> All fishes have cold blood :
> Thus no fish is a whale,
> And consequently no whale is a fish.

Take also an example with an affirmative minor :

> No Mohamedan is a Jew ;
> Some Turks are Jews :
> Therefore some Turks are not Mohamedans.

As the guiding principle for this figure I therefore give, for the mood with the negative minor : *Cui repugnat nota, etiam repugnat notatum;* and for the mood with the affirmative minor : *Notato repugnat id cui nota repugnat.* Translated these may be thus combined : Two subjects which stand in opposite relations to one predicate have a negative relation to each other.

The third case is that in which we place two judgments

together in order to investigate the relation of their *predicates*. Hence arises the *third figure*, in which accordingly the middle appears in both premises as the subject. It is also here the *tertium comparationis*, the measure which is applied to both the conceptions which are to be investigated, or, as it were, a chemical reagent, with which we test them both in order to learn from their relation to it what relation exists between themselves. Thus, then, the conclusion declares whether a relation of subject and predicate exists between the two, and to what extent this is the case. Accordingly, what exhibits itself in this figure is reflection concerning two properties which we are inclined to regard either as *incompatible*, or else as *inseparable*, and in order to decide this we attempt to make them the predicates of one subject in two judgments. From this it results either that both properties belong to the same thing, consequently their *compatibility*, or else that a thing has the one but not the other, consequently their *separableness*. The former in all moods with two affirmative premisses, the latter in all moods with one negative; for example:

Some brutes can speak;
All brutes are irrational:
Therefore some irrational beings can speak.

According to Kant (*Die Falsche Spitzfinigkeit*, § 4) this inference would only be conclusive if we added in thought: "Therefore some irrational beings are brutes." But this seems to be here quite superfluous and by no means the natural process of thought. But in order to carry out the same process of thought directly by means of the first figure I must say:

" All brutes are irrational;
Some beings that can speak are brutes,"

which is clearly not the natural course of thought; indeed the conclusion which would then follow, "Some beings that can speak are irrational," would have to be converted in order to preserve the conclusion which the third figure gives of itself, and at which the whole course of thought has aimed. Let us take another example:

> All alkalis float in water;
> All alkalis are metals:
> Therefore some metals float in water.

When this is transposed into the first figure the minor must be converted, and thus runs: "Some metals are alkalis." It therefore merely asserts that some metals lie

in the sphere "alkalis," thus , while our

actual knowledge is that all alkalis lie in the sphere

"metals," thus: It follows that if the first

figure is to be regarded as the only normal one, in order to think naturally we would have to think less than we know, and to think indefinitely while we know definitely. This assumption has too much against it. Thus in general it must be denied that when we draw inferences in the second and third figures we tacitly convert a proposition. On the contrary, the third, and also the second, figure exhibits just as rational a process of thought as the first. Let us now consider another example of the other class of the third figure, in which the separableness of two predicates is the result; on account of which one premiss must here be negative:

> No Buddhist believes in a God;
> Some Buddhists are rational:
> Therefore some rational beings do not believe in a God.

As in the examples given above the *compatibility* of two properties is the problem of reflection, now their *separableness* is its problem, which here also must be decided by comparing them with *one* subject and showing that *one* of them is present in it without the *other*.　Thus the end is directly attained, while by means of the first figure it could only be attained indirectly.　For in order to reduce the syllogism to the first figure we must convert the minor, and therefore say: "Some rational beings are Buddhists," which would be only a faulty expression of its meaning, which really is: "Some Buddhists are yet certainly rational."

As the guiding principle of this figure I therefore give: for the affirmative moods: *Ejusdem rei notæ, modo sit altera universalis, sibi invicem sunt notæ particulares;* and for the negative moods: *Nota rei competens, notæ eidem repugnanti, particulariter repugnat, modo sit altera universalis.*　Translated: If two predicates are affirmed of one subject, and at least one of them universally, they are also affirmed of each other particularly; and, on the contrary, they are denied of each other particularly whenever one of them contradicts the subject of which the other is affirmed; provided always that either the contradiction or the affirmation be universal.

In the *fourth figure* the subject of the major has to be compared with the predicate of the minor; but in the conclusion they must both exchange their value and position, so that what was the subject of the major appears as the predicate of the conclusion, and what was the predicate of the minor appears as the subject of the conclusion.　By this it becomes apparent that this figure is merely the *first*, wilfully turned upside down, and by no means the expression of a real process of thought natural to the reason.

On the other hand, the first three figures are the ectypes of three real and essentially different operations of thought. They have this in common, that they consist in the comparison of two judgments; but such a comparison only becomes fruitful when these judgments have *one* conception in common.　If we present the premises to our imagination under the sensible form of two rods, we can think of this conception as a clasp that links them to each other; indeed in lecturing one might provide oneself with such rods. On the other hand, the three figures are distinguished by this, that those judgments are compared either with reference to the subjects of both, or to the predicates of both, or lastly, with reference to the subject of the one and the predicate of the other. Since now every conception has the property of being subject or predicate only because it is already part of a judgment, this confirms my view that in the syllogism only judgments are primarily compared, and conceptions only because they are parts of judgments. In the comparison of two judgments, however, the essential question is, in *respect of what* are they compared? not *by what means* are they compared? The former consists of the concepts which are different in the two judgments; the latter consists of the middle, that is, the conception which is identical in both. It is therefore not the right point of view which Lambert, and indeed really Aristotle, and almost all the moderns have taken in starting from the *middle* in the analysis of syllogisms, and making it the principal matter and its position the essential characteristic of the syllogisms. On the contrary, its roll is only secondary, and its position a consequence of the logical value of the conceptions which are really to be compared in the syllogism. These may be compared to two substances which are to be chemically tested, and the middle to the reagent by which they are tested. It therefore always takes the place which the conceptions to be compared leave vacant, and does not appear again in the conclusion. It is selected according to our knowledge of its relation to both the conceptions and its suitableness for the place it has to take up. Therefore in many cases we can change it at pleasure for another without affecting the syllogism. For example, in the syllogism:

> All men are mortal;
> Caius is a man:

I can exchange the middle " man" for "animal existence." In the syllogism :

> All diamonds are stones ;
> All diamonds are combustible :

I can exchange the middle "diamond" for "anthracite."
As an external mark by which we can recognise at once
the figure of a syllogism the middle is certainly very
useful. But as the fundamental characteristic of a thing
which is to be explained, we must take what is essential
to it ; and what is essential here is, whether we place two
propositions together in order to compare their predicates
or their subjects, or the predicate of the one and the
subject of the other.

Therefore, in order as premisses to yield a conclusion,
two judgments must have a conception in common ;
further, they must not both be negative, nor both particular ; and lastly, in the case in which the conceptions to
be compared are the subjects of both, they must not both
be affirmative.

The voltaic pile may be regarded as a sensible image of
the syllogism. Its point of indifference, at the centre,
represents the middle, which holds together the two premisses, and by virtue of which they have the power of
yielding a conclusion. The two different conceptions, on
the other hand, which are really what is to be compared,
are represented by the two opposite poles of the pile.
Only because these are brought together by means of
their two conducting wires, which represent the copulas
of the two judgments, is the spark emitted upon their
contact—the new light of the conclusion.

CHAPTER XI.[1]

ON RHETORIC.

ELOQUENCE is the faculty of awakening in others our view of a thing, or our opinion about it, of kindling in them our feeling concerning it, and thus putting them in sympathy with us. And all this by conducting the stream of our thought into their minds, through the medium of words, with such force as to carry their thought from the direction it has already taken, and sweep it along with ours in its course. The more their previous course of thought differs from ours, the greater is this achievement. From this it is easily understood how personal conviction and passion make a man eloquent; and in general, eloquence is more the gift of nature than the work of art; yet here, also, art will support nature.

In order to convince another of a truth which conflicts with an error he firmly holds, the first rule to be observed, is an easy and natural one: *let the premisses come first, and the conclusion follow.* Yet this rule is seldom observed, but reversed; for zeal, eagerness, and dogmatic positiveness urge us to proclaim the conclusion loudly and noisily against him who adheres to the opposed error. This easily makes him shy, and now he opposes his will to all reasons and premisses, knowing already to what conclusion they lead. Therefore we ought rather to keep the conclusion completely concealed, and only advance the premisses

[1] This chapter is connected with the conclusion of § 9 of the first volume.

distinctly, fully, and in different lights. Indeed, if possible, we ought not to express the conclusion at all. It will come necessarily and regularly of its own accord into the reason of the hearers, and the conviction thus born in themselves will be all the more genuine, and will also be accompanied by self-esteem instead of shame. In difficult cases we may even assume the air of desiring to arrive at a quite opposite conclusion from that which we really have in view. An example of this is the famous speech of Antony in Shakspeare's "Julius Cæsar."

In defending a thing many persons err by confidently advancing everything imaginable that can be said for it, mixing up together what is true, half true, and merely plausible. But the false is soon recognised, or at any rate felt, and throws suspicion also upon the cogent and true arguments which were brought forward along with it. Give then the true and weighty pure and alone, and beware of defending a truth with inadequate, and therefore, since they are set up as adequate, sophistical reasons; for the opponent upsets these, and thereby gains the appearance of having upset the truth itself which was supported by them, that is, he makes *argumenta ad hominem* hold good as *argumenta ad rem*. The Chinese go, perhaps, too far the other way, for they have the saying: "He who is eloquent and has a sharp tongue may always leave half of a sentence unspoken; and he who has right on his side may confidently yield three-tenths of his assertion."

CHAPTER XII.[1]

FROM the analysis of the different functions of our intellect given in the whole of the preceding chapters, it is clear that for a correct use of it, either in a theoretical or a practical reference, the following conditions are demanded: (1.) The correct apprehension through perception of the real things taken into consideration, and of all their essential properties and relations, thus of all *data*. (2.) The construction of correct conceptions out of these; thus the connotation of those properties under correct abstractions, which now become the material of the subsequent thinking. (3.) The comparison of those conceptions both with the perceived object and among themselves, and with the rest of our store of conceptions, so that correct judgments, pertinent to the matter in hand, and fully comprehending and exhausting it, may proceed from them; thus the right *estimation* of the matter. (4.) The placing together or *combination* of those judgments as the premisses of *syllogisms*. This may be done very differently according to the choice and arrangement of the judgments, and yet the actual *result* of the whole operation primarily depends upon it. What is really of importance here is that from among so many possible combinations of those different judgments which have to do with the matter free deliberation should hit upon the very ones which serve the purpose and are decisive. But if in the first function, that is, in the apprehension through perception

[1] This chapter is connected with § 14 of the first volume.

of the things and relations, any single essential point has been overlooked, the correctness of all the succeeding operations of the mind cannot prevent the result from being false; for there lie the data, the material of the whole investigation. Without the certainty that these are correctly and completely collected, one ought to abstain, in important matters, from any definite decision.

A conception is *correct;* a judgment is *true;* a body is *real;* and a relation is *evident.* A proposition of immediate certainty is an *axiom.* Only the fundamental principles of logic, and those of mathematics drawn *a priori* from intuition or perception, and finally also the law of causality, have immediate certainty. A proposition of indirect certainty is a maxim, and that by means of which it obtains its certainty is the proof. If immediate certainty is attributed to a proposition which has no such certainty, this is a *petitio principii.* A proposition which appeals directly to the empirical perception is an *assertion:* to confront it with such perception demands judgment. Empirical perception can primarily afford us only *particular,* not universal truths. Through manifold repetition and confirmation such truths indeed obtain a certain universality also, but it is only comparative and precarious, because it is still always open to attack. But if a proposition has absolute universality, the perception to which it appeals is not empirical but *a priori.* Thus Logic and Mathematics alone are absolutely certain sciences; but they really teach us only what we already knew beforehand. For they are merely explanations of that of which we are conscious *a priori,* the forms of our own knowledge, the one being concerned with the forms of thinking, the other with those of perceiving. Therefore we spin them entirely out of ourselves. All other scientific knowledge is empirical.

A proof proves *too much* if it extends to things or cases of which that which is to be proved clearly does not hold good; therefore it is refuted apagogically by these. The *deductio ad absurdum* properly consists in this, that we take a false assertion which has been made as the major proposition of a syllogism, then add to it a correct minor, and arrive at a conclusion which clearly contradicts facts of experience or unquestionable truths. But by some round-about way such a refutation must be possible of every false doctrine. For the defender of this will yet certainly recognise and admit some truth or other, and then the consequences of this, and on the other hand those of the false assertion, must be followed out until we arrive at two propositions which directly contradict each other. We find many examples in Plato of this beautiful artifice of genuine dialectic.

A *correct hypothesis* is nothing more than the true and complete expression of the present fact, which the originator of the hypothesis has intuitively apprehended in its real nature and inner connection. For it tells us only what really takes place here.

The opposition of the *analytical* and *synthetical* methods we find already indicated by Aristotle, yet perhaps first distinctly described by Proclus, who says quite correctly: "Μεθοδοι δε παραδιδονται· καλλιστη μεν ή δια της ανα-λυσεως επ᾽ αρχην ὁμολογουμενην αναγουσα το ζητουμενον· ήν και Πλατων, ὡς φασι, Λαοδαμαντι παρεδωκεν. κ. τ. λ." (*Methodi traduntur sequentes: pulcherrima quidem ea, quæ per analysin quæsitum refert ad principium, de quo jam convenit ; quam etiam Plato Laodamanti tradidisse dicitur.*) "*In Primum Euclidis Librum,*" L. iii. Certainly the analytical method consists in referring what is given to an admitted principle ; the synthetical method, on the contrary, in deduction from such a principle. They are therefore analogous to the επαγωγη and απαγωγη explained in chapter ix. ; only the latter are not used to establish propositions, but always to overthrow them. The analytical method proceeds from the facts ; the particular, to the principle or rule ; the universal, or from the consequents to the reasons ; the other conversely. Therefore it would be much more correct to call them *the inductive and the deductive methods*, for the customary names are unsuitable and do not fully express the things.

If a philosopher tries to begin by thinking out the methods in accordance with which he will philosophise, he is like a poet who first writes a system of æsthetics in order to poetise in accordance with it. Both of them may be compared to a man who first sings himself a tune and afterwards dances to it. The thinking mind must find its way from original tendency. Rule and application, method and achievement, must, like matter and form, be inseparable. But after we have reached the goal we may consider the path we have followed. Æsthetics and methodology are, from their nature, younger than poetry and philosophy; as grammar is younger than language, thorough bass younger than music, and logic younger than thought.

This is a fitting place to make, in passing, a remark by means of which I should like to check a growing evil while there is yet time. That Latin has ceased to be the language of all scientific investigations has the disadvantage that there is no longer an immediately common scientific literature for the whole of Europe, but national literatures. And thus every scholar is primarily limited to a much smaller public, and moreover to a public hampered with national points of view and prejudices. Then he must now learn the four principal European languages, as well as the two ancient languages. In this it will be a great assistance to him that the *termini technici* of all sciences (with the exception of mineralogy) are, as an inheritance from our predecessors, Latin or Greek. Therefore all nations wisely retain these. Only the Germans have hit upon the unfortunate idea of wishing to Germanise the *termini technici* of all the sciences. This has two great disadvantages. First, the foreign and also the German scholar is obliged to learn all the technical terms of his science twice. which. when there are many—for example, in Anatomy—is an incredibly tiresome and lengthy business. If the other nations were not in this respect wiser than the Germans, we would have the trouble of learning every *terminus technicus* five times. If the Germans carry this further, foreign men of learning will leave their books altogether unread; for besides this fault they are for the most part too diffuse, and are written in a careless, bad, and often affected and objectionable style, and besides are generally conceived with a rude disregard of the reader and his requirements. Secondly, those Germanised forms of the *termini technici* are almost throughout long, patched-up, stupidly chosen, awkward, jarring words, not clearly separated from the rest of the language, which therefore impress themselves with difficulty upon the memory, while the Greek and Latin expressions chosen by the ancient and memorable founders of the sciences possess the whole of the opposite good qualities, and easily impress themselves on the memory by their sonorous sound. What an ugly, harsh-sounding word, for instance, is *"Stickstoff"* instead of *azot!* *"Verbum," "substantiv," "adjectiv,"* are remembered and distinguished more easily than *"Zeitwort," "Nennwort," "Beiwort,"* or even *"Umstandswort"* instead of *"adverbium."* In Anatomy it is quite unsupportable, and moreover vulgar and low. Even *"Pulsader"* and *"Blutader"* are more exposed to momentary confusion than *"Arterie"* and *"Vene;"* but utterly bewildering are such expressions as *"Fruchthälter," "Fruchtgang,"* and *"Fruchtleiter"* instead of *"uterus," "vagina,"* and *"tuba Faloppii,"* which yet every doctor must know, and which he will find sufficient in all European languages. In the same way *"Speiche"* and *"Ellenbogenröhre"* instead of *"radius"* and *"ulna,"* which all Europe has understood for thousands of years. Wherefore then this clumsy, confusing, drawling, and awkward Germanising? Not less objectionable is the translation of the technical terms in Logic, in which our gifted professors of philosophy are the creators of a new terminology, and almost every one of them has his own. With G. E. Schulze, for example, the subject is called "*Grundbegriff*," the predicate "*Beilegungsbegriff;*" then there are "*Beilegungsschlüsse*," "*Voraussetzungsschlüsse*," and "*Entgegensetzungsschlüsse;*" the judgments have "*Grösse*," "*Beschaffenheit*," "*Verhältniss*," and "*Zuverlässigkeit*," i.e., quantity, quality, relation, and modality. The same perverse influence of this Germanising mania is to be found in all the sciences. The Latin and Greek expressions have the further advantage that they stamp the scientific conception as such, and distinguish it from the words of common intercourse, and the ideas which cling to them through association; while, for example, "*Speisebrei*" instead of *chyme* seems to refer to the food of little children, and "*Lungensack*" instead of *pleura*, and "*Herzbeutel*" instead of *pericardium* seem to have been invented by butchers rather than anatomists. Besides this, the most immediate necessity of learning the ancient languages depends upon the old *termini technici*, and they are more and more in danger of being neglected through the use of living languages in learned investigations. But if it comes to this, if the spirit of the ancients bound up with their languages disappears from a liberal education, then coarseness, insipidity, and vulgarity will take possession of the whole of literature. For the works of the ancients are the pole-star of every artistic or literary effort; if it sets they are lost. Even now we can observe from the miserable and puerile style of most writers that they have never written Latin.[1] The study of the classical authors is very properly called the study of *Humanity*, for through it the student first becomes a *man* again, for he enters

---

[1] A principal use of the study of the ancients is that it preserves us from *verbosity ;* for the ancients always take pains to write concisely and pregnantly, and the error of almost all moderns is verbosity, which the most recent try to make up for by suppressing syllables and letters. Therefore we ought to pursue the study of the ancients all our life, although reducing the time devoted to it. The ancients knew that we ought not to write as we speak. The moderns, on the other hand, are not even ashamed to print lectures they have delivered.

into the world which was still free from all the absurdities of the Middle Ages and of romanticism, which afterwards penetrated so deeply into mankind in Europe that even now every one comes into the world covered with it, and has first to strip it off simply to become a man again. Think not that your modern wisdom can ever supply the place of that initiation into manhood; ye are not, like the Greeks and Romans, born freemen, unfettered sons of nature. Ye are first the sons and heirs of the barbarous Middle Ages and of their madness, of infamous priestcraft, and of half-brutal, half-childish chivalry. Though both now gradually approach their end, yet ye cannot yet stand on your own feet. Without the school of the ancients your literature will degenerate into vulgar gossip and dull philistinism. Thus for all these reasons it is my well-intended counsel that an end be put at once to the Germanising mania condemned above.

I shall further take the opportunity of denouncing here the disorder which for some years has been introduced into German orthography in an unprecedented manner. Scribblers of every species have heard something of conciseness of expression, but do not know that this consists in the careful omission of everything super-fluous (to which, it is true, the whole of their writings belong), but imagine they can arrive at it by clipping the words as swindlers clip coin; and every syllable which appears to them superfluous, because they do not feel its value, they cut off without more ado. For example, our ancestors, with true tact, said " *Beweis* " and " *Verweis;* " but, on the other hand, " *Nachweisung.*" The fine distinc-tion analogous to that between " *Versuch* " and " *Versu-chung,*" "*Betracht* " and "*Betrachtung,*" is not perceptible to dull ears and thick skulls; therefore they have invented the word " *Nachweis,*" which has come at once into gene-ral use, for this only requires that an idea should be thoroughly awkward and a blunder very gross. Accord-ingly a similar amputation has already been proposed in in-

numerable words; for example, instead of " *Untersuchung* "
is written " *Untersuch ;* " nay, even instead of " *allmälig,*'
" *mälig ;* " instead of " *beinahe,*" " *nahe ;* " instead of " *be-
ständig,*" " *ständig.*" If a Frenchman took upon himself
to write " *près* " instead of " *presque,*" or if an Englishman
wrote " *most* " instead of " *almost,*" they would be laughed
at by every one as fools; but in Germany whoever does
this sort of thing passes for a man of originality. Chemists
already write " *löslich* " and " *unlöslich* " instead of " *unauf-
löslich,*" and if the grammarians do not rap them over
the knuckles they will rob the language of a valuable
word. Knots, shoe-strings, and also conglomerates of
which the cement is softened, and all analogous things
are " *löslich* " (can be loosed); but what is " *auflöslich*"
(soluble), on the other hand, is whatever vanishes in a
liquid, like salt in water. " *Auflösen* " (to dissolve) is the
terminus ad hoc, which says this and nothing else, marking
out a definite conception; but our acute improvers of the
language wish to empty it into the general rinsing-pan
" *lösen* " (to loosen); they would therefore in consistency be
obliged to make " *lösen* " also take the place everywhere
of " *ablösen* " (to relieve, used of guards), " *auslösen* " (to
release), " *einlösen* " (to redeem), &c., and in these, as in
the former case, deprive the language of definiteness of
expression. But to make the language poorer by a word
means to make the thought of the nation poorer by a
conception. Yet this is the tendency of the united efforts
of almost all our writers of books for the last ten or
twenty years. For what I have shown here by *one* example can be supported by a hundred others, and the
meanest stinting of syllables prevails like a disease. The
miserable wretches actually count the letters, and do not
hesitate to mutilate a word, or to use one in a false sense,
whenever by doing so they can gain two letters. He
who is capable of no new thoughts will at least bring new
words to market, and every ink-slinger regards it as his
vocation to improve the language. Journalists practise

this most shamelessly; and since their papers, on account of the trivial nature of their contents, have the largest public, indeed a public which for the most part reads nothing else, a great danger threatens the language through them. I therefore seriously advise that they should be subjected to an orthographical censorship, or that they should be made to pay a fine for every unusual or mutilated word; for what could be more improper than that changes of language should proceed from the lowest branch of literature? Language, especially a relatively speaking original language like German, is the most valuable inheritance of a nation, and it is also an exceedingly complicated work of art, easily injured, and which cannot again be restored, therefore a *noli me tangere.* Other nations have felt this, and have shown great piety towards their languages, although far less complete than German. Therefore the language of Dante and Petrarch differs only in trifles from that of to-day; Montaigne is still quite readable, and so also is Shakspeare in his oldest editions. For a German indeed it is good to have somewhat long words in his mouth; for he thinks slowly, and they give him time to reflect. But this prevailing economy of language shows itself in yet more character-istic phenomena. For example, in opposition to all logic and grammar, they use the imperfect for the perfect and pluperfect; they often stick the auxiliary verb in their pocket; they use the ablative instead of the genitive; for the sake of omitting a couple of logical particles they make such intricate sentences that one has to read them four times over in order to get at the sense; for it is only the paper and not the reader's time that they care to spare. In proper names, after the manner of Hotten-tots, they do not indicate the case either by inflection or article: the reader may guess it. But they are specially fond of contracting the double vowel and dropping the lengthening *h*, those letters sacred to prosody; which is just the same thing as if we wanted to banish η and ω

from Greek, and make ε and *o* take their place. **Whoever**
writes *Scham, Märchen, Mass, Spass,* ought also to write
Lon, Son, Stat, Sat, Jar, Al, &c.   But since writing is the
copy of speech, posterity will imagine that one ought
to speak as one writes; and then of the German language
there will only remain a narrow, mouth-distorting, jarring
noise of consonants, and all prosody will be lost.   The
spelling "*Literatur*" instead of the correct "*Litteratur*"
is also very much liked, because it saves a letter.   In
defence of this the participle of the verb *linere* is given
as the root of the word.   But *linere* means to smear;
therefore the favoured spelling might actually be correct
for the greater part of German bookmaking; so that one
could distinguish a very small "*Litteratur*" from a very
extensive "*Literatur.*"   In order to write concisely let a
man improve his style and shun all useless gossip and
chatter, and then he will not need to cut out syllables
and letters on account of the dearness of paper.   But
to write so many useless pages, useless sheets, useless
books, and then to want to make up this waste of
time and paper at the cost of the innocent syllables and
letters—that is truly the superlative of what is called
in English being penny wise and pound foolish.   It is to
be regretted that there is no German Academy to take
charge of the language against literary *sans-culottism,*
especially in an age when even those who are ignorant
of the ancient language venture to employ the press.
I have expressed my mind more fully on the whole subject of the inexcusable mischief being done at the present
day to the German language in my "Parerga," vol. ii.
chap. 23.

In my essay on the principle of sufficient reason, § 51,
I already proposed a first *classification of the sciences* in
accordance with the form of the principle of sufficient
reason which reigns in them ; and I also touched upon
it again in §§ 7 and 15 of the first volume of this work.
I will give here a small attempt at such a classification,

which will yet no doubt be susceptible of much improvement and perfecting :—

I. Pure *a priori* Sciences.
 1. The doctrine of the ground of being.
  (*a.*) In space : Geometry.
  (*b.*) In time : Arithmetic and Algebra.
 2. The doctrine of the ground of knowing : Logic.

II. Empirical or *a posteriori* Sciences. All based upon the ground of becoming, *i.e.*, the law of causalty, and upon the three modes of that law.
 1. The doctrine of causes.
  (*a.*) Universal: Mechanics, Hydrodynamics, Physics, Chemistry.
  (*b.*) Particular: Astronomy, Mineralogy, Geology, Technology, Pharmacy.
 2. The doctrine of stimuli.
  (*a.*) Universal: Physiology of plants and animals, together with the ancillary science, Anatomy.
  (*b.*) Particular: Botany, Zoology, Zootomy, Comparative Physiology, Pathology, Therapeutics.
 3. The doctrine of motives.
  (*a.*) Universal: Ethics, Psychology.
  (*b.*) Particular: Jurisprudence, History.

Philosophy or Metaphysics, as the doctrine of consciousness and its contents in general, or of the whole of experience as such, does not appear in the list, because it does not at once pursue the investigation which the principle of sufficient reason prescribes, but first has this principle itself as its object. It is to be regarded as the thorough bass of all sciences, but belongs to a higher class than they do, and is almost as much related to art as to science. As in music every particular period must correspond to the tonality to which thorough bass has advanced, so every author, in proportion to the line he follows, must bear the stamp of the philosophy which prevails in his time. But besides this, every science has also its special philosophy; and therefore we speak of the philosophy of botany, of zoology, of history, &c. By this we must reasonably understand nothing more than the chief results of each science itself, regarded and comprehended from the highest, that is the most general, point of view which is possible within that science. These general results connect themselves directly with general philosophy, for they supply it with important data, and relieve it from the labour of seeking these itself in the philosophically raw material of the special sciences. These special philosophies therefore stand as a mediating link between their special sciences and philosophy proper. For since the latter has to give the most general explanations concerning the whole of things, these must also be capable of being brought down and applied to the individual of every species of thing. The philosophy of each science, however, arises independently of philosophy in general, from the data of its own science itself. Therefore it does not need to wait till that philosophy at last be found; but if worked out in advance it will certainly agree with the true universal philosophy. This, on the other hand, must be capable of receiving confirmation and illustration from the philosophies of the particular sciences; for the most general truth must be capable of being proved through the more special truths. Goethe has afforded a beautiful example of the philosophy of zoology in his reflections on Dalton's and Pander's skeletons of rodents (*Hefte zur Morphologie*, 1824). And like merit in connection with the same science belongs to Kielmayer, Delamark, Geoffroy St. Hilaire, Cuvier, and many others, in that they have all brought out clearly the complete analogy, the inner relationship, the permanent type, and systematic connection of animal forms. Empirical sciences pursued purely for their own sake and without philosophical tendency are

like a face without eyes. They are, however, a suitable
occupation for men of good capacity who yet lack the
highest faculties, which would even be a hindrance to
minute investigations of such a kind. Such men concen-
trate their whole power and their whole knowledge upon
one limited field, in which, therefore, on condition of remaining in entire ignorance of everything else, they can
attain to the most complete knowledge possible; while
the philosopher must survey all fields of knowledge, and
indeed to a certain extent be at home in them; and
thus that complete knowledge which can only be attained by the study of detail is necessarily denied him.
Therefore the former may be compared to those Geneva
workmen of whom one makes only wheels, another only
springs, and a third only chains. The philosopher, on
the other hand, is like the watchmaker, who alone produces a whole out of all these which has motion and
significance. They may also be compared to the musi-
cians of an orchestra, each of whom is master of his own
instrument; and the philosopher, on the other hand, to the
conductor, who must know the nature and use of every
instrument, yet without being able to play them all, or
even one of them, with great perfection. Scotus Erigena
includes all sciences under the name *Scientia*, in opposition to philosophy, which he calls *Sapientia*. The same
distinction was already made by the Pythagoreans; as
may be seen from Stobæus (*Floril.*, vol. i. p. 20), where
it is very clearly and neatly explained. But a much
happier and more piquant comparison of the relation of
the two kinds of mental effort to each other has been
so often repeated by the ancients that we no longer know
to whom it belongs. Diogenes Laertius (ii. 79) attributes
it to Aristippus, Stobæus (*Floril.*, tit. iv. 110) to Aristo of
Chios; the Scholiast of Aristotle ascribes it to him (p. 8 of
the Berlin edition), but Plutarch (*De Puer. Educ.*, c. 10)
attributes it to Bio—" *Qui ajebat, sicut Penelopes proci,*

*quum non possent cum Penelope concumbere, rem cum ejus
ancillis habuissent; ita qui philosophiam nequeunt appre-
hendere eos in alliis nullius pretii diciplinis sese conterere."*
In our predominantly empirical and historical age it can
do no harm to recall this.

CHAPTER XIII.[1]

ON THE METHODS OF MATHEMATICS.

EUCLID's method of demonstration has brought forth from its own womb its most striking parody and caricature in the famous controversy on the theory of parallels, and the attempts, which are repeated every year, to prove the eleventh axiom. This axiom asserts, and indeed supports its assertion by the indirect evidence of a third inter-secting line, that two lines inclining towards each other (for that is just the meaning of "less than two right angles") if produced far enough must meet—a truth which is supposed to be too complicated to pass as self-evident, and therefore requires a demonstration. Such a demonstration, however, cannot be produced, just because there is nothing that is not immediate. This scruple of conscience reminds me of Schiller's question of law:—

"For years I have used my nose for smelling. Have I, then, actually a right to it that can be proved?" Indeed it seems to me that the logical method is hereby reduced to absurdity. Yet it is just through the controversies about this, together with the vain attempts to prove what is *directly* certain as merely *indirectly* certain, that the self-sufficingness and clearness of intuitive evidence appears in contrast with the uselessness and difficulty of logical proof—a contrast which is no less instructive than amusing. The direct certainty is not allowed to be valid here, because it is no mere logical certainty following from the conceptions, thus resting only upon the relation of the

[1] This chapter is connected with § 15 of the first volume.

predicate to the subject, according to the principle of contradiction. That axiom, however, is a synthetical proposition *a priori*, and as such has the guarantee of pure, not empirical, perception, which is just as immediate and certain as the principle of contradiction itself, from which all demonstrations first derive their certainty. Ultimately this holds good of every geometrical theorem, and it is quite arbitrary where we draw the line between what is directly certain and what has first to be demonstrated. It surprises me that the eighth axiom is not rather attacked. "Figures which coincide with each other are equal to each other." For "coinciding with each other" is either a mere tautology or something purely empirical which does not belong to pure perception but to external sensuous experience. It presupposes that the figures may be moved ; but only matter is movable in space. Therefore this appeal to coincidence leaves pure space—the one element of geometry—in order to pass over to what is material and empirical.

The reputed motto of the Platonic lecture-room, " Αγεω-μετρητος μηδεις εισιτω," of which mathematicians are so proud, was no doubt inspired by the fact that Plato regarded the geometrical figures as intermediate existences between the eternal Ideas and particular things, as Aristotle frequently mentions in his "Metaphysics" (especially i. c. 6, p. 887, 998, *et Scholia*, p. 827, ed. Berol.) Moreover, the opposition between those self-existent eternal forms, or Ideas, and the transitory individual things, was most easily made comprehensible in geometrical figures, and thereby laid the foundation of the doctrine of Ideas, which is the central point of the philosophy of Plato, and indeed his only serious and decided theoretical dogma. In expounding it, therefore, he started from geometry. In the same sense we are told that he regarded geometry as a preliminary exercise through which the mind of the pupil accustomed itself to deal with incorporeal objects, having hitherto in practical life had only to do with corporeal things (*Schol. in Aristot.*, p. 12, 15). This, then, is the sense in which Plato recommended geometry to the philosopher; and therefore one is not justified in extending it further. I rather recommend, as an investigation of the influence of mathematics upon our mental powers, and their value for scientific culture in general, a very thorough and learned discussion, in the form of a review of a book by Whewell in the *Edinburgh Review* of January 1836. Its author, who afterwards published it with some other discussions, with his name, is Sir W. Hamilton, Professor of Logic and Metaphysics in Scotland. This work has also found a German translator, and has appeared by itself under the title, "*Ueber den Werth und Unwerth der Mathematik*" *aus dem Englishen*, 1836. The conclusion the author arrives at is that the value of mathematics is only indirect, and lies in the application to ends which are only attainable through them; but in themselves mathematics leave the mind where they find it, and are by no means conducive to its general culture and development, nay, even a decided hindrance. This conclusion is not only proved by thorough dianoiological investigation of the mathematical activity of the mind, but is also confirmed by a very learned accumulation of examples and authorities. The only direct use which is left to mathematics is that it can accustom restless and unsteady minds to fix their attention. Even Descartes, who was yet himself famous as a mathematician, held the same opinion with regard to mathematics. In the "*Vie de Descartes par Baillet*," 1693, it is said, Liv. ii. c. 6, p. 54: "*Sa propre expérience l'avait convaincu du peu d'utilité des mathématiques, surtout lorsqu'on ne les cultive que pour elles mêmes. . . . Il ne voyait rien de moins solide, que de s'occuper de nombres tout simples et de figures imaginaires,*" &c.

CHAPTER XIV.

ON THE ASSOCIATION OF IDEAS.

THE presence of ideas and thoughts in our consciousness is as strictly subordinated to the principle of sufficient reason in its different forms as the movement of bodies to the law of causality. It is just as little possible that a thought can appear in the mind without an occasion as that a body can be set in motion without a cause. Now this occasion is either *external*, thus an impression of the senses, or *internal*, thus itself also a thought which introduces another thought by means of *association*. This again depends either upon a relation of reason and consequent between the two; or upon similarity, even mere analogy; or lastly upon the circumstance that they were both first apprehended at the same time, which again may have its ground in the proximity in space of their objects. The last two cases are denoted by the word *à propos*. The predominance of one of these three bonds of association of thoughts over the others is characteristic of the intellectual worth of the man. The first named will predominate in thoughtful and profound minds, the second in witty, ingenious, and poetical minds, and the third in minds of limited capacity. Not less characteristic is the degree of facility with which one thought recalls others that stand in any kind of relation to it: this constitutes the activeness of the mind. But the impossibility of the appearance of a thought without its sufficient occasion, even when there is the strongest desire to call it up, is proved by all the cases in which we weary ourselves in vain to *recollect* something, and go through the whole store of our thoughts in order to find any one that may be associated with the one we seek; if we find the former, the latter is also found. Whoever wishes to call up something in his memory first seeks for a thread with which it is connected by the association of thoughts. Upon this depends mnemonics: it aims at providing us with easily found occasioners or causes for all the conceptions, thoughts, or words which are to be preserved. But the worst of it is that these occasioners themselves have first to be recalled, and this again requires an occasioner. How much the occasion accomplishes in memory may be shown in this way. If we have read in a book of anecdotes say fifty anecdotes, and then have laid it aside, immediately afterwards we will sometimes be unable to recollect a single one of them. But if the occasion comes, or if a thought occurs to us which has any analogy with one of those anecdotes, it immediately comes back to us; and so with the whole fifty as opportunity offers. The same thing holds good of all that we read. Our immediate remembrance of words, that is, our remembrance of them without the assistance of mnemonic contrivances, and with it our whole faculty of speech, ultimately depends upon the direct association of thoughts. For the learning of language consists in this, that once for all we so connect a conception with a word that this word will always occur to us along with this conception, and this conception will always occur to us along with this word. We have afterwards to repeat the same process in learning every new language; yet if we learn a language for passive and not for active use—that is, to read, but not to speak, as, for example, most of us learn Greek—then the connection is one-sided, for the conception occurs to us along with the word, but the word does not always occur to us along with the conception. The same procedure as in language becomes apparent in the particular case, in the learning of every new proper name. But sometimes we do not trust ourselves to connect directly the name of *this* person, or town, river, mountain, plant, animal, &c., with the thought of each so firmly that it will call each of them up of itself; and then we assist ourselves mnemonically, and connect the image of the person or thing with any perceptible quality the name of which occurs in that of the person or thing. Yet this is only a temporary prop to lean on; later we let it drop, for the association of thoughts becomes an immediate support.

The search of memory for a clue shows itself in a peculiar manner in the case of a dream which we have forgotten on awaking, for in this case we seek in vain for that which a few minutes before occupied our minds with the strength of the clearest present, but now has entirely disappeared. We grasp at any lingering impression by which may hang the clue that by virtue of association would call that dream back again into our consciousness. According to Kieser, " *Tellurismus*," Bd. ii. § 271, memory even of what passed in magnetic-somnambular sleep may possibly sometimes be aroused by a sensible sign found when awake. It depends upon the same impossibility of the appearance of a thought without its occasion that if we propose to do anything at a definite time, this can only take place if we either think of nothing else till then, or if at the determined time we are *reminded* of it by something, which may either be an external impression arranged beforehand or a thought which is itself again brought about in the regular way. Both, then, belong to the class of motives. Every morning when we awake our consciousness is a *tabula rasa*, which, however, quickly fills itself again. First it is the surroundings of the previous evening which now reappear, and remind us of what we thought in these surroundings; to this the events of the previous day link themselves on; and so one thought rapidly recalls the others, till all that occupied us yesterday is there again. Upon the fact that this takes place properly depends the health of the mind, as opposed to madness, which, as is shown in the third book, consists in the existence of great blanks in the memory of past events. But how completely sleep breaks the thread of memory, so that each morning it has to be taken up again, we see in particular cases of the incompleteness of this operation. For example, sometimes we cannot recall in the morning a melody which the night before ran in our head till we were tired of it.

The cases in which a thought or a picture of the fancy suddenly came into our mind without any conscious occasion seem to afford an exception to what has been said. Yet this is for the most part an illusion, which rests on the fact that the occasion was so trifling and the thought itself so vivid and interesting, that the former is instantly driven out of consciousness. Yet sometimes the cause of such an instantaneous appearance of an idea may be an internal physical impression either of the parts of the brain on each other or of the organic nervous system upon the brain.

In general our internal process of thought is in reality not so simple as the theory of it; for here it is involved in many ways. To make the matter clear to our imagination, let us compare our consciousness to a sheet of water of some depth. Then the distinctly conscious thoughts are merely the surface; while, on the other hand, the indistinct thoughts, the feelings, the after sensation of perceptions and of experience generally, mingled with the special disposition of our own will, which is the kernel of our being, is the mass of the water. Now the mass of the whole consciousness is more or less, in proportion to the intellectual activity, in constant motion, and what rise to the surface, in consequence of this, are the clear pictures of the fancy or the distinct, conscious thoughts expressed in words and the resolves of the will. The whole process of our thought and purpose seldom lies on the surface, that is, consists in a combination of distinctly thought judgments; although we strive against this in order that we may be able to explain our thought to ourselves and others. But ordinarily it is in the obscure depths of the mind that the rumination of the materials received from without takes place, through which they are worked up into thoughts; and it goes on almost as unconsciously as the conversion of nourishment into the humours and substance of the body. Hence it is that we can often give no account of the origin of our deepest thoughts. They are the birth of our mysterious inner life. Judgments, thoughts, purposes, rise from out that deep unexpectedly and to our own surprise. A letter brings us unlooked-for and important news, in consequence of which our thoughts and motives are disordered; we get rid of the matter for the present, and think no more about it; but next day, or on the third or fourth day after, the whole situation sometimes stands distinctly before us, with what we have to do in the circumstances. Consciousness is the mere surface of our mind, of which, as of the earth, we do not know the inside, but only the crust.

But in the last instance, or in the secret of our inner being, what sets in activity the association of thought itself, the laws of which were set forth above, is the *will*, which urges its servant the intellect, according to the measure of its powers, to link thought to thought, to recall the similar, the contemporaneous, to recognise reasons and consequents. For it is to the interest of the will that, in general, one should think, so that one may be well equipped for all cases that may arise. Therefore the form of the principle of sufficient reason which governs the association of thoughts and keeps it active is ultimately the law of motivation. For that which rules the sensorium, and determines it to follow the analogy or other association of thoughts in this or that direction, is the will of the thinking subject. Now just as here the laws of the connection of ideas subsist only upon the basis of the will, so also in the real world the causal connection of bodies really subsists only upon the basis of the will, which manifests itself in the phenomena of this world. On this account the explanation from causes is never absolute and exhaustive, but leads back to forces of nature as their condition, and the inner being of the latter is just the will as thing in itself. In saying this, however, I have certainly anticipated the following book.

But because now the *outward* (sensible) occasions of the presence of our ideas, just as well as the *inner* occasions (those of association), and both independently of each other, constantly affect the consciousness, there arise from this the frequent interruptions of our course of thought, which introduce a certain cutting up and confusion of our thinking. This belongs to its imperfections which cannot be explained away, and which we shall now consider in a separate chapter.

CHAPTER XV.

ON THE ESSENTIAL IMPERFECTIONS OF THE INTELLECT.

OUR self-consciousness has not space but only time as its form, and therefore we do not think in three dimensions, as we perceive, but only in *one*, thus in a line, without breadth or depth. This is the source of the greatest of the essential imperfections of our intellect. We can know all things only in *succession*, and can become conscious of only one at a time, indeed even of this one only under the condition that for the time we forget everything else, thus are absolutely unconscious of everything else, so that for the time it ceases to exist as far as we are concerned. In respect of this quality our intellect may be compared to a telescope with a very narrow field of vision; just because our consciousness is not stationary but fleeting. The intellect apprehends only successively, and in order to grasp one thing must let another go, retaining nothing but traces of it, which are ever becoming weaker. The thought which is vividly present to me now must after a little while have escaped me altogether; and if a good night's sleep intervene, it may be that I shall never find it again, unless it is connected with my personal interests, that is, with my will, which always commands the field.

Upon this imperfection of the intellect depends the disconnected and often *fragmentary nature of* our course of thought, which I have already touched on at the close of last chapter; and from this again arises the unavoidable *distraction* of our thinking. Sometimes external impres-

sions of sense throng in upon it, disturbing and interrupt-
ing it, forcing different kinds of things upon it every
moment; sometimes *one* thought draws in *another* by the
bond of association, and is now itself dislodged by it;
sometimes, lastly, the intellect itself is not capable of
fixing itself very long and continuously at a time upon
one thought, but as the eye when it gazes long at one
object is soon unable to see it any more distinctly, because
the outlines run into each other and become confused,
until finally all is obscure, so through long-continued
reflection upon one subject our thinking also is gradually
confused, becomes dull, and ends in complete stupor.
Therefore after a certain time, which varies with the
individual, we must for the present give up every meditation or deliberation which has had the fortune to remain
undisturbed, but yet has not been brought to an end,
even if it concerns a matter which is most important and
pertinent to us; and we must dismiss from our consciousness the subject which interests us so much, however
heavily our anxiety about it may weigh upon us, in order
to occupy ourselves now with insignificant and indifferent
things. During this time that important subject no
longer exists for us; it is like the heat in cold water,
latent. If now we resume it again at another time, we
approach it like a new thing, with which we become
acquainted anew, although more quickly, and the agreeable or disagreeable impression of it is also produced
anew upon our will. We ourselves, however, do not
come back quite unchanged. For with the physical
composition of the humours and tension of the nerves,
which constantly changes with the hours, days, and years,
our mood and point of view also changes. Moreover, the
different kinds of ideas which have been there in the
meantime have left an echo behind them, the tone of
which influences the ideas which follow. Therefore the
same thing appears to us at different times, in the morning, in the evening, at mid-day, or on another day, often

very different; opposite views of it now press upon each other and increase our doubt. Hence we speak of sleeping upon a matter, and for important determinations we demand a long time for consideration. Now, although this quality of our intellect, as springing from its weakness, has its evident disadvantages, yet, on the other hand, it affords the advantage that after the distraction and the physical change we return to our subject as comparatively new beings, fresh and strange, and thus are able to see it repeatedly in very different lights. From all this it is plain that human consciousness and thought is in its nature necessarily fragmentary, on account of which the theoretical and practical results which are achieved by piecing together such fragments are for the most part defective. In this our thinking consciousness is like a magic lantern, in the focus of which only one picture can appear at a time, and each, even if it represents the noblest objects, must yet soon pass away in order to make room for others of a different, and even most vulgar, description. In practical matters the most important plans and resolutions are formed in general; but others are subordinated to these as means to an end, and others again are subordinated to these, and so on down to the particular case that has to be carried out *in concreto*. They do not, however, come to be carried out in the order of their dignity, but while we are occupied with plans which are great and general, we have to contend with the most trifling details and the cares of the moment. In this way our consciousness becomes still more desultory. In general, theoretical occupations of the mind unfit us for practical affairs, and *vice versâ*.

In consequence of the inevitably distracted and fragmentary nature of all our thinking, which has been pointed out, and the mingling of ideas of different kinds thereby introduced, to which even the noblest human minds are subject, we really have only *half a consciousness* with which to grope about in the labyrinth of our life and the

obscurity of our investigations; bright moments sometimes illuminate our path like lightning. But what is
to be expected of heads of which even the wisest is every
night the scene of the strangest and most senseless dreams,
and which has to take up its meditations again on awakening from these? Clearly a consciousness which is subject
to such great limitations is little suited for solving the
riddle of the world; and such an endeavour would necessarily appear strange and pitiful to a being of a higher
order whose intellect had not time as its form, and whose
thinking had thus true completeness and unity Indeed
it is really wonderful that we are not completely confused
by the very heterogeneous mixture of ideas and fragments
of thought of every kind which are constantly crossing each
other in our minds, but are yet always able to see our
way again and make everything agree together. Clearly
there must exist a simpler thread upon which everything
ranges itself together: but what is this? Memory alone
is not sufficient, for it has essential limitations of which
I shall speak shortly, and besides this, it is exceedingly
imperfect and untrustworthy. The *logical ego* or even
the *transcendental synthetic unity of apperception* are expressions and explanations which will not easily serve
to make the matter comprehensible; they will rather
suggest to many:

"'Tis true your beard is curly, yet it will not draw you the bolt."

Kant's proposition, "The *I think* must accompany all
our ideas," is insufficient; for the "I" is an unknown
quantity, *i.e.*, it is itself a secret. That which gives unity
and connection to consciousness in that it runs through
all its ideas, and is thus its substratum, its permanent
supporter, cannot itself be conditioned by consciousness,
therefore cannot be an idea. Rather it must be the *prius*
of consciousness, and the root of the tree of which that
is the fruit. This, I say, is the *will*. It alone is unchangeable and absolutely identical, and has brought

forth consciousness for its own ends. Therefore it is also the will which gives it unity and holds together all its ideas and thoughts, accompanying them like a continuous harmony. Without it the intellect would no longer have the unity of consciousness, as a mirror in which now this and now that successively presents itself, or at the most only so much as a convex mirror whose rays unite in an imaginary point behind its surface. But the *will* alone is that which is permanent and unchangeable in consciousness. It is the will which holds together all thoughts and ideas as means to its ends, and tinges them with the colour of its own character, its mood, and its interests, commands the attention, and holds in its hand the train of motives whose influence ultimately sets memory and the association of ideas in activity; at bottom it is the will that is spoken of whenever "I" appears in a judgment. Thus it is the true and final point of unity of consciousness, and the bond of all its functions and acts; it does not itself, however, belong to the intellect, but is only its root, source, and controller.

From the *form of time and the single dimension* of the series of ideas, on account of which, in order to take up one, the intellect must let all the others fall, there follows not only its distraction, but also its *forgetfulness.* Most of what it lets fall it never takes up again; especially since the taking up again is bound to the principle of sufficient reason, and thus demands an occasion which the association of thoughts and motivation have first to supply; an occasion, however, which may be the more remote and smaller in proportion as our sensibility for it is heightened by our interest in the subject. But memory, as I have already shown in the essay on the principle of sufficient reason, is not a store-house, but merely a faculty acquired by practice of calling up ideas at pleasure, which must therefore constantly be kept in practice by use; for otherwise it will gradually be lost. Accordingly the knowledge even of the learned man exists only *virtualiter* as an acquired facility in calling up certain ideas; *actualiter*, on the other hand, it also is confined to one idea, and is only conscious of this one at a time. Hence arises a strange contrast between what he knows *potentiâ* and what he knows *actu;* that is, between his knowledge and what he thinks at any moment: the former is an immense and always somewhat chaotic mass, the latter is a single distinct thought. The relation resembles that between the innumerable stars of the heavens and the limited field of vision of the telescope; it appears in a striking manner when upon some occasion he wishes to call distinctly to his remembrance some particular circumstance in his knowledge, and time and trouble are required to produce it from that chaos. Rapidity in doing this is a special gift, but is very dependent upon day and hour; therefore memory sometimes refuses us its service, even in things which at another time it has readily at hand. This consideration calls us in our studies to strive more to attain to correct insight than to increase our learning, and to lay it to heart that the *quality* of knowledge is more important than its *quantity.* The latter imparts to books only thickness, the former thoroughness and also style; for it is an *intensive* quantity, while the other is merely *extensive.* It consists in the distinctness and completeness of the conceptions, together with the purity and accuracy of the knowledge of perception which forms their foundation; therefore the whole of knowledge in all its parts is penetrated by it, and in proportion as it is so is valuable or trifling. With a small quantity, but of good quality, one achieves more than with a very large quantity of bad quality.

The most perfect and satisfactory knowledge is that of perception, but it is limited absolutely to the particular, the individual. The combination of the many and the different in *one* idea is only possible through the *conception*, that is, through the omission of the differences; therefore this is a very imperfect manner of presenting things to the mind. Certainly the particular also can be directly comprehended as a universal, if it is raised to the (Platonic) Idea; but in this process, which I have analysed in the third book, the intellect already passes beyond the limits of individuality, and therefore of time; moreover it is only an exception.

These inner and essential imperfections of the intellect are further increased by a disturbance which, to a certain extent, is external to it, but yet is unceasing—the influence exerted by the will upon all its operations whenever it is in any way concerned in their result. Every passion, indeed every inclination and aversion, tinges the objects of knowledge with its colour. Of most common occurrence is the falsifying of knowledge which is brought about by wishes and hopes, for they picture to us the scarcely possible as probable and well nigh certain, and make us almost incapable of comprehending what is opposed to it: fear acts in a similar way; and every preconceived opinion, every partiality, and, as has been said, every interest, every emotion and inclination of the will, acts in an analogous manner.

To all these imperfections of the intellect we have finally to add this, that it grows old with the brain, that is, like all physiological functions, it loses its energy in later years, whereby all its imperfections are then much increased.

The defective nature of the intellect here set forth will not, however, surprise us if we look back at its origin and destiny as established by me in the second book. Nature has produced it for the service of an individual will. Therefore it is only designed to know things so far as they afford the motives of such a will, but not to fathom them or comprehend their true being. Human intellect is only a higher gradation of the intellect of the brutes; and as this is entirely confined to the present, our intellect also bears strong traces of this limitation.

Therefore our memory and recollection is something very imperfect. How little of all that we have done, experienced, learnt, or read, can we recall! And even this little for the most part only laboriously and imperfectly. For the same reasons is it so very difficult for us to keep ourselves free from the impressions of the present. Unconsciousness is the original and natural condition of all things, and therefore also the basis from which, in particular species of beings, consciousness results as their highest efflorescence; wherefore even then unconsciousness always continues to predominate. Accordingly most existences are without consciousness; but yet they act according to the laws of their nature, *i.e.*, of their will. Plants have at most a very weak analogue of consciousness; the lowest species of animals only the dawn of it. But even after it has ascended through the whole series of animals to man and his reason, the unconsciousness of plants, from which it started, still remains the foundation, and may be traced in the necessity for sleep, and also in all those essential and great imperfections, here set forth, of every intellect produced through physiological functions; and of another intellect we have no conception.

The imperfections here proved to be *essential* to the intellect are constantly increased, however, in particular cases, by *non-essential* imperfections. The intellect is never in *every* respect what it possibly might be. The perfections possible to it are so opposed that they exclude each other. Therefore no man can be at once Plato and Aristotle, or Shakspeare and Newton, or Kant and Goethe. The imperfections of the intellect, on the contrary, consort very well together; therefore in reality it for the most part remains far below what it might be. Its functions depend upon so very many conditions, which we can only comprehend as anatomical and physiological, in the *phenomenon* in which alone they are given us, that a decidedly excelling intellect, even in *one* respect alone, is among the rarest of natural phenomena. Therefore the productions of such an

intellect are preserved through thousands of years, indeed
every relic of such a highly favoured individual becomes
a most valuable treasure.　From such an intellect down
to that which approaches imbecility the gradations are
innumerable.　And primarily, in conformity with these
gradations, the *mental horizon* of each of us varies very
much from the mere comprehension of the present, which
even the brute has, to that which also embraces the next
hour, the day, even the morrow, the week, the year, the
life, the century, the thousand years, up to that of the consciousness which has almost always present, even though
obscurely dawning, the horizon of the infinite, and whose
thoughts therefore assume a character in keeping with
this.　Further, that difference among intelligences shows
itself in the rapidity of their thinking, which is very important, and which may be as different and as finely graduated as that of the points in the radius of a revolving disc.
The remoteness of the consequents and reasons to which
any one's thought can extend seems to stand in a certain
relation to the rapidity of his thinking, for the greatest
exertion of thought-power in general can only last quite
a short time, and yet only while it lasts can a thought be
thought out in its complete unity.　It therefore amounts
to this, how far the intellect can pursue it in so short a
time, thus what length of path it can travel in it.　On
the other hand, in the case of some, rapidity may be made
up for by the greater duration of that time of perfectly
concentrated thought.　Probably the slow and lasting
thought makes the mathematical mind, while rapidity of
thought makes the genius.　The latter is a flight, the
former a sure advance upon firm ground, step by step.
Yet even in the sciences, whenever it is no longer a
question of mere quantities, but of understanding the
nature of phenomena, this last kind of thinking is inadequate.　This is shown, for example, by Newton's theory
of colour, and later by Biot's nonsense about colour rings,
which yet agrees with the whole atomistic method of

treating light among the French, with its *molécules de lumière*, and in general with their fixed idea of reducing everything in nature to mere mechanical effects. Lastly, the great individual diversity of intelligence we are speaking about shows itself excellently in the *degrees of the clearness of understanding*, and accordingly in the distinctness of *the whole thinking*. To one man that is to understand which to another is only in some degree to observe; the one is already done and at the goal while the other is only at the beginning; to the one that is the solution which to the other is only the problem. This depends on the *quality of thought* and knowledge, which was already referred to above. As in rooms the degree of light varies, so does it in minds. We can detect this *quality of the whole thought* as soon as we have read only a few pages of an author. For in doing so we have been obliged to understand both with his understanding and in his sense; and therefore before we know all that he has thought we see already how he thinks, what is the *formal* nature, the *texture* of his thinking, which remains the same in everything about which he thinks, and whose expression is the train of thought and the style. In this we feel at once the pace, the flexibleness and lightness, even indeed the soaring power of his mind; or, on the contrary, its dulness, formality, lameness and leaden quality. For, as language is the expression of the mind of a nation, style is the more immediate expression of the mind of an author than even his physiognomy. We throw a book aside when we observe that in it we enter an obscurer region than our own, unless we have to learn from it mere facts, not thoughts. Apart from mere facts, only that author will afford us profit whose understanding is keener and clearer than our own, who forwards our thinking instead of hindering it, like the dull mind that will force us to keep pace with the toad-like course of its thought; thus that author with whose mind it gives

us sensible relief and assistance sometimes to think, by
whom we feel ourselves borne where we could not have
gone alone.   Goethe once said to me that if he read a
page of Kant he felt as if he entered a brightly lighted
room.   Inferior minds are so not merely because they
are distorted, and therefore judge falsely, but primarily
through the *indistinctness* of their whole thinking, which
may be compared to seeing through a bad telescope,
when all the outlines appear indistinct and as if ob-
literated, and the different objects run into each other.
The weak understanding of such minds shrinks from
the demand for distinctness of conceptions, and therefore
they do not themselves make this claim upon it, but put
up with haziness; and to satisfy themselves with this they
gladly have recourse to *words*, especially such as denote
indefinite, very abstract, unusual conceptions which are
hard to explain; such, for example, as infinite and finite,
sensible and supersensible, the Idea of being, Ideas of
the reason, the absolute, the Idea of the good, the
divine, moral freedon, power of spontaneous generation,
the absolute Idea, subject-object, &c.   The like of these
they confidently fling about, imagine they really express
thoughts, and expect every one to be content with them;
for the highest summit of wisdom which they can see is
to have at command such ready-made words for every
possible question.   This immense *satisfaction in words* is
thoroughly characteristic of inferior minds.   It depends
simply upon their incapacity for distinct conceptions,
whenever these must rise above the most trivial and
simple relations.   Hence upon the weakness and indolence
of their intellect, and indeed upon the secret consciousness of this, which in the case of scholars is bound up
with the early learnt and hard necessity of passing themselves off as thinking beings, to meet which demand in
all cases they keep such a suitable store of ready-made
words.   It must really be amusing to see a professor of
philosophy of this kind in the chair, who *bonâ fide* delivers

such a juggle of words destitute of thoughts, quite sincerely, under the delusion that they are really thoughts,
and in front of him the students, who just as *bonâ fide, i.e.,*
under the same delusion, listen attentively and take notes,
while yet in reality neither the one nor the other goes
beyond the words, but rather these words themselves, together with the audible scratching of pens, are the only
realities in the whole matter. This peculiar *satisfaction in
words* has more than anything else to do with the per-
petuation of errors For, relying on the words and phrases
received from his predecessors, each one confidently passes
over obscurities and problems, and thus these are pro-
pagated through centuries from book to book; and the
thinking man, especially in youth, is in doubt whether it
may be that he is incapable of understanding it, or that
there is really nothing here to understand ; and similarly,
whether for others the problem which they all slink past
with such comical seriousness by the same path is no
problem at all, or whether it is only that they will not
see it. Many truths remain undiscovered simply on this
account, that no one has the courage to look the problem
in the face and grapple with it. On the contrary, the
distinctness of thought and clearness of conceptions
peculiar to eminent minds produces the effect that even
known truths when brought forward by them gain new
light, or at least a new stimulus. If we hear them or read
them, it is as if we exchanged a bad telescope for a good
one. Let one only read, for example, in Euler's " Letters
to the Princess," his exposition of the fundamental truths
of mechanics and optics. Upon this rests the remark of
Diderot in the *Neveu de Rameau,* that only the perfect
masters are capable of teaching really well the elements of
a science; just because it is only they who really understand the questions, and for them words never take the
place of thoughts.

But we ought to know that inferior minds are the
rule, good minds the exception, eminent minds very rare,

and genius a portent.   How otherwise could a human
race consisting of about eight hundred million individuals
have left so much after six thousand years to discover, to
invent, to think out, and to say ?   The intellect is calculated for the support of the individual alone, and as a rule
it is only barely sufficient even for this.   But nature has
wisely been very sparing of conferring a larger measure ;
for the man of limited intelligence can survey the few
and simple relations which lie within reach of his narrow
sphere of action, and can control the levers of them with
much greater ease than could the eminently intellectual
man who commands an incomparably larger sphere and
works with long levers.   Thus the insect sees everything
on its stem or leaf with the most minute exactness, and
better than we, and yet is not aware of the man who
stands within three steps of it.   This is the reason of the
slyness of half-witted persons, and the ground of the
paradox : *Il y a un mystère dans l'esprit des gens qui
n'en ont pas.*   For practical life genius is about as useful
as an astral telescope in a theatre.   Thus, with regard
to the intellect nature is highly *aristocratic.*   The distinctions which it has established are greater than those
which are made in any country by birth, rank, wealth,
or caste.   But in the aristocracy of intellect, as in other
aristocracies, there are many thousands of plebeians for
one nobleman, many millions for one prince, and the great
multitude of men are mere populace, mob, rabble, *la
canaille.*   Now certainly there is a glaring contrast between the scale of rank of nature and that of convention,
and their agreement is only to be hoped for in a golden
age.   Meanwhile those who stand very high in the one
scale of rank and in the other have this in common, that
for the most part they live in exalted isolation, to which
Byron refers when he says :—

> " To feel me in the solitude of kings
> Without the power that makes them bear a crown."
> —*Proph. of Dante,* c. **1.**

For intellect is a differentiating, and therefore a separating principle. Its different grades, far more than those of mere culture, give to each man different conceptions, in consequence of which each man lives to a certain extent in a different world, in which he can directly meet those only who are like himself, and can only attempt to speak to the rest and make himself understood by them from a distance. Great differences in the grade and in the cultivation of the understanding fix a wide gulf between man and man, which can only be crossed by benevolence; for it is, on the contrary, the unifying principle, which identifies every one else with its own self. Yet the connection remains a moral one; it cannot become intellectual. Indeed, when the degree of culture is about the same, the conversation between a man of great intellect and an ordinary man is like the journey together of two men, one of whom rides on a spirited horse and the other goes on foot. It soon becomes very trying to both of them, and for any length of time impossible. For a short way the rider can indeed dismount, in order to walk with the other, though even then the impatience of his horse will give him much to do.

But the public could be benefited by nothing so much as by the recognition of that *intellectual aristocracy of nature*. By virtue of such recognition it would comprehend that when facts are concerned, thus when the matter has to be decided from experiments, travels, codes, histories, and chronicles, the normal mind is certainly sufficient; but, on the other hand, when mere thoughts are in question, especially those thoughts the material or data of which are within reach of every one, thus when it is really only a question of *thinking before* others, decided reflectiveness, native eminence, which only nature bestows, and that very seldom, is inevitably demanded, and no one deserves to be heard who does not at once give proofs of this. If the public could be brought to see this for itself, it would no longer waste the time which is sparingly measured out to it for its culture on the productions of ordinary minds, thus on the innumerable botches of poetry and philosophy which are produced every day. It would no longer seize always what is newest, in the childish delusion that books, like eggs, must be enjoyed while they are fresh, but would confine itself to the works of the few select and chosen minds of all ages and nations, would strive to learn to know and understand them, and might thus by degrees attain to true culture. And then, also, those thousands of uncalled-for productious which, like tares, hinder the growth of the good wheat would be discontinued.

CHAPTER XVI.[1]

ON THE PRACTICAL USE OF REASON AND ON STOICISM.

IN the seventh chapter I have shown that, in the theoretical sphere, procedure based upon *conceptions* suffices for mediocre achievements only, while great achievements, on the other hand, demand that we should draw from perception itself as the primary source of all knowledge. In the practical sphere, however, the converse is the case. Here determination by what is perceived is the way of the brutes, but is unworthy of man, who has *conceptions* to guide his conduct, and is thus emancipated from the power of what is actually perceptibly present, to which the brute is unconditionally given over. In proportion as a man makes good this prerogative his conduct may be called *rational*, and only in this sense can we speak of *practical reason*, not in the Kantian sense, the inadmissibility of which I have thoroughly exposed in my prize essay on the foundation of morals.

It is not easy, however, to let oneself be determined by *conceptions* alone; for the directly present external world, with its perceptible reality, intrudes itself forcibly even on the strongest mind. But it is just in conquering this impression, in destroying its illusion, that the human spirit shows its worth and greatness. Thus if incitements to lust and pleasure leave it unaffected, if the threats and fury of enraged enemies do not shake it, if the entreaties of erring friends do not make its

---

[1] This chapter is connected with § 16 of the first volume.

purpose waver, and the delusive forms with which pre-concerted plots surround it leave it unmoved, if the scorn of fools and of the vulgar herd does not disturb it nor trouble it as to its own worth, then it seems to stand under the influence of a spirit-world, visible to it alone (and this is the world of conceptions), before which that perceptibly present world which lies open to all dissolves like a phantom.   But, on the other hand, what gives to the external world and visible reality their great power over the mind is their nearness and directness.   As the magnetic needle, which is kept in its position by the combined action of widely distributed forces of nature embracing the whole earth, can yet be perturbed and set in violent oscillation by a small piece of iron, if only it comes quite close to it, so even a great mind can some-times be disconcerted and perturbed by trifling events and insignificant men, if only they affect it very closely, and the deliberate purpose can be for the moment shaken by a trivial but immediately present counter motive. For the influence of the motives is subject to a law which is directly opposed to the law according to which weights act on a balance, and in consequence of it a very small motive, which, however, lies very near to us, can out-weigh one which in itself is much stronger, but which only affects us from a distance.   But it is this quality of the mind, by reason of which it allows itself to be determined in accordance with this law, and does not withdraw itself from it by the strength of actual practical reason, which the ancients denoted by *animi impotentia*, which really signifies *ratio regendæ voluntatis impotens*. Every *emotion* (*animi perturbatio*) simply arises from the fact that an idea which affects our will comes so exces-sively near to us that it conceals everything else from us, and we can no longer see anything but it, so that for the moment we become incapable of taking account of things of another kind.   It would be a valuable safe-guard against this if we were to bring ourselves to regard the present, by the assistance of imagination, as if it were past, and should thus accustom our apperception to the epistolary style of the Romans. Yet conversely we are very well able to regard what is long past as so vividly present that old emotions which have long been asleep are thereby reawakened in their full strength. Thus also no one would be irritated or disconcerted by a misfortune, a disappointment, if reason always kept present to him what man really is: the most needy of creatures, daily and hourly abandoned to innumerable misfortunes, great and small, το δειλοτατον ζωον, who has therefore to live in constant care and fear. Herodotus already says, "Παν εστι ανθρωπος συμφορα" (*homo totus est calamitas*).

The application of reason to practice primarily accomplishes this. It reconstructs what is one-sided and defective in knowledge of mere perception, and makes use of the contrasts or oppositions which it presents, to correct each other, so that thus the objectively true result is arrived at. For example, if we look simply at the bad action of a man we will condemn him; on the other hand, if we consider merely the need that moved him to it, we will compassionate him: reason, by means of its conceptions, weighs the two, and leads to the conclusion that he must be restrained, restricted, and curbed by a proportionate punishment.

I am again reminded here of Seneca's saying: "*Si vis tibi omnia subjicere, te subjice rationi.*" Since, however, as was shown in the fourth book, the nature of suffering is positive, and that of pleasure negative, he who takes abstract or rational knowledge as the rule of his conduct, and therefore constantly reflects on its consequences and on the future, will very frequently have to practise *sustine et abstine*, for in order to obtain the life that is most free from pain he generally sacrifices its keenest joys and pleasures, mindful of Aristotle's "ὁ φρονιμος το αλυπον διωκει, ου το ἡδυ" (*quod dolore vacat, non quod suave est, persequitur vir prudens*). Therefore with him the future constantly borrows from the present, instead of the present borrowing from the future, as is the case with a frivolous fool, who thus becomes impoverished and finally bankrupt. In the case of the former reason must, for the most part, assume the *rôle* of a churlish mentor, and unceasingly call for renunciations, without being able to promise anything in return, except a fairly painless existence. This rests on the fact that reason, by means of its conceptions, surveys the *whole* of life, whose outcome, in the happiest conceivable case, can be no other than what we have said.

When this striving after a painless existence, so far as it might be attainable by the application of and strict adherence to rational reflection and acquired knowledge of the true nature of life, was carried out with the greatest consistency and to the utmost extreme, it produced cynicism, from which stoicism afterwards proceeded. I wish briefly here to bring this out more fully for the sake of establishing more firmly the concluding exposition of our first book.

All ancient moral systems, with the single exception of that of Plato, were guides to a happy life. Accordingly in them the end of virtue was entirely in this life, not beyond death. For to them it is only the right path to a truly happy life; and on this account the wise choose it. Hence arise those lengthy debates chiefly preserved for us by Cicero, those keen and constantly renewed investigations, whether virtue quite alone and in itself is really sufficient for a happy life, or whether this further requires some external condition; whether the virtuous and wise may also be happy on the rack and the wheel, or in the bull of Phalaris; or whether it does not go as far as this. For certainly this would be the touchstone of an ethical system of this kind; the practice of it must give happiness directly and unconditionally. If it cannot do this it does not accomplish what it ought, and must be rejected. It is therefore with truth and in accordance with the Christian point of view that Augustine prefaces his exposition of the moral systems of the ancients (*De Civ. Dei*, Lib. xix. c. 1) with the explanation : "*Exponenda sunt nobis argumenta mortalium, quibus sibi ipsi beatitudinem facere* IN HUJUS VITÆ INFELICITATE *moliti sunt; ut ab eorum rebus vanis spes nostra quid differat clarescat. De finibus bonorum et malorum multa inter se philosophi disputarunt; quam quæstionem maxima intentione versantes, invenire conati sunt, quid efficiat hominem beatum : illud enim est finis bonorum.*" I wish to place beyond all doubt the eudæmonistic end which we have ascribed to all ancient ethics by several express statements of the ancients themselves. Aristotle says in the "*Eth. Magna*," i. 4: "Ἡ εὐδαιμονια εν τῳ ευ ζην εστι, το δε ευ ζην εν τῳ κατα τας αρετας ζην." (*Felicitas in bene vivendo posita est : verum bene vivere est in eo positum, ut secundum virtutem vivamus*), with which may be compared "*Eth. Nicom.*," i. 5. "*Cic. Tusc.*," v. 1 : "*Nam, quum ea causa impulerit eos, qui primi se ad philosophiæ studia contulerunt, ut, omnibus rebus posthabitis, totos se in optimo vitæ statu exquirendo collocarent ; profecto spe beate vivendi tantam in eo studio curam operamque posuerunt.*" According to Plutarch (*De Repugn. Stoic.*, c. xviii.) Chrysippus said : "Το κατα κακιαν ζην τῳ κακοδαιμονως ζην ταυτον εστι." (*Vitiose vivere idem est quod vivere infeliciter.*) Ibid., c. 26 : "Ἡ φρονησις ουχ ἑτερον εστι της ευδαιμονιας καθ' ἑαυτο, αλλ' ευδαιμονια." (*Prudentia nihil differt a felicitate, estque ipsa adeo felicitas.*) "Stob. Ecl.," Lib. ii. c. 7 : "Τελος δε φασιν ειναι το ευδαιμονειν, ου ἑνεκα παντα πραττεται." (*Finem esse dicunt felicitatem, cujus causa fiunt omnia.*) "Ευδαιμονιαν συνωνυμειν τῳ τελει λεγουσι." (*Finem bonorum et felicitatem synonyma esse dicunt.*) "Arrian Diss. Epict.," i. 4 : "Ἡ αρετη ταυτην εχει την επαγγελιαν, ευδαιμονιαν ποιησαι." (*Virtus profitetur, se felicitatem præstare.*) Sen., Ep. 90: "*Ceterum (sapientia) ad beatum statum tendit, illo ducit, illo vias aperit.*"—Id., Ep. 108 : "*Illud admoneo auditionem philosophorum, lectionemque, ad propositum beatæ vitæ tra- hendum.*"

The ethics of the Cynics also adopted this end of the happiest life, as the Emperor Julian expressly testifies (Orat. vi.) : "*Της Κυνικης δε φιλοσοφιας σκοπος μεν εστι και τελος, ὡσπερ δη και πασης φιλοσοφιας, το ευδαιμονειν· το δε ευδαιμονειν εν τῳ ζην κατα φυσιν, αλλα μη προς τας των πολλων δοξας.*" (*Cynicæ philosophiæ ut etiam omnis philosophiæ, scopus et finis est feliciter vivere : felicitas vitæ autem in eo posita est, ut secundum naturam vivatur, nec vero secundum opiniones multitudinis.*) Only the Cynics followed quite a peculiar path to this end, a path directly opposed to the ordinary one—the path of extreme priva- tion. They start from the insight that the motions of the will which are brought about by the objects which attract and excite it, and the wearisome, and for the most part vain, efforts to attain these, or, if they are attained, the fear of losing them, and finally the loss itself, produce far greater pain than the want of all these objects ever can. Therefore, in order to attain to the life that is most free from pain, they chose the path of the extremest desti- tution, and fled from all pleasures as snares through which one was afterwards handed over to pain. But after this they could boldly scorn happiness and its caprices. This is the *spirit of cynicism.* Seneca dis- tinctly expresses it in the eighth chapter, "*De Tranquili- tate Animi:*" "*Cogitandum est, quanto levior dolor sit, non habere, quam perdere : et intelligemus paupertati eo mino- rem tormentorum, quo minorem damnorum esse materiam.*" Then : "*Tolerabilius est, faciliusque, non acquirere, quam amittere. . . . Diogenes effecit, ne quid sibi eripi posset, . . . qui se fortuitis omnibus exuit. . . . Videtur mihi dixisse ; age tuum negotium, fortuna : nihil apud Diogenem jam tuum est.*" The parallel passage to this last sentence is the quotation of Stobæus (*Ecl.* ii. 7) : "*Διογενης εφη νομι- ζειν ὁραν την Τυχην ενορωσαν αυτον και λεγουσαν· τουτον*

δ'ου δυναμαι βαλεειν κυνα λυσσητηρα." (*Diogenes credere
se dixit, videre Fortunam, ipsum intuentem, ac dicentem :
aut hunc non potui tetigisse canem rabiosum.*) The same
spirit of cynicism is also shown in the epitaph on Diogenes,
in Suidas, under the word Φιλισκος, and in " Diogenes
Laertius," vi. 2 :

> " Γηρασκει μεν χαλκος υπο χρονου· αλλα σον ουτι
> Κυδος ὁ πας αιων, Διογενης, καϑελει·
> Μουνος επει βιοτης αυταρκεα δοξαν εδειξας
> Θνητοις, και ζωης οιμον ελαφροτατην."

> (*Æra quidem absumit tempus, sed tempore numquam
> Interitura tua est gloria, Diogenes :
> Quandoquidem ad vitam miseris mortalibus æquam
> Monstrata est facilis, te duce, et ampla via.*)

Accordingly the fundamental thought of cynicism is that
life in its simplest and nakedest form, with the hardships
that belong to it by nature, is the most endurable, and is
therefore to be chosen; for every assistance, convenience,
gratification, and pleasure by means of which men seek to
make life more agreeable only brings with it new and
greater ills than originally belonged to it. Therefore we
may regard the following sentence as the expression of the
kernel of the doctrine of cynicism: " Διογενης εβοα πολ-
λακις λεγων, τον των ανθωπων βιον ραδιον υπο των θεων
δεδοσθαι, αποκεκρυφθαι δε αυτον ζητουντων μελιπηκτα
και μυρα και τα παραπλησια." (*Diogenes clamabat sæpius,
hominum vitam facilem a diis dari, verum occultari illam
quærentibus mellita cibaria, unguenta et his similia. (Diog.,
Laert.,* vi. 2.) And further : " Δεον, αντι των αχρηστων
πονων, τους κατα φυσιν ἑλομενους, ζην ευδαιμονως· παρα την
ανοιαν κακοδαιμονουσι. . . . τον αυτον χαρακτηρα του βιου
λεγων διεξαγειν, ὁνπερ και ʽΗρακλης, μηδεν ελευθηριας
προκρινων." (*Quum igitur, repudiatis inutilibus laboribus,
naturales insequi, ac vivere beate debeamus, per summam de-
mentiam infelices sumus. . . . eandem vitæ formam, quam
Hercules, se vivere affirmans, nihil libertati præferens.
Ibid.*) Therefore the old, genuine Cynics, Antisthenes,

Diogenes, Krates, and their disciples had once for all re-
nounced every possession, all conveniences and pleasures,
in order to escape for ever from the troubles and cares,
the dependence and the pains, which are inevitably
bound up with them and are not counterbalanced by
them. Through the bare satisfaction of the most pressing wants and the renunciation of everything superfluous
they thought they would come off best. Accordingly they
contented themselves with what in Athens or Corinth
was to be had almost for nothing, such as lupines, water,
an old threadbare cloak, a wallet, and a staff. They
begged occasionally, as far as was necessary to supply
such wants, but they never worked. Yet they accepted
absolutely nothing that exceeded the wants referred to
above. Independence in the widest sense was their aim.
They occupied their time in resting, going about, talking
with all men, and much mocking, laughing, and joking;
their characteristic was carelessness and great cheerful-
ness. Since now in this manner of life they had no aims
of their own, no purposes or ends to pursue, thus were
lifted above the sphere of human action, and at the same
time always enjoyed complete leisure, they were admirably fitted, as men of proved strength of mind, to be the
advisers and admonishers of the rest. Therefore Apuleius
says (*Florid.*, iv.): "*Crates, ut lar familiaris apud homines
suæ ætatis cultus est. Nulla domus ei unquam clausa erat:
nec erat patrisfamilias tam absconditum secretum, quin eo
tempestive Crates interveniret, litium omnium et jurgiorum
inter propinquos disceptator et arbiter.*" Thus in this, as in
so many other respects, they show a great likeness to the
mendicant friars of modern times, that is, to the better
and more genuine among them, whose ideal may be seen
in the Capucine Christoforo in Manzoni's famous romance.
Yet this resemblance lies only in the effects, not in the
cause. They agree in the result, but the fundamental
thought of the two is quite different. With the friars, as
with the Sannyâsis, who are akin to them, it is an aim

which transcends life; but with the Cynics it is only the conviction that it is easier to reduce their wishes and their wants to the *minimum*, than to attain to the *maximum* in their satisfaction, which indeed is impossible, for with their satisfaction the wishes and wants grow *ad infinitum;* therefore, in order to reach the goal of all ancient ethics, the greatest happiness possible in this life, they took the path of renunciation as the shortest and easiest: "ὅθεν και τον Κυνισμον ειρηκασιν συντομον επ' αρετην ὁδον." (*Unde Cynismum dixere compendiosam ad virtutem viam.*) *Diog. Laert.,* vi. 9. The fundamental difference between the spirit of cynicism and that of asceticism comes out very clearly in the humility which is essential to the ascetic, but is so foreign to the Cynic that, on the contrary, he is distinguished beyond everything else for pride and scorn :—

> "*Sapiens uno minor est Jove, dives,*
> *Liber, honoratus, pulcher, rex denique regum.*"—*Hor.*

On the other hand, the view of life held by the Cynics agrees in spirit with that of J. J. Rousseau as he expounds it in the "*Discours sur l'Origine de l'Inégalité.*" For he also would wish to lead us back to the crude state of nature, and regards the reduction of our wants to the minimum as the surest path to happiness. For the rest, the Cynics were exclusively *practical* philosophers : at least no account of their theoretical philosophy is known to me.

Now the Stoics proceeded from them in this way—they changed the practical into the theoretical. They held that the *actual* dispensing with everything that can be done without is not demanded, but that it is sufficient that we should regard possessions and pleasures constantly as *dispensable*, and as held in the hand of chance; for then the actual deprivation of them, if it should chance to occur, would neither be unexpected nor fall heavily. One might always have and enjoy everything; only one

must ever keep present the conviction of the worthlessness and dispensableness of these good things on the one
hand, and of their uncertainty and perishableness on the
other, and therefore prize them all very little, and be
always ready to give them up. Nay more, he who must
actually dispense with these things in order not to be
moved by them, thereby shows that in his heart he
holds them to be truly good things, which one must put
quite out of sight if one is not to long after them. The
wise man, on the other hand, knows that they are not
good things at all, but rather perfectly indifferent things,
ἀδιάφορα, in any case προηγμένα. Therefore if they
present themselves he will accept them, but yet is always
ready to let them go again, if chance, to which they belong, should demand them back; for they are των ουκ εφ'
ἡμιν. In this sense, Epictetus, chap. vii., says that the
wise man, like one who has landed from a ship, &c., will
also let himself be comforted by a wife or a child, but yet
will always be ready, whenever the captain calls, to let
them go again. Thus the Stoics perfected the theory of
equanimity and independence at the cost of the practice,
for they reduced everything to a mental process, and by
arguments, such as are presented in the first chapter of
Epictetus, sophisticated themselves into all the amenities
of life. But in doing so they left out of account that
everything to which one is accustomed becomes a need,
and therefore can only be given up with pain; that the
will does not allow itself to be played with, cannot enjoy
without loving the pleasures; that a dog does not remain
indifferent if one draws a piece of meat through its mouth,
and neither does a wise man if he is hungry; and that
there is no middle path between desiring and renouncing.
But they believed that they satisfied their principles if,
sitting at a luxurious Roman table, they left no dish
untasted, yet at the same time protested that they were
each and all of them mere προηγμένα, not αγαθα; or in
plain English, if they eat, drank, and were merry, yet

gave no thanks to God for it all, but rather made fastidious
faces, and persisted in boldly asserting that they gained
nothing whatever from the whole feast. This was the
expedient of the Stoics; they were therefore mere brag-
garts, and stand to the Cynics in much the same relation
as well-fed Benedictines and Augustines stand to Francis-
cans and Capucines. Now the more they neglected
practice, the more they refined the theory. I shall here
add a few proofs and supplementary details to the exposition of it given at the close of our first book.

If we search in the writings of the Stoics which remain to us, all of which are unsystematically composed,
for the ultimate ground of that irrefragible equanimity
which is unceasingly demanded of us, we find no other
than the knowledge that the course of the world is entirely
independent of our will, and consequently, that the evil
which befalls us is inevitable. If we have regulated our
claims by a correct insight into this, then mourning,
rejoicing, fearing, and hoping are follies of which we are
no longer capable. Further, especially in the commen-
taries of Arrian, it is surreptitiously assumed that all that
is ουκ εφ' ἡμιν (*i.e.*, does not depend upon us) is at once
also ου προς ἡμας (*i.e.*, does not concern us). Yet it
remains true that all the good things of life are in the
power of chance, and therefore whenever it makes use of
this power to deprive us of them, we are unhappy if we
have placed our happiness in them. From this unworthy
fate we are, in the opinion of the Stoics, delivered by the
right use of reason, by virtue of which we regard all these
things, never as ours, but only as lent to us for an indefinite time; only thus can we never really lose them.
Therefore Seneca says (Ep. 98): "*Si, quid humanarum
rerum varietas possit, cogitaverit, ante quam senserit*," and
Diogenes Laertius (vii. 1. 87): "Ισον δε εστι το κατ' αρετην
ζην τῳ κατ' εμπειριαν των φυσει συμβαινοντων ζην." (*Secundum virtutem vivere idem est, quod secundum experientiam
eorum, quæ secundum naturam accidunt, vivere.*) The pas-

sage in Arrian's "Discourses of Epictetus," B. iii., c. 24, 84–89, is particularly in point here; and especially, as a proof of what I have said in this reference in § 16 of the first volume, the passage: "Τουτο γας εστι το αιτιον τοις ανθροποις παντων των κακων το τας προληψεις τας κοινας μη δυνασθαι εφαρμοζειν τοις επι μερους," Ibid. iv., 1. 42. (*Hæc enim causa est hominibus omnium malorum, quod anticipationes generales rebus singularibus accommodare non possunt.*) Similarly the passage in "Marcus Aurelius" (iv. 29): "Ει ξενος κοσμου ο μη γνωριζων τα εν αυτῳ οντα, ουχ ἡττον ξενος και ο μη γνωριζων τα γιγνομενα;" that is: "If he is a stranger to the universe who does not know what is in it, no less is he a stranger who does not know how things go on in it." Also Seneca's eleventh chapter, "*De Tranquilitate Animi*," is a complete proof of this view. The opinion of the Stoics amounts on the whole to this, that if a man has watched for a while the juggling illusion of happiness and then uses his reason, he must recognise both the rapid changes of the dice and the intrinsic worthlessness of the counters, and therefore must henceforth remain unmoved. Taken generally the Stoical point of view may be thus expressed: our suffering always arises from the want of agreement between our wishes and the course of the world. Therefore one of these two must be changed and adapted to the other. Since now the course of things is not in our power (ουκ εφ' ἡμιν), we must direct our volitions and desires according to the course of things: for the will alone is εφ' ἡμιν. This adaptation of volition to the course of the external world, thus to the nature of things, is very often understood under the ambiguous κατα φυσιν ζην. See the "Discourses of Epictetus," ii. 17, 21, 22. Seneca also denotes this point of view (Ep. 119) when he says: "*Nihil interest, utrum non desideres, an habeas. Summa rei in utroque est eadem: non torqueberis.*" Also Cicero (*Tusc.* iv. 26) by the words: "*Solum habere velle, summa dementia est.*"

Similarly Arrian (iv. 1. 175): "Ου γαρ εκπληρωσει των επιθυμουμενων ελευθερια παρασκευαζεται, αλλα ανασκευῃ της επιθυμιας." (*Non enim explendis desideriis libertas comparatur, sed tollenda cupiditate.*)

The collected quotations in the "*Historia Philosophiæ Græco-Romanæ*" of Ritter and Preller may be taken as proofs of what I have said, in the place referred to above, about the ὁμολογουμενως ζην of the Stoics. Also the saying of Seneca (Ep. 31, and again Ep. 74): "*Perfecta virtus est æqualitas et tenor vitæ per omnia consonans sibi.*" The following passage of Seneca's indicates the spirit of the Stoa generally (Ep. 92): "*Quid est beata vita? Securitas et perpetua tranquillitas. Hanc dabit animi magnitudo, dabit constantia bene judicati tenax.*" A systematical study of the Stoics will convince every one that the end of their ethics, like that of the ethics of Cynicism from which they sprang, is really nothing else than a life as free as possible from pain, and therefore as happy as possible. Whence it follows that the Stoical morality is only a special form of *Eudæmonism.* It has not, like the Indian, the Christian, and even the Platonic ethics, a metaphysical tendency, a transcendental end, but a completely immanent end, attainable in this life; the steadfast serenity (αταραξια) and unclouded happiness of the wise man, whom nothing can disturb. Yet it cannot be denied that the later Stoics, especially Arrian, sometimes lose sight of this end, and show a really ascetic tendency, which is to be attributed to the Christian and Oriental spirit in general which was then already spreading. If we consider closely and seriously the goal of Stoicism, that αταραξια, we find in it merely a hardening and insensibility to the blow of fate which a man attains to because he keeps ever present to his mind the shortness of life, the emptiness of pleasure, the instability of happiness, and has also discerned that the difference between happiness and unhappiness is very much less than our anticipation of both is wont to represent. But this is

yet no state of happiness; it is only the patient endurance of sufferings which one has foreseen as irremediable.   Yet magnanimity and worth consist in this, that
one should bear silently and patiently what is irremediable, in melancholy peace, remaining always the same,
while others pass from rejoicing to despair and from despair to rejoicing.   Accordingly one may also conceive of
Stoicism as a spiritual hygiene, in accordance with which,
just as one hardens the body against the influences of
wind and weather, against fatigue and exertion, one has
also to harden one's mind against misfortune, danger, loss,
injustice, malice, perfidy, arrogance, and the folly of men.

I remark further, that the καθήκοντα of the Stoics,
which Cicero translates *officia*, signify as nearly as possible *Obliegenheiten*, or that which it befits the occasion
to do; English, *incumbencies;* Italian, *quel che tocca a me di
fare, o di lasciare*, thus what *it behoves* a reasonable man
to do. Cf. *Diog. Laert.*, vii. 1. 109. Finally, the *pantheism* of the Stoics, though absolutely inconsistent with
many an exhortation of Arrian, is most distinctly expressed by Seneca : " *Quid est Deus? Mens universi. Quid
est Deus? Quod vides totum, et quod non vides totum. Sic
demum magnitudo sua illi redditur, qua nihil majus ex-
cogitari potest: si solus est omnia, opus suum et extra et
intra tenet.*" (*Quæst. Natur.* 1, *præfatio* 12.)

CHAPTER XVII.[1]

ON MAN'S NEED OF METAPHYSICS.

WITH the exception of man, no being wonders at its own existence; but it is to them all so much a matter of course that they do not observe it. The wisdom of nature speaks out of the peaceful glance of the brutes; for in them the will and the intellect are not yet so widely separated that they can be astonished at each other when they meet again. Thus here the whole phenomenon is still firmly attached to the stem of nature from which it has come, and is partaker of the unconscious omniscience of the great mother. Only after the inner being of nature (the will to live in its objectification) has ascended, vigorous and cheerful, through the two series of unconscious existences, and then through the long and broad series of animals, does it attain at last to reflection for the first time on the entrance of reason, thus in man. Then it marvels at its own works, and asks itself what it itself is. Its wonder however is the more serious, as it here stands for the first time consciously in the presence of *death*, and besides the finiteness of all existence, the vanity of all effort forces itself more or less upon it. With this reflection and this wonder there arises therefore for man alone, the *need for a metaphysic;* he is accordingly an *animal metaphysicum.* At the beginning of his consciousness certainly he also accepts himself as a matter of course. This does not last long however, but very early, with the first dawn of reflection, that wonder already appears, which is

[1] This chapter is connected with § 15 of the first volume.

some day to become the mother of metaphysics. In agreement with this Aristotle also says at the beginning of his metaphysics: "Διά γαρ το θαυμαζειν οί ανθρωποι και νυν και το πρωτον ηρξαντο φιλοσοφειν." (*Propter admirationem enim et nunc et primo inceperunt homines philosophari.*) Moreover, the special philosophical disposition consists primarily in this, that a man is capable of wonder beyond the ordinary and everyday degree, and is thus induced to make the *universal* of the phenomenon his problem, while the investigators in the natural sciences wonder only at exquisite or rare phenomena, and their problem is merely to refer these to phenomena which are better known. The lower a man stands in an intellectual regard the less of a problem is existence itself for him; everything, how it is, and that it is, appears to him rather a matter of course. This rests upon the fact that his intellect still remains perfectly true to its original destiny of being serviceable to the will as the medium of motives, and therefore is closely bound up with the world and nature, as an integral part of them. Consequently it is very far from comprehending the world in a purely objective manner, freeing itself, so to speak, from the whole of things, opposing itself to this whole, and so for a while becoming as if self-existent. On the other hand, the philosophical wonder which springs from this is conditioned in the individual by higher development of the intellect, yet in general not by this alone; but without doubt it is the knowledge of death, and along with this the consideration of the suffering and misery of life, which gives the strongest impulse to philosophical reflection and metaphysical explanation of the world. If our life were endless and painless, it would perhaps occur to no one to ask why the world exists, and is just the kind of world it is; but everything would just be taken as a matter of course. In accordance with this we find that the interest which philosophical and also religious systems inspire has always its strongest hold in the dogma of some kind of

existence after death; and although the most recent
systems seem to make the existence of their gods the
main point, and to defend this most zealously, yet in
reality this is only because they have connected their
special dogma of immortality with this, and regard the one
as inseparable from the other: only on this account is it
of importance to them. For if one could establish their
doctrine of immortality for them in some other way, their
lively zeal for their gods would at once cool, and it would
give place almost to complete indifference if, conversely,
the absolute impossibility of immortality were proved to
them; for the interest in the existence of the gods would
vanish with the hope of a closer acquaintance with
them, to the residuum which might connect itself with
their possible influence on the events of this present life.
But if one could prove that continued existence after
death is incompatible with the existence of gods, because,
let us say, it pre-supposes originality of being, they would
soon sacrifice the gods to their own immortality and become zealous for Atheism. The fact that the materialistic
systems, properly so-called, and also absolute scepticism,
have never been able to obtain a general or lasting influence, depends upon the same grounds.

Temples and churches, pagodas and mosques, in all
lands and in all ages, in splendour and vastness, testify to
the metaphysical need of man, which, strong and ineradic-
able, follows close upon his physical need. Certainly
whoever is satirically inclined might add that this metaphysical need is a modest fellow who is content with poor
fare. It sometimes allows itself to be satisfied with
clumsy fables and insipid tales. If only imprinted early
enough, they are for a man adequate explanations of his
existence and supports of his morality. Consider, for
example, the Koran. This wretched book was sufficient
to found a religion of the world, to satisfy the metaphysical
need of innumerable millions of men for twelve hundred
years, to become the foundation of their morality, and of

no small contempt for death, and also to inspire them to bloody wars and most extended conquests. We find in it the saddest and the poorest form of Theism. Much may be lost through the translations; but I have not been able to discover one single valuable thought in it. Such things show that metaphysical capacity does not go hand in hand with the metaphysical need. Yet it will appear that in the early ages of the present surface of the earth this was not the case, and that those who stood considerably nearer than we do to the beginning of the human race and the source of organic nature, had also both greater energy of the intuitive faculty of knowledge, and a truer disposition of mind, so that they were capable of a purer, more direct comprehension of the inner being of nature, and were thus in a position to satisfy the metaphysical need in a more worthy manner. Thus originated in the primitive ancestors of the Brahmans, the Rishis, the almost super-human conceptions which were afterwards set down in the Upanishads of the Vedas.

On the other hand, there have never been wanting persons who were interested in deriving their living from that metaphysical need, and in making the utmost they could out of it. Therefore among all nations there are monopolists and farmers-general of it—the priests. Yet their trade had everywhere to be assured to them in this way, that they received the right to impart their metaphysical dogmas to men at a very early age, before the judgment has awakened from its morning slumber, thus in early childhood; for then every well-impressed dogma, however senseless it may be, remains for ever. If they had to wait till the judgment is ripe, their privileges could not continue.

A second, though not a numerous class of persons, who derive their support from the metaphysical need of man, is constituted by those who live by *philosophy*. By the Greeks they were called Sophists, by the moderns they are called Professors of Philosophy. Aristotle (*Metaph.,*

ii. 2) without hesitation numbers Aristippus among the Sophists. In Diogenes Laertius (ii. 65) we find that the reason of this is that he was the first of the Socratics who accepted payment for his philosophy; on account of which Socrates also returned him his present. Among the moderns also those who live *by* philosophy are not only, as a rule, and with the rarest exceptions, quite different from those who live *for* philosophy, but they are very often the opponents, the secret and irreconcilable enemies of the latter. For every true and important philosophical achievement will overshadow their own too much, and, moreover, cannot adapt itself to the views and limitations of their guild. Therefore it is always their endeavour to prevent such a work from making its way; and for this purpose, according to the age and circumstances in each case, the customary means are suppressing, concealing, hushing up, ignoring and keeping secret, or denying, disparaging, censuring, slandering and distorting, or, finally, denouncing and persecuting. Hence many a great man has had to drag himself wearily through life unknown, unhonoured, unrewarded, till at last, after his death, the world became undeceived as to him and as to them. In the meanwhile they had attained their end, had been accepted by preventing him from being accepted, and, with wife and child, had lived *by* philosophy, while he lived *for* it. But if he is dead, then the thing is reversed; the new generation of the former class, which always exists, now becomes heir to his achievements, cuts them down to its own measure, and now lives *by* him. That Kant could yet live both *by* and *for* philosophy depended on the rare circumstance that, for the first time since *Divus Antoninus* and *Divus Julianus*, a philosopher sat on the throne. Only under such auspices could the "Critique of Pure Reason" have seen the light. Scarcely was the king dead than we see that Kant also, seized with fear, because he belonged to the guild, modified, expurgated, and spoiled his masterpiece in the second edition, and yet was soon in danger of losing his place; so that Campe invited him to come to him, in Brunswick, and live with him as the instructor of his family (Ring., *Ansichten aus Kant's Leben,* p. 68). University philosophy is, as a rule, mere juggling. Its real aim is to impart to the students, in the deepest ground of their thought, that tendency of mind which the ministry that appoints to the professorships regards as consistent with its views. The ministry may also be perfectly right in this from a statesman's point of view; only the result of it is that such philosophy of the chair is a *nervis alienis mobile lignum,* and cannot be regarded as serious philosophy, but as the mere jest of it. Moreover, it is at any rate just that such inspection or guidance should extend only to the philosophy of the chair, and not to the real philosophy that is in earnest. For if anything in the world is worth wishing for—so well worth wishing for that even the ignorant and dull herd in its more reflective moments would prize it more than silver and gold—it is that a ray of light should fall on the obscurity of our being, and that we should gain some explanation of our mysterious existence, in which nothing is clear but its misery and its vanity. But even if this is in itself attainable, it is made impossible by imposed and compulsory solutions.

We shall now subject to a general consideration the different ways of satisfying this strong metaphysical need.

By *metaphysics* I understand all knowledge that pretends to transcend the possibility of experience, thus to transcend nature or the given phenomenal appearance of things, in order to give an explanation of that by which, in some sense or other, this experience or nature is conditioned; or, to speak in popular language, of that which is behind nature, and makes it possible. But the great original diversity in the power of understanding, besides the cultivation of it, which demands much leisure, makes so great a difference between men, that as soon as a people has emerged from the state of savages, no *one* metaphysic can serve for them all. Therefore among civilised nations we find throughout two different kinds of metaphysics, which are distinguished by the fact that the one has its evidence *in itself*, the other *outside itself*. Since the metaphysical systems of the first kind require reflection, culture, and leisure for the recognition of their evidence, they can be accessible only to a very small number of men; and, moreover, they can only arise and maintain their existence in the case of advanced civilisation. On the other hand, the systems of the second kind exclusively are for the great majority of men who are not capable of thinking, but only of believing, and who are not accessible to reasons, but only to authority. These systems may therefore be called metaphysics of the people, after the analogy of poetry of the people, and also wisdom of the people, by which is understood proverbs. These systems, however, are known under the name of religions, and are found among all nations, not excepting even the most savage. Their evidence is, as has been said, external, and as such is called revelation, which is authenticated by signs and miracles. Their arguments are principally threats of eternal, and indeed also temporal evils, directed against unbelievers, and even against mere doubters. As *ultima ratio theologorum*, we find among many nations the stake or things similar to it. If they seek a different authentication, or if they make use of other arguments, they already make the transition into the systems of the first kind, and may degenerate into a mixture of the two, which brings more danger than advantage, for their invaluable prerogative of being imparted to *children* gives them the surest guarantee of the permanent possession of the mind, for thereby their dogmas grow into a kind of second inborn intellect, like the twig upon the grafted tree; while, on the other hand, the systems of the first kind only appeal to grown-up people, and in them always find a system of the second kind already in possession of their convictions. Both kinds of metaphysics, whose difference may be briefly expressed by the words reasoned conviction and faith, have this in common, that every one of their particular systems stands in a hostile relation to all the others of its kind. Between those of the first kind war is waged only with word and pen ; between those of the second with fire and sword as well. Several of the latter owe their propagation in part to this last kind of polemic, and all have by degrees divided the earth between them, and indeed with such decided authority that the peoples of the earth are distinguished and separated more according to them than according to nationality or government. They alone *reign*, each in its own province. The systems of the first kind, on the contrary, are at the most *tolerated*, and even this only because, on account of the small number of their adherents, they are for the most part not considered worth the trouble of combating with fire and sword—although, where it seemed necessary, these also have been employed against them with effect; besides, they occur only in a sporadic form. Yet in general they have only been endured in a tamed and subjugated condition, for the system of the second kind which prevailed in the country ordered them to conform their teaching more or less closely to its own. Sometimes it not only subjugated them, but even employed their services and used them as a support, which is however a dangerous experiment. For these systems of the first kind, since they are deprived of power, believe they may advance themselves by craft, and never entirely lay aside a secret ill-will which at times comes unexpectedly into prominence and inflicts injuries which are hard to heal. For they are further made the more dangerous by the fact that all the real sciences, not even excepting the most innocent, are their secret allies against the systems of the second kind, and without themselves being openly at war with the latter, suddenly and unexpectedly do great mischief in their province. Besides, the attempt which is aimed at by the enlistment referred to of the services of the systems of the first kind by the second—the attempt to add an inner authentication to a system whose original authentication was external, is in its nature perilous; for, if it were capable of such an authentication, it would never have required an external one. And in general it is always a hazardous thing to attempt to place a new foundation under a finished structure. Moreover, how should a religion require the suffrage of a philosophy ? It has everything upon its side—revelation, tradition, miracles, prophecies, the protection of the government, the highest rank, as is due to the truth, the consent and reverence of all, a thousand temples in which it is proclaimed and practised, bands of sworn priests, and, what is more than all, the invaluable privilege of being allowed to imprint its doctrines on the mind at the tender age of childhood, whereby they became almost like innate ideas. With such wealth of means at its disposal, still to desire the assent of poor philosophers it must be more covetous, or to care about their contradiction it must be more fearful, than seems to be compatible with a good conscience.

To the distinction established above between metaphysics of the first and of the second kind, we have yet to add the following:—A system of the first kind, thus a philosophy, makes the claim, and has therefore the obligation, in everything that it says, *sensu stricto et proprio*, to be true, for it appeals to thought and conviction. A religion, on the other hand, being intended for the innumerable multitude who, since they are incapable of examination and thought, would never comprehend the profoundest and most difficult truths *sensu proprio*, has only the obligation to be true *sensu allegorico*. Truth cannot appear naked before the people. A symptom of this *allegorical* nature of religions is the *mysteries* which are to be found perhaps in them all, certain dogmas which cannot even be distinctly thought, not to speak of being literally true. Indeed, perhaps it might be asserted that some absolute contradictions, some actual absurdities, are an essential ingredient in a complete religion, for these are just the

stamp of its allegorical nature, and the only adequate
means of making the ordinary mind and the uncultured
understanding *feel* what would be incomprehensible to it,
that religion has ultimately to do with quite a different
order of things, with an order of *things in themselves*, in
the presence of which the laws of this phenomenal world,
in conformity with which it must speak, vanish; and that
therefore not only the contradictory but also the comprehensible dogmas are really only allegories and accommo-
dations to the human power of comprehension. It seems
to me that it was in this spirit that Augustine and even
Luther adhered to the mysteries of Christianity in opposi-
sition to Pelagianism, which sought to reduce everything
to the dull level of comprehensibility. From this point of
view it is also conceivable how Tertullian could say in all
seriousness : *"Prorsus credibile est, quia ineptum est : ... cer-
tum est, quia impossibile "* (*De Carne Christi*, c. 5). This *allegorical* nature of religions makes them independent of the
proofs which are incumbent on philosophy, and in general
withdraws them from investigation. Instead of this
they require faith, that is, a voluntary admission that
such is the state of the case. Since, then, faith guides
action, and the allegory is always so framed that, as
regards the practical, it leads precisely to that which
the truth *sensu proprio* would also lead to, religion is
justified in promising to those who believe eternal salvation. Thus we see that in the main, and for the great majority, who cannot apply themselves to thought, religions
very well supply the place of metaphysics in general, the
need of which man feels to be imperative. They do this
partly in a practical interest, as the guiding star of their
action, the unfurled standard of integrity and virtue, as
Kant admirably expresses it; partly as the indispensable
comfort in the heavy sorrows of life, in which capacity
they fully supply the place of an objectively true metaphysic, because they lift man above himself and his existence in time, as well perhaps as such a metaphysic ever

could. In this their great value and indeed necessity shows itself very clearly. For Plato says, and says rightly, " φιλόσοφον πλῆθος ἀδύνατον εἶναι " (*vulgus philosophum esse impossible est. De Rep.*, vi. p. 89, *Bip.*) On the other hand, the only stumbling-stone is this, that religions never dare to confess their allegorical nature, but have to assert that they are true *sensu proprio*. They thereby encroach on the province of metaphysics proper, and call forth the antagonism of the latter, which has therefore expressed itself at all times when it was not chained up. The controversy which is so perseveringly carried on in our own day between supernaturalists and rationalists also rests on the failure to recognise the allegorical nature of all religion. Both wish to have Christianity true *sensu proprio;* in this sense the former wish to maintain it without deduction, as it were with skin and hair; and thus they have a hard stand to make against the knowledge and general culture of the age. The latter wish to explain away all that is properly Christian; whereupon they retain something which is neither *sensu proprio* nor *sensu allegorico* true, but rather a mere platitude, little better than Judaism, or at the most a shallow Pelagianism, and, what is worst, an abject optimism, absolutely foreign to Christianity proper. Moreover, the attempt to found a religion upon reason removes it into the other class of metaphysics, that which has its authentication *in itself*, thus to the foreign ground of the philosophical systems, and into the conflict which these wage against each other in their own arena, and consequently exposes it to the light fire of scepticism and the heavy artillery of the " Critique of Pure Reason;" but for it to venture there would be clear presumption.

It would be most beneficial to both kinds of metaphysics that each of them should remain clearly separated from the other and confine itself to its own province, that it may there be able to develop its nature fully. Instead of which, through the whole Christian era, the endeavour has been to bring about a fusion of the two, for the dogmas and conceptions of the one have been carried over into the other, whereby both are spoiled. This has taken place in the most open manner in our own day in that strange hermaphrodite or centaur, the so-called philosophy of religion, which, as a kind of gnosis, endeavours to interpret the given religion, and to explain what is true *sensu allegorico* through something which is true *sensu proprio*. But for this we would have to know and possess the truth *sensu proprio* already; and in that case such an interpretation would be superfluous. For to seek first to find metaphysics, *i.e.*, the truth *sensu proprio*, merely out of religion by explanation and interpretation would be a doubtful and dangerous undertaking, to which one would only make up one's mind if it were proved that truth, like iron and other base metals, could only be found in a mixed, not in a pure form, and therefore one could only obtain it by reduction from the mixed ore.

Religions are necessary for the people, and an inestimable benefit to them. But if they oppose themselves to the progress of mankind in the knowledge of the truth, they must with the utmost possible forbearance be set aside. And to require that a great mind—a Shakspeare; a Goethe—should make the dogmas of any religion implicitly, *bonâ fide et sensu proprio*, his conviction is to require that a giant should put on the shoe of a dwarf.

Religions, being calculated with reference to the power of comprehension of the great mass of men, can only have indirect, not immediate truth. To require of them the latter is as if one wished to read the letters set up in the form-chase, instead of their impression. The value of a religion will accordingly depend upon the greater or less content of truth which it contains under the veil of allegory, and then upon the greater or less distinctness with which it becomes visible through this veil, thus upon the transparency of the latter. It almost seems that, as the oldest languages are the most perfect, so also are the oldest religions. If I were to take the results of my philosophy as the standard of truth, I would be obliged to concede to Buddhism the pre-eminence over the rest. In any case it must be a satisfaction to me to see my teaching in such close agreement with a religion which the majority of men upon the earth hold as their own; for it numbers far more adherents than any other. This agreement, however, must be the more satisfactory to me because in my philosophising I have certainly not been under its influence. For up till 1818, when my work appeared, there were very few, exceedingly incomplete and scanty, accounts of Buddhism to be found in Europe, which were almost entirely limited to a few essays in the earlier volumes of "Asiatic Researches," and were principally concerned with the Buddhism of the Burmese. Only since then has fuller information about this religion gradually reached us, chiefly through the profound and instructive essays of the meritorious member of the St. Petersburg Academy, J. J. Schmidt, in the proceedings of his Academy, and then little by little through several English and French scholars, so that I was able to give a fairly numerous list of the best works on this religion in my work, " *Ueber den Willen in der Natur,*" under the heading *Sinologie.* Unfortunately Csoma Körösi, that persevering Hungarian, who, in order to study the language and sacred writings of Buddhism, spent many years in Tibet, and for the most part in Buddhist monasteries, was carried off by death just as he was beginning to work out for us the results of his researches. I cannot, however, deny the pleasure with which I read, in his provisional accounts, several passages cited directly from the Kahgyur itself; for example, the following conversation of the dying Buddha with Brahma, who is doing him homage: "There is a description of their conversation on the subject of creation,—by whom was the world made? Shakya asks several questions of Brahma,—whether was it he who made or produced such and such things, and endowed or blessed them with such and such virtues or properties,—whether was it he who caused the several revolutions in the destruction and regeneration of the world. He denies that he had ever done anything to that effect. At last he himself asks Shakya how the world was made,—by whom? Here are attributed all changes in the world to the moral works of the animal beings, and it is stated that in the world all is illusion, there is no reality in the things; all is empty. Brahma, being instructed in his doctrine, becomes his follower" (Asiatic Researches, vol. xx. p. 434).

I cannot place, as is always done, the fundamental difference of all religions in the question whether they are monotheistic, polytheistic, pantheistic, or atheistic, but only in the question whether they are optimistic or pessimistic, that is, whether they present the existence of the world as justified by itself, and therefore praise and value it, or regard it as something that can only be conceived as the consequence of our guilt, and therefore properly ought not to be, because they recognise that pain and death cannot lie in the eternal, original, and immutable order of things, in that which in every respect ought to be. The power by virtue of which Christianity was able to overcome first Judaism, and then the heathenism of Greece and Rome, lies solely in its pessimism, in the confession that our state is both exceedingly wretched and sinful, while Judaism and heathenism were optimistic. That truth, profoundly and painfully felt by all, penetrated, and bore in its train the need of redemption.

I turn to a general consideration of the other kind of metaphysics, that which has its authentication in itself, and is called *philosophy*. I remind the reader of its origin, mentioned above, in a *wonder* concerning the world and our own existence, inasmuch as these press upon the intellect as a riddle, the solution of which therefore occupies mankind without intermission. Here, then, I wish first of all to draw attention to the fact that this could not be

the case if, in Spinoza's sense, which in our own day has
so often been brought forward again under modern forms
and expositions as pantheism, the world were an "*absolute
substance*," and therefore an *absolutely necessary existence.*
For this means that it exists with so great a necessity
that beside it every other necessity comprehensible to our
understanding as such must appear as an accident. It
would then be something which comprehended in itself
not only all actual but also all possible existence, so that,
as Spinoza indeed declares, its possibility and its actuality
would be absolutely one. Its non-being would therefore
be impossibility itself; thus it would be something the
non-being or other-being of which must be completely
inconceivable, and which could therefore just as little be
thought away as, for example, space or time. And since,
further, *we ourselves* would be parts, modes, attributes, or
accidents of such an absolute substance, which would be
the only thing that, in any sense, could ever or anywhere
exist, our and its existence, together with its properties,
would necessarily be very far from presenting itself to us
as remarkable, problematical, and indeed as an unfathomable and ever-disquieting riddle, but, on the contrary,
would be far more self-evident than that two and two
make four. For we would necessarily be incapable of
thinking anything else than that the world is, and is,
as it is; and therefore we would necessarily be as little
conscious of its existence *as such, i.e.,* as a problem for
reflection, as we are of the incredibly fast motion of our
planet.

All this, however, is absolutely not the case. Only to
the brutes, who are without thought, does the world and
existence appear as a matter of course; to man, on the
contrary, it is a problem, of which even the most uneducated and narrow-minded becomes vividly conscious in
certain brighter moments, but which enters more distinctly
and more permanently into the consciousness of each one
of us the clearer and more enlightened that conscious-

ness is, and the more material for thought it has acquired through culture, which all ultimately rises, in minds that are naturally adapted for philosophising, to Plato's " θαυμα-ζειν, μαλα φιλοσοφικον παθος " (*mirari, valde philosophicus affectus*), that is, to that *wonder* which comprehends in its whole magnitude that problem which unceasingly occupies the nobler portion of mankind in every age and in every land, and gives it no rest. In fact, the pendulum which keeps in motion the clock of metaphysics, that never runs down, is the consciousness that the non-existence of this world is just as possible as its existence. Thus, then, the Spinozistic view of it as an absolutely necessary existence, that is, as something that absolutely and in every sense ought to and must be, is a false one. Even simple Theism, since in its cosmological proof it tacitly starts by inferring the previous non-existence of the world from its existence, thereby assumes beforehand that the world is something contingent. Nay, what is more, we very soon apprehend the world as something the non-existence of which is not only conceivable, but indeed preferable to its existence. Therefore our wonder at it easily passes into a brooding over the *fatality* which could yet call forth its existence, and by virtue of which such stupendous power as is demanded for the production and maintenance of such a world could be directed so much against its own interest. The philosophical astonishment is therefore at bottom perplexed and melancholy; philosophy, like the overture to " Don Juan," commences with a minor chord. It follows from this that it can neither be Spinozism nor optimism. The more special nature, which has just been indicated, of the astonishment which leads us to philosophise clearly springs from the sight of the *suffering and the wickedness* in the world, which, even if they were in the most just proportion to each other, and also were far outweighed by good, are yet something which absolutely and in general ought not to be. But since now nothing can come out of nothing, these also must have their germ in the origin or in the kernel of the world itself. It is hard for us to assume this if we look at the magnitude, the order and completeness, of the physical world, for it seems to us that what had the power to produce such a world must have been able to avoid the suffering and the wickedness. That assumption (the truest expression of which is Ormuzd and Ahrimines), it is easy to conceive, is hardest of all for Theism. Therefore the freedom of the will was primarily invented to account for wickedness. But this is only a concealed way of making something out of nothing, for it assumes an *Operari* that proceeded from no *Esse* (see *Die beiden Grundprobleme der Ethik*, p. 58, *et seq.*; second edition, p. 57 *et seq.*) Then it was sought to get rid of evil by attributing it to matter, or to unavoidable necessity, whereby the devil, who is really the right *Expediens ad hoc*, was unwillingly set aside. To evil also belongs *death;* but wickedness is only the throwing of the existing evil from oneself on to another. Thus, as was said above, it is wickedness, evil, and death that qualify and intensify the philosophical astonishment. Not merely that the world exists, but still more that it is such a wretched world, is the *punctum pruriens* of metaphysics, the problem which awakens in mankind an unrest that cannot be quieted by scepticism nor yet by criticism.

We find *physics* also (in the widest sense of the word) occupied with the explanation of the phenomena in the world. But it lies in the very nature of its explanations themselves that they cannot be sufficient. Physics cannot stand on its own feet, but requires a metaphysic to lean upon, whatever airs it may give itself towards the latter. For it explains the phenomena by something still more unknown than they are themselves; by laws of nature, resting upon forces of nature, to which the power of life also belongs. Certainly the whole present condition of all things in the world, or in nature, must necessarily be explicable from purely physical causes. But such an explanation—supposing one actually succeeded so far as to be able to give it—must always just as necessarily be tainted with two imperfections (as it were with two sores, or like Achilles with the vulnerable heel, or the devil with the horse's hoof), on account of which everything so explained really remains still unexplained.   First with this imperfection, that the *beginning* of every explanatory chain of causes and effects, *i.e.*, of connected changes, can absolutely *never* be reached, but, just like the limits of the world in space and time, unceasingly recedes *in infinito*. Secondly with this, that the whole of the efficient causes out of which everything is explained constantly rest upon something which is completely inexplicable, the original *qualities* of things and the *natural forces* which play a prominent part among them, by virtue of which they produce a specific kind of effect, *e.g.*, weight, hardness, impulsive force, elasticity, warmth, electricity, chemical forces &c., and which now remain in every explanation which is given, like an unknown quantity, which absolutely cannot be eliminated, in an otherwise perfectly solved algebraical equation.   Accordingly there is no fragment of clay, however little worth, that is not entirely composed of inexplicable qualities.   Thus these two inevitable defects in every purely physical, *i.e.*, causal, explanation show that such an explanation can only be *relative*, and that its whole method and nature cannot be the only one, the ultimate and thus the sufficient one, *i.e.*, cannot be the method of explanation that can ever lead to the satisfactory solution of the difficult riddle of things, and to the true understanding of the world and existence; but that the physical explanation in general and as such requires further a *metaphysical* explanation, which affords us the key to all its assumptions, but just on this account must necessarily follow quite a different path.   The first step to this is that one should bring to distinct consciousness and firmly retain the difference of the two, hence the difference between *physics* and *metaphysics*.   It rests in general on the Kantian distinction between *phenomenon*

and *thing in itself*.   Just because Kant held the latter to
be absolutely unknowable, there was, according to him,
no *metaphysics*, but merely immanent knowledge, *i.e.*, *physics*, which throughout can speak only of phenomena, and
also a critique of the reason which strives after metaphysics.   Here, however, in order to show the true point of
connection between my philosophy and that of Kant, I
shall anticipate the second book, and give prominence to
the fact that Kant, in his beautiful exposition of the compatibility of freedom and necessity (Critique of Pure
Reason, first edition, p. 532–554; and Critique of Practical Reason, p. 224–231 of Rosenkranz's edition), shows
how one and the same action may in one aspect be perfectly explicable as necessarily arising from the character
of the man, the influence to which he has been subject in
the course of his life, and the motives which are now present to him, but yet in another aspect must be regarded
as the work of his free will; and in the same sense he
says, § 53 of the "Prolegomena:" "Certainly natural necessity will belong to every connection of cause and effect in
the world of sense; yet, on the other hand, freedom will be
conceded to that cause which is not itself a phenomenon
(though indeed it is the ground of phenomena), thus
nature and freedom may without contradiction be attributed to the same thing, but in a different reference—in
the one case as a phenomenon, in the other case as a thing
in itself." What, then, Kant teaches of the phenomenon of
man and his action my teaching extends to *all* phenomena
in nature, in that it makes the *will* as a thing in itself
their foundation. This proceeding is justified first of all
by the fact that it must not be assumed that man is
specifically *toto genere* radically different from the other
beings and things in nature, but rather that he is different
only in degree.   I turn back from this premature digression to our consideration of the inadequacy of physics to
afford us the ultimate explanation of things.   I say, then,
everything certainly is physical, but yet nothing is explic-

able physically. As for the motion of the projected bullet, so also for the thinking of the brain, a physical explanation must ultimately be in itself possible, which would make the latter just as comprehensible as is the former. But even the former, which we imagine we understand so perfectly, is at bottom as obscure to us as the latter; for what the inner nature of expansion in space may be—of impenetrability, mobility, hardness, elasticity, and gravity remains, after all physical explanations, a mystery, just as much as thought. But because in the case of thought the inexplicable appears most immediately, a spring was at once made here from physics to metaphysics, and a substance of quite a different kind from all corporeal substances was hypostatised—a soul was set up in the brain. But if one had not been so dull as only to be capable of being struck by the most remarkable of phenomena, one would have had to explain digestion by a soul in the stomach, vegetation by a soul in the plant, affinity by a soul in the reagents, nay, the falling of a stone by a soul in the stone. For the quality of every unorganised body is just as mysterious as the life in the living body. In the same way, therefore, the physical explanation strikes everywhere upon what is metaphysical, by which it is annihilated, i.e., it ceases to be explanation. Strictly speaking, it may be asserted that no natural science really achieves anything more than what is also achieved by Botany: the bringing together of similars, classification. A physical system which asserted that its explanations of things—in the particular from causes, and in general from forces—were really sufficient, and thus exhausted the nature of the world, would be the true *Naturalism*. From Leucippus, Democritus, and Epicurus down to the *Système de la Nature*, and further, to Delamark, Cabanis, and to the materialism that has again been warmed up in the last few years, we can trace the persistent attempt to set up a *system of physics without metaphysics*, that is, a system which would make the phenomenon the thing in itself. But all their explanations seek to conceal from the explainers themselves and from others that they simply assume the principal matter without more ado. They endeavour to show that all phenomena, even those of mind, are physical. And they are right; only they do not see that all that is physical is in another aspect also metaphysical. But, without Kant, this is indeed difficult to see, for it presupposes the distinction of the phenomenon from the thing in itself. Yet without this Aristotle, much as he was inclined to empiricism, and far as he was removed from the Platonic hyperphysics, kept himself free from this limited point of view. He says : "*Ει μεν ουν μη εστι τις ἑτερα ουσια παρα τας φυσει συνεστηκυιας, ἡ φυσικη αν ειη πρωτη επιστημη· ει δε εστι τις ουσια ακινητος, αὑτη προτερα και φιλοσοφια πρωτη, και καθολου οὑτως, ὁτι πρωτη· και περι του οντος ᾗ ον, ταυτης αν ειη θεωρησαι.*" (*Si igitur non est aliqua alia substantia, præter eas, quæ natura consistunt, physica profecto prima scientia esset : quodsi autem est aliqua substantia immobilis, hæc prior et philosophia prima, et universalis sic, quod prima ; et de ente, prout ens est, speculari hujus est*), "Metaph.," v. 1. Such an *absolute system of physics* as is described above, which leaves room for no *metaphysics*, would make the *Natura naturata* into the *Natura naturans;* it would be physics established on the throne of metaphysics, yet it would comport itself in this high position almost like Holberg's theatrical would-be politician who was made burgomaster. Indeed behind the reproach of atheism, in itself absurd, and for the most part malicious, there lies, as its inner meaning and truth, which gives it strength, the obscure conception of such an absolute system of physics without metaphysics. Certainly such a system would necessarily be destructive of ethics; and while Theism has falsely been held to be inseparable from morality, this is really true only of *metaphysics in general, i.e.,* of the knowledge that the order of nature is not the only and absolute order of things. Therefore we may set up this as the necessary *Credo* of all just and

good men: "I believe in metaphysics." In this respect it
is important and necessary that one should convince oneself of the untenable nature of an *absolute system of physics,*
all the more as this, the true *naturalism,* is a point of view
which of its own accord and ever anew presses itself upon
a man, and can only be done away with through profound
speculation. In this respect, however, all kinds of systems
and faiths, so far and so long as they are accepted, certainly
serve as a substitute for such speculation. But that a
fundamentally false view presses itself upon man of its
own accord, and must first be skilfully removed, is explicable from the fact that the intellect is not originally
intended to instruct us concerning the nature of things,
but only to show us their relations, with reference to our
will; it is, as we shall find in the second book, only the
medium of motives. Now, that the world schematises
itself in the intellect in a manner which exhibits quite a
different order of things from the absolutely true one,
because it shows us, not their kernel, but only their outer
shell, happens accidentally, and cannot be used as a
reproach to the intellect; all the less as it nevertheless
finds in itself the means of rectifying this error, in that it
arrives at the distinction between the phenomenal appearance and the inner being of things, which distinction
existed in substance at all times, only for the most part
was very imperfectly brought to consciousness, and therefore was inadequately expressed, indeed often appeared in
strange clothing. The Christian mystics, when they call
it the *light of nature,* declare the intellect to be inadequate
to the comprehension of the true nature of things. It is,
as it were, a mere surface force, like electricity, and does
not penetrate to the inner being.

The insufficiency of pure naturalism appears, as we have
said, first of all, on the empirical path itself, through the
circumstance that every physical explanation explains the
particular from its cause; but the chain of these causes, as
we know *a priori,* and therefore with perfect certainty,

runs back to infinity, so that absolutely no cause could
ever be the first. Then, however, the effect of every cause
is referred to a law of nature, and this finally to a force of
nature, which now remains as the absolutely inexplicable.
But this inexplicable, to which all phenomena of this so
clearly given and naturally explicable world, from the
highest to the lowest, are referred, just shows that the
whole nature of such explanation is only conditional, as
it were only *ex concessis*, and by no means the true and
sufficient one; therefore I said above that physically
everything and nothing is explicable. That absolutely
inexplicable element which pervades all phenomena, which
is most striking in the highest, *e.g.*, in generation, but yet
is just as truly present in the lowest, *e.g.*, in mechanical
phenomena, points to an entirely different kind of order
of things lying at the foundation of the physical order,
which is just what Kant calls the order of things in
themselves, and which is the goal of metaphysics. But,
secondly, the insufficiency of pure naturalism comes out
clearly from that fundamental philosophical truth, which
we have fully considered in the first half of this book, and
which is also the theme of the " Critique of Pure Reason ;"
the truth that every *object*, both as regards its objective
existence in general and as regards the manner (forms) of
this existence, is throughout conditioned by the knowing
subject, hence is merely a phenomenon, not a thing in
itself. This is explained in § 7 of the first volume, and it
is there shown that nothing can be more clumsy than that,
after the manner of all materialists, one should blindly take
the objective as simply given in order to derive everything
from it without paying any regard to the subjective, through
which, however, nay, in which alone the former exists.
Samples of this procedure are most readily afforded us
by the fashionable materialism of our own day, which
has thereby become a philosophy well suited for barbers'
and apothecaries' apprentices. For it, in its innocence,
matter, assumed without reflection as absolutely real, is

the thing in self, and the one capacity of a thing in itself is impulsive force, for all other qualities can only be manifestations of this.

With naturalism, then, or the purely physical way of looking at things, we shall never attain our end; it is like a sum that never comes out. Causal series without beginning or end, fundamental forces which are inscrutable, endless space, beginningless time, infinite divisibility of matter, and all this further conditioned by a knowing brain, in which alone it exists just like a dream, and without which it vanishes—constitute the labyrinth in which naturalism leads us ceaselessly round. The height to which in our time the natural sciences have risen in this respect entirely throws into the shade all previous centuries, and is a summit which mankind reaches for the first time. But however great are the advances which *physics* (understood in the wide sense of the ancients) may make, not the smallest step towards *metaphysics* is thereby taken, just as a plane can never obtain cubical content by being indefinitely extended. For all such advances will only perfect our knowledge of the *phenomenon;* while *metaphysics* strives to pass beyond the phenomenal appearance itself, to that which so appears. And if indeed it had the assistance of an entire and complete experience, it would, as regards the main point, be in no way advantaged by it. Nay, even if one wandered through all the planets and fixed stars, one would thereby have made no step in *metaphysics*. It is rather the case that the greatest advances of physics will make the need of metaphysics ever more felt; for it is just the corrected, extended, and more thorough knowledge of nature which, on the one hand, always undermines and ultimately overthrows the metaphysical assumptions which till then have prevailed, but, on the other hand, presents the problem of metaphysics itself more distinctly, more correctly, and more fully, and separates it more clearly from all that is merely physical; moreover, the more perfectly and accurately known nature of the particular thing more pressingly demands the explanation of the whole and the general, which, the more correctly, thoroughly, and completely it is known empirically, only presents itself as the more mysterious. Certainly the individual, simple investigator of nature, in a special branch of physics, does not at once become clearly conscious of all this ; he rather sleeps contentedly by the side of his chosen maid, in the house of Odysseus, banishing all thoughts of Penelope (cf. ch. 12 at the end). Hence we see at the present day the *husk of nature* investigated in its minutest details, the intestines of intestinal worms and the vermin of vermin known to a nicety. But if some one comes, as, for example, I do, and speaks of the *kernel of nature,* they will not listen ; they even think it has nothing to do with the matter, and go on sifting their husks. One finds oneself tempted to call that over-microscopical and micrological investigator of nature the cotquean of nature. But those persons who believe that crucibles and retorts are the true and only source of all wisdom are in their own way just as perverse as were formerly their antipodes the Scholastics. As the latter, absolutely confined to their abstract conceptions, used these as their weapons, neither knowing nor investigating anything outside them, so the former, absolutely confined to their empiricism, allow nothing to be true except what their eyes behold, and believe they can thus arrive at the ultimate ground of things, not discerning that between the phenomenon and that which manifests itself in it, the thing in itself, there is a deep gulf, a radical difference, which can only be cleared up by the knowledge and accurate delimitation of the subjective element of the phenomenon, and the insight that the ultimate and most important conclusions concerning the nature of things can only be drawn from self-consciousness ; yet without all this one cannot advance a step beyond what is directly given to the senses, thus can get no further than to the problem. Yet, on the other hand, it is to be observed that the most perfect possible knowledge of nature is the corrected *statement of the problem* of metaphysics. Therefore no one ought to venture upon this without having first acquired a knowledge of all the branches of natural science, which, though general, shall be thorough, clear, and connected. For the problem must precede its solution. Then, however, the investigator must turn his glance inward; for the intellectual and ethical phenomena are more important than the physical, in the same proportion as, for example, animal magnetism is a far more important phenomenon than mineral magnetism. The last fundamental secret man carries within himself, and this is accessible to him in the most immediate manner; therefore it is only here that he can hope to find the key to the riddle of the world and gain a clue to the nature of all things. The special province of metaphysics thus certainly lies in what has been called mental philosophy.

> " The ranks of living creatures thou dost lead
> Before me, teaching me to know my brothers
> In air and water and the silent wood :
>
> .   .   .   .
>
> Then to the cave secure thou leadest me,
> Then show'st me mine own self, and in my breast
> The deep, mysterious miracles unfold." [1]

Finally, then, as regards the *source or the foundation* of metaphysical knowledge, I have already declared myself above to be opposed to the assumption, which is even repeated by Kant, that it must lie *in mere conceptions.* In no knowledge can conceptions be what is first; for they are always derived from some perception. What has led, however, to that assumption is probably the example of mathematics. Mathematics can leave perception altogether, and, as is especially the case in algebra, trigonometry, and analysis, can operate with purely abstract conceptions, nay, with conceptions which are represented

---

[1] [Bayard Taylor's translation of Faust, vol. i. 180. Trs.]

only by signs instead of words, and can yet arrive at a perfectly certain result, which is still so remote that any one who adhered to the firm ground of perception could not arrive at it. But the possibility of this depends, as Kant has clearly shown, on the fact that the conceptions of mathematics are derived from the most certain and definite of all perceptions, from the *a priori* and yet intuitively known relations of quantity, and can therefore be constantly realised again and controlled by these, either arithmetically, by performing the calculations which are merely indicated by those signs, or geometrically, by means of what Kant calls the construction of the conceptions. This advantage, on the other hand, is not possessed by the conceptions out of which it was believed metaphysics could be built up; such, for example, as essence, being, substance, perfection, necessity, reality, finite, infinite, absolute, ground, &c. For such conceptions are by no means original, as fallen from heaven, or innate; but they also, like all conceptions, are derived from perceptions; and as, unlike the conceptions of mathematics, they do not contain the mere form of perception, but more, empirical perceptions must lie at their foundation. Thus nothing can be drawn from them which the empirical perceptions did not also contain, that is, nothing which was not a matter of experience, and which, since these conceptions are very wide abstractions, we would receive with much greater certainty at first hand from experience. For from conceptions nothing more can ever be drawn than the perceptions from which they are derived contain. If we desire pure conceptions, *i.e.*, such as have no empirical source, the only ones that can be produced are those which concern space and time, *i.e.*, the merely formal part of perception, consequently only the mathematical conceptions, or at most also the conception of causality, which indeed does not originate in experience, but yet only comes into consciousness by means of it (first in sense-perception); therefore experience indeed is only possible by means of it; but it also is only

valid in the sphere of experience, on which account Kant
has shown that it only serves to communicate the connection of experience, and not to transcend it; that thus it
admits only of physical application, not of metaphysical.
Certainly only its *a priori* origin can give apodictic certainty
to any knowledge; but this limits it to the mere *form* of
experience in general, for it shows that it is conditioned
by the subjective nature of the intellect. Such knowledge,
then, far from taking us beyond experience, gives only one
part of experience itself, the *formal* part, which belongs
to it throughout, and therefore is universal, consequently
mere form without content. Since now metaphysics can
least of all be confined to this, it must have also *empirical*
sources of knowledge; therefore that preconceived idea of
a metaphysic to be found purely *a priori* is necessarily vain.
It is really a *petitio principii* of Kant's, which he expresses
most distinctly in § 1 of the Prolegomena, that metaphysics
must not draw its fundamental conceptions and principles
from experience. In this it is assumed beforehand that
only what we knew *before* all experience can extend
beyond all possible experience. Supported by this, Kant
then comes and shows that all such knowledge is nothing
more than the form of the intellect for the purpose of
experience, and consequently can never lead beyond experience, from which he then rightly deduces the impossibility of all metaphysics. But does it not rather seem
utterly perverse that in order to discover the secret of
experience, *i.e.*, of the world which alone lies before us, we
should look quite away from it, ignore its content, and
take and use for its material only the empty forms of
which we are conscious *a priori?* Is it not rather in
keeping with the matter that *the science of experience in
general*, and as such, should also be drawn from experience?
Its problem itself is given it empirically; why should
not the solution of it call in the assistance of experience?
Is it not senseless that he who speaks of the nature of
things should not look at things themselves, but should

confine himself to certain abstract conceptions? The task of metaphysics is certainly not the observation of particular experiences, but yet it is the correct explanation of experience as a whole. Its foundation must therefore, at any rate, be of an empirical nature. Indeed the *a priori* nature of a part of human knowledge will be apprehended by it as a given *fact,* from which it will infer the subjective origin of the same. Only because the consciousness of its *a priori* nature accompanies it is it called by Kant *transcendental* as distinguished from *transcendent,* which signifies "passing beyond all possibility of experience," and has its opposite in *immanent, i.e.,* remaining within the limits of experience. I gladly recall the original meaning of this expression introduced by Kant, with which, as also with that of the Categories, and many others, the apes of philosophy carry on their game at the present day. Now, besides this, the source of the knowledge of metaphysics is not *outer* experience alone, but also *inner.* Indeed, what is most peculiar to it, that by which the decisive step which alone can solve the great question becomes possible for it, consists, as I have fully and thoroughly proved in " *Ueber den Willen in der Natur,"* under the heading, " *Physische Astronomie,"* in this, that at the right place it combines outer experience with inner, and uses the latter as a key to the former.

The origin of metaphysics in empirical sources of knowledge, which is here set forth, and which cannot fairly be denied, deprives it certainly of that kind of apodictic certainty which is only possible through knowledge *a priori.* This remains the possession of logic and mathematics—sciences, however, which really only teach what every one knows already, though not distinctly. At most the primary elements of natural science may also be deduced from knowledge *a priori.* By this confession metaphysics only surrenders an ancient claim, which, according to what has been said above, rested upon misunderstanding, and against which the great diversity and changeableness of metaphysical systems, and also the constantly accompanying scepticism, in every age has testified. Yet against the possibility of metaphysics in general this changeableness cannot be urged, for the same thing affects just as much all branches of natural science, chemistry, physics, geology, zoology, &c., and even history has not remained exempt from it. But when once, as far as the limits of human intellect allow, a true system of metaphysics shall have been found, the unchangeableness of a science which is known *a priori* will yet belong to it; for its foundation can only be *experience in general*, and not the particular and special experiences by which, on the other hand, the natural sciences are constantly modified and new material is always being provided for history. For experience as a whole and in general will never change its character for a new one.

The next question is: How can a science drawn from experience pass beyond it and so merit the name of metaphysics ? It cannot do so perhaps in the same way as we find a fourth number from three proportionate ones, or a triangle from two sides and an angle. This was the way of the pre-Kantian dogmatism, which, according to certain laws known to us *a priori*, sought to reason from the given to the not given, from the consequent to the reason, thus from experience to that which could not possibly be given in any experience. Kant proved the impossibility of a metaphysic upon this path, in that he showed that although these laws were not drawn from experience, they were only valid for experience. He therefore rightly taught that in such a way we cannot transcend the possibility of all experience. But there are other paths to metaphysics. The whole of experience is like a cryptograph, and philosophy the deciphering of it, the correctness of which is proved by the connection appearing everywhere. If this whole is only profoundly enough comprehended, and the inner experience is connected with the outer, it must be capable of being *interpreted*, *explained* from itself. Since Kant has irrefutably proved to us that experience in general proceeds from two elements, the forms of knowledge and the inner nature of things, and that these two may be distinguished in experience from each other, as that of which we are conscious *a priori* and that which is added *a posteriori*, it is possible, at least in general, to say, what in the given experience, which is primarily merely phenomenal, belongs to the *form* of this phenomenon, conditioned by the intellect, and what, after deducting this, remains over for the *thing in itself.* And although no one can discern the thing in itself through the veil of the forms of perception, on the other hand every one carries it in himself, indeed is it himself; therefore in self-consciousness it must be in some way accessible to him, even though only conditionally. Thus the bridge by which metaphysics passes beyond experience is nothing else than that analysis of experience into phenomenon and thing in itself in which I have placed Kant's greatest merit. For it contains the proof of a kernel of the phenomenon different from the phenomenon itself. This can indeed never be entirely separated from the phenomenon and regarded in itself as an *ens extramundanum*, but is always known only in its relations to and connections with the phenomenon itself. But the interpretation and explanation of the latter, in relation to the former, which is its inner kernel, is capable of affording us information with regard to it which does not otherwise come into consciousness. In this sense, then, metaphysics goes beyond the phenomenon, *i.e.*, nature, to that which is concealed in or behind it (το μετα το φυσικον), always regarding it, however, merely as that which manifests itself in the phenomenon, not as independent of all phenomenal appearance; it therefore remains immanent, and does not become transcendent. For it never disengages itself entirely from experience, but remains merely its interpretation and explanation, since it never speaks of the thing in itself otherwise than in its relation to the phenomenon. This at least is the sense in which I, with reference throughout to the limitations of human knowledge proved by Kant, have attempted to solve the problem of metaphysics. Therefore his Prolegomena to future metaphysics will be valid and suitable for mine also. Accordingly it never really goes beyond experience, but only discloses the true understanding of the world which lies before it in experience. It is neither, according to the definition of metaphysics which even Kant repeats, a science of mere conceptions, nor is it a system of deductions from *a priori* principles, the uselessness of which for the *end* of metaphysics has been shown by Kant. But it is rational knowledge, drawn from perception of the external actual world and the information which the most intimate fact of self-consciousness affords us concerning it, deposited in distinct conceptions. It is accordingly the science of experience; but its subject and its source is not particular experiences, but the totality of all experience. I completely accept Kant's doctrine that the world of experience is merely phenomenal, and that the *a priori* knowledge is valid only in relation to phenomena; but I add that just as phenomenal appearance, it is the manifestation of that which appears, and with him I call this the thing in itself. This must therefore express its nature and character in the world of experience, and consequently it must be possible to interpret these from this world, and indeed from the matter, not the mere form, of experience. Accordingly philosophy is nothing but the correct and universal understanding of experience itself, the true exposition of its meaning and content. To this the metaphysical, *i.e.*, that which is merely clothed in the phenomenon and veiled in its forms, is that which is related to it as thought to words.

Such a deciphering of the world with reference to that which manifests itself in it must receive its confirmation from itself, through the agreement with each other in which it places the very diverse phenomena of the world, and which without it we do not perceive. If we find a document the alphabet of which is unknown, we endeavour to make it out until we hit upon an hypothesis as to the significance of the letters in accordance with which they make up comprehensible words and connected sentences. Then, however, there remains no doubt as to the correctness of the deciphering, because it is not possible that the agreement and connection in which all the letters of that writing are placed by this explanation is merely accidental, and that by attributing quite a different value to the letters we could also recognise words and sentences in this arrangement of them. In the same way the deciphering of the world must completely prove itself from itself. It must throw equal light upon all the phenomena of the world, and also bring the most heterogeneous into agreement, so that the contradiction between those which are most in contrast may be abolished. This proof from itself is the mark of genuineness. For every false deciphering, even if it is suitable for some phenomena, will conflict all the more glaringly with the rest. So, for example, the optimism of Leibnitz conflicts with the palpable misery of existence ; the doctrine of Spinoza, that the world is the only possible and absolutely necessary substance, is incompatible with our wonder at its existence and nature ; the Wolfian doctrine, that man obtains his *Existentia* and *Essentia* from a will foreign to himself, is contradicted by our moral responsibility for the actions which proceed with strict necessity from these, in conflict with the motives ; the oft-repeated doctrine of the progressive development of man to an ever higher perfection, or in general of any kind of becoming by means of the process of the world, is opposed to the *a priori* knowledge that at any point of time an infinite time has already run its course, and consequently all that is supposed to come with time would necessarily have already existed ; and in this way an interminable list might be given of the contradictions of dogmatic assumptions with the given reality of things. On the other hand, I must deny that any doctrine of my philosophy could fairly be added to such a list, because each of them has been thought out in the presence of the perceived reality, and none of them has its root in abstract conceptions alone. There is yet in it a fundamental thought which is applied to all the phenomena of the world as their key; but it proves itself to be the right alphabet at the application of which all words and sentences have sense and significance. The discovered answer to a riddle shows itself to be the right one by the fact that all that is said in the riddle is suitable to it. In the same way my doctrine introduces agreement and connection into the confusion of the contrasting phenomena of this world, and solves the innumerable contradictions which, when regarded from any other point of view, it presents. Therefore, so far, it is like a sum that comes out right, yet by no means in the sense that it leaves no problem over to solve, no possible question unanswered. To assert anything of that sort would be a presumptuous denial of the limits of human knowledge in general. Whatever torch we may kindle, and whatever space it may light, our horizon will always remain bounded by profound night. For the ultimate solution of the riddle of the world must necessarily be concerned with the things in themselves, no longer with the phenomena. But all our forms of knowledge are adapted to the phenomena alone; therefore we must comprehend everything through coexistence, succession, and causal relations. These forms, however, have meaning and significance only with reference to the phenomenon; the things in themselves and their possible relations cannot be apprehended by means of those forms. Therefore the actual, positive solution of the riddle of the world must be something that human intellect is absolutely incapable of grasping and thinking; so that if a being of a higher kind were to come and take all pains to impart it to us, we would be absolutely incapable of understanding anything of his expositions. Those, therefore, who profess to know the ultimate, *i.e.*, the first ground of things, thus a primordial being, an absolute, or whatever else they choose to call it, together with the process, the reasons, motives, or whatever it may be, in consequence of which the world arises from it, or springs, or falls, or is produced, set in existence, "discharged," and ushered forth, are playing tricks, are vain boasters, when indeed they are not charlatans.

I regard it as a great excellence of my philosophy that all its truths have been found independently of each other, by contemplation of the real world; but their unity and agreement, about which I had been unconcerned, has always afterwards appeared of itself. Hence also it is rich, and has wide-spreading roots in the ground of perceptible reality, from which all nourishment of abstract truths springs; and hence, again, it is not wearisome—a quality which, to judge from the philosophical writings of the last fifty years, one might regard as essential to philosophy. If, on the other hand, all the doctrines of a philosophy are merely deduced the one out of the other, and ultimately indeed all out of one first principle, it must be poor and meagre, and consequently wearisome, for nothing can follow from a proposition except what it really already says itself. Moreover, in this case everything depends upon the correctness of *one* proposition, and by a single mistake in the deduction the truth of the whole would be endangered. Still less security is given by the systems which start from an intellectual intuition, *i.e.*, a kind of ecstasy or clairvoyance. All knowledge so obtained must be rejected as subjective, individual, and consequently problematical. Even if it actually existed it would not be communicable, for only the normal knowledge of the brain is communicable; if it is abstract, through conceptions and words; if purely perceptible or concrete, through works of art.

If, as so often happens, metaphysics is reproached with having made so little progress, it ought also to be considered that no other science has grown up like it under constant oppression, none has been so hampered and hindered from without as it has always been by the religion of every land, which, everywhere in possession of a monopoly of metaphysical knowledge, regards metaphysics as a weed growing beside it, as an unlicensed worker, as a horde of gipsies, and as a rule tolerates it only under the condition that it accommodates itself to serve and follow it. For where has there ever been true freedom of thought? It has been vaunted sufficiently; but whenever it wishes to go further than perhaps to differ about the subordinate dogmas of the religion of the country, a holy shudder seizes the prophets of tolerance, and they say: "Not a step further!" What progress of metaphysics was possible under such oppression? Nay, this constraint which the privileged metaphysics exercises is not confined to the *communication* of thoughts, but extends to *thinking* itself, for its dogmas are so firmly imprinted in the tender, plastic, trustful, and thoughtless age of childhood, with studied solemnity and serious airs, that from that time forward they grow with the brain, and almost assume the nature of innate thoughts, which some philosophers have therefore really held them to be, and still more have pretended to do so. Yet nothing can so firmly resist the comprehension of even the *problem* of metaphysics as a previous solution of it intruded upon and early implanted in the mind. For the necessary starting-point for all genuine philosophy is the deep feeling of the Socratic: "This one thing I know, that I know nothing." The ancients were in this respect in a better position than we are, for their national religions certainly limited somewhat the imparting of thoughts; but they did not interfere with the freedom of thought itself, because they were not formally and solemnly impressed upon children, and in general were not taken so seriously. Therefore in metaphysics the ancients are still our teachers.

Whenever metaphysics is reproached with its small progress, and with not having yet reached its goal in spite of such sustained efforts, one ought further to consider that in the meanwhile it has constantly performed the invaluable service of limiting the boundless claims of the privileged metaphysics, and yet at the same time combating naturalism and materialism proper, which are called forth by it as an inevitable reaction. Consider to what a pitch the arrogance of the priesthood of every religion would rise if the belief in their doctrines was as firm and blind as they really wish. Look back also at the wars, disturbances, rebellions, and revolutions in Europe from the eighth to the eighteenth century; how few will be found that have not had as their essence, or their pretext, some controversy about beliefs, thus a metaphysical problem, which became the occasion of exciting nations against each other. Yet is that whole thousand years a continual slaughter, now on the battlefield, now on the scaffold, now in the streets, in metaphysical interests! I wish I had an authentic list of all crimes which Christianity has really prevented, and all good deeds it has really performed, that I might be able to place them in the other scale of the balance.

Lastly, as regards the *obligations* of metaphysics, it has only one ; for it is one which endures no other beside it—the obligation to be *true*. If one would impose other obligations upon it besides this, such as to be spiritualistic, optimistic, monotheistic, or even only to be moral, one cannot know beforehand whether this would not interfere with the fulfilment of that first obligation, without which all its other achievements must clearly be worthless. A given philosophy has accordingly no other standard of its value than that of truth. For the rest, philosophy is essentially *world-wisdom :* its problem is the world. It has to do with this alone, and leaves the gods in peace—expects, however, in return, to be left in peace by them.

Supplements to the Second Book.

" 'Ihr folget falscher Spur,
    Denkt nicht, wir scherzen !
Ist nicht der Kern der Natur
    Menschen im Herzen ? ' "
                        —GOETHE.

SUPPLEMENTS TO THE SECOND BOOK

CHAPTER XVIII.[1]

ON THE POSSIBILITY OF KNOWING THE THING IN ITSELF.

IN 1836 I already published, under the title "*Ueber den Willen in der Natur*" (second ed., 1854; third ed., 1867), the most essential supplement to this book, which contains the most peculiar and important step in my philosophy, the transition from the phenomenon to the thing in itself, which Kant gave up as impossible. It would be a great mistake to regard the foreign conclusions with which I have there connected my expositions as the real material and subject of that work, which, though small as regards its extent, is of weighty import. These conclusions are rather the mere occasion starting from which I have there expounded that fundamental truth of my philosophy with so much greater clearness than anywhere else, and brought it down to the empirical knowledge of nature. And indeed this is done most exhaustively and stringently under the heading "*Physische Astronomie;*" so that I dare not hope ever to find a more correct or accurate expression of that core of my philosophy than is given there. Whoever desires to know my philosophy thoroughly and to test it seriously must therefore give attention before everything to that section. Thus, in general, all that is said in that little work would form the chief content of these supplements, if it had not to be excluded on account of having preceded

---

[1] This chapter is connected with § 18 of the first volume.

them; but, on the other hand, I here take for granted that it is known, for otherwise the very best would be wanting.

I wish now first of all to make a few preliminary observations from a general point of view as to the sense in which we can speak of a knowledge of the thing in itself and of its necessary limitation.

What is *knowledge?* It is primarily and essentially *idea.* What is *idea?* A very complicated *physiological* process in the brain of an animal, the result of which is the consciousness of a *picture* there. Clearly the relation between such a picture and something entirely different from the animal in whose brain it exists can only be a very indirect one. This is perhaps the simplest and most comprehensible way of disclosing the *deep gulf between the ideal and the real.* This belongs to the things of which, like the motion of the earth, we are not directly conscious; therefore the ancients did not observe it, just as they did not observe the motion of the earth. Once pointed out, on the other hand, first by Descartes, it has ever since given philosophers no rest. But after Kant had at last proved in the most thorough manner the complete diversity of the ideal and the real, it was an attempt, as bold as it was absurd, yet perfectly correctly calculated with reference to the philosophical public in Germany, and consequently crowned with brilliant results, to try to assert the *absolute identity* of the two by dogmatic utterances, on the strength of a pretended intellectual intuition. In truth, on the contrary, a subjective and an objective existence, a being for self and a being for others, a consciousness of one's own self, and a consciousness of other things, is given us directly, and the two are given in such a fundamentally different manner that no other difference can compare with this. About himself every one knows directly, about all others only very indirectly. This is the fact and the problem.

Whether, on the other hand, through further processes

in the interior of a brain, general conceptions (*Universalia*) are abstracted from the perceptible ideas or images that have arisen within it, for the assistance of further combinations, whereby knowledge becomes *rational*, and is now called *thinking*—this is here no longer the essential question, but is of subordinate significance. For all such *conceptions* receive their content only from the perceptible idea, which is therefore *primary knowledge*, and has consequently alone to be taken account of in an investigation of the relation between the ideal and the real. It therefore shows entire ignorance of the problem, or at least it is very inept, to wish to define that relation as that between *being* and *thinking*. Thinking has primarily only a relation to *perceiving*, but *perception* has a relation to the *real being* of what is perceived, and this last is the great problem with which we are here concerned. Empirical being, on the other hand, as it lies before us, is nothing else than simply being given in perception; but the relation of the latter to *thinking* is no riddle, for the conceptions, thus the immediate materials of thought, are obviously *abstracted* from perception, which no reasonable man can doubt. It may be said in passing that one can see how important the choice of expressions in philosophy is from the fact that that inept expression condemned above, and the misunderstanding which arose from it, became the foundation of the whole Hegelian pseudo-philosophy, which has occupied the German public for twenty-five years.

If, however, it should be said: "The perception is itself the knowledge of the thing in itself: for it is the effect of that which is outside of us, and as this *acts*, so it *is:* its action is just its being;" to this we reply: (1.) that the law of causality, as has been sufficiently proved, is of subjective origin, as well as the sensation from which the perception arises; (2.) that at any rate time and space, in which the object presents itself, are of subjective origin; (3.) that if the being of the object consists simply in its action, this means that it consists merely in the changes which it brings about in others; therefore itself and in itself it is nothing at all. Only of *matter* is it true, as I have said in the text, and worked out in the essay on the principle of sufficient reason, at the end of § 21, that its being consists in its action, that it is through and through only causality, thus is itself causality objectively regarded; hence, however, it is also nothing in itself (ἡ ὕλη το αληθινον ψευδος, *materia mendacium verax*), but as an ingredient in the perceived object, is a mere abstraction, which for itself alone can be given in no experience. It will be fully considered later on in a chapter of its own. But the perceived object must be something *in itself*, and not merely something *for others*. For otherwise it would be altogether merely idea, and we would have an absolute idealism, which would ultimately become theoretical egoism, with which all reality disappears and the world becomes a mere subjective phantasm. If, however, without further question, we stop altogether at the *world as idea*, then certainly it is all one whether I explain objects as ideas in my head or as phenomena exhibiting themselves in time and space; for time and space themselves exist only in my head. In this sense, then, an identity of the ideal and the real might always be affirmed; only, after Kant, this would not be saying anything new. Besides this, however, the nature of things and of the phenomenal world would clearly not be thereby exhausted; but with it we would always remain still upon the ideal side. The *real* side must be something *toto genere* different from *the world as idea*, it must be that which things are *in themselves;* and it is this entire diversity between the ideal and the real which Kant has proved in the most thorough manner.

Locke had denied to the senses the knowledge of things as they are in themselves; but Kant denied this also to the perceiving *understanding*, under which name I here comprehend what he calls the *pure* sensibility, and, as it is given *a priori*, the law of causality which brings about the empirical perception. Not only are both right, but we can also see quite directly that a contradiction lies in the assertion that a thing is known as it is in and for itself, *i.e.*, outside of knowledge. For all knowing is, as we have said, essentially a perceiving of ideas; but my perception of ideas, just because it is mine, can never be identical with the inner nature of the thing outside of me. The being in and for itself, of everything, must necessarily be *subjective ;* in the idea of another, however, it exists just as necessarily as *objective*—a difference which can never be fully reconciled. For by it the whole nature of its existence is fundamentally changed; as objective it presupposes a foreign subject, as whose idea it exists, and, moreover, as Kant has shown, has entered forms which are foreign to its own nature, just because they belong to that foreign subject, whose knowledge is only possible by means of them. If I, absorbed in this reflection, perceive, let us say lifeless bodies, of easily surveyed magnitude and regular, comprehensible form, and now attempt to conceive this spatial existence, in its three dimensions, as their being in itself, consequently as the existence which to the things is subjective, the impossibility of the thing is at once apparent to me, for I can never think those objective forms as the being which to the things is subjective, rather I become directly conscious that what I there perceive is only a picture produced in my brain, and existing only for me as the knowing subject, which cannot constitute the ultimate, and therefore subjective, being in and for itself of even these lifeless bodies. But, on the other hand, I must not assume that even these lifeless bodies exist only in my idea, but, since they have inscrutable qualities, and, by virtue of these, activity, I must concede to them a *being in itself* of some kind. But this very inscrutableness of the properties, while, on the one hand, it certainly points to something which exists independently of our knowledge, gives also, on the other hand, the empirical proof that our knowledge, because it consists simply in *framing ideas* by means of subjective forms, affords us always mere *phenomena,* not the true being of things.   This is the explanation of the fact that in all that we know there remains hidden from us a certain something, as quite inscrutable, and we are obliged to confess that we cannot thoroughly understand even the commonest and simplest phenomena.   For it is not merely the highest productions of nature, living creatures, or the *complicated* phenomena of the unorganised world that remain inscrutable to us, but even every rock-crystal, every iron-pyrite, by reason of its crystallographical, optical, chemical, and electrical properties, is to the searching consideration and investigation an abyss of incomprehensibilities and mysteries.   This could not be the case if we knew things as they are in themselves ; for then at least the simpler phenomena, the path to whose qualities was not barred for us by ignorance, would necessarily be thoroughly comprehensible to us, and their whole being and nature would be able to pass over into our knowledge.   Thus it lies not in the defectiveness of our acquaintance with things, but in the nature of knowledge itself.   For if our perception, and consequently the whole empirical comprehension of the things that present themselves to us, is already essentially and in the main determined by our faculty of knowledge, and conditioned by its forms and functions, it cannot but be that things exhibit themselves in a manner which is quite different from their own inner nature, and therefore appear as in a mask, which allows us merely to assume what is concealed beneath it, but never to know it; hence, then, it gleams through as an inscrutable mystery, and never can the nature of anything entire and without reserve pass over into knowledge; but much less can any real thing be construed *a priori,* like a mathematical problem.   Thus the empirical inscrutableness of all natural things is a proof *a posteriori* of the ideality and merely phenomenal-actuality of their empirical existence.

According to all this, upon the path of *objective know-*

ledge, hence starting from the *idea*, one will never get beyond the idea, *i.e.*, the phenomenon. One will thus remain at the outside of things, and will never be able to penetrate to their inner nature and investigate what they are in themselves, *i.e.*, for themselves. So far I agree with Kant. But, as the counterpart of this truth, I have given prominence to this other truth, that we are not merely the *knowing subject*, but, in another aspect, we ourselves also belong to the inner nature that is to be known, *we ourselves are the thing in itself;* that therefore a *way from within* stands open for us to that inner nature belonging to things themselves, to which we cannot penetrate *from without*, as it were a subterranean passage, a secret alliance, which, as if by treachery, places us at once within the fortress which it was impossible to take by assault from without. The thing in itself can, as such, only come into consciousness quite directly, in this way, that *it is itself conscious of itself:* to wish to know it objectively is to desire something contradictory. Everything objective is idea, therefore appearance, mere phenomenon of the brain.

Kant's chief result may in substance be thus concisely stated : " All conceptions which have not at their foundation a perception in space and time (sensuous intuition), that is to say then, which have not been drawn from such a perception, are absolutely empty, *i.e.*, give no knowledge. But since now perception can afford us only *phenomena*, not things in themselves, we have also absolutely no knowledge of things in themselves." I grant this of everything, with the single exception of the knowledge which each of us has of his own *willing :* this is neither a perception (for all perception is spatial) nor is it empty ; rather it is more real than any other. Further, it is not *a priori*, like merely formal knowledge, but entirely *a posteriori ;* hence also we cannot anticipate it in the particular case, but are hereby often convicted of error concerning ourselves. In fact, our *willing* is the one opportunity which we have of understanding from within any event which exhibits itself without, consequently the one thing which is known to us *immediately*, and not, like all the rest, merely given in the idea.   Here, then, lies the datum which alone is able to become the key to everything else, or, as I have said, the single narrow door to the truth. Accordingly we must learn to understand nature from ourselves, not conversely ourselves from nature.   What is known to us immediately must give us the explanation of what we only know indirectly, not conversely.   Do we perhaps understand the rolling of a ball when it has received an impulse more thoroughly than our movement when we feel a motive?   Many may imagine so, but I say it is the reverse.   Yet we shall attain to the knowledge that what is essential in both the occurrences just mentioned is identical; although identical in the same way as the lowest audible note of harmony is the same as the note of the same name ten octaves higher.

Meanwhile it should be carefully observed, and I have always kept it in mind, that even the inward experience which we have of our own will by no means affords us an exhaustive and adequate knowledge of the thing in itself. This would be the case if it were entirely an immediate experience; but it is effected in this way: the will, with and by means of the corporisation, provides itself also with an intellect (for the sake of its relations to the external world), and through this now knows itself as will in self-consciousness (the necessary counterpart of the external world); this knowledge therefore of the thing in itself is not fully adequate.   First of all, it is bound to the form of the idea, it is apprehension, and as such falls asunder into subject and object.   For even in self-consciousness the I is not absolutely simple, but consists of a knower, the intellect, and a known, the will.   The former is not known, and the latter does not know, though both unite in the consciousness of an I.   But just on this account that I is not thoroughly *intimate* with itself, as it were transparent, but is opaque, and therefore remains a riddle to itself, thus even in inner knowledge there also exists a difference between the true being of its object and the apprehension of it in the knowing subject. Yet inner knowledge is free from two forms which belong to outer knowledge, the form of *space* and the form of *causality*, which is the means of effecting all sense-perception. On the other hand, there still remains the form of *time*, and that of being known and knowing in general. Accordingly in this inner knowledge the thing in itself has indeed in great measure thrown off its veil, but still does not yet appear quite naked. In consequence of the form of time which still adheres to it, every one knows his will only in its successive *acts*, and not as a whole, in and for itself: therefore no one knows his character *a priori*, but only learns it through experience and always incompletely. But yet the apprehension, in which we know the affections and acts of our own will, is far more immediate than any other. It is the point at which the thing in itself most directly enters the phenomenon and is most closely examined by the knowing subject; therefore the event thus intimately known is alone fitted to become the interpreter of all others.

For in every emergence of an act of will from the obscure depths of our inner being into the knowing consciousness a direct transition occurs of the thing in itself, which lies outside time, into the phenomenal world. Accordingly the act of will is indeed only the closest and most distinct *manifestation* of the thing in itself; yet it follows from this that if all other manifestations or phenomena could be known by us as directly and inwardly, we would be obliged to assert them to be that which the will is in us. Thus in this sense I teach that the inner nature of everything is *will*, and I call will the thing in itself. Kant's doctrine of the unknowableness of the thing in itself is hereby modified to this extent, that the thing in itself is only not absolutely and from the very foundation knowable, that yet by far the most immediate of its phenomena, which by this immediateness is *toto genere* distinguished from all the rest, represents it for us; and accordingly we have to refer the whole world of phenomena to that one in which the thing in itself appears in the very thinnest of veils, and only still remains phenomenon in so far as my intellect, which alone is capable of knowledge, remains ever distinguished from me as the willing subject, and moreover does not even in *inner* perfection put off the form of knowledge of *time*.

Accordingly, even after this last and furthest step, the question may still be raised, what that will, which exhibits itself in the world and as the world, ultimately and absolutely is in itself? *i.e.*, what it is, regarded altogether apart from the fact that it exhibits itself as will, or in general *appears*, *i.e.*, in general is *known*. This question can never be answered: because, as we have said, becoming known is itself the contradictory of being in itself, and everything that is known is as such only phenomenal. But the possibility of this question shows that the thing in itself, which we know most directly in the will, may have, entirely outside all possible phenomenal appearance, ways of existing, determinations, qualities, which are absolutely unknowable and incomprehensible to us, and which remain as the nature of the thing in itself, when, as is explained in the fourth book, it has voluntarily abrogated itself as *will*, and has therefore retired altogether from the phenomenon, and for our knowledge, *i.e.*, as regards the world of phenomena, has passed into empty nothingness. If the will were simply and absolutely the thing in itself this nothing would also be *absolute*, instead of which it expressly presents itself to us there as only *relative*.

I now proceed to supplement with a few considerations pertinent to the subject the exposition given both in our second book and in the work " *Ueber den Willen in der Natur*," of the doctrine that what makes itself known to us in the most immediate knowledge as will is also that which objectifies itself at different grades in all the phenomena of this world; and I shall begin by citing a number of psychological facts which prove that first of all in our own consciousness the will always appears as primary and fundamental, and throughout asserts its superiority to the intellect, which, on the other hand, always presents itself as secondary, subordinate, and conditioned. This proof is the more necessary as all philosophers before me, from the first to the last, place the true being or the kernel of man in the *knowing* consciousness, and accordingly have conceived and explained the I, or, in the case of many of them, its transcendental hypostasis called soul, as primarily and essentially *knowing*, nay, *thinking*, and only in consequence of this, secondarily and derivatively, as *willing*. This ancient and universal radical error, this enormous πρωτον ψευδος and fundamental ὑστερον προτερον, must before everything be set aside, and instead of it the true state of the case must be brought to perfectly distinct consciousness. Since, however, this is done here for the first time, after thousands of years of philosophising, some fulness of statement will be appropriate. The remarkable phenomenon, that in this most essential point all philosophers have erred, nay, have exactly reversed the truth, might, especially in the case of those of the Christian era, be partly explicable from the fact that they all had the intention of presenting man as distinguished as widely as possible from the brutes, yet at the same time obscurely felt that the difference between them lies in the intellect, not in the will; whence there arose unconsciously within them an inclination to make the intellect the essential and principal thing, and even to explain volition as a mere function of the intellect. Hence also the conception of a soul is not only inadmissible, because it is a transcendent hypostasis, as is proved by the "Critique of Pure Reason," but it becomes the source of irremediable errors, because in its "simple substance" it establishes beforehand an indivisible unity of knowledge and will, the separation of which is just the path to the truth. That conception must therefore appear no more in philosophy, but may be left to German doctors and physiologists, who, after they have laid aside scalpel and spattle, amuse themselves by philosophising with the conceptions they received when they were confirmed. They might certainly try their luck in England. The French physiologists and zootomists have (till lately) kept themselves free from that reproach.

The first consequence of their common fundamental error, which is very inconvenient to all these philosophers, is this : since in death the knowing consciousness obviously perishes, they must either allow death to be the annihilation of the man, to which our inner being is opposed, or they must have recourse to the assumption of a continued existence of the knowing consciousness, which requires a strong faith, for his own experience has sufficiently proved to every one the thorough and complete dependence of the knowing consciousness upon the brain, and one can just as easily believe in digestion without a stomach as in a knowing consciousness without a brain. My philosophy alone leads out of this dilemma, for it for the first time places the true being of man not in the consciousness but in the will, which is not essentially bound up with consciousness, but is related to consciousness, *i.e.*, to knowledge, as substance to accident, as something illuminated to the light, as the string to the resounding-board, and which enters consciousness from within as the corporeal world does from without. Now we can comprehend the indestructibleness of this our real kernel and true being, in spite of the evident ceasing of consciousness in death, and the corresponding non-existence of it before birth. For the intellect is as perishable as the brain, whose product or rather whose action it is. But the brain, like the whole organism, is the product or phenomenon, in short, the subordinate of the will, which alone is imperishable.

CHAPTER XIX.[1]

ON THE PRIMACY OF THE WILL IN SELF-CONSCIOUSNESS.

THE will, as the thing in itself, constitutes the inner, true, and indestructible nature of man; in itself, however, it is unconscious. For consciousness is conditioned by the intellect, and the intellect is a mere accident of our being; for it is a function of the brain, which, together with the nerves and spinal cord connected with it, is a mere fruit, a product, nay, so far, a parasite of the rest of the organism; for it does not directly enter into its inner constitution, but merely serves the end of self-preservation by regulating the relations of the organism to the external world. The organism itself, on the other hand, is the visibility, the objectivity, of the individual will, the image of it as it presents itself in that very brain (which in the first book we learned to recognise as the condition of the objective world in general), therefore also brought about by its forms of knowledge, space, time, and causality, and consequently presenting itself as extended, successively acting, and material, *i.e.*, as something operative or efficient. The members are both directly felt and also perceived by means of the senses only in the brain. According to this one may say: The intellect is the secondary phenomenon; the organism the primary phenomenon, that is, the immediate manifestation of the will; the will is metaphysical, the intellect physical;—the intellect, like its objects, is merely phenomenal appearance; the will alone is the thing in itself. Then, in a more and more *figurative sense*,

[1] This chapter is connected with § 19 of the first volume.

thus by way of simile : The will is the substance of man, the intellect the accident; the will is the matter, the intellect is the form; the will is warmth, the intellect is light.

We shall now first of all verify and also elucidate this thesis by the following facts connected with the inner life of man; and on this opportunity perhaps more will be done for the knowledge of the inner man than is to be found in many systematic psychologies.

1. Not only the consciousness of other things, *i.e.*, the apprehension of the external world, but also *self-consciousness*, contains, as was mentioned already above, a knower and a known; otherwise it would not be *consciousness*. For *consciousness* consists in knowing; but knowing requires a knower and a known; therefore there could be no self-consciousness if there were not in it also a known opposed to the knower and different from it. As there can be no object without a subject, so also there can be no subject without an object, *i.e.*, no knower without something different from it which is known. Therefore a consciousness which is through and through pure intelligence is impossible. The intelligence is like the sun, which does not illuminate space if there is no object from which its rays are reflected. The knower himself, as such, cannot be known; otherwise he would be the known of another knower. But now, as the *known* in self-consciousness we find exclusively the *will*. For not merely willing and purposing in the narrowest sense, but also all striving, wishing, shunning, hoping, fearing, loving, hating, in short, all that directly constitutes our own weal and woe, desire and aversion, is clearly only affection of the will, is a moving, a modification of willing and not-willing, is just that which, if it takes outward effect, exhibits itself as an act of will proper.[1] In all knowledge, however, the known is first

[1] It is remarkable that Augustine already knew this. In the fourteenth book, "*De Civ. Dei*," c. 6, he speaks of the *affectionibus animi*, which in the preceding book he had brought under four categories, *cupiditas, timor, lætitia, tristitia*, and says: "*Voluntas est quippe in omnibus, imo omnes nihil*

and essential, not the knower; for the former is the πρω-
τοτυπος, the latter the εκτυπος. Therefore in self-consciousness also the known, thus the will, must be what is
first and original; the knower, on the other hand, only what
is secondary, that which has been added, the mirror. They
are related very much as the luminous to the reflecting
body; or, again, as the vibrating strings to the resounding-
board, in which case the note produced would be consciousness. We may also regard the plant as a like symbol of
consciousness. It has, we know, two poles, the root and the
corona: the former struggling into darkness, moisture, and
cold, the latter into light, dryness, and warmth; then,
as the point of indifference of the two poles, where they
part asunder, close to the ground, the collum (*rhizoma, le
collet*). The root is what is essential, original, perennial,
the death of which involves that of the corona, is thus the
primary; the corona, on the other hand, is the ostensible,
but it has sprung from something else, and it passes away
without the root dying; it is thus secondary. The root
represents the will, the corona the intellect, and the point
of indifference of the two, the collum, would be the *I*,
which, as their common termination, belongs to both. This
I is the *pro tempore* identical subject of knowing and willing, whose identity I called in my very first essay (on the
principle of sufficient reason), and in my first philosophical
wonder, the miracle κατ εξοχην. It is the temporal starting-point and connecting-link of the whole phenomenon,
i.e., of the objectification of the will: it conditions indeed
the phenomenon, but is also conditioned by it. This comparison may even be carried to the individual nature of
men. As a large corona commonly springs only from a
large root, so the greatest intellectual capabilities are only
found in connection with a vehement and passionate will.
A genius of a phlegmatic character and weak passions

---

*aliud, quam voluntates sunt: nam
quid est cupiditas et lætitia, nisi voluntas in eorum consensionem, quæ
volumus? et quid est metus atque tristitia, nisi voluntas in dissensionem ab
his, quæ nolumus? cet.*"

would resemble those succulent plants that, with a considerable corona consisting of thick leaves, have very small roots; will not, however, be found. That vehemence of will and passionateness of character are conditions of heightened intelligence exhibits itself physiologically through the fact that the activity of the brain is conditioned by the movement which the great arteries running towards the *basis cerebri* impart to it with each pulsation; therefore an energetic pulse, and even, according to Bichat, a short neck, is a requisite of great activity of the brain. But the opposite of the above certainly occurs: vehement desires, passionate, violent character, along with weak intellect, *i.e.*, a small brain of bad conformation in a thick skull. This is a phenomenon as common as it is repulsive: we might perhaps compare it to beetroot.

2. But in order not merely to describe consciousness figuratively, but to know it thoroughly, we have first of all to find out what appears in the same way in every consciousness, and therefore, as the common and constant element, will also be the essential. Then we shall consider what distinguishes *one* consciousness from another, which accordingly will be the adventitious and secondary element.

Consciousness is positively only known to us as a property of animal nature; therefore we must not, and indeed cannot, think of it otherwise than as *animal consciousness*, so that this expression is tautological. Now, that which in *every* animal consciousness, even the most imperfect and the weakest, is always present, nay, lies at its foundation, is an immediate sense of *longing*, and of the alternate satisfaction and non-satisfaction of it, in very different degrees. This we know to a certain extent *a priori*. For marvellously different as the innumerable species of animals are, and strange as some new form, never seen before, appears to us, we yet assume beforehand its inmost nature, with perfect certainty, as well known, and indeed fully confided to us. We know that the animal *wills*, indeed also *what* it wills, existence, well-being, life, and propagation; and since in this we presuppose with perfect certainty identity with us, we do not hesitate to attribute to it unchanged all the affections of will which we know in ourselves, and speak at once of its desire, aversion, fear, anger, hatred, love, joy, sorrow, longing, &c. On the other hand, whenever phenomena of mere knowledge come to be spoken of we fall at once into uncertainty. We do not venture to say that the animal conceives, thinks, judges, knows: we only attribute to it with certainty ideas in general; because without them its *will* could not have those emotions referred to above. But with regard to the definite manner of knowing of the brutes and the precise limits of it in a given species, we have only indefinite conceptions, and make conjectures. Hence our understanding with them is also often difficult, and is only brought about by skill, in consequence of experience and practice. Here then lie distinctions of consciousness. On the other hand, a longing, desiring, wishing, or a detesting, shunning, and not wishing, is proper to every consciousness: man has it in common with the polyp. This is accordingly the essential element in and the basis of every consciousness. The difference of the manifestations of this in the different species of animal beings depends upon the various extension of their sphere of knowledge, in which the motives of those manifestations lie. We understand directly from our own nature all actions and behaviour of the brutes which express movements of the will; therefore, so far, we sympathise with them in various ways. On the other hand, the gulf between us and them results simply and solely from the difference of intellect. The gulf which lies between a very sagacious brute and a man of very limited capacity is perhaps not much greater than that which exists between a blockhead and a man of genius; therefore here also the resemblance between them in another aspect, which springs from the likeness of their inclinations and emotions, and assimilates them again to each other, sometimes appears with surprising promi-

nence, and excites astonishment. This consideration makes
it clear that in all animal natures the *will* is what is
primary and substantial, the *intellect* again is secondary,
adventitious, indeed a mere tool for the service of the
former, and is more or less complete and complicated,
according to the demands of this service. As a species of
animals is furnished with hoofs, claws, hands, wings, horns,
or teeth according to the aims of its will, so also is it furnished with a more or less developed brain, whose function
is the intelligence necessary for its endurance. The more
complicated the organisation becomes, in the ascending
series of animals, the more numerous also are its wants,
and the more varied and specially determined the objects
which are capable of satisfying them ; hence the more complicated and distant the paths by which these are to be
obtained, which must now be all known and found : therefore in the same proportion the ideas of the animal must
be more versatile, accurate, definite, and connected, and
also its attention must be more highly strung, more sustained, and more easily roused, consequently its intellect
must be more developed and perfect. Accordingly we
see the organ of intelligence, the cerebral system, together
with all the organs of sense, keep pace with the increasing
wants and the complication of the organism ; and the increase of the part of consciousness that has to do with
ideas (as opposed to the willing part) exhibits itself in a
bodily form in the ever-increasing proportion of the brain
in general to the rest of the nervous system, and of the
cerebrum to the cerebellum ; for (according to Flourens)
the former is the workshop of ideas, while the latter is the
disposer and orderer of movements. The last step which
nature has taken in this respect is, however, dispropor-
tionately great. For in man not only does the faculty
of ideas of *perception*, which alone existed hitherto,
reach the highest degree of perfection, but the *abstract*
idea, thought, *i.e., reason*, and with it reflection, is added.
Through this important advance of the intellect, thus

of the secondary part of consciousness, it now gains a preponderance over the primary part, in so far as it becomes henceforward the predominantly active part. While in the brute the immediate sense of its satisfied or unsatisfied desire constitutes by far the most important part of its consciousness, and the more so indeed the lower the grade of the animal, so that the lowest animals are only distinguished from plants by the addition of a dull idea, in man the opposite is the case. Vehement as are his desires, even more vehement than those of any brute, rising to the level of passions, yet his consciousness remains continuously and predominantly occupied and filled with ideas and thoughts. Without doubt this has been the principal occasion of that fundamental error of all philosophers on account of which they make thought that which is essential and primary in the so-called soul, *i.e.*, in the inner or spiritual life of man, always placing it first, but will, as a mere product of thought, they regard as only a subordinate addition and consequence of it. But if willing merely proceeded from knowing, how could the brutes, even the lower grades of them, with so very little knowledge, often show such an unconquerable and vehement will? Accordingly, since that fundamental error of the philosophers makes, as it were, the accident the substance, it leads them into mistaken paths, which there is afterwards no way of getting out of. Now this relative predominance of the *knowing* consciousness over the *desiring*, consequently of the secondary part over the primary, which appears in man, may, in particular exceptionally favoured individuals, go so far that at the moments of its highest ascendancy, the secondary or knowing part of consciousness detaches itself altogether from the willing part, and passes into free activity for itself, *i.e.*, untouched by the will, and consequently no longer serving it. Thus it becomes purely objective, and the clear mirror of the world, and from it the conceptions of genius then arise. which are the subject of our third book.

3. If we run through the series of grades of animals downwards, we see the intellect always becoming weaker and less perfect, but we by no means observe a corresponding degradation of the will. Rather it retains everywhere its identical nature and shows itself in the form of great attachment to life, care for the individual and the species, egoism and regardlessness of all others, together with the emotions that spring from these. Even in the smallest insect the will is present, complete and entire; it wills what it wills as decidedly and completely as the man. The difference lies merely in *what* it wills, *i.e.*, in the motives, which, however, are the affair of the intellect. It indeed, as the secondary part of consciousness, and bound to the bodily organism, has innumerable degrees of completeness, and is in general essentially limited and imperfect. The *will*, on the contrary, as original and the thing in itself, can never be imperfect, but every act of will is all that it can be. On account of the simplicity which belongs to the will as the thing in itself, the metaphysical in the phenomenon, its nature admits of no degrees, but is always completely itself. Only its *excitement* has degrees, from the weakest inclination to the passion, and also its susceptibility to excitement, thus its vehemence from the phlegmatic to the choleric temperament. The *intellect*, on the other hand, has not merely degrees of *excitement*, from sleepiness to being in the vein, and inspiration, but also degrees of its nature, of the completeness of this, which accordingly rises gradually from the lowest animals, which can only obscurely apprehend, up to man, and here again from the fool to the genius. The *will* alone is everywhere completely itself. For its function is of the utmost simplicity; it consists in willing and not willing, which goes on with the greatest ease, without effort, and requires no practice. Knowing, on the contrary, has multifarious functions, and never takes place entirely without effort, which is required to fix the attention and to make clear the object, and at a higher

stage is certainly needed for thinking and deliberation ; therefore it is also capable of great improvement through exercise and education. If the intellect presents a simple, perceptible object to the will, the latter expresses at once its approval or disapproval of it, and this even if the intellect has laboriously inquired and pondered, in order from numerous data, by means of difficult combinations, ultimately to arrive at the conclusion as to which of the two seems to be most in conformity with the interests of the will. The latter has meanwhile been idly resting, and when the conclusion is arrived at it enters, as the Sultan enters the Divan, merely to express again its monotonous approval or disapproval, which certainly may vary in degree, but in its nature remains always the same.

This fundamentally different nature of the will and the intellect, the essential simplicity and originality of the former, in contrast to the complicated and secondary character of the latter, becomes still more clear to us if we observe their remarkable interaction within us, and now consider in the particular case, how the images and thoughts which arise in the intellect move the will, and how entirely separated and different are the parts which the two play. We can indeed perceive this even in actual events which excite the will in a lively manner, while primarily and in themselves they are merely objects of the intellect. But, on the one hand, it is here not so evident that this reality primarily existed only in the intellect; and, on the other hand, the change does not generally take place so rapidly as is necessary if the thing is to be easily surveyed, and thereby become thoroughly comprehensible. Both of these conditions, however, are fulfilled if it is merely thoughts and phantasies which we allow to act on the will. If, for example, alone with ourselves, we think over our personal circumstances, and now perhaps vividly present to ourselves the menace of an actually present danger and the possibility of an unfortunate issue, anxiety at once compresses the heart, and the blood ceases to circulate in the veins. But if then the intellect passes to the possibility of an opposite issue, and lets the imagination picture the long hoped for happiness thereby attained, all the pulses quicken at once with joy and the heart feels light as a feather, till the intellect awakes from its dream. Thereupon, suppose that an occasion should lead the memory to an insult or injury once suffered long ago, at once anger and bitterness pour into the breast that was but now at peace. But then arises, called up by accident, the image of a long-lost love, with which the whole romance and its magic scenes is connected; then that anger will at once give place to profound longing and sadness. Finally, if there occurs to us some former humiliating incident, we shrink together, would like to sink out of sight, blush with shame, and often try forcibly to distract and divert our thoughts by some loud exclamation, as if to scare some evil spirit. One sees, the intellect plays, and the will must dance to it. Indeed the intellect makes the will play the part of a child which is alternately thrown at pleasure into joyful or sad moods by the chatter and tales of its nurse. This depends upon the fact that the will is itself without knowledge, and the understanding which is given to it is without will. Therefore the former is like a body which is moved, the latter like the causes which set it in motion, for it is the medium of motives. Yet in all this the primacy of the will becomes clear again, if this will, which, as we have shown, becomes the sport of the intellect as soon as it allows the latter to control it, once makes its supremacy in the last instance felt by prohibiting the intellect from entertaining certain ideas, absolutely preventing certain trains of thought from arising, because it knows, *i.e.*, learns from that very intellect, that they would awaken in it some one of the emotions set forth above. It now bridles the intellect, and compels it to turn to other things. Hard as this often may be, it must yet be accomplished as soon as the will is in earnest about it, for the resistance in this case does not proceed from the intellect, which always remains indifferent, but from the will itself, which in one respect has an inclination towards an idea that in another respect it abhors. It is in itself interesting to the will simply because it excites it, but at the same time abstract knowledge tells it that this idea will aimlessly cause it a shock of painful or unworthy emotion : it now decides in conformity with this abstract knowledge, and compels the obedience of the intellect. This is called " being master of oneself." Clearly the master here is the will, the servant the intellect, for in the last instance the will always keeps the upper hand, and therefore constitutes the true core, the inner being of man. In this respect the title *Ηγεμονικον* would belong to the *will ;* yet it seems, on the other hand, to apply to the *intellect,* because it is the leader and guide, like the *valet de place* who conducts a stranger. In truth, however, the happiest figure of the relation of the two is the strong blind man who carries on his shoulders the lame man who can see.

The relation of the will to the intellect here explained may also be further recognised in the fact that the intellect is originally entirely a stranger to the purposes of the will. It supplies the motives to the will, but it only learns afterwards, completely *a posteriori,* how they have affected it, as one who makes a chemical experiment applies the reagents and awaits the result. Indeed the intellect remains so completely excluded from the real decisions and secret purposes of its own will that sometimes it can only learn them like those of a stranger, by spying upon them and surprising them, and must catch the will in the act of expressing itself in order to get at its real intentions. For example, I have conceived a plan, about which, however, I have still some scruple, but the feasibleness of which, as regards its possibility, is completely uncertain, for it depends upon external and still undecided circumstances. It would therefore certainly be un-

necessary to come to a decision about it at present, and so
for the time I leave the matter as it is. Now in such a case
I often do not know how firmly I am already attached to
that plan in secret, and how much, in spite of the scruple,
I wish to carry it out: that is, my intellect does not
know. But now only let me receive news that it is prac-
ticable, at once there rises within me a jubilant, irresistible gladness, that passes through my whole being and
takes permanent possession of it, to my own astonishment.
For now my intellect learns for the first time how firmly
my will had laid hold of that plan, and how thoroughly
the plan suited it, while the intellect had regarded it as
entirely problematical, and had with difficulty been able
to overcome that scruple. Or in another case, I have
entered eagerly into a contract which I believed to be
very much in accordance with my wishes. But as the
matter progresses the disadvantages and burdens of it are
felt, and I begin to suspect that I even repent of what I
so eagerly pursued ; yet I rid myself of this feeling by
assuring myself that even if I were not bound I would
follow the same course. Now, however, the contract is
unexpectedly broken by the other side, and I perceive with
astonishment that this happens to my great satisfaction
and relief. Often we don't know what we wish or what
we fear. We may entertain a wish for years without even
confessing it to ourselves, or even allowing it to come to
clear consciousness ; for the intellect must know nothing
about it, because the good opinion which we have of ourselves might thereby suffer. But if it is fulfilled we learn
from our joy, not without shame, that we have wished this.
For example, the death of a near relation whose heir we
are. And sometimes we do not know what we really fear,
because we lack the courage to bring it to distinct con-
sciousnesss. Indeed we are often in error as to the real
motive from which we have done something or left it
undone, till at last perhaps an accident discovers to us the
secret, and we know that what we have held to be the

motive was not the true one, but another which we had
not wished to confess to ourselves, because it by no means
accorded with the good opinion we entertained of ourselves. For example, we refrain from doing something
on purely moral grounds, as we believe, but afterwards we
discover that we were only restrained by fear, for as soon
as all danger is removed we do it. In particular cases
this may go so far that a man does not even guess the
true motive of his action, nay, does not believe himself
capable of being influenced by such a motive; and yet it
is the true motive of his action. We may remark in
passing that in all this we have a confirmation and explanation of the rule of Larochefoucauld : " *L'amour-propre
est plus habile que le plus habile homme du monde ;* " nay,
even a commentary on the Delphic γνωθι σαυτον and its
difficulty. If now, on the contrary, as all philosophers
imagine, the intellect constituted our true nature and the
purposes of the will were a mere result of knowledge, then
only the motive from which we imagined that we acted
would be decisive of our moral worth ; in analogy with
the fact that the intention, not the result, is in this respect
decisive. But really then the distinction between imagined
and true motive would be impossible. Thus all cases here
set forth, to which every one who pays attention may
observe analogous cases in himself, show us how the
intellect is so strange to the will that it is sometimes
even mystified by it : for it indeed supplies it with
motives, but does not penetrate into the secret workshop
of its purposes. It is indeed a confidant of the will, but
a confidant that is not told everything. This is also
further confirmed by the fact, which almost every one will
some time have the opportunity of observing in himself,
that sometimes the intellect does not thoroughly trust the
will. If we have formed some great and bold purpose,
which as such is yet really only a promise made by the
will to the intellect, there often remains within us a slight
unconfessed doubt whether we are quite in earnest about

it, whether in carrying it out we will not waver or draw back, but will have sufficient firmness and persistency to fulfil it. It therefore requires the deed to convince us ourselves of the sincerity of the purpose.

All these facts prove the absolute difference of the will and the intellect, the primacy of the former and the sub-ordinate position of the latter.

4. The *intellect* becomes tired; the *will* is never tired. After sustained work with the head we feel the tiredness of the brain, just like that of the arm after sustained bodily work. All *knowing* is accompanied with effort; *willing*, on the contrary, is our very nature, whose mani-festations take place without any weariness and entirely of their own accord. Therefore, if our will is strongly excited, as in all emotions, thus in anger, fear, desire, grief, &c., and we are now called upon to know, perhaps with the view of correcting the motives of that emotion, the violence which we must do ourselves for this purpose is evidence of the transition from the original natural activity proper to ourselves to the derived, indirect, and forced activity. For the will alone is αυτοματος, and therefore ακαματος και αγηρατος ἡματα παντα (*lassitu-dinis et senii expers in sempiternum*). It alone is active without being called upon, and therefore often too early and too much, and it knows no weariness. Infants who scarcely show the first weak trace of intelligence are already full of self-will: through unlimited, aimless roar-ing and shrieking they show the pressure of will with which they swell, while their willing has yet no object, *i.e.*, they will without knowing what they will. What Cabanis has observed is also in point here: "*Toutes ces passions, qui se succèdent d'une mannière si rapide, et se peignent avec tant de naïveté, sur le visage mobile des enfants. Tandis que les faibles muscles de leurs bras et de leurs jambes savent encore a peine former quelque mouvemens indécis, les muscles de la face expriment déja par des mouvemens dis-tincts presque toute la suite des affections générales propres a*

la nature humaine: et l'observateur attentif reconnait facile-ment dans ce tableau les traits caractéristiques de l'homme futur" (*Rapports du Physique et Moral*, vol. i. p. 123). The intellect, on the contrary, develops slowly, following the completion of the brain and the maturity of the whole organism, which are its conditions, just because it is merely a somatic function. It is because the brain attains its full size in the seventh year that from that time forward children become so remarkably intelligent, inquisitive, and reasonable. But then comes puberty; to a certain extent it affords a support to the brain, or a resounding-board, and raises the intellect at once by a large step, as it were by an octave, corresponding to the lowering of the voice by that amount. But at once the animal desires and passions that now appear resist the reasonableness that has hitherto prevailed and to which they have been added. Further evidence is given of the indefatigable nature of the will by the fault which is, more or less, peculiar to all men by nature, and is only overcome by education—*precipitation*. It consists in this, that the will hurries to its work before the time. This work is the purely active and executive part, which ought only to begin when the explorative and deliberative part, thus the work of knowing, has been completely and thoroughly carried out. But this time is seldom waited for. Scarcely are a few data concerning the circumstances before us, or the event that has occurred, or the opinion of others conveyed to us, superficially comprehended and hastily gathered together by knowledge, than from the depths of our being the will, always ready and never weary, comes forth unasked, and shows itself as terror, fear, hope, joy, desire, envy, grief, zeal, anger, or courage, and leads to rash words and deeds, which are generally followed by repentance when time has taught us that the hegemoni-con, the intellect, has not been able to finish half its work of comprehending the circumstances, reflecting on their connection, and deciding what is prudent, because the will did not wait for it, but sprang forward long before its time with " Now it is my turn !" and at once began the active work, without the intellect being able to resist, as it is a mere slave and bondman of the will, and not, like it, αυτοματος, nor active from its own power and its own impulse ; therefore it is easily pushed aside and silenced by a nod of the will, while on its part it is scarcely able, with the greatest efforts, to bring the will even to a brief pause, in order to speak. This is why the people are so rare, and are found almost only among Spaniards, Turks, and perhaps Englishmen, who even under circumstances of provocation *keep the head uppermost,* imperturbably proceed to comprehend and investigate the state of affairs, and when others would already be beside themselves, *con mucho sosiego,* still ask further questions, which is something quite different from the indifference founded upon apathy and stupidity of many Germans and Dutchmen. Iffland used to give an excellent representation of this admirable quality, as Hetmann of the Cossacks, in Benjowski, when the conspirators have enticed him into their tent and hold a rifle to his head, with the warning that they will fire it if he utters a cry, Iffland blew into the mouth of the rifle to try whether it was loaded. Of ten things that annoy us, nine would not be able to do so if we understood them thoroughly in their causes, and therefore knew their necessity and true nature; but we would do this much oftener if we made them the object of reflection before making them the object of wrath and indignation. For what bridle and bit are to an unmanageable horse the intellect is for the will in man ; by this bridle it must be controlled by means of instruction, exhortation, culture, &c., for in itself it is as wild and impetuous an impulse as the force that appears in the descending waterfall, nay, as we know, it is at bottom identical with this. In the height of anger, in intoxication, in despair, it has taken the bit between its teeth, has run away, and follows its original nature. In the *Mania sine delirio* it has lost bridle and bit altogether, and shows now most distinctly its original nature, and that the intellect is as different from it as the bridle from the horse. In this condition it may also be compared to a clock which, when a certain screw is taken away, runs down without stopping.

Thus this consideration also shows us the will as that which is original, and therefore metaphysical; the intellect, on the other hand, as something subordinate and physical. For as such the latter is, like everything physical, subject to *vis inertiæ*, consequently only active if it is set agoing by something else, the will, which rules it, manages it, rouses it to effort, in short, imparts to it the activity which does not originally reside in it. Therefore it willingly rests whenever it is permitted to do so, often declares itself lazy and disinclined to activity; through continued effort it becomes weary to the point of complete stupefaction, is exhausted, like the voltaic pile, through repeated shocks. Hence all continuous mental work demands pauses and rest, otherwise stupidity and incapacity ensue, at first of course only temporarily; but if this rest is persistently denied to the intellect it will become excessively and continuously fatigued, and the consequence is a permanent deterioration of it, which in an old man may pass into complete incapacity, into childishness, imbecility, and madness. It is not to be attributed to age in and for itself, but to long-continued tyrannical over-exertion of the intellect or brain, if this misfortune appears in the last years of life. This is the explanation of the fact that Swift became mad, Kant became childish, Walter Scott, and also Wordsworth, Southey, and many *minorum gentium*, became dull and incapable. Goethe remained to the end clear, strong, and active-minded, because he, who was always a man of the world and a courtier, never carried on his mental occupations with self-compulsion. The same holds good of Wieland and of Kuebel, who lived to the age of ninety-one, and also of Voltaire. Now all this proves how very subordinate and physical and what a mere tool the intellect is. Just on this account it requires, during almost a third part of its lifetime, the entire suspension of its activity in sleep, *i.e.*, the rest of the brain, of which it is the mere function, and which therefore just as truly precedes it as the stomach precedes digestion, or as a body precedes its impulsion, and with which in old age it flags and decays. The will, on the contrary, as the thing in itself, is never lazy, is absolutely untiring, its activity is its essence, it never ceases willing, and when, during deep sleep, it is forsaken of the intellect, and therefore cannot act outwardly in accordance with motives, it is active as the vital force, cares the more uninterruptedly for the inner economy of the organism, and as *vis naturæ medicatrix* sets in order again the irregularities that have crept into it. For it is not, like the intellect, a function of the body; *but the body is its function;* therefore it is, *ordine rerum*, prior to the body, as its metaphysical substratum, as the in-itself of its phenomenal appearance. It shares its unwearying nature, for the time that life lasts, with the heart, that *primum mobile* of the organism, which has therefore become its symbol and synonym. Moreover, it does not disappear in the old man, but still continues to will what it has willed, and indeed becomes firmer, more inflexible, than it was in youth, more implacable, self-willed, and unmanageable, because the intellect has become less susceptible: therefore in old age the man can perhaps only be matched by taking advantage of the weakness of his intellect.

Moreover, the prevailing *weakness* and *imperfection* of the intellect, as it is shown in the want of judgment, narrow-mindedness, perversity, and folly of the great majority of men, would be quite inexplicable if the intellect were not subordinate, adventitious, and merely instrumental, but the immediate and original nature of the so-called soul, or in general of the inner man: as all philosophers have hitherto assumed it to be. For how could the original nature in its immediate and peculiar function so constantly err and fail? The *truly* original in human consciousness, the *willing*, always goes on with perfect success; every being wills unceasingly, capably, and decidedly. To regard the immorality in the will as an imperfection of it would be a fundamentally false point of view. For morality has rather a source which really lies above nature, and therefore its utterances are in contradiction with it. Therefore morality is in direct opposition to the natural will, which in itself is completely egoistic; indeed the pursuit of the path of morality leads to the abolition of the will. On this subject I refer to our fourth book and to my prize essay, "*Ueber das Fundament der Moral.*"

5. That the *will* is what is real and essential in man, and the *intellect* only subordinate, conditioned, and produced, is also to be seen in the fact that the latter can carry on its function with perfect purity and correctness only so long as the will is silent and pauses. On the other hand, the function of the intellect is disturbed by every observable excitement of the will, and its result is falsified by the intermixture of the latter; but the converse does not hold, that the intellect should in the same way be a hindrance to the will. Thus the moon cannot shine when the sun is in the heavens, but when the moon is in the heavens it does not prevent the sun from shining.

A great *fright* often deprives us of our senses to such an extent that we are petrified, or else do the most absurd things; for example, when fire has broken out run right into the flames. *Anger* makes us no longer know what we do, still less what we say. *Zeal*, therefore called blind, makes us incapable of weighing the arguments of others, or even of seeking out and setting in order our own. *Joy* makes us inconsiderate, reckless, and foolhardy, and *desire* acts almost in the same way. *Fear* prevents us from seeing and laying hold of the resources that are still present, and often lie close beside us. Therefore for overcoming sudden dangers, and also for fighting with opponents and enemies, the most essential qualifications are *coolness and presence of mind.* The former consists in the silence of the will so that the intellect can act; the latter in the undisturbed activity of the intellect under the pressure of events acting on the will; therefore the former is the condition of the latter, and the two are nearly related; they are seldom to be found, and always only in a limited degree. But they are of inestimable advantage, because they permit the use of the intellect just at those times when we stand most in need of it, and therefore confer decided superiority. He who is without them only knows what he should have done or said when the opportunity has passed. It is very appropriately said of him who is violently moved, *i.e.,* whose will is so strongly excited that it destroys the purity of the function of the intellect, he is *disarmed;* for the correct knowledge of the circumstances and relations is our defence and weapon in the conflict with things and with men. In this sense Balthazar Gracian says: "*Es la passion enemiga declarada de la cordura*" (Passion is the declared enemy of prudence). If now the intellect were not something completely different from the will, but, as has been hitherto supposed, knowing and willing had the same root, and were equally original functions of an absolutely simple nature, then with the rousing and heightening of the will, in which the emotion consists, the intellect would necessarily also be heightened; but, as we have seen, it is rather hindered and depressed by this; whence the ancients called emotion *animi perturbatio.* The intellect is really like the reflecting surface of water, but the water itself is like the will, whose disturbance therefore at once destroys the clearness of that mirror and the distinctness of its images. The *organism* is the will itself, is embodied will, *i.e.,* will objectively perceived in the brain. Therefore many of its functions, such as respiration, circulation, secretion of bile, and muscular power, are heightened and accelerated by the pleasurable, and in general the healthy, emotions. The *intellect*, on the other hand, is the mere function of the brain, which is only nourished and supported by the organism as a parasite. Therefore every perturbation of the *will*, and with it of the *organism*, must disturb and paralyse the function of the brain, which exists for itself and for no other wants than its own, which are simply rest and nourishment.

But this disturbing influence of the activity of the will upon the intellect can be shown, not only in the perturbations brought about by emotions, but also in many other, more gradual, and therefore more lasting falsifications of thought by our inclinations. *Hope* makes us regard what we wish, and *fear* what we are apprehensive of, as probable and near, and both exaggerate their object. Plato (according to Ælian, V.H., 13, 28) very beautifully called hope the dream of the waking. Its nature lies in this, that the will, when its servant the intellect is not able to produce what it wishes, obliges it at least to picture it before it, in general to undertake the roll of comforter, to appease its lord with fables, as a nurse a child, and so to dress these out that they gain an appearance of likelihood. Now in this the intellect must do violence to its own nature, which aims at the truth, for it compels it, contrary to its own laws, to regard as true things which are neither true nor probable, and often scarcely possible, only in order to appease, quiet, and send to sleep for a while the restless and unmanageable *will*. Here we see clearly who is master and who is servant. Many may well have observed that if a matter which is of importance to them may turn out in several different ways, and they have brought all of these into one disjunctive judgment which in their opinion is complete, the actual result is yet quite another, and one wholly unexpected by them : but perhaps they will not have considered this, that this result was then almost always the one which was unfavourable to them. The explanation of this is, that while their *intellect* intended to survey the possibilities completely, the worst of all remained quite invisible to it; because the *will*, as it were, covered it with its hand, that is, it so mastered the intellect that it was quite incapable of glancing at the worst case of all, although, since it actually came to pass, this was also the most probable case. Yet in very melancholy dispositions, or in those that have become prudent through experience like this, the process is reversed, for here apprehension plays the part which was formerly played by hope. The first appearance of danger throws them into groundless anxiety. If the intellect begins to investigate the matter it is rejected as incompetent, nay, as a deceitful sophist, because the heart is to be believed, whose fears are now actually allowed to pass for arguments as to the reality and greatness of the danger. So then the intellect dare make no search for good reasons on the other side, which, if left to itself, it would soon recognise, but is obliged at once to picture to them the most unfortunate issue, even if it itself can scarcely think this issue possible :

> " Such as we know is false, yet dread in sooth,
> Because the worst is ever nearest truth."
> —BYRON (*Lara*, c. 1).

Love and *hate* falsify our judgment entirely. In our enemies we see nothing but faults—in our loved ones nothing but excellences, and even their faults appear to us amiable. Our *interest*, of whatever kind it may be, exercises a like secret power over our judgment; what is in conformity with it at once seems to us fair, just, and reasonable; what runs contrary to it presents itself to us, in perfect seriousness, as unjust and outrageous, or injudicious and absurd. Hence so many prejudices of position, profession, nationality, sect, and religion. A conceived hypothesis gives us lynx-eyes for all that confirms it, and makes us blind to all that contradicts it. What is opposed to our party, our plan, our wish, our hope, we often cannot comprehend and grasp at all, while it is clear to every one else; but what is favourable to these, on the other hand, strikes our eye from afar. What the heart opposes the head will not admit. We firmly retain many errors all through life, and take care never to examine their ground, merely from a fear, of which we ourselves are conscious, that we might make the discovery that we had so long believed and so often asserted what is false. Thus then is the intellect daily befooled and corrupted by the impositions of inclination. This has been very beautifully expressed by Bacon of Verulam in the words: *Intellectus* LUMINIS SICCI *non est; sed recipit infusionem a voluntate et affectibus: id quod generat ad quod vult scientias: quod enim mavult homo, id potius credit. Innumeris modis, iisque interdum imperceptibilibus, affectus intellectum imbuit et inficit (Org. Nov.,* i. 14). Clearly it is also this that opposes all new fundamental opinions in the sciences and all refutations of sanctioned errors, for one will not easily see the truth of that which convicts one of incredible want of thought. It is explicable, on this ground alone, that the truths of Goethe's doctrine of colours, which are so clear and simple, are still denied by the physicists; and thus Goethe himself has had to learn what a much harder position one has if one promises men instruction than if one promises them amusement. Hence it is much more fortunate to be born a poet than a philosopher. But the more obstinately an error was held by the other side, the more shameful does the conviction afterwards become. In the case of an overthrown system, as in the case of a conquered army, the most prudent is he who first runs away from it.

A trifling and absurd, but striking example of that mysterious and immediate power which the will exercises over the intellect, is the fact that in doing accounts we make mistakes much oftener in our own favour than to our disadvantage, and this without the slightest dishonest intention, merely from the unconscious tendency to diminish our *Debit* and increase our *Credit.*

Lastly, the fact is also in point here, that when advice is given the slightest aim or purpose of the adviser generally outweighs his insight, however great it may be; therefore we dare not assume that he speaks from the latter when we suspect the existence of the former. How little perfect sincerity is to be expected even from otherwise honest persons whenever their interests are in any way concerned we can gather from the fact that we so often deceive ourselves when hope bribes us, or fear befools us, or suspicion torments us, or vanity flatters us, or an hypothesis blinds us, or a small aim which is close at hand injures a greater but more distant one; for in this we see the direct and unconscious disadvantageous influence of the will upon knowledge. Accordingly it ought not to surprise us if in asking advice the will of the person asked directly dictates the answer even before the question could penetrate to the forum of his judgment.

I wish in a single word to point out here what will be fully explained in the following book, that the most perfect knowledge, thus the purely objective comprehension of the world, *i.e.*, the comprehension of genius, is conditioned by a silence of the will so profound that while it lasts even the individuality vanishes from consciousness and the man remains *as the pure subject of knowing*, which is the correlative of the *Idea*.

The disturbing influence of the will upon the intellect, which is proved by all these phenomena, and, on the other hand, the weakness and frailty of the latter, on account of which it is incapable of working rightly whenever the will is in any way moved, gives us then another proof that the will is the radical part of our nature, and acts with original power, while the intellect, as adventitious and in many ways conditioned, can only act in a subordinate and conditional manner.

There is no direct disturbance of the will by the intellect corresponding to the disturbance and clouding of knowledge by the will that has been shown. Indeed we cannot well conceive such a thing. No one will wish to construe as such the fact that motives wrongly taken up lead the will astray, for this is a fault of the intellect in its own function, which is committed quite within its own province, and the influence of which upon the will is entirely indirect. It would be plausible to attribute *irresolution* to this, for in its case, through the conflict of the motives which the intellect presents to the will, the latter is brought to a standstill, thus is hindered. But when we consider it more closely, it becomes very clear that the cause of this hindrance does not lie in the activity of the *intellect* as such, but entirely in *external objects* which are brought about by it, for in this case they stand in precisely such a relation to the will, which is here interested, that they draw it with nearly equal strength in different directions. This real cause merely acts *through* the intellect as the medium of motives, though certainly under the assumption that it is keen enough to comprehend the objects in their manifold relations. Irresolution, as a trait of character, is just as much conditioned by qualities of the will as of the intellect. It is certainly not peculiar to exceedingly limited minds, for their weak understanding does not allow them to discover such manifold qualities and relations in things, and moreover is so little fitted for the exertion of reflection and pondering these, and then the probable consequences of each step, that they rather decide at once according to the first impression, or according to some simple rule of conduct. The converse of this occurs in the case of persons of considerable understanding. Therefore, whenever such persons also possess a tender care for their own well-being, *i.e.*, a very sensitive egoism, which constantly desires to come off well and always to be safe, this introduces a certain anxiety at every step, and thereby irresolution. This quality therefore indicates throughout not a want of understanding but a want of courage. Yet very eminent minds survey the relations and their probable developments with such rapidity and certainty, that if they are only supported by some courage they thereby acquire that quick decision and resolution that fits them to play an important part in the affairs of the world, if time and circumstances afford them the opportunity.

The only decided, direct restriction and disturbance which the will can suffer from the intellect as such may indeed be the quite exceptional one, which is the consequence of an abnormally preponderating development of the intellect, thus of that high endowment which has been defined as genius. This is decidedly a hindrance to the energy of the character, and consequently to the power of action. Hence it is not the really great minds that make historical characters, because they are capable of bridling and ruling the mass of men and carrying out the affairs of the world; but for this persons of much less capacity of mind are qualified when they have great firmness, decision, and persistency of will, such as is quite inconsistent with very high intelligence. Accordingly, where this very high intelligence exists we actually have a case in which the intellect directly restricts the will.

6. In opposition to the hindrances and restrictions which it has been shown the intellect suffers from the will, I wish now to show, in a few examples, how, conversely, the functions of the intellect are sometimes aided and heightened by the incitement and spur of the will; so that in this also we may recognise the primary nature of the one and the secondary nature of the other, and it may become clear that the intellect stands to the will in the relation of a tool.

A motive which affects us strongly, such as a yearning desire or a pressing need, sometimes raises the intellect to a degree of which we had not previously believed it capable. Difficult circumstances, which impose upon us the necessity of certain achievements, develop entirely new talents in us, the germs of which were hidden from us, and for which we did not credit ourselves with any capacity. The understanding of the stupidest man becomes keen when objects are in question that closely concern his wishes; he now observes, weighs, and distinguishes with the greatest delicacy even the smallest circumstances that have reference to his wishes or fears. This has much to do with the cunning of half-witted persons, which is often remarked with surprise. On this account Isaiah rightly says, *vexatio dat intellectum*, which is therefore also used as a proverb. Akin to it is the German proverb, "*Die Noth ist die Mutter der Künste*" ("Necessity is the mother of the arts"); when, however, the fine arts are to be excepted, because the heart of every one of their works, that is, the conception, must proceed from a perfectly will-less, and only thereby purely objective, perception, if they are to be genuine. Even the understanding of the brutes is increased considerably by necessity, so that in cases of difficulty they accomplish things at which we are astonished. For example, they almost all calculate that it is safer not to run away when they believe they are not seen; therefore the hare lies still in the furrow of the field and lets the sportsman pass close to it; insects, when they cannot escape, pretend to be dead, &c. We may obtain a fuller knowledge of this influence from the special history of the self-education of the wolf, under the spur of the great difficulty of its position in civilised Europe; it is to be found in the second letter of Leroy's excellent book, "*Lettres sur l'intelligence et la perfectibilité des animaux.*" Immediately afterwards, in the third letter, there follows the high school of the fox, which in an equally difficult position has far less physical strength. In its case, however, this is made up for by great understanding; yet only through the constant struggle with want on the one hand and danger on the other, thus under the spur of the will, does it attain that high degree of cunning which distinguishes it especially in old age. In all these enhancements of the intellect the will plays the part of a rider who with the

spur urges the horse beyond the natural measure of its
strength.

In the same way the memory is enhanced through the
pressure of the will.   Even if it is otherwise weak, it
preserves perfectly what has value for the ruling passion.
The lover forgets no opportunity favourable to him, the
ambitious man forgets no circumstance that can forward
his plans, the avaricious man never forgets the loss he has
suffered, the proud man never forgets an injury to his
honour, the vain man remembers every word of praise and
the most trifling distinction that falls to his lot.   And this
also extends to the brutes: the horse stops at the inn
where once long ago it was fed; dogs have an excellent
memory for all occasions, times, and places that have
afforded them choice morsels; and foxes for the different
hiding-places in which they have stored their plunder.

Self-consideration affords opportunity for finer observations in this regard.   Sometimes, through an interruption,
it has entirely escaped me what I have just been thinking
about, or even what news I have just heard.   Now if the
matter had in any way even the most distant personal
interest, the after-feeling of the impression which it made
upon the *will* has remained.   I am still quite conscious
how far it affected me agreeably or disagreeably, and also
of the special manner in which this happened, whether,
even in the slightest degree, it vexed me, or made me
anxious, or irritated me, or depressed me, or produced the
opposite of these affections.   Thus the mere relation of
the thing to my will is retained in the memory after the
thing itself has vanished, and this often becomes the clue
to lead us back to the thing itself.   The sight of a man
sometimes affects us in an analogous manner, for we
remember merely in general that we have had something
to do with him, yet without knowing where, when, or
what it was, or who he is.   But the sight of him still
recalls pretty accurately the feeling which our dealings
with him excited in us, whether it was agreeable or dis-

agreeable, and also in what degree and in what way. Thus our memory has preserved only the response of the will, and not that which called it forth. We might call what lies at the foundation of this process the memory of the heart; it is much more intimate than that of the head. Yet at bottom the connection of the two is so far-reaching that if we reflect deeply upon the matter we will arrive at the conclusion that memory in general requires the support of a will as a connecting point, or rather as a thread upon which the memories can range themselves, and which holds them firmly together, or that the will is, as it were, the ground to which the individual memories cleave, and without which they could not last; and that therefore in a pure intelligence, *i.e.*, in a merely knowing and absolutely will-less being, a memory cannot well be conceived. Accordingly the improvement of the memory under the spur of the ruling passion, which has been shown above, is only the higher degree of that which takes place in all retention and recollection; for its basis and condition is always the will. Thus in all this also it becomes clear how very much more essential to us the will is than the intellect. The following facts may also serve to confirm this.

The intellect often obeys the will; for example, if we wish to remember something, and after some effort succeed; so also if we wish now to ponder something carefully and deliberately, and in many such cases. Sometimes, again, the intellect refuses to obey the will; for example, if we try in vain to fix our minds upon something, or if we call in vain upon the memory for something that was intrusted to it. The anger of the will against the intellect on such occasions makes its relation to it and the difference of the two very plain. Indeed the intellect, vexed by this anger, sometimes officiously brings what was asked of it hours afterwards, or even the following morning, quite unexpectedly and unseasonably. On the other hand, the will never really obeys the intellect; but the latter is only the

ministerial council of that sovereign; it presents all kinds
of things to the will, which then selects what is in conformity with its nature, though in doing so it determines
itself with necessity, because this nature is unchangeable
and the motives now lie before it.   Hence no system of
ethics is possible which moulds and improves the will
itself.   For all teaching only affects *knowledge,* and knowledge never determines the will itself, *i.e.,* the *fundamental
character* of willing, but only its application to the circumstances present.   Rectified knowledge can only modify
conduct so far as it proves more exactly and judges more
correctly what objects of the will's choice are within its
reach; so that the will now measures its relation to things
more correctly, sees more clearly what it desires, and consequently is less subject to error in its choice.   But over the
will itself, over the main tendency or fundamental maxim
of it, the intellect has no power.   To believe that knowledge really and fundamentally determines the will is like
believing that the lantern which a man carries by night is
the *primum mobile* of his steps.   Whoever, taught by experience or the admonitions of others, knows and laments a fundamental fault of his character, firmly and honestly forms
the intention to reform and give it up; but in spite of this, on
the first opportunity, the fault receives free course.   New repentance, new intentions, new transgressions.   When this
has been gone through several times he becomes conscious
that he cannot improve himself, that the fault lies in his
nature and personality, indeed is one with this.   Now he
will blame and curse his nature and personality, will have
a painful feeling, which may rise to anguish of consciousness, but to change these he is not able.   Here we see that
which condemns and that which is condemned distinctly
separate: we see the former as a merely theoretical faculty,
picturing and presenting the praiseworthy, and therefore
desirable, course of life, but the other as something real
and unchangeably present, going quite a different way in
spite of the former: and then again the first remaining

behind with impotent lamentations over the nature of the other, with which, through this very distress, it again identifies itself. Will and intellect here separate very distinctly. But here the will shows itself as the stronger, the invincible, unchangeable, primitive, and at the same time as the essential thing in question, for the intellect deplores its errors, and finds no comfort in the correctness of the *knowledge,* as its own function. Thus the intellect shows itself entirely secondary, as the spectator of the deeds of another, which it accompanies with impotent praise and blame, and also as determinable from without, because it learns from experience, weighs and alters its precepts. Special illustrations of this subject will be found in the "*Parerga,*" vol. ii. § 118 (second ed., § 119.) Accordingly, a comparison of our manner of thinking at different periods of our life will present a strange mixture of permanence and changeableness. On the one hand, the moral tendency of the man in his prime and the old man is still the same as was that of the boy ; on the other hand, much has become so strange to him that he no longer knows himself, and wonders how he ever could have done or said this and that. In the first half of life to-day for the most part laughs at yesterday, indeed looks down on it with contempt; in the second half, on the contrary, it more and more looks back at it with envy. But on closer examination it will be found that the changeable element was the *intellect,* with its functions of insight and knowledge, which, daily appropriating new material from without, presents a constantly changing system of thought, while, besides this, it itself rises and sinks with the growth and decay of the organism. The will, on the contrary, the basis of this, thus the inclinations, passions, and emotions, the character, shows itself as what is unalterable in consciousness. Yet we have to take account of the modifications that depend upon physical capacities for enjoyment, and hence upon age. Thus, for example, the eagerness for sensuous pleasure will show itself in childhood as a love of dainties, in youth and manhood as the tendency to sensuality, and in old age again as a love of dainties.

7. If, as is generally assumed, the will proceeded from knowledge, as its result or product, then where there is much will there would necessarily also be much knowledge, insight, and understanding. This, however, is absolutely not the case; rather, we find in many men a strong, *i.e.*, decided, resolute, persistent, unbending, wayward, and vehement will, combined with a very weak and incapable understanding, so that every one who has to do with them is thrown into despair, for their will remains inaccessible to all reasons and ideas, and is not to be got at, so that it is hidden, as it were, in a sack, out of which it wills blindly. Brutes have often violent, often stubborn wills, but yet very little understanding. Finally, plants only will without any knowledge at all.

If willing sprang merely from knowledge, our *anger* would necessarily be in every case exactly proportionate to the occasion, or at least to our relation to it, for it would be nothing more than the result of the present knowledge. This, however, is rarely the case; rather, anger generally goes far beyond the occasion. Our fury and rage, the *furor brevis*, often upon small occasions, and without error regarding them, is like the raging of an evil spirit which, having been shut up, only waits its opportunity to dare to break loose, and now rejoices that it has found it. This could not be the case if the foundation of our nature were a *knower*, and willing were merely a result of *knowledge;* for how came there into the result what did not lie in the elements? The conclusion cannot contain more than the premisses. Thus here also the will shows itself as of a nature quite different from knowledge, which only serves it for communication with the external world, but then the will follows the laws of its own nature without taking from the intellect anything but the occasion.

The intellect, as the mere tool of the will, is as different from it as the hammer from the smith. So long as in a conversation the intellect alone is active it remains *cold*. It is almost as if the man himself were not present. Moreover, he cannot then, properly speaking, compromise himself, but at the most can make himself ridiculous. Only when the will comes into play is the man really present: now he becomes *warm*, nay, it often happens, *hot*. It is always the will to which we ascribe the warmth of life; on the other hand, we say the *cold* understanding, or to investigate a thing *coolly, i.e.,* to think without being influenced by the will. If we attempt to reverse the relation, and to regard the will as the tool of the intellect, it is as if we made the smith the tool of the hammer.

Nothing is more provoking, when we are arguing against a man with reasons and explanations, and taking all pains to convince him, under the impression that we have only to do with his *understanding*, than to discover at last that he *will* not understand; that thus we had to do with his *will*, which shuts itself up against the truth and brings into the field wilful misunderstandings, chicaneries, and sophisms in order to intrench itself behind its understanding and its pretended want of insight. Then he is certainly not to be got at, for reasons and proofs applied against the will are like the blows of a phantom produced by mirrors against a solid body. Hence the saying so often repeated, "*Stat pro ratione voluntas.*" Sufficient evidence of what has been said is afforded by ordinary life. But unfortunately proofs of it are also to be found on the path of the sciences. The recognition of the most important truths, of the rarest achievements, will be looked for in vain from those who have an interest in preventing them from being accepted, an interest which either springs from the fact that such truths contradict what they themselves daily teach, or else from this, that they dare not make use of them and teach them; or if all this be not the case they will not accept them, because the watchword of mediocrity will always be, *Si quelqu'un*

excelle parmi nous, qu'il aille exceller ailleurs, as Helvetius
has admirably rendered the saying of the Ephesian in the
fifth book of Cicero's "*Tusculanœ*" (c. 36), or as a saying
of the Abyssinian Fit Arari puts it, "Among quartzes
adamant is outlawed." Thus whoever expects from this
always numerous band a just estimation of what he has
done will find himself very much deceived, and perhaps
for a while he will not be able to understand their behaviour, till at last he finds out that while he applied
himself to *knowledge* he had to do with the *will*, thus is
precisely in the position described above, nay, is really
like a man who brings his case before a court the judges
of which have all been bribed. Yet in particular cases he
will receive the fullest proof that their will and not their
insight opposed him, when one or other of them makes up
his mind to plagiarism. Then he will see with astonishment what good judges they are, what correct perception
of the merit of others they have, and how well they know
how to find out the best, like the sparrows, who never
miss the ripest cherries.

The counterpart of the victorious resistance of the will
to knowledge here set forth appears if in expounding our
reasons and proofs we have the will of those addressed
with us. Then all are at once convinced, all arguments
are telling, and the matter is at once clear as the day.
This is well known to popular speakers. In the one case,
as in the other, the will shows itself as that which has
original power, against which the intellect can do nothing.

8. But now we shall take into consideration the individual qualities, thus excellences and faults of the will
and character on the one hand, and of the intellect on the
other, in order to make clear, in their relation to each
other, and their relative worth, the complete difference
of the two fundamental faculties. History and experience teach that the two appear quite independently of
each other. That the greatest excellence of mind will not
easily be found combined with equal excellence of char-

acter is sufficiently explained by the extraordinary rarity
of both, while their opposites are everywhere the order of
the day; hence we also daily find the latter in union.
However, we never infer a good will from a superior mind,
nor the latter from the former, nor the opposite from the
opposite, but every unprejudiced person accepts them
as perfectly distinct qualities, the presence of which
each for itself has to be learned from experience. Great
narrowness of mind may coexist with great goodness of
heart, and I do not believe Balthazar Gracian was right
in saying (*Discreto*, p. 406), "*No ay simple, que no sea
malicioso*" ("There is no simpleton who would not be malicious "), though he has the Spanish proverb in his favour,
"*Nunca la necedad anduvo sin malicia*" ("Stupidity is
never without malice"). Yet it may be that many stupid
persons become malicious for the same reason as many
hunchbacks, from bitterness on account of the neglect
they have suffered from nature, and because they think
they can occasionally make up for what they lack in
understanding through malicious cunning, seeking in this
a brief triumph. From this, by the way, it is also comprehensible why almost every one easily becomes malicious in the presence of a very superior mind. On the
other hand, again, stupid people have very often the reputation of special good-heartedness, which yet so seldom
proves to be the case that I could not help wondering
how they had gained it, till I was able to flatter myself
that I had found the key to it in what follows. Moved
by a secret inclination, every one likes best to choose
for his more intimate intercourse some one to whom
he is a little superior in understanding, for only in this
case does he find himself at his ease, because, according to
Hobbes, "*Omnis animi voluptas, omnisque alacritas in eo
sita est, quod quis habeat, quibuscum conferens se, possit
magnifice sentire de se ipso*" (*De Cive*, i. 5). For the
same reason every one avoids him who is superior to himself; wherefore Lichtenberg quite rightly observes : "To

certain men a man of mind is a more odious production
than the most pronounced rogue." And similarly Helvetius says: *"Les gens médiocres ont un instinct sûr et prompt,
pour connaître et fuir les gens d'esprit."* And Dr. Johnson
assures us that "there is nothing by which a man exas-
perates most people more than by displaying a superior
ability of brilliancy in conversation. They seem pleased
at the time, but their envy makes them curse him
in their hearts" (Boswell; aet. anno 74). In order to
bring this truth, so universal and so carefully concealed,
more relentlessly to light, I add the expression of it by
Merck, the celebrated friend of Goethe's youth, from his
story *"Lindor:"* "He possessed talents which were given
him by nature and acquired by himself through learning;
and thus it happened that in most society he left the
worthy members of it far behind. If, in the moment of
delight at the sight of an extraordinary man, the public
swallows these superiorities also, without actually at once
putting a bad construction upon them, yet a certain impression of this phenomenon remains behind, which, if it is
often repeated, may on serious occasions have disagreeable
future consequences for him who is guilty of it. Without
any one consciously noting that on this occasion he was
insulted, no one is sorry to place himself tacitly in the
way of the advancement of this man. Thus on this account great mental superiority isolates more than anything else, and makes one, at least silently, hated. Now
it is the opposite of this that makes stupid people so generally liked; especially since many can only find in them
what, according to the law of their nature referred to
above, they must seek. Yet this the true reason of such
an inclination no one will confess to himself, still less to
others; and therefore, as a plausible pretext for it, will
impute to those he has selected a special goodness of
heart, which, as we have said, is in reality only very
rarely and accidentally found in combination with mental
incapacity. Want of understanding is accordingly by no

means favourable or akin to goodness of character. But, on the other hand, it cannot be asserted that great understanding is so; nay, rather, no scoundrel has in general been without it. Indeed even the highest intellectual eminence can coexist with the worst moral depravity. An example of this is afforded by Bacon of Verulam : " Ungrateful, filled with the lust of power, wicked and base, he at last went so far that, as Lord Chancellor and the highest judge of the realm, he frequently allowed himself to be bribed in civil actions. Impeached before his peers, he confessed himself guilty, was expelled by them from the House of Lords, and condemned to a fine of forty thousand pounds and imprisonment in the Tower" (see the review of the latest edition of Bacon's Works in the *Edinburgh Review*, August 1837). Hence also Pope called him "the wisest, brightest, meanest of mankind " ("Essay on Man," iv. 282). A similar example is afforded by the historian Guicciardini, of whom Rosini says in the *Notizie Storiche*, drawn from good contemporary sources, which is given in his historical romance " *Luisa Strozzi* : " " *Da coloro, che pongono l'ingegno e il sapere al di sopra di tutte le umane qualità, questo uomo sarà riguardato come fra i più grandi del suo secolo : ma da quelli, che reputano la virtù dovere andare innanzi a tutto, non potra esecrarsi abbastanza la sua memoria. Esso fu il più crudele fra i cittadini a perseguitare, uccidere e confinare,*" &c.[1]

If now it is said of one man, "He has a good heart, though a bad head," but of another, " He has a very good head, yet a bad heart," every one feels that in the first case the praise far outweighs the blame—in the other case the reverse. Answering to this, we see that if some one has done a bad deed his friends and he himself try to remove the guilt from the *will* to the *intellect*, and to give out that

[1] By those who place mind and learning above all other human qualities this man will be reckoned the greatest of his century. But by those who let virtue take precedence of everything else his memory can never be execrated enough. He was the cruelest of the citizens in persecuting, putting to death, and banishing.

faults of the heart were faults of the head ; roguish tricks
they will call *errors*, will say they were merely want of
understanding, want of reflection, light-mindedness, folly ;
nay, if need be, they will plead a paroxysm, momentary
mental aberration, and if a heavy crime is in question,
even madness, only in order to free the *will* from the guilt.
And in the same way, we ourselves, if we have caused
a misfortune or injury, will before others and ourselves
willingly impeach our *stultitia*, simply in order to escape
the reproach of *malitia*. In the same way, in the case of
the equally unjust decision of the judge, the difference,
whether he has erred or been bribed, is so infinitely great.
All this sufficiently proves that the *will* alone is the real
and essential, the kernel of the man, and the *intellect*
is merely its tool, which may be constantly faulty without
the will being concerned. The accusation of want of
understanding is, at the moral judgment-seat, no accusation at all ; on the contrary, it even gives privileges.
And so also, before the courts of the world, it is everywhere sufficient to deliver a criminal from all punishment
that his guilt should be transferred from his will to his
intellect, by proving either unavoidable error or mental
derangement, for then it is of no more consequence than
if hand or foot had slipped against the will. I have fully
discussed this in the appendix, " *Ueber die Intellektuelle
Freiheit*," to my prize essay on the freedom of the will,
to which I refer to avoid repetition.

Everywhere those who are responsible for any piece of
work appeal, in the event of its turning out unsatisfac-
torily, to their good intentions, of which there was no
lack. Hereby they believe that they secure the essential,
that for which they are properly answerable, and their
true self ; the inadequacy of their faculties, on the other
hand, they regard as the want of a suitable tool.

If a man is *stupid*, we excuse him by saying that he
cannot help it ; but if we were to excuse a *bad* man on
the same grounds we would be laughed at. And yet the

one, like the other, is innate. This proves that the will is the man proper, the intellect merely its tool.

Thus it is always only our *willing* that is regarded as depending upon ourselves, *i.e.*, as the expression of our true nature, and for which we are therefore made responsible. Therefore it is absurd and unjust if we are taken to task for our beliefs, thus for our knowledge: for we are obliged to regard this as something which, although it changes in us, is as little in our power as the events of the external world. And here, also, it is clear that the *will* alone is the inner and true nature of man; the *intellect*, on the contrary, with its operations, which go on as regularly as the external world, stands to the will in the relation of something external to it, a mere tool.

High mental capacities have always been regarded as the gift of nature or the gods; and on that account they have been called *Gaben, Begabung, ingenii dotes*, gifts (a man highly gifted), regarding them as something different from the man himself, something that has fallen to his lot through favour. No one, on the contrary, has ever taken this view of moral excellences, although they also are innate; they have rather always been regarded as something proceeding from the man himself, essentially belonging to him, nay, constituting his very self. But it follows now from this that the will is the true nature of man; the intellect, on the other hand, is secondary, a tool, a gift.

Answering to this, all religions promise a reward beyond life, in eternity, for excellences of the *will* or heart, but none for excellences of the head or understanding. Virtue expects its reward in that world; prudence hopes for it in this; genius, again, neither in this world nor in that; it is its own reward. Accordingly the will is the eternal part, the intellect the temporal.

Connection, communion, intercourse among men is based, as a rule, upon relations which concern the *will*, not upon such as concern the *intellect*. The first kind of communion may be called the *material*, the other the *formal*. Of the former kind are the bonds of family and relationship, and further, all connections that rest upon any common aim or interest, such as that of trade or profession, of the corporation, the party, the faction, &c. In these it merely amounts to a question of views, of aims; along with which there may be the greatest diversity of intellectual capacity and culture. Therefore not only can any one live in peace and unity with any one else, but can act with him and be allied to him for the common good of both. Marriage also is a bond of the heart, not of the head. It is different, however, with merely formal communion, which aims only at an exchange of thought; this demands a certain equality of intellectual capacity and culture. Great differences in this respect place between man and man an impassable gulf: such lies, for example, between a man of great mind and a fool, between a scholar and a peasant, between a courtier and a sailor. Natures as heterogeneous as this have therefore trouble in making themselves intelligible so long as it is a question of exchanging thoughts, ideas, and views. Nevertheless close *material* friendship may exist between them, and they may be faithful allies, conspirators, or men under mutual pledges. For in all that concerns the will alone, which includes friendship, enmity, honesty, fidelity, falseness, and treachery, they are perfectly homogeneous, formed of the same clay, and neither mind nor culture make any difference here; indeed here the ignorant man often shames the scholar, the sailor the courtier. For at the different grades of culture there are the same virtues and vices, emotions and passions; and although somewhat modified in their expression, they very soon mutually recognise each other even in the most heterogeneous individuals, upon which the similarly disposed agree and the opposed are at enmity.

Brilliant qualities of mind win admiration, but never affection; this is reserved for the moral, the qualities of the character. Every one will choose as his friend the honest, the good-natured, and even the agreeable, complaisant man, who easily concurs, rather than the merely able man. Indeed many will be preferred to the latter, on account of insignificant, accidental, outward qualities which just suit the inclination of another. Only the man who has much mind himself will wish able men for his society; his friendship, on the other hand, he will bestow with reference to moral qualities; for upon this depends his really high appreciation of a man in whom a single good trait of character conceals and expiates great want of understanding. The known goodness of a character makes us patient and yielding towards weaknesses of understanding, as also towards the dulness and childishness of age. A distinctly noble character along with the entire absence of intellectual excellence and culture presents itself as lacking nothing; while, on the contrary, even the greatest mind, if affected with important moral faults, will always appear blamable. For as torches and fireworks become pale and insignificant in the presence of the sun, so intellect, nay, genius, and also beauty, are outshone and eclipsed by the goodness of the heart. When this appears in a high degree it can make up for the want of those qualities to such an extent that one is ashamed of having missed them. Even the most limited understanding, and also grotesque ugliness, whenever extraordinary goodness of heart declares itself as accompanying them, become as it were transfigured, outshone by a beauty of a higher kind, for now a wisdom speaks out of them before which all other wisdom must be dumb. For goodness of heart is a transcendent quality; it belongs to an order of things that reaches beyond this life, and is incommensurable with any other perfection. When it is present in a high degree it makes the heart so large that it embraces the world, so that now everything lies within it, no longer without; for it identifies all natures with its own. It then extends to others also that boundless indulgence which otherwise each one only bestows on himself. Such a man is incapable of becoming angry; even if the malicious mockery and sneers of others have drawn attention to his own intellectual or physical faults, he only reproaches himself in his heart for having been the occasion of such expressions, and therefore, without doing violence to his own feelings, proceeds to treat those persons in the kindest manner, confidently hoping that they will turn from their error with regard to him, and recognise themselves in him also. What is wit and genius against this?—what is Bacon of Verulam?

Our estimation of our own selves leads to the same result as we have here obtained by considering our estimation of others. How different is the self-satisfaction which we experience in a moral regard from that which we experience in an intellectual regard! The former arises when, looking back on our conduct, we see that with great sacrifices we have practised fidelity and honesty, that we have helped many, forgiven many, have behaved better to others than they have behaved to us; so that we can say with King Lear, "I am a man more sinned against than sinning;" and to its fullest extent if perhaps some noble deed shines in our memory. A deep seriousness will accompany the still peace which such a review affords us; and if we see that others are inferior to us here, this will not cause us any joy, but we will rather deplore it, and sincerely wish that they were as we are. How entirely differently does the knowledge of our intellectual superiority affect us! Its ground bass is really the saying of Hobbes quoted above: *Omnis animi voluptas, omnisque alacritas in eo sita est, quod quis habeat, quibuscum conferens se, possit magnifice sentire de se ipso.* Arrogant, triumphant vanity, proud, contemptuous looking down on others, inordinate delight in the consciousness of decided and considerable superiority, akin to pride of physical advantages, —that is the result here. This opposition between the two kinds of self-satisfaction shows that the one concerns our true inner and eternal nature, the other a more external, merely temporal, and indeed scarcely more than a mere physical excellence. The *intellect* is in fact simply the function of the brain; the *will*, on the contrary, is that whose function is the whole man, according to his being and nature.

If, looking without us, we reflect that $\dot{o}\ \beta\iota os\ \beta\rho\alpha\chi vs,\ \dot{\eta}$ $\delta\epsilon\ \tau\epsilon\chi\nu\eta\ \mu\alpha\kappa\rho\alpha$ (*vita brevis, ars longa*), and consider how the greatest and most beautiful minds, often when they have scarcely reached the summit of their power, and the greatest scholars, when they have only just attained to a thorough knowledge of their science, are snatched away by death, we are confirmed in this, that the meaning and end of life is not intellectual but moral.

The complete difference between the mental and moral qualities displays itself lastly in the fact that the intellect suffers very important changes through time, while the will and character remain untouched by it. The new-born child has as yet no use of its understanding, but obtains it within the first two months to the extent of perception and apprehension of the things in the external world—a process which I have described more fully in my essay, "*Ueber das Sehn und die Farben*," p. 10 of the second (and third) edition. The growth of reason to the point of speech, and thereby of thought, follows this first and most important step much more slowly, generally only in the third year; yet the early childhood remains hopelessly abandoned to silliness and folly, primarily because the brain still lacks physical completeness, which, both as regards its size and texture, it only attains in the seventh year. But then for its energetic activity there is still wanting the antagonism of the genital system; it therefore only begins with puberty. Through this, how-ever, the intellect has only attained to the *capacity* for its psychical improvement; this itself can only be won by practice, experience, and instruction. Thus as soon as the mind has escaped from the folly of childhood it falls into the snares of innumerable errors, prejudices, and chimeras, sometimes of the absurdest and crudest kind, which it obstinately sticks to, till experience gradually removes them, and many of them also are insensibly lost. All this takes many years to happen, so that one grants it majority indeed soon after the twentieth year, yet has placed full maturity, years of discretion, not before the fortieth year. But while this psychical education, resting upon help from without, is still in process of growth, the inner *physical* energy of the brain already begins to sink again. This has reached its real calminating point about the thirtieth year, on account of its dependence upon the pressure of blood and the effect of the pulsation upon the brain, and through this again upon the predominance of the arterial over the venous system, and the fresh tenderness of the brain fibre, and also on account of the energy of the genital system. After the thirty-fifth year a slight diminution of the physical energy of the brain becomes noticeable, which, through the gradually approaching predominance of the venous over the arterial system, and also through the increasing firmer and drier consistency of the brain fibre, more and more takes place, and would be much more observable if it were not that, on the other hand, the psychical perfecting, through exercise, experience, increase of knowledge, and acquired skill in the use of it, counteracts it—an antagonism which fortunately lasts to an advanced age, for the brain becomes more and more like a worn-out instrument. But yet the diminution of the original energy of the intellect, resting entirely upon organic conditions, continues, slowly indeed, but unceasingly : the faculty of original conception, the imagination, the plastic power, the memory, become noticeably weaker; and so it goes on step by step downwards into old age, garrulous, without memory, half-unconscious, and ultimately quite childish.

The will, on the contrary, is not affected by all this becoming, this change and vicissitude, but is from beginning to end unalterably the same. *Willing* does not require to be learned like *knowing*, but succeeds perfectly at once. The new-born child makes violent movements, rages, and cries; it wills in the most vehement manner, though it does not yet know what it wills. For the medium of motives, the intellect, is not yet fully developed. The will is in darkness concerning the external world, in which its objects lie, and now rages like a prisoner against the walls and bars of his dungeon. But little by little it becomes light: at once the fundamental traits of universal human willing, and, at the same time, the individual modification of it here present, announce themselves. The already appearing character shows itself indeed at first in weak and uncertain outline, on account of the defective service of the intellect, which has to present it with motives; but to the attentive observer it soon declares its complete presence, and in a short time it becomes unmistakable. The characteristics appear which last through the whole of life; the principal tendencies of the will, the easily excited emotions, the ruling passion, declare themselves. Therefore the events at school stand to those of the future life for the most part as the dumb-show in " Hamlet" that precedes the play to be given at the court, and foretells its content in the form of pantomime, stands to the play itself. But it is by no means possible to prognosticate in the same way the future intellectual capacities of the man from those shown in the boy; rather as a rule the *ingenia præcocia,* prodigies, turn out block-heads; genius, on the contrary, is often in childhood of slow conception, and comprehends with difficulty, just because it comprehends deeply. This is how it is that every one relates laughing and without reserve the follies and stupidities of his childhood. For example, Goethe, how he threw all the kitchen crockery out of the window (*Dichtung und Wahrheit,* vol. i. p. 7); for we know that all this only concerns what changes. On the other hand, a prudent man will not favour us with the bad features, the malicious or deceitful actions, of his youth, for he feels that they also bear witness to his present character. I have been told that when Gall, the phrenologist and investigator of man, had to put himself into connection with a man as yet unknown to him, he used to get him to speak about his youthful years and actions, in order, if possible, to gather from these the distinctive traits of his character; because this must still be the same now. This is the reason why we are indifferent to the follies and want of understanding of our youthful years, and even look back on them with smiling satisfaction, while the bad features of character even of that time, the ill-natured actions and the misdeeds then committed exist even in old age as inextinguishable reproaches, and trouble our consciences. Now, just as the character appears complete, so it remains unaltered to old age. The advance of age, which gradually consumes the intellectual powers, leaves the moral qualities untouched. The goodness of the heart still makes the old man honoured and loved when his head already shows the weaknesses which are the commencement of second childhood. Gentleness, patience, honesty, veracity, disinterestedness, philanthropy, &c., remain through the whole life, and are not lost through the weaknesses of old age; in every clear moment of the worn-out old man they come forth undiminished, like the sun from the winter clouds. And, on the other hand, malice, spite, avarice, hard-heartedness, infidelity, egoism, and baseness of every kind also remain undiminished to our latest years. We would not believe but would laugh at any one who said to us, "In former years I was a malicious rogue, but now I am an honest and noble-minded man." Therefore Sir Walter Scott, in the "Fortunes of Nigel," has shown very beautifully, in the case of the old usurer, how burning avarice, egoism, and injustice are still in their full strength, like a poisonous plant in autumn, when the intellect has already become childish. The only alterations that take place in our inclinations are those which result directly from the decrease of our physical strength, and with it of our capacities for enjoyment. Thus voluptuousness will make way for intemperance, the love of splendour for avarice, and vanity for ambition;

just like the man who before he has a beard will wear a
false one, and later, when his own beard has become grey,
will dye it brown. Thus while all organic forces, muscular power, the senses, the memory, wit, understanding,
genius, wear themselves out, and in old age become dull,
the will alone remains undecayed and unaltered: the
strength and the tendency of willing remains the same.
Indeed in many points the will shows itself still more
decided in age: thus, in the clinging to life, which, it is
well known, increases; also in the firmness and persistency
with regard to what it has once embraced, in obstinacy;
which is explicable from the fact that the susceptibility of
the intellect for other impressions, and thereby the movement of the will by motives streaming in upon it, has
diminished. Hence the implacable nature of the anger
and hate of old persons—

> " The young man's wrath is like light straw on fire,
> But like red-hot steel is the old man's ire."
>
> *—Old Ballad.*

From all these considerations it becomes unmistakable
to the more penetrating glance that, while the *intellect* has
to run through a long series of gradual developments, but
then, like everything physical, must encounter decay, the
will takes no part in this, except so far as it has to contend at first with the imperfection of its tool, the intellect,
and, again, at last with its worn-out condition, but itself
appears perfect and remains unchanged, not subject to
the laws of time and of becoming and passing away in it.
Thus in this way it makes itself known as that which
is metaphysical, not itself belonging to the phenomenal
world.

9. The universally used and generally very well understood expressions *heart* and *head* have sprung from a true
feeling of the fundamental distinction here in question;
therefore they are also apt and significant, and occur in
all languages. *Nec cor nec caput habet,* says Seneca of the
Emperor Claudius (*Ludus de morte Claudii Cæsaris,* c. 8).

The heart, this *primum mobile* of the animal life, has with perfect justice been chosen as the symbol, nay, the synonym, of the *will,* as the primary kernel of our phenomenon, and denotes this in opposition to the intellect, which is exactly identical with the head. All that, in the widest sense, is matter of the will, as wish, passion, joy, grief, goodness, wickedness, also what we are wont to understand under "Gemüth," and what Homer expresses through φιλον ἦτορ, is attributed to the *heart.* Accordingly we say : He has a bad heart ;—his heart is in the thing ;—it comes from his heart ;—it cut him to the heart ;—it breaks his heart ;—his heart bleeds ;—the heart leaps for joy ;—who can see the heart of man ?—it is heart-rending, heart-crushing, heart-breaking, heart-inspiring, heart-touching ;—he is good-hearted, hard-hearted, heartless, stout-hearted, faint-hearted, &c. &c. Quite specially, however, love affairs are called affairs of the heart, *affaires de cœur ;* because the sexual impulse is the focus of the will, and the selection with reference to it constitutes the chief concern of natural, human volition, the ground of which I shall show in a full chapter supplementary to the fourth book. Byron in "Don Juan," c. xi. v. 34, is satirical about love being to women an affair of the head instead of an affair of the heart. On the other hand, the *head* denotes everything that is matter of *knowledge.* Hence a man of head, a good head, a fine head, a bad head, to lose one's head, to keep one's head uppermost, &c. Heart and head signifies the whole man. But the head is always the second, the derived ; for it is not the centre but the highest efflorescence of the body. When a hero dies his heart is embalmed, not his brain ; on the other hand, we like to preserve the skull of the poet, the artist, and the philosopher. So Raphael's skull was preserved in the Academia di S. Luca at Rome, though it has lately been proved not to be genuine ; in Stockholm in 1820 the skull of Descartes was sold by auction.[1]

[1] The *Times* of 18th October 1845 ; from the *Athenæum.*

A true feeling of the real relation between will, intellect, and life is also expressed in the Latin language. The intellect is *mens, νους* ; the will again is *animus,* which comes from *anima,* and this from *ανεμων. Anima* is the life itself, the breath, *ψυχη* ; but *animus* is the living principle, and also the will, the subject of inclinations, intentions, passions, emotions ; hence also *est mihi animus,—fert animus,—*for "I have a desire to," also *animi causa,* &c. ; it is the Greek *θυμος,* the German "Gemüth," thus the heart but not the head. *Animi perturbatio* is an emotion ; *mentis perturbatio* would signify insanity. The predicate *immortalis* is attributed to *animus,* not to *mens.* All this is the rule gathered from the great majority of passages ; though in the case of conceptions so nearly related it cannot but be that the words are sometimes interchanged. Under *ψυχη* the Greeks appear primarily and originally to have understood the vital force, the living principle, whereby at once arose the dim sense that it must be something metaphysical, which consequently would not be reached by death. Among other proofs of this are the investigations of the relation between *νους* and *ψυχη* preserved by Stobæus (*Ecl.,* Lib. i. c. 51, § 7, 8).

10. Upon what depends the *identity of the person?* Not upon the matter of the body ; it is different after a few years. Not upon its form, which changes as a whole and in all its parts ; all but the expression of the glance, by which, therefore, we still know a man even after many years ; which proves that in spite of all changes time produces in him something in him remains quite untouched by it. It is just this by which we recognise him even after the longest intervals of time, and find the former man entire. It is the same with ourselves, for, however old we become, we yet feel within that we are entirely the same as we were when we were young, nay, when we were still children. This, which unaltered always remains quite the same, and does not grow old along with us, is really the

kernel of our nature, which does not lie in time. It is assumed that the identity of the person rests upon that of consciousness. But by this is understood merely the connected recollection of the course of life; hence it is not sufficient. We certainly know something more of our life than of a novel we have formerly read, yet only very little. The principal events, the interesting scenes, have impressed themselves upon us; in the remainder a thousand events are forgotten for one that has been retained. The older we become the more do things pass by us without leaving any trace. Great age, illness, injury of the brain, madness, may deprive us of memory altogether, but the identity of the person is not thereby lost. It rests upon the identical *will* and the unalterable character of the person. It is it also which makes the expression of the glance unchangeable. In the *heart* is the man, not in the head. It is true that, in consequence of our relation to the external world, we are accustomed to regard as our real self the subject of knowledge, the knowing I, which wearies in the evening, vanishes in sleep, and in the morning shines brighter with renewed strength. This is, however, the mere function of the brain, and not our own self. Our true self, the kernel of our nature, is what is behind that, and really knows nothing but willing and not willing, being content and not content, with all the modifications of this, which are called feelings, emotions, and passions. This is that which produces the other, does not sleep with it when it sleeps, and in the same way when it sinks in death remains uninjured. Everything, on the contrary, that belongs to *knowledge* is exposed to oblivion; even actions of moral significance can sometimes, after years, be only imperfectly recalled, and we no longer know accurately and in detail how we acted on a critical occasion. But the *character itself*, to which the actions only testify, cannot be forgotten by us; it is now still quite the same as then. The will itself, alone and for itself, is permanent, for it alone is unchangeable, indestructible, not growing old, not physical, but metaphysical, not belonging to the phenomenal appearance, but to that itself which so appears. How the identity of consciousness also, so far as it goes, depends upon it I have shown above in chapter 15, so I need not dwell upon it further here.

11. Aristotle says in passing, in his book on the comparison of the desirable, "To live well is better than to live" (βελτιον του ζην το ευ ζην, Top. iii. 2). From this we might infer, by double contraposition, not to live is better than to live badly. This is also evident to the intellect; yet the great majority live very badly rather than not at all. This clinging to life cannot therefore have its ground in the *object* of life, since life, as was shown in the fourth book, is really a constant suffering, or at the least, as will be shown further on in the 28th chapter, a business which does not cover its expenses; thus that clinging to life can only be founded in the *subject* of it. But it is not founded in the *intellect*, it is no result of reflection, and in general is not a matter of choice; but this willing of life is something that is taken for granted: it is a *prius* of the intellect itself. We ourselves are the will to live, and therefore we must live, well or ill. Only from the fact that this clinging to a life which is so little worth to them is entirely *a priori* and not *a posteriori* can we explain the excessive fear of death that dwells in every living thing, which Rochefoucauld has expressed in his last reflection, with rare frankness and naïveté, and upon which the effect of all tragedies and heroic actions ultimately rest, for it would be lost if we prized life only according to its objective worth. Upon this inexpressible *horror mortis* is also founded the favourite principle of all ordinary minds, that whosoever takes his own life must be mad; yet not less the astonishment, mingled with a certain admiration, which this action always excites even in thinking minds, because it is so opposed to the nature of all living beings that in a certain sense we are forced to admire him who is able to perform it. For suicide proceeds from a purpose

of the intellect, but our will to live is a *prius* of the intellect. Thus this consideration also, which will be fully discussed in chapter 28, confirms the primacy of the will in self-consciousness.

12. On the other hand, nothing proves more clearly the secondary, dependent, conditioned nature of the *intellect* than its periodical intermittance. In deep sleep all knowing and forming of ideas ceases. But the kernel of our nature, the metaphysical part of it which the organic functions necessarily presuppose as their *primum mobile*, must never pause if life is not to cease, and, moreover, as something metaphysical and therefore incorporeal, it requires no rest. Therefore the philosophers who set up a *soul* as this metaphysical kernel, *i.e.*, an originally and essentially *knowing* being, see themselves forced to the assertion that this soul is quite untiring in its perceiving and knowing, therefore continues these even in deep sleep; only that we have no recollection of this when we awake. The falseness of this assertion, however, was easy to see whenever one had rejected that *soul* in consequence of Kant's teaching. For sleep and waking prove to the unprejudiced mind in the clearest manner that knowing is a secondary function and conditioned by the organism, just like any other. Only the *heart* is untiring, because its beating and the circulation of the blood are not directly conditioned by nerves, but are just the original manifestation of the will. Also all other physiological functions governed merely by ganglionic nerves, which have only a very indirect and distant connection with the brain, are carried on during sleep, although the secretions take place more slowly; the beating of the heart itself, on account of its dependence upon respiration, which is conditioned by the cerebral system (*medulla oblongata*), becomes with it a little slower. The stomach is perhaps most active in sleep, which is to be attributed to its special consensus with the now resting brain, which occasions mutual disturbances. The *brain* alone, and with it knowing, pauses entirely in

deep sleep. For it is merely the minister of foreign affairs, as the ganglion system is the minister of the interior. The brain, with its function of knowing, is only a *vedette* established by the will for its external ends, which, up in the watch-tower of the head, looks round through the windows of the senses and marks where mischief threatens and where advantages are to be looked for, and in accordance with whose report the will decides. This *vedette*, like every one engaged on active service, is then in a condition of strain and effort, and therefore it is glad when, after its watch is completed, it is again withdrawn, as every watch gladly retires from its post. This withdrawal is going to sleep, which is therefore so sweet and agreeable, and to which we are so glad to yield; on the other hand, being roused from sleep is unwelcome, because it recalls the *vedette* suddenly to its post. One generally feels also after the beneficent systole the reappearance of the difficult diastole, the reseparation of the intellect from the will. A so-called *soul*, which was originally and radically a *knowing* being, would, on the contrary, necessarily feel on awaking like a fish put back into water. In sleep, when merely the vegetative life is carried on, the will works only according to its original and essential nature, undisturbed from without, with no diminution of its power through the activity of the brain and the exertion of knowing, which is the heaviest organic function, yet for the organism merely a means, not an end; therefore, in sleep the whole power of the will is directed to the maintenance and, where it is necessary, the improvement of the organism. Hence all healing, all favourable crises, take place in sleep; for the *vis naturæ medicatrix* has free play only when it is delivered from the burden of the function of knowledge. The embryo which has still to form the body therefore sleeps continuously, and the new-born child the greater part of its time. In this sense Burdach (*Physiologie*, vol. iii. p. 484) quite rightly declares sleep to be the *original state*.

With reference to the brain itself, I account to myself for the necessity of sleep more fully through an hypothesis which appears to have been first set up in Neumann's book, " *Von den Krankheiten des Menschen*," 1834, vol. 4, § 216. It is this, that the nutrition of the brain, thus the renewal of its substance from the blood, cannot go on while we are awake, because the very eminent organic function of knowing and thinking would be disturbed or put an end to by the low and material function of nutrition. This explains the fact that sleep is not a purely negative condition, a mere pausing of the activity of the brain, but also shows a positive character. This makes itself known through the circumstance that between sleep and waking there is no mere difference of degree, but a fixed boundary, which, as soon as sleep intervenes, declares itself in dreams which are completely different from our immediately preceding thoughts. A further proof of this is that when we have dreams which frighten us we try in vain to cry out, or to ward off attacks, or to shake off sleep; so that it is as if the connecting-link between the brain and the motor nerves, or between the cerebrum and the cerebellum (as the regulator of movements) were abolished; for the brain remains in its isolation and sleep holds us fast as with brazen claws. Finally, the positive character of sleep can be seen in the fact that a certain degree of strength is required for sleeping. Therefore too great fatigue or natural weakness prevent us from seizing it, *capere somnum.* This may be explained from the fact that the *process of nutrition* must be introduced if sleep is to ensue: the brain must, as it were, begin to feed. Moreover, the increased flow of blood into the brain during sleep is explicable from the nutritive process; and also the position of the arms laid together above the head, which is instinctively assumed because it furthers this process: also why children, so long as their brain is still growing, require a great deal of sleep, while in old age, on the other hand, when a certain atrophy of the brain, as of all the parts, takes place, sleep is short; and finally why excessive sleep produces a certain dulness of consciousness, the consequence of a certain hypertrophy of the brain, which in the case of habitual excess of sleep may become permanent and produce imbecility: ανιη και πολυς ὑπνος (*noxæ est etiam multus somnus*), Od. 15, 394. The need of sleep is therefore directly proportionate to the intensity of the brain-life, thus to the clearness of the consciousness. Those animals whose brain-life is weak and dull sleep little and lightly; for example, reptiles and fishes: and here I must remind the reader that the winter sleep is sleep almost only in name, for it is not an inaction of the brain alone, but of the whole organism, thus a kind of apparent death. Animals of considerable intelligence sleep deeply and long. Men also require more sleep the more developed, both as regards quantity and quality, and the more active their brain is. Montaigne relates of himself that he had always been a long sleeper, that he had passed a large part of his life in sleeping, and at an advanced age still slept from eight to nine hours at a time (Liv. iii., chap. 13). Descartes also is reported to have slept a great deal (Baillet, *Vie de Descartes*, 1693, p. 288). Kant allowed himself seven hours for sleep, but it was so hard for him to do with this that he ordered his servant to force him against his will, and without listening to his remonstrances, to get up at the set time (Jachmann, *Immanuel Kant*, p. 162). For the more completely awake a man is, *i.e.*, the clearer and more lively his consciousness, the greater for him is the necessity of sleep, thus the deeper and longer he sleeps. Accordingly much thinking or hard brain-work increases the need of sleep. That sustained muscular exertion also makes us sleepy is to be explained from the fact that in this the brain continuously, by means of the *medulla oblongata*, the spinal marrow, and the motor nerves, imparts the stimulus to the muscles which affects their irritability, and in this way it exhausts its strength.

The fatigue which we observe in the arms and legs has accordingly its real seat in the brain ; just as the pain which these parts feel is really experienced in the brain ; for it is connected with the motor nerves, as with the nerves of sense. The muscles which are not actuated from the brain—for example, those of the heart—accordingly never tire. The same grounds explain the fact that both during and after great muscular exertion we cannot think acutely. That one has far less energy of mind in summer than in winter is partly explicable from the fact that in summer one sleeps less ; for the deeper one has slept, the more completely awake, the more lively, is one afterwards. This, however, must not mislead us into extending sleep unduly, for then it loses in intension, *i.e.*, in deepness and soundness, what it gains in extension ; whereby it becomes mere loss of time. This is what Goethe means when he says (in the second part of " Faust ") of morning slumber : " Sleep is husk : throw it off." Thus in general the phenomenon of sleep most specially confirms the assertion that consciousness, apprehension, knowing, thinking, is nothing original in us, but a conditioned and secondary state. It is a luxury of nature, and indeed its highest, which it can therefore the less afford to pursue without interruption the higher the pitch to which it has been brought. It is the product, the efflorescence of the cerebral nerve-system, which is itself nourished like a parasite by the rest of the organism. This also agrees with what is shown in our third book, that knowing is so much the purer and more perfect the more it has freed and severed itself from the will, whereby the purely objective, the æsthetic comprehension appears. Just as an extract is so much the purer the more it has been separated from that out of which it is extracted and been cleared of all sediment. The opposite is shown by the *will*, whose most immediate manifestation is the whole organic life, and primarily the untiring heart.

This last consideration is related to the theme of the

following chapter, to which it therefore makes the transition: yet the following observation belongs to it. In magnetic somnambulism the consciousness is doubled: two trains of knowledge, each connected in itself, but quite different from each other, arise ; the waking consciousness knows nothing of the somnambulent. But the will retains in both the same character, and remains throughout identical; it expresses in both the same inclinations and aversions. For the function may be doubled, but not the true nature.

CHAPTER XX.[1]

OBJECTIFICATION OF THE WILL IN THE ANIMAL ORGANISM.

BY *objectification* I understand the self-exhibition in the real corporeal world. However, this world itself, as was fully shown in the first book and its supplements, is throughout conditioned by the knowing subject, thus by the intellect, and therefore as such is absolutely inconceivable outside the knowledge of this subject; for it primarily consists simply of ideas of perception, and as such is a phenomenon of the brain. After its removal the thing in itself would remain. That this is the *will* is the theme of the second book, and is there proved first of all in the human organism and in that of the brutes.

The knowledge of the external world may also be defined as the *consciousness of other things,* in opposition to *self-consciousness.* Since we have found in the latter that its true object or material is the will, we shall now, with the same intention, take into consideration the consciousness of other things, thus objective knowledge. Now here my thesis is this : *that which in self-consciousness, thus subjectively is the intellect, presents itself in the consciousness of other things, thus objectively, as the brain; and that which in self-consciousness, thus subjectively, is the will, presents itself in the consciousness of other things, thus objectively, as the whole organism.*

To the evidence which is given in support of this proposition, both in our second book and in the first two chapters of the treatise " *Ueber den Willen in der Natur,*"

---

[1] This chapter is connected with § 20 of the first volume.

I add the following supplementary remarks and illustrations.

Nearly all that is necessary to establish the first part of this thesis has already been brought forward in the preceding chapter, for in the necessity of sleep, in the alterations that arise from age, and in the differences of the anatomical conformation, it was proved that the intellect is of a secondary nature, and depends absolutely upon a single organ, the brain, whose function it is, just as grasping is the function of the hand; that it is therefore physical, like digestion, not metaphysical, like the will. As good digestion requires a healthy, strong stomach, as athletic power requires muscular sinewy arms, so extraordinary intelligence requires an unusually developed, beautifully formed brain of exquisitely fine texture and animated by a vigorous pulse. The nature of the will, on the contrary, is dependent upon no organ, and can be prognosticated from none. The greatest error in Gall's phrenology is that he assigns organs of the brain for moral qualities also. Injuries to the head, with loss of brain substance, affect the intellect as a rule very disadvantageously: they result in complete or partial imbecility or forgetfulness of language, permanent or temporary, yet sometimes only of one language out of several which were known, also in the loss of other knowledge possessed, &c., &c. On the other hand, we never read that after a misfortune of this kind the *character* has undergone a change, that the man has perhaps become morally worse or better, or has lost certain inclinations or passions, or assumed new ones; never. For the will has not its seat in the brain, and moreover, as that which is metaphysical, it is the *prius* of the brain, as of the whole body, and therefore cannot be altered by injuries of the brain. According to an experiment made by Spallanzani and repeated by Voltaire,[1] a

---

[1] *Spallanzani, Risultati di esperienze sopra la riproduzione della testa nelle lumache terrestri:* in the *Memorie di matematica e fisica della* *Società Italiana,* Tom. i. p. 581. *Voltaire, Les colimaçons du révérend père l'escarbotier.*

snail that has had its head cut off remains alive, and after
some weeks a new head grows on, together with horns;
with this consciousness and ideas again appear; while till
then the snail had only given evidence of blind will
through unregulated movements.   Thus here also we find
the will as the substance which is permanent, the intellect,
on the contrary, conditioned by its organ, as the changing
accident. It may be defined as the regulator of the will.

It was perhaps Tiedemann who first compared the
cerebral nervous system to a *parasite* (*Tiedemann und
Trevirann's Journal für Physiologie*, Bd. i. § 62).   The
comparison is happy; for the brain, together with the
spinal cord and nerves which depend upon it, is, as it were,
implanted in the organism, and is nourished by it without
on its part *directly* contributing anything to the support of
the economy of the organism; therefore there can be life
without a brain, as in the case of brainless abortions, and
also in the case of tortoises, which live for three weeks
after their heads have been cut off; only the *medulla
oblongata*, as the organ of respiration, must be spared.
Indeed a hen whose whole brain Flourens had cut away
lived for ten months and grew.   Even in the case of men
the destruction of the brain does not produce death
directly, but only through the medium of the lungs, and
then of the heart (*Bichat, Sur la Vie et la Mort*, Part ii.,
art. ii. § 1).   On the other hand, the brain controls the
relations to the external world; this alone is its office,
and hereby it discharges its debt to the organism which
nourishes it, since its existence is conditioned by the
external relations.   Accordingly the brain alone of all the
parts requires sleep, because its *activity* is completely distinct from its *support;* the former only consumes both
strength and substance, the latter is performed by the rest
of the organism as the nurse of the brain : thus because
its activity contributes nothing to its continued existence
it becomes exhausted, and only when it pauses in sleep
does its nourishment go on unhindered.

The second part of our thesis, stated above, will require a fuller exposition even after all that I have said about it in the writings referred to. I have shown above, in chapter 18, that the thing in itself, which must lie at the foundation of every phenomenon, and therefore of our own phenomenal existence also, throws off in self-consciousness *one* of its phenomenal forms—space, and only retains the other—time. On this account it presents itself here more immediately than anywhere else, and we claim it as will, according to its most undisguised manifestation. But no *permanent substance*, such as matter is, can present itself in time alone, because, as § 4 of the first volume showed, such a substance is only possible through the intimate union of space and time. Therefore, in self-consciousness the will is not apprehended as the enduring substratum of its impulses, therefore is not perceived as a permanent substance; but only its individual acts, such as purposes, wishes, and emotions, are known successively and during the time they last, directly, yet not perceptibly. The knowledge of the will in self-consciousness is accordingly not a *perception* of it, but a perfectly direct becoming aware of its successive impulses. On the other hand, for the knowledge which is directed *outwardly*, brought about by the senses and perfected in the understanding, which, besides time, has also space for its form, which two it connects in the closest manner by means of the function of the understanding, causality, whereby it really becomes *perception*—this knowledge presents to itself *perceptibly* what in inner immediate apprehension was conceived as will, as *organic body*, whose particular movements visibly present to us the acts, and whose parts and forms visibly present to us the sustained efforts, the fundamental character, of the individually given will, nay, whose pain and comfort are perfectly immediate affections of this will itself.

We first become aware of this identity of the body with the will in the individual actions of the two, for in these what is known in self-consciousness as an immediate, real act of will, at the same time and unseparated, exhibits itself outwardly as movement of the body; and every one beholds the purposes of his will, which are instantaneously brought about by motives which just as instantaneously appear at once as faithfully copied in as many actions of his body as his body itself is copied in his shadow; and from this, for the unprejudiced man, the knowledge arises in the simplest manner that his body is merely the outward manifestation of his will, *i.e.*, the way in which his will exhibits itself in his perceiving intellect, or his will itself under the form of the idea. Only if we forcibly deprive ourselves of this primary and simple information can we for a short time marvel at the process of our own bodily action as a miracle, which then rests on the fact that between the act of will and the action of the body there is really no causal connection, for they are directly *identical*, and their apparent difference only arises from the circumstance that here what is one and the same is apprehended in two different modes of knowledge, the outer and the inner. Actual willing is, in fact, inseparable from doing and in the strictest sense only that is an act of will which the deed sets its seal to. Mere resolves of the will, on the contrary, till they are carried out, are only intentions, and are therefore matter of the intellect alone; as such they have their place merely in the brain, and are nothing more than completed calculations of the relative strength of the different opposing motives. They have, therefore, certainly great probability, but no infallibility. They may turn out false, not only through alteration of the circumstances, but also from the fact that the estimation of the effect of the respective motives upon the will itself was erroneous, which then shows itself, for the deed is untrue to the purpose: therefore before it is carried out no resolve is certain. The *will itself*, then, is operative only in real action; hence in muscular action, and consequently in *irritability*. Thus the *will* proper objectifies itself in this. The cerebrum is the place of motives, where, through these, the will becomes choice, *i.e.*, becomes more definitely determined by motives. These motives are ideas, which, on the occasion of external stimuli of the organs of sense, arise by means of the functions of the brain, and are also worked up into conceptions, and then into resolves. When it comes to the real act of will these motives, the workshop of which is the cerebrum, act through the medium of the cerebellum upon the spinal cord and the motor nerves which proceed from it, which then act upon the muscles, yet merely as *stimuli* of their irritability; for galvanic, chemical, and even mechanical stimuli can effect the same contraction which the motor nerve calls forth. Thus what was *motive* in the brain acts, when it reaches the muscle through the nerves, as mere stimulus. Sensibility in itself is quite unable to contract a muscle. This can only be done by the muscle itself, and its capacity for doing so is called *irritability*, i.e., *susceptibility to stimuli*. It is exclusively a property of the muscle, as sensibility is exclusively a property of the nerve. The latter indeed gives the muscle the *occasion* for its contraction, but it is by no means it that, in some mechanical way, draws the muscle together; but this happens simply and solely on account of the *irritability*, which is a power of the muscle itself. Apprehended from without this is a *Qualitas occulta*, and only self-consciousness reveals it as the *will*. In the causal chain here briefly set forth, from the effect of the motive lying outside us to the contraction of the muscle, the will does not in some way come in as the last link of the chain; but it is the metaphysical substratum of the irritability of the muscle : thus it plays here precisely the same part which in a physical or chemical chain of causes is played by the mysterious forces of nature which lie at the foundation of the process—forces which as such are not themselves involved as links in the causal chain, but impart to all the links of it the capacity to act, as I have fully shown in § 26 of the first volume. Therefore we would ascribe the contraction of the muscle also to a similar mysterious force of nature, if it were not that this contraction is disclosed to us by an entirely different source of knowledge—self-consciousness as *will.* Hence, as was said above, if we start from the will our own muscular movement appears to us a miracle ; for indeed there is a strict causal chain from the external motive to the muscular action ; but the will itself is not included as a link in it, but, as the metaphysical substratum of the possibility of an action upon the muscle through brain and nerve, lies at the foundation of the present muscular action also ; therefore the latter is not properly its *effect* but its *manifestation.* As such it enters the world of idea, the form of which is the law of causality, a world which is entirely different from the *will* in itself : and thus, if we start from the *will,* this manifestation has, for attentive reflection, the appearance of a miracle, but for deeper investigation it affords the most direct authentication of the great truth that what appears in the phenomenon as body and its action is in itself *will.* If now perhaps the motor nerve that leads to my hand is severed, the will can no longer move it. This, however, is not because the hand has ceased to be, like every part of my body, the objectivity, the mere visibility, of my will, or in other words, that the irritability has vanished, but because the effect of the motive, in consequence of which alone I can move my hand, cannot reach it and act on its muscles as a stimulus, for the line of connection between it and the brain is broken. Thus really my will is, in this part, only deprived of the effect of the motive. The will objectifies itself directly, in irritability, not in sensibility.

In order to prevent all misunderstandings about this important point, especially such as proceed from physiology pursued in a purely empirical manner, I shall explain the whole process somewhat more thoroughly. My doctrine asserts that the whole body is the will itself, exhibiting itself in the perception of the brain ; consequently, having entered into its forms of knowledge. From this it follows that the will is everywhere equally present in the whole body, as is also demonstrably the case, for the organic functions are its work no less than the animal. But how, then, can we reconcile it with this, that the *voluntary* actions, those most undeniable expressions of the will, clearly originate in the brain, and thus only through the spinal cord reach the nerve fibres, which finally set the limbs in motion, and the paralysis or severing of which therefore prevents the possibility of voluntary movement? This would lead one to think that the will, like the intellect, has its seat only in the brain, and, like it, is a mere function of the brain.

Yet this is not the case: but the whole body is and remains the exhibition of the will in perception, thus the will itself objectively perceived by means of the functions of the brain. That process, however, in the case of the acts of will, depends upon the fact that the will, which, according to my doctrine, expresses itself in every phenomenon of nature, even in vegetable and inorganic phenomena, appears in the bodies of men and animals as a *conscious will*. A *consciousness*, however, is essentially a unity, and therefore always requires a central point of unity. The necessity of consciousness is, as I have often explained, occasioned by the fact that in consequence of the increased complication, and thereby more multifarious wants, of an organism, the acts of its will must be guided by *motives*, no longer, as in the lower grades, by mere stimuli. For this purpose it had at this stage to appear provided with a knowing consciousness, thus with an intellect, as the medium and place of the motives. This intellect, if itself objectively perceived, exhibits itself as the brain, together with its appendages, spinal cord, and nerves. It is the brain now in which, on the occasion of external impressions, the ideas arise which become motives for the will. But in the *rational* intellect they undergo besides this a still further working up, through reflection and deliberation. Thus such an intellect must first of all

unite in *one* point all impressions, together with the
working up of them by its functions, whether to mere
perception or to conceptions, a point which will be, as it
were, the focus of all its rays, in order that that unity of
consciousness may arise which is the *theoretical ego*, the
supporter of the whole consciousness, in which it presents
itself as identical with the *willing ego*, whose mere function
of knowledge it is.   That point of unity of consciousness,
or the theoretical ego, is just Kant's synthetic unity of
apperception, upon which all ideas string themselves as
on a string of pearls, and on account of which the "I
think," as the thread of the string of pearls, "must be
capable of accompanying all our ideas."[1] This assembling-
place of the motives, then, where their entrance into the
single focus of consciousness takes place, is the brain.
Here, in the non-rational consciousness, they are merely
perceived; in the *rational* consciousness they are elucidated
by conceptions, thus are first thought in the abstract and
compared; upon which the will chooses, in accordance
with its individual and immutable character, and so the
purpose results which now, by means of the cerebellum,
the spinal cord, and the nerves, sets the outward limbs in
motion.   For although the will is quite directly present in
these, inasmuch as they are merely its manifestation, yet
when it has to move according to motives, or indeed
according to reflection, it requires such an apparatus for
the apprehension and working up of ideas into such
motives, in conformity with which its acts here appear as
resolves: just as the nourishment of the blood with chyle
requires a stomach and intestines, in which this is prepared, and then as such is poured into the blood through
the *ductus thoracicus*, which here plays the part which the
spinal cord plays in the former case.   The matter may be
most simply and generally comprehended thus: the will is
immediately present as irritability in all the muscular
fibres of the whole body, as a continual striving after

[1] Cf. Ch. 22.

activity in general. Now if this striving is to realise itself, thus to manifest itself as movement, this movement must as such have some direction; but this direction must be *determined* by something, *i.e.*, it requires a guide, and this is the nervous system. For to the mere irritability, as it lies in the muscular fibres and in itself is pure will, all directions are alike; thus it determines itself in no direction, but behaves like a body which is equally drawn in all directions; it remains at rest. Since the activity of the nerves comes in as motive (in the case of reflex movements as a stimulus), the striving force, *i.e.*, the irritability, receives a definite direction, and now produces the movements. Yet those external acts of will which require no motives, and thus also no working up of mere stimuli into ideas in the brain, from which motives arise, but which follow immediately upon stimuli, for the most part inward stimuli, are the reflex movements, starting only from the spinal cord, as, for example, spasms and cramp, in which the will acts without the brain taking part. In an analogous manner the will carries on the organic life, also by nerve stimulus, which does not proceed from the brain. Thus the will appears in every muscle as irritability, and is consequently of itself in a position to contract them, yet only *in general;* in order that some definite contraction should take place at a given moment, there is required here, as everywhere, a cause, which in this case must be a stimulus. This is everywhere given by the nerve which goes into the muscle. If this nerve is in connection with the brain, then the contraction is a conscious act of will, *i.e.*, takes place in accordance with motives, which, in consequence of *external* impressions, have arisen as ideas in the brain. If the nerve is *not* in connection with the brain, but with the *sympathicus maximus*, then the contraction is involuntary and unconscious, an act connected with the maintenance of the organic life, and the nerve stimulus which causes it is occasioned by *inward* impressions; for example, by the pressure upon the stomach of the food received, or of the chyme upon the intestines, or of the in-flowing blood upon the walls of the heart, in accordance with which the act is digestion, or *motus peristalticus*, or beating of the heart, &c.

But if now, in this process, we go one step further, we find that the muscles are the product of the blood, the result of its work of condensation, nay, to a certain extent they are merely solidified, or, as it were, clotted or crystallised blood; for they have taken up into themselves, almost unaltered, its fibrin (*cruor*) and its colouring matter (*Burdach's Physiologie*, Bd. v. § 686). But the force which forms the muscle out of the blood must not be assumed to be different from that which afterwards moves it as irritability, upon nerve stimulus, which the brain supplies; in which case it then presents itself in self-consciousness as that which we call *will*. The close connection between the blood and irritability is also shown by this, that where, on account of imperfection of the lesser circulation, part of the blood returns to the heart unoxidised, the irritability is also uncommonly weak, as in the batrachia. Moreover, the movement of the blood, like that of the muscle, is independent and original; it does not, like irritation, require the influence of the nerve, and is even independent of the heart, as is shown most clearly by the return of the blood through the veins to the heart; for here it is not propelled by a *vis a tergo*, as in the case of the arterial circulation; and all other mechanical explanations, such as a power of suction of the right ventricle of the heart, are quite inadequate. (See *Burdach's Physiologie*, Bd. 4, § 763, and *Rösch, Ueber die Bedeutung des Blutes*, § 11, *seq.*) It is remarkable to see how the French, who recognise nothing but mechanical forces, controvert each other with insufficient grounds upon both sides; and Bichat ascribes the flowing back of the blood through the veins to the pressure of the walls of the capillary tubes, and Magendie, on the other hand, to the continued action of the impulse of the heart (*Précis de Physiologie par Magendie*, vol. ii. p.

389). That the movement of the blood is also independent of the nervous system, at least of the cerebral nervous system, is shown by the fetus, which (according to *Müller's Physiologie*), without brain and spinal cord, has yet circulation of the blood. And Flourens also says : " *Le mouvement du cœur, pris en soi, et abstraction faite de tout ce qui n'est pas essentiellement lui, comme sa durée, son énergie, ne dépend ni immédiatement, ni coinstantanément, du système nerveux central, et conséquemment c'est dans tout autre point de ce système que dans les centres nerveux eux-mêmes, qu'il faut chercher le principe primitif et immédiat de ce mouvement* " (*Annales des sciences naturelles p. Audouin et Brougniard*, 1828, vol. 13). Cuvier also says : " *La circulation survit à la déstruction de tout l'encéphale et de toute la moëlle épiniaire (Mém. de l'acad. d. sc.*, 1823, vol. 6; *Hist. d. l'acad. p. Cuvier,*" p. cxxx). " *Cor primum vivens et ultimum moriens,*" says Haller. The beating of the heart ceases at last in death. The blood has made the vessels themselves ; for it appears in the ovum earlier than they do; they are only its path, voluntarily taken, then beaten smooth, and finally gradually condensed and closed up; as Kaspar Wolff has already taught: " *Theorie der Generation,*" § 30–35. The motion of the heart also, which is inseparable from that of the blood, although occasioned by the necessity of sending blood into the lungs, is yet an original motion, for it is independent of the nervous system and of sensibility, as Burdach fully shows. " In the heart," he says, " appears, with the maximum of irritability, a minimum of sensibility " (*loc. cit.*, § 769). The heart belongs to the muscular system as well as to the blood or vascular system; from which, however, it is clear that the two are closely related, indeed constitute one whole. Since now the metaphysical substratum of the force which moves the muscle, thus of irritability, is the *will*, the will must also be the metaphysical substratum of the force which lies at the foundation of the movement and the formations of the blood, as that by which the muscles are produced. The course of

the arteries also determines the form and size of all the
limbs; consequently the whole form of the body is determined by the course of the blood. Thus in general the
blood, as it nourishes all the parts of the body, has also,
as the primary fluidity of the organism, produced and
framed them out of itself. And the nourishment which
confessedly constitutes the principal function of the blood
is only the continuance of that original production of
them. This truth will be found thoroughly and excellently
explained in the work of Rösch referred to above: " *Ueber
die Bedeutung des Blutes,*" 1839. He shows that the blood
is that which first has life and is the source both of the
existence and of the maintenance of all the parts; that all
the organs have sprung from it through secretion, and
together with them, for the management of their functions,
the nervous system, which appears now as *plastic,* ordering
and arranging the life of the particular parts within, now
as *cerebral,* controlling the relation to the external world.
" The blood," he says, p. 25, " was flesh and nerve at once,
and at the same moment at which the muscle freed itself
from it the nerve, severed in like manner, remained
opposed to the flesh." Here it is a matter of course that
the blood, before those solid parts have been secreted from
it, has also a somewhat different character from afterwards;
it is then, as Rösch defines it, the chaotic, animated, slimy,
primitive fluid, as it were an organic emulsion, in which
all subsequent parts are *implicite* contained: moreover, it
has not the red colour quite at the beginning. This disposes of the objection which might be drawn from the fact
that the brain and the spinal cord begin to form before the
circulation of the blood is visible or the heart appears.
In this reference also Schultz says (*System der Circulation,*
§ 297): " We do not believe that the view of Baūmgärten,
according to which the nervous system is formed earlier
than the blood, can consistently be carried out; for
Baūmgärten reckons the appearance of the blood only from
the formation of the corpuscles, while in the embryo and

in the series of animals blood appears much earlier in the form of a pure plasma." The blood of invertebrate animals never assumes the red colour; but we do not therefore, with Aristotle, deny that they have any. It is well worthy of note that, according to the account of Justinus Kerner (*Geschichte zweier Somnambulen*, § 78), a somnambulist of a very high degree of clairvoyance, says: "I am as deep in myself as ever a man can be led; the force of my mortal life seems to me to have its source in the blood, whereby, through the circulation in the veins, it communicates itself, by means of the nerves, to the whole body, and to the brain, which is the noblest part of the body, and above the blood itself."

From all this it follows that the will objectifies itself most immediately in the blood as that which originally makes and forms the organism, perfects it by growth, and afterwards constantly maintains it, both by the regular renewal of all the parts and by the extraordinary restoration of any part that may have been injured. The first productions of the blood are its own vessels, and then the muscles, in the irritability of which the will makes itself known to self-consciousness; but with this also the heart, which is at once vessel and muscle, and therefore is the true centre and *primum mobile* of the whole life. But for the individual life and subsistence in the external world the will now requires two assistant systems: *one* to govern and order its inner and outer activity, and *another* for the constant renewal of the mass of the blood; thus a controller and a sustainer. It therefore makes for itself the nervous and the intestinal systems; thus the *functiones animales* and the *functiones naturales* associate themselves in a subsidiary manner with the *functiones vitales*, which are the most original and essential. In the *nervous system*, accordingly, the will only objectifies itself in an indirect and secondary way; for this system appears as a mere auxiliary organ, as a contrivance by means of which the will attains to a knowledge of those occasions, internal and external,

upon which, in conformity with its aims, it must express
itself; the internal occasions are received by the *plastic*
nervous system, thus by the sympathetic nerve, this *cere-*
brum abdominale, as mere stimuli, and the will thereupon
reacts on the spot without the brain being conscious; the
outward occasions are received by the brain, as *motives*,
and the will reacts through conscious actions directed outwardly. Therefore the whole nervous system constitutes,
as it were, the antennæ of the will, which it stretches
towards within and without. The nerves of the brain and
spinal cord separate at their roots into sensory and motory
nerves. The sensory nerves receive the knowledge from
without, which now accumulates in the thronging brain,
and is there worked up into ideas, which arise primarily as
motives. But the motory nerves bring back, like couriers,
the result of the brain function to the muscle, upon which
it acts as a stimulus, and the irritability of which is the
immediate manifestation of the will. Presumably the
plastic nerves also divide into sensory and motory, although
on a subordinate scale. The part which the ganglia play
in the organism we must think of as that of a diminutive
brain, and thus the one throws light upon the other. The
ganglia lie wherever the organic functions of the vegetative
system require care. It is as if there the will was not
able by its direct and simple action to carry out its aims,
but required guidance, and consequently control; just as
when in some business a man's own memory is not sufficient, and he must constantly take notes of what he does.
For this end mere knots of nerves are sufficient for the
interior of the organism, because everything goes on within
its own compass. For the exterior, on the other hand,
a very complicated contrivance of the same kind is required. This is the brain with its feelers, which it
stretches into the outer world, the nerves of sense. But
even in the organs which are in communication with this
great nerve centre, in very simple cases the matter does
not need to be brought before the highest authority, but a

subordinate one is sufficient to determine what is needed; such is the spinal cord, in the reflex actions discovered by Marshall Hall, such as sneezing, yawning, vomiting, the second half of swallowing, &c. &c. The will itself is present in the whole organism, since this is merely its visible form; the nervous system exists everywhere merely for the purpose of making the *direction* of an action possible by a control of it, as it were to serve the will as a mirror, so that it may see what it does, just as we use a mirror to shave by. Hence small sensoria arise within us for special, and consequently simple, functions, the ganglia; but the chief sensorium, the brain, is the great and skilfully contrived apparatus for the complicated and multifarious functions which have to do with the ceaselessly and irregularly changing external world. Wherever in the organism the nerve threads run together in a ganglion, there, to a certain extent, an animal exists for itself and shut off, which by means of the ganglion has a kind of weak knowledge, the sphere of which is, however, limited to the part from which these nerves directly come. But what actuates these parts to such *quasi* knowledge is clearly the *will;* indeed we are utterly unable to conceive it otherwise. Upon this depends the *vita propria* of each part, and also in the case of insects, which, instead of a spinal cord, have a double string of nerves, with ganglia at regular intervals, the capacity of each part to continue alive for days after being severed from the head and the rest of the trunk; and finally also the actions which in the last instance do not receive their motives from the brain, *i.e.,* instinct and natural mechanical skill. Marshall Hall, whose discovery of the reflex movements I have mentioned above, has given us in this the *theory of involuntary movements.* Some of these are normal or physiological; such are the closing of the places of ingress to and egress from the body, thus of the *sphincteres vesicæ et ani* (proceeding from the nerves of the spinal cord); the closing of the eyelids in sleep (from the fifth pair of

nerves), of the larynx (from *N. vagus*) if food passes over
it or carbonic acid tries to enter; also swallowing, from
the pharynx, yawning and sneezing, respiration, entirely
in sleep and partly when awake; and, lastly, the erection,
ejaculation, as also conception, and many more.   Some,
again, are abnormal and pathological; such are stammer-
ing, hiccoughing, vomiting, also cramps and convulsions of
every kind, especially in epilepsy, tetanus, in hydrophobia
and otherwise ; finally, the convulsive movements produced
by galvanic or other stimuli, and which take place without
feeling or consciousness in paralysed limbs, *i.e.*, in limbs
which are out of connection with the brain, also the convulsions of beheaded animals, and, lastly, all movements
and actions of children born without brains.   All cramps
are a rebellion of the nerves of the limbs against the
sovereignty of the brain; the normal reflex movements, on
the other hand, are the legitimate autocracy of the subordinate officials.   These movements are thus all involuntary, because they do not proceed from the brain, and
therefore do not take place in accordance with motives,
but follow upon mere stimuli.   The stimuli which occasion
them extend only to the spinal cord or the *medulla oblongata*, and from there the reaction directly takes place which
effects the movement.   The spinal cord has the same relation to these involuntary movements as the brain has to
motive and action, and what the sentient and voluntary
nerve is for the latter the incident and motor nerve is
for the former.   That yet, in the one as in the other, that
which really moves is the *will* is brought all the more
clearly to light because the involuntarily moved muscles
are for the most part the same which, under other circumstances, are moved from the brain in the voluntary actions,
in which their *primum mobile* is intimately known to us
through self-consciousness as the *will*.   Marshall Hall's
excellent book " On the Diseases of the Nervous System "
is peculiarly fitted to bring out clearly the difference be-

tween volition and will, and to confirm the truth of my
fundamental doctrine.

For the sake of illustrating all that has been said, let us
now call to mind that case of the origination of an organism which is most accessible to our observation. Who
makes the chicken in the egg? Some power and skill
coming from without, and penetrating through the shell?
Oh no! The chicken makes itself, and the force which
carries out and perfects this work, which is complicated,
well calculated, and designed beyond all expression, breaks
through the shell as soon as it is ready, and now performs
the outward actions of the chicken, under the name of
will. It cannot do both at once; previously occupied
with the perfecting of the organism, it had no care for
without. But after it has completed the former, the latter
appears, under the guidance of the brain and its feelers,
the senses, as a tool prepared beforehand for this end, the
service of which only begins when it grows up in self-
consciousness as intellect, which is the lantern to the steps
of the will, its ἡγεμονικον, and also the supporter of the
objective external world, however limited the horizon of
this may be in the consciousness of a hen. But what the
hen is now able to do in the external world, through the
medium of this organ, is, as accomplished by means of
something secondary, infinitely less important than what
it did in its original form, for it made itself.

We became acquainted above with the cerebral nervous
system as an *assistant organ* of the will, in which it therefore objectifies itself in a secondary manner. As thus the
cerebral system, although not directly coming within the
sphere of the life-functions of the organism, but only
governing its relations to the outer world, has yet the
organism as its basis, and is nourished by it in return for
its services; and as thus the cerebral or animal life is to be
regarded as the production of the organic life, the brain
and its function, knowledge, thus the intellect, belong
indirectly and in a subordinate manner to the manifesta-

tion of the *will*. The will objectifies itself also in it, as
will to apprehend the external world, thus as *will to know*.
Therefore great and fundamental as is the difference in
us between willing and knowing, the ultimate substratum
of both is yet the same, the *will*, as the real inner nature
of the whole phenomenon. But knowing, the intellect,
which presents itself in self-consciousness entirely as
secondary, is to be regarded not only as the accident of
the will, but also as its work, and thus, although in a
circuitous manner, is yet to be referred to it. As the
intellect presents itself physiologically as the function of
an organ of the body, metaphysically it is to be regarded
as a work of the will, whose objectification or visible
appearance is the whole body. Thus the will *to know*,
objectively perceived, is the brain; as the will *to go*,
objectively perceived, is the foot; the will *to grasp*, the
hand; the will *to digest*, the stomach; the will *to beget*, the
genitals, &c. This whole objectification certainly ultimately exists only for the brain, as its perception : in this
the will exhibits itself as organised body. But so far as
the brain knows, it is *itself* not known, but is the *knower*,
the subject of all knowledge. So far, however, as in objective perception, *i.e.*, in the consciousness of *other things*, thus
secondarily, *it is known*, it belongs, as an organ of the body,
to the objectification of the will. For the whole process
is the *self-knowledge of the will ;* it starts from this and
returns to it, and constitutes what Kant has called the
phenomenon in opposition to the thing in itself. Therefore
that which is *known*, that which is *idea*, is the *will ;* and
this idea is what we call body, which, as extended in space
and moving in time, exists only by means of the functions of
the brain, thus only in it. That, on the other hand, which
knows, which *has that idea*, is the *brain*, which yet does
not know itself, but only becomes conscious of itself subjectively as intellect, *i.e.*, as the *knower*. That which
when regarded from within is the faculty of knowledge is
when regarded from without the brain. This brain is a

part of that body, just because it itself belongs to the objectification of the *will*, the will's *will to know* is objectified in it, its tendency towards the external world. Accordingly the brain, and therefore the intellect, is certainly conditioned immediately by the body, and this again by the brain, yet only indirectly, as spatial and corporeal, in the world of perception, not in itself, *i.e.*, as will. Thus the whole is ultimately the will, which itself becomes idea, and is that unity which we express by I. The brain itself, so far as it is *perceived*—thus in the consciousness of other things, and hence secondarily—is only idea. But in itself, and so far as it *perceives*, it is the will, because this is the real substratum of the whole phenomenon; its will to know objectifies itself as brain and its functions. We may take the voltaic pile as an illustration, certainly imperfect, but yet to some extent throwing light upon the nature of the human phenomenon, as we here regard it. The metals, together with the fluid, are the body; the chemical action, as the basis of the whole effect, is the will, and the electric current resulting from it, which produces shock and spark, is the intellect. But *omne simile claudicat*.

Quite recently the *physiatrical* point of view has at last prevailed in pathology. According to it diseases are themselves a curative process of nature, which it introduces to remove, by overcoming its causes, a disorder which in some way has got into the organism. Thus in the decisive battle, the crisis, it is either victorious and attains its end, or else is defeated. This view only gains its full rationality from our standpoint, which shows the *will* in the vital force, that here appears as *vis naturæ medicatrix*, the will which lies at the foundation of all organic functions in a healthy condition, but now, when disorder has entered, threatening its whole work, assumes dictatorial power in order to subdue the rebellious forces by quite extraordinary measures and entirely abnormal operations (the disease), and bring everything back to the right track.

On the other hand, that the *will itself* is sick, as Brandis
repeatedly expresses himself in his book, " *Ueber die
Anwendung der Kälte*," which I have quoted in the first
part of my essay, " *Ueber den Willen in der Natur*," is a
gross misunderstanding.   When I weigh this, and at the
same time observe that in his earlier book, " *Ueber die
Lebenskraft*," of 1795, Brandis betrayed no suspicion that
this force is in itself the will, but, on the contrary, says
there, page 13 : " It is impossible that the vital force can be
that which we only know through our consciousness, for
most movements take place without our consciousness.
The assertion that this, of which the only characteristic
known to us is consciousness, also affects the body without consciousness is at the least quite arbitrary and
unproved ; " and page 14: " Haller's objections to the
opinion that all living movements are the effect of the
soul are, as I believe, quite unanswerable; " when I further reflect that he wrote his book, " *Ueber die Anwendung
der Kälte*," in which all at once the will appears so decidedly
as the vital force, in his seventieth year, an age at which
no one as yet has conceived for the first time original
fundamental thoughts ; when, lastly, I bear in mind that
he makes use of my exact expressions, " will and idea,"
and not of those which are far more commonly used by
others, " the faculties of desire and of knowledge," I am
now convinced, contrary to my earlier supposition, that he
borrowed his fundamental thought from me, and with the
usual honesty which prevails at the present day in the
learned world, said nothing about it.   The particulars
about this will be found in the second (and third) edition
of my work, " *Ueber den Willen in der Natur*," p. 14.

Nothing is more fitted to confirm and illustrate the
thesis with which we are occupied in this chapter than
Bichat's justly celebrated book, " *Sur la vie et la mort*."
His reflections and mine reciprocally support each other,
for his are the physiological commentary on mine, and
mine are the philosophical commentary on his, and one

will best understand us both by reading us together. This refers specially to the first half of his work, entitled "*Recherches physiologiques sur la vie.*" He makes the foundation of his expositions the opposition of the *organic* to the *animal* life, which corresponds to mine of the will to the intellect. Whoever looks at the sense, not at the words, will not allow himself to be led astray by the fact that he ascribes the will to the animal life; for by will, as is usual, he only understands conscious volition, which certainly proceeds from the brain, where, however, as was shown above, it is not yet actual willing, but only deliberation upon and estimation of the motives, the conclusion or product of which at last appears as the act of will. All that I ascribe to the *will* proper he ascribes to the *organic* life, and all that I conceive as *intellect* is with him the *animal* life : the latter has with him its seat in the brain alone, together with its appendages : the former, again, in the whole of the remainder of the organism. The complete opposition in which he shows that the two stand to each other corresponds to that which with me exists between the will and the intellect. As anatomist and physiologist he starts from the objective, that is, from the consciousness of other things ; I, as a philosopher, start from the subjective, self-consciousness ; and it is a pleasure to see how, like the two voices in a duet, we advance in harmony with each other, although each expresses something different. Therefore, let every one who wishes to understand me read him ; and let every one who wishes to understand him, better than he understood himself, read me. Bichat shows us, in article 4, that the *organic* life begins earlier and ends later than the *animal* life ; consequently, since the latter also rests in sleep, has nearly twice as long a duration ; then, in articles 8 and 9, that the organic life performs everything perfectly, at once, and of its own accord ; the animal life, on the other hand, requires long practice and education. But he is most interesting in the sixth article, where he shows that the *animal* life is completely limited to the intellectual operations, therefore goes on coldly and indifferently, while the emotions and passions have their seat in the *organic* life, although the occasions of them lie in the animal, *i.e.*, the cerebral, life. Here he has ten valuable pages which I wish I could quote entire.   On page 50 he says : " *Il est sans doute éton-nant, que les passions n'ayent jamais leur terme ni leur origine dans les divers organs de la vie animale ; qu'au contraire les parties servant aux fonctions internes, soient constamment affectées par elles, et même les déterminent sui-vant l'état où elles se trouvent.   Tel est cependant ce que la stricte observation nous prouve.   Je dis d'abord que l'effet de toute espèce de passion, constamment étranger à la vie animale, est de faire naître un changement, une altération quelconque dans la vie organique.*"   Then he shows in detail how anger acts on the circulation of the blood and the beating of the heart, then how joy acts, and lastly how fear ; next, how the lungs, the stomach, the intestines, the liver, glands, and pan-creas are affected by these and kindred emotions, and how grief diminishes the nutrition ; and then how the animal, that is, the brain life, is untouched by all this, and quietly goes on its way. He refers to the fact that to signify intel-lectual operations we put the hand to the head, but, on the contrary, we lay it on the heart, the stomach, the bowels, if we wish to express our love, joy, sorrow, or hatred ; and he remarks that he must be a bad actor who when he spoke of his grief would touch his head, and when he spoke of his mental effort would touch his heart; and also that while the learned make the so-called soul reside in the head, the common people always indicate the well-felt difference between the affections of the intellect and the will by the right expression, and speak, for example, of a capable, clever, fine head; but, on the other hand, say a good heart, a feeling heart, and also " Anger boils in my veins," " Stirs my gall," " My bowels leap with joy," " Jealousy poisons my blood," &c.   " *Les chants sont le lan-gage des passions, de la vie organique, comme la parole ordi-*

naire est celui de l'entendement, de la vie animale : la déclamation, tient le milieu, elle anime la langue froide du cerveau par la langue expressive des organes intérieurs, du cœur, du foie, de l'estomac," &c. His conclusion is : *"La vie organique est le terme où aboutissent, et le centre d'où partent les passions."* Nothing is better fitted than this excellent and thorough book to confirm and bring out clearly that the body is only the embodied (*i.e.*, perceived by means of the brain functions, time, space, and causality) will itself, from which it follows that the will is the primary and original, the intellect, as mere brain function, the subordinate and derived. But that which is most worthy of admiration, and to me most pleasing, in Bichat's thought is, that this great anatomist, on the path of his purely physiological investigations, actually got so far as to explain the unalterable nature of the *moral character* from the fact that only the *animal* life, thus the functions of the brain, are subject to the influence of education, practice, culture, and habit, but the moral character belongs to the *organic* life, *i.e.*, to all the other parts, which cannot be modified from without. I cannot refrain from giving the passage; it occurs in article 9, § 2 : *" Telle est donc la grande différence des deux vies de l'animal"* (cerebral or animal and organic life) *"par rapport à l'inégalité de perfection des divers systèmes de fonctions, dont chacune résulte ; savoir, que dans l'une la prédominance ou l'infériorité d'un système relativement aux autres, tient presque toujours à l'activité ou à l'inertie plus grandes de ce système, à l'habitude d'agir ou de ne pas agir ; que dans l'autre, au contraire, cette prédominance ou cette infériorité sont immédiatement liées a la texture des organes, et jamais à leur éducation. Voilà pourquoi le tempérament physique et le* CHARACTÈRE MORAL *ne sont point susceptible de changer par l'éducation, qui modifie si prodigieusement les actes de la vie animale ; car, comme nous l'avons vu, tous deux* APPARTIENNENT À LA VIE ORGANIQUE. *La charactère est, si je puis m'exprimer ainsi, la physionomie des passions ; le tempérament est celle des fonc-*

tions internes: or les unes et les autres étant toujours les mêmes, ayant une direction que l'habitude et l'exercice ne dérangent jamais, il est manifeste que le tempérament et le charactère doivent être aussi soustraits à l'empire de l'éducation. Elle peut modérer l'influence du second, perfectionner assez le jugement et la réflection, pour rendre leur empire supérieur au sien, fortifier la vie animal afin qu'elle résiste aux impulsions de l'organique. Mais vouloir par elle dénaturer le charactère, adoucir ou exalter les passions dont il est l'expression habituelle, agrandir ou resserrer leur sphère, c'est une entreprise analogue a celle d'un médecin qui essaierait d'élever ou d'abaisser de quelque degrés, et pour toute la vie, la force de contraction ordinaire au cœur dans l'état de santé, de précipiter ou de ralentir habituellement le mouvement naturel aux artères, et qui est nécessaire à leur action, etc. Nous observerions à ce médecin, que la circulation, la respiration, etc., ne sont point sous le domaine de la volonté (volition), quelles ne peuvent être modifiées par l'homme, sans passer à l'état maladif, etc. Faisons la même observation à ceux qui croient qu'on change le charactère, et par-là même les PASSIONS, *puisque celles-ci sont un* PRODUIT DE L'ACTION DE TOUS LES ORGANES INTERNES, *ou qu'elles y ont au moins spécialement leur siège."* The reader who is familiar with my philosophy may imagine how great was my joy when I discovered, as it were, the proof of my own convictions in those which were arrived at upon an entirely different field, by this extraordinary man, so early taken from the world.

A special authentication of the truth that the organism is merely the visibility of the will is also afforded us by the fact that if dogs, cats, domestic cocks, and indeed other animals, bite when violently angry, the wounds become mortal; nay, if they come from a dog, may cause hydrophobia in the man who is bitten, without the dog being mad or afterwards becoming so. For the extremest anger is only the most decided and vehement will to annihilate its object; this now appears in the assumption by the saliva of an injurious, and to a certain extent magically acting, power, and springs from the fact that the will and the organism are in truth one. This also appears from the fact that intense vexation may rapidly impart to the mother's milk such a pernicious quality that the sucking child dies forthwith in convulsions (*Most, Ueber sympathetische Mittel,* p. 16).

NOTE ON WHAT HAS BEEN SAID ABOUT BICHAT

BICHAT has, as we have shown above, cast a deep glance into human nature, and in consequence has given an exceedingly admirable exposition, which is one of the most profound works in the whole of French literature. Now, sixty years later, M. Flourens suddenly appears with a polemic against it in his work, "*De la vie et de l'intelligence,*" and makes so bold as to declare without ceremony that all that Bichat has brought to light on this important subject, which was quite his own, is false. And what does he oppose to him in the field? Counter reasons? No, counter assertions [1] and authorities, indeed, which are as inadmissible as they are remarkable—Descartes and Gall! M. Flourens is by conviction a Cartesian, and to him Descartes, in the year 1858, is still "*le philosophe par excellence.*" Now Descartes was certainly a great man, yet only as a forerunner. In the whole of his dogmas, on the other hand, there is not a word of truth; and to appeal to these as authorities at this time of day is simply absurd. For in the nineteenth century a Cartesian in philosophy is just what a follower of Ptolemy would be in astronomy, or a follower of Stahl in chemistry. But for M. Flourens the dogmas of Descartes are articles of faith. Descartes has taught, *les volontés sont des pensées :* therefore this is the case, although every one feels within himself that willing and thinking are as different as white and black. Hence I have been able above, in chapter 19, to prove and explain this fully and thoroughly, and always under the guidance of experience. But above all, according to Descartes, the oracle of M. Flourens, there are two fundamentally different substances, body and soul. Consequently M. Flourens, as an orthodox Cartesian, says : "*Le premier point est de séparer, même par les mots, ce qui est du corps de ce qui est de l'âme*" (i. 72). He informs us further that this "*âme réside uniquement et exclusivement dans le cerveau*" (ii. 137); from whence, according to a passage of Descartes, it sends the *spiritus animales* as couriers to the muscles, yet can only itself be affected by the brain ;

---

[1] "*Tout ce qui est relatif à l'entendement appartient à la vie animale,*" dit Bichat, et jusque-là point de doute; "*tout ce qui est relatif aux passions appartient à la vie organique,*"—et ceci est absolument faux. Indeed ? —decrevit Florentius magnus.

therefore the passions have their seat (*siège*) in the heart, which is altered by them, yet their place (*place*) in the brain. Thus, really thus, speaks the oracle of M. Flourens, who is so much edified by it, that he even utters it twice after him (i. 33 and ii. 135), for the unfailing conquest of the ignorant Bichât, who knows neither soul nor body, but merely an animal and an organic life, and whom he then here condescendingly informs that we must thoroughly distinguish the parts where the passions have their *seat* (*siègent*) from those which they *affect*. According to this, then, the passions *act* in one place while they *are* in another. Corporeal things are wont to act only where they are, but with an immaterial soul the case may be different. But what in general may he and his oracle really have thought in this distinction of *place* and *siège*, of *siéger* and *affecter ?* The fundamental error of M. Flourens and Descartes springs really from the fact that they confound the motives or occasions of the passions, which, as ideas, certainly lie in the intellect, *i.e.*, in the brain, with the passions themselves, which, as movements of the will, lie in the whole body, which (as we know) is the perceived will itself. M. Flourens' second authority is, as we have said, Gall. I certainly have said, at the beginning of this twentieth chapter (and already in the earlier edition) : "The greatest error in Gall's phrenology is, that he makes the brain the organ of moral qualities also." But what I censure and reject is precisely what M. Flourens praises and admires, for he bears in his heart the doctrine of Descartes : "*Les volontés sont des pensées.*" Accordingly he says, p. 144 : "*Le premier service que Gall a rendu à la physiologie (?) a été de rammener le moral à l'intellectuel, et de faire voir que les facultés morales et les facultés intellectuelles sont du même ordre, et de les placer toutes, autant les unes que les autres, uniquement et exclusivement dans le cerveau.*" To a certain extent my whole philosophy, but especially the nineteenth chapter of this volume, consists of the refutation of this fundamental error. M. Flourens, on the contrary, is never tired of extolling this as a great truth and Gall as its discoverer ; for example, p. 147 : "*Si j'en étais à classer les services que nous a rendu Gall, je dirais que le premier a été de rammener les qualités morales au cerveau;*"—p. 153 : "*Le cerveau seul est l'organe de l'âme, et de l'âme dans toute la plénitude de ses fonctions*" (we see the simple soul of Descartes still always lurks in the background, as the kernel of the matter) ; "*il est le siège de toutes les facultés intellectuelles. . . . Gall a rammené* LE MORAL A L'INTELLECTUEL, *il a rammené les qualités morales au même siège, au même organe, que les facultés intellectuelles.*" Oh how must Bichât and I be ashamed of ourselves in the presence of such wisdom ! But, to speak seriously, what can be more disheartening, or rather more shocking, than to see the true and profound rejected and the false and perverse extolled ; to live to find that important truths, deeply hidden, and extracted late and with difficulty, are to be torn down, and the old, stale, and late conquered errors set up in their place ; nay, to be compelled to fear that through such procedure the advances of human knowledge, so hardly achieved, will be broken off ! But let us quiet our fears; for *magna est vis veritatis et prævalebit.* M. Flourens is unquestionably a man of much merit, but he has chiefly acquired it upon the experimental path. Just those truths, however, which are of the greatest importance cannot be brought out by experiments, but only by reflection and penetration. Now Bichat by his reflection and penetration has here brought a truth to light which is of the number of those which are unattainable by the experimental efforts of M. Flourens, even if, as a true and consistent Cartesian, he tortures a hundred more animals to death. But he ought betimes to have observed and thought something of this : "Take care, friend, for it burns." The presumption and self-sufficiency, however, such as is only imparted by superficiality combined with a false obscurity, with which M. Flourens undertakes to refute a thinker like Bichat by counter assertions, old wives' beliefs, and futile authorities, indeed to reprove and instruct him, and even almost to mock at him, has its origin in the nature of the Academy and its *fauteuils.* Throned upon these, and saluting each other mutually as *illustre confrère,* gentlemen cannot avoid making themselves equal with the best who have ever lived, regarding themselves as oracles, and therefore fit to decree what shall be false and what true. This impels and entitles me to say out plainly for once, that the really superior and privileged minds, who now and then are born for the enlightenment of the rest, and to whom certainly Bichat belongs, are so "by the grace of God," and accordingly stand to the Academy (in which they have generally occupied only the forty-first *fauteuil*) and to its *illustres confrères,* as born princes to the numerous representatives of the people, chosen from the crowd. Therefore a secret awe should warn these gentlemen of the Academy (who always exist by the score) before they attack such a man,—unless they have most cogent reasons to present, and not mere contradictions and appeals to *placita* of Descartes, which at the present day is quite absurd.

END OF VOL. II.